Obtaining
Venture Financing

Obtaining
Venture Financing

A Guide for Entrepreneurs

James W. Henderson
Baylor University

Lexington Books
D.C. Heath and Company/Lexington, Massachusetts/Toronto

Library of Congress Cataloging-in-Publication Data

Henderson, James W.
  Obtaining venture financing.

  Includes index.
  1. Venture capital—United States.   I. Title.
HG4963.H44   1987   658.1'5224   85-40234
ISBN 0-669-10931-2 (alk. paper)
ISBN 0-669-27670-7 (pbk.: alk. paper)

Published simultaneously in Canada
Printed in the United States of America
Casebound International Standard Book Number: 0-669-10931-2
Paperbound International Standard Book Number: 0-669-27670-7
Library of Congress Catalog Card Number: 85-40234

The paper used in this publication meets the minimum requirements of American National Standard for Information Sciences—Permanence of Paper for Printed Library Materials, ANSI Z39.48-1984. ♾

Year and number of this printing:
91 92 93 94   10 9 8 7 6 5

Contents

Figures and Tables

Figures

Tables

Preface and Acknowledgments

Much of the growth and development of the U.S. economy can be attributed directly to the entrepreneurial spirit of the owners and managers of the nation's small businesses. Through their innovative behavior and willingness to risk their own capital, these individuals provide the stimulus that energizes the economy at large.

This book was developed to provide a basic understanding of the principles, tools of analysis, and related information that are useful to the owners of emerging businesses interested in financing practices and alternatives. This book goes beyond the typical guide to securing venture capital. It is more than a "How to" book on preparing a business plan or a step-by-step guide in securing an SBA guaranteed loan. Instead, the principles of venture evaluation and financing are presented in a clear and systematic manner. The business life-cycle approach is used in both the analytical presentation and organization of the book. Financing practices are different at different stages of business development. What works for a growing firm at a later stage in its development would likely not have worked in the startup stage. These principles must be understood in order to take the generalized presentation of this book and put them into practice in specific financing situations.

The one thing that is certain in today's world is change. Environments change rapidly, and one's ability to adjust to those changes is usually the difference between success and failure. By the time you read this book, it is likely that the institutional environment will have changed somewhat. But while the practices may differ in degree, the principles are still applicable. Herein lies the strength of the presentation. By focusing on the principles of financing and evaluation, the entrepreneur can adjust to an environment where practices are changing.

Many individuals contributed directly and indirectly to the completion of this project. I would like to thank my colleagues who read and provided comments on early versions of this manuscript: Lucian Conway, John T. Rose, Tom Harrison, Richard E. Walker, and Terry S. Maness. To the anonymous reviewers, your time and thoughtful comments have resulted in an improved presentation. To my students at Baylor University, your insights and enthusiastic response have meant a great deal to me over the years. Needless to mention, any mistakes that remain are solely my responsibility.

Finally, I would like to express my appreciation to my wife Betsy and sons Luke and Jesse, who have given me their unconditional love and support over the years. Without their understanding, the time away from them would have been much more difficult. The importance of this material is timeless and that has been my motivation. As recorded in Proverbs 24:3,4, "Any enterprise is built by wise planning, becomes strong through common sense, and profits wonderfully by keeping abreast of the facts." It is my desire that this book will prove to be a reliable resource in helping you put these principles into practice.

Obtaining
Venture Financing

1

Introduction and Overview

There is a commonly held belief that a small firm represents a riskier investment opportunity than its larger counterpart. As a result of this perception, small firms have been effectively shut out of both the commercial paper and bond markets, forcing an almost exclusive reliance on the commercial banking industry as the primary source of external capital. If it is true that there is a higher degree of risk associated with small size, then this limitation represents an efficient market decision. However, if there is no correlation between size and risk, then firm size should not be a criterion in capital market decisions.

Based on current empirical research, the evidence to support the claim of a significant positive correlation between risk and firm size is inconclusive. So why does the market perceive such a correlation? There are two possible explanations. First, financial markets may not be equipped to accurately assess the risk associated with the small firm. The individuals responsible for making funding decisions have systematically limited the types of situations they will consider. Thus, they lack experience in evaluating certain types of businesses and identifying the degree of risk associated with them.

A second, more likely explanation is that the small business concern is usually limited in its capacity to provide the types of information used to determine relative levels of risk. Economies of scale do exist in gathering, processing, and disseminating information. The small firm may not have the expertise available to provide the sophisticated financial planning models that are commonly generated in larger corporations. In addition, cost considerations may prevent the small firm from supplying audited financial statements, which provide a much greater level of assurance than other types of financial data.

The result is an information gap between what funding sources require to evaluate venture opportunities and what entrepreneurs typically provide. The solution to narrowing this information gap is to educate entrepreneurs in the information requirements of the capital markets. The more the entrepreneur knows about the way that capital sources evaluate risk and the kinds of information they need to do so, the greater the likelihood of successfully tapping into the formal capital market.

The Parameters for Defining Business

A **closely held business** is defined as one that is privately owned by a small group of related individuals. This group, usually composed of relatives, friends, or other close associates, is actively involved in the management of the firm and runs the operation to benefit the group. The vast majority of the 14 million businesses operating in the United States are closely held and most can be classified as small businesses by the size standards established by the Small Business Administration. Businesses that are small usually remain small because of the attitudes and goals of the owner, not because of any inherent efficiencies of small size. However, there is a significant number of businesses that are temporarily small solely because they are new and emerging in their respective markets.

These emerging firms can be more accurately classified as "entrepreneurial ventures" than "small businesses." A small business is one "that is independently owned and operated, not dominant in its field, and does not engage in any new marketing or innovative practices," whereas the "entrepreneurial venture is one . . . [where] the principal goals . . . are profitability and growth and the business is characterized by innovative strategic practices" (Carland et al. 1984).

The small business is operated by and for the benefit of one individual or a small group of individuals who are usually closely related. The personality of the business is closely tied to that of the owner, who is directly involved in all or almost all aspects of the enterprise. This type of operation usually has a very loose organizational structure managed by the founder of the business and a few close associates.

A business that has grown to the point where one individual can no longer effectively manage and control all aspects of the enterprise will take on a completely different managerial and organizational structure. Professional managers who have little or no ownership interests are hired and the day-to-day control of the operation becomes less centralized. However, growth does not occur randomly or by chance; it is anticipated and planned for. The owner of an entrepreneurial venture will establish goals for growth and profitability, use strategic management techniques in planning ways to achieve these goals, and practice innovative behavior to guarantee that they are reached.

The Entrepreneurial Venture and Economic Development

Available data indicate that a substantial portion of the growth and expansion of the U.S. economy is directly attributable to the small business sector. Firms with fewer than 100 employees (numbering around 2.5 million) were responsible for over half of the new employment generated economy-wide during the 1976–1982 period (*State of Small Business* 1985). These jobs, however, were not equally distributed among these firms. A study by Birch and McCracken (1982) indicates that the bulk of these jobs was generated by fewer than 15 percent of the firms in question.

Thus, it is apparent that there is a relatively small number of growth-oriented entrepreneurial ventures around the country (approximately 400,000) that are responsible for the majority of the job creation, innovation, and development in the economy. The dilemma that policymakers are faced with today involves providing a supportive environment for the growth-oriented entrepreneur that in turn will further the development goals of the economy at large. However, this objective must be balanced against the equally important one of promoting (or at least not impeding) the opportunities for the small business owner who is interested primarily in furthering personal goals and providing a primary income source for self and family. The challenge is to identify the two groups, understand their unique problems and opportunities, and develop strategies to assist in furthering their personal ambitions and business objectives.

Understanding the distinctive characteristics of small businesses and entrepreneurial ventures is a necessary prerequisite to promoting economic growth and development in each sector. Policies that impact on one will probably have little effect on the other. For example, the elimination of double taxation on corporate dividends will have a negligible impact on most small businesses and even those run by growth-oriented entrepreneurs who retain most of their earnings to internally finance their growth. However, the same policy is likely to have a significant impact on the mature firm, which exists in a stable economic environment and regularly pays dividends to its shareholders. Another example is the investment tax credit. Firms that have small equipment requirements or little interest in expansion will have virtually no vested interest in this tax incentive for capital investment. On the other hand, firms planning to substantially increase their plant size are keenly interested in the investment tax credit.

Life-Cycle Stages and Business Activity

Although every business is uniquely situated and subject to a different operating environment, a careful examination will reveal that many features are similar, regardless of business type or structure. As a firm grows and develops, it moves through various stages in its life cycle. Each stage in the life cycle offers a different risk/reward opportunity and, as a result, attracts only those funding sources with the same risk/reward propensity. Thus, the likelihood of attracting a particular investor or lender will depend as much on the stage of the business life cycle as the term nature of the funding request.

The major misconception about the business life cycle is that firms begin in the early developmental stages and either progress through startup, growth, and maturity or fail in the process. Many firms do follow this develop-and-grow pattern, while others seem to reach a certain economic plateau and stay there indefinitely. The one thing that is certain about the business development process is that there is no single pattern that ensures success.

The challenge in studying business development with the life-cycle model is to recognize, first, that stages are not defined by unique time periods; rather, they are defined by the common problems, issues, and activities confronting the entrepreneur. Second, the decision to stabilize, grow, or quit can be made at any stage of the life cycle. In many cases, personal goals and ambitions determine whether the entrepreneur will use the business as a foundation for expansion or simply maintain a stable and profitable enterprise. Finally, finances are not always the determining factor in the entrepreneur's decision. Time and energy also play an important role. It is the human factor that makes the study of the development process challenging and exciting.

The stages of the business life cycle can be categorized as: 1) development, 2) expansion, and 3) acquisition. Each of these stages can be divided into distinct substages. The following discussion will examine the life-cycle stages in terms of the problems, issues, and activities associated with each stage.

Development Stage

The development stage of a business is characterized by a high level of risk associated with the new venture. Much of the financing available at this stage takes the form of equity capital. There are three distinct stages within this category: seed, startup, and early growth.

Seed Stage. The seed stage of a business is the initial period where the main activity is to investigate and research a concept or simply prove that an idea has some merit. By definition, these activities occur *prior* to the actual startup of a venture; thus, this stage is often referred to as the "pre-startup" or "research and development" stage. The entrepreneur will use capital at this stage to develop the venture concept to the point that his/her vision becomes a reality for the funding source.

The research and development activities taking place during the seed stage are typically very costly. With no sales revenues to offset the expenses, the entrepreneur has few formal funding sources to explore. In addition to the basic research often needed to prove a technology, this stage is characterized by research into the market feasibility of the venture—preparing the marketing and business plans. These activities are essential if the venture concept is to progress beyond the idea stage and gain credibility in the formal venture capital community, where a much larger amount of the startup financing is available.

At this early stage of development, there is little or no formal organizational structure. In fact, the entrepreneur is more often than not the entire management team. Businesses can remain in this stage indefinitely. However, if the concept does not reach the startup stage in one to five years, there is little likelihood that it ever will.

Startup Stage. Companies that have progressed beyond the conceptual stage and are actually ready to develop and market a product/service are in the startup stage. With market research completed and a business plan prepared, the newly assembled management team, composed of founder and close associates, is ready to test the developed venture concept by seeking funds in the formal capital markets. Although informal funding sources are still the most feasible at this stage, venture capitalists have an increased interest.

Business firms at this stage are still in the process of being organized. The formal structure is very loose and the primary goal of the operation is survival. Although a product may be available, it has not yet begun selling to any degree, which means the firm is still experiencing significant losses.

A primary activity at this stage of a venture is the further development of a product or concept. It may be necessary to come up with a prototype or conduct a market test. Most entrepreneurs do not have the resources to remain at this stage for more than one to three years.

Early-Growth Stage. The early-growth stage of a business is sometimes referred to as the "first stage." The management team is still composed of the founder and associates. Their energies are directed toward securing the resources that will enable the business to grow. A more formal organizational structure with clearly defined functional responsibilities is being developed. Most or all of the seed and startup capital has been expended in conceptualizing the venture, developing a prototype, and test marketing the product. The business is, for the first time, prepared to promote and market the product formally. Funding at this stage is for the purpose of initiating this process.

Equity sources are still the best option available to the firm, even at this later stage. The informal market is typically too small to meet the increased capital needs, so the venture capital industry is the primary source of capital at this stage.

Profits range from negative, to breakeven, to marginally positive. At this stage, the personal ambitions of the entrepreneur play an important role in determining the direction that the venture takes. The entrepreneur who has limited ambitions can maintain the status quo and view the company solely as a source of personal income. The more ambitious entrepreneur will, however, exploit past success and expand the operation. The status quo entrepreneur will maintain the business at this stage indefinitely. The growth-oriented entrepreneur will either successfully move into the expansion stage within one to two years or dissolve the business.

Expansion Stage

If the venture is to progress successfully beyond the early development stage, the cash-generating capacity of the business must be used to establish borrowing power in the credit markets. It is possible for a venture to reach this stage in the life cycle and fail to successfully enter the expansion stage. The result is not always dissolution. Many companies reach this point with a strong enough customer base to guarantee a sales volume and level of profit that will keep the operation viable. As long as market conditions do not change dramatically or management prove ineffective, a business can remain at this point indefinitely.

Rapid-Growth Stage. At the beginning of this life-cycle stage, a firm may or may not be generating a profit. However, as sales growth accelerates, the capital requirements of the company also accelerate because of increased inventory levels and growing accounts receivable. The rate of growth that a firm can support internally is limited by its ability to generate cash from operations. Financing at this stage usually takes the form of an operating capital loan, which allows the firm to support a sales growth rate that exceeds the rate of growth of operating cash flow. It is at this stage of the business life cycle that the institutionalized debt market, especially the commercial banking industry, becomes a viable source of funds.

If a business is to successfully pass through this stage, the entrepreneur must carefully monitor growth to ensure that it does not exceed the firm's ability to generate cash—both internally and externally. Cash sources are extremely important at this stage because of the requirements of a rapidly expanding employee and customer base.

The entrepreneur's management style will begin to shift its focus from managing the current operation to planning for the future. Aggressive planning is essential in a rapidly changing business environment. An operation committed to a growth strategy must develop a strategic planning ability if it is to avoid the cash shortages that are so common at this stage.

Because of the extreme time pressures placed on the entrepreneur, the firm is likely to hire its first professional managers and begin delegating certain responsibilities. The firm's organizational structure becomes increasingly complex and is usually divided along the functional lines of finance, accounting, marketing, and administration.

The successful entrepreneur must be careful at this stage to maintain a balanced perspective. The entrepreneur's ego can become a source of conflict with managers, employees, family, and friends. Many entrepreneurs will go through a period where they feel they can "walk on water" and expand into products or markets that neither complement their operation nor match their individual expertise.

Firms that successfully navigate through this stage often emerge without the founding entrepreneur. It is not unusual for the founder to sell out during this stage and either move on to another venture or be forced out by investors or creditors because of an inability to direct the maturing operation.

Sustained-Growth Stage. Businesses that reach the sustained-growth stage of the life cycle are always profitable. This stage will see the firm's first major expansion in facilities, the penetration of a new geographic market, or the development of a new product line. As the firm matures and advances into this later stage, its alternative funding options increase substantially. The firm can choose to fund an expansion either with debt or with equity, based on the relative cost of funds.

At this stage, the goal of management is to repeat the successes and avoid the failures of the previous stages. Operational planning and financial budgeting become increasingly important management tools. The rapid-growth stage tends to introduce inefficiencies in the system that must be corrected in order for the company to maintain the financial gains of the earlier stage.

The firm will have an extensive organizational structure. Management will become increasingly professional in its composition and more decentralized in its decision making. Because of its size and resources, the company has the ability to indefinitely remain a viable force in the market. The major threats to this stable position are complacency and inflexibility, which create an unwillingness or inability to respond to environmental change.

Bridge Stage. This stage is also referred to as the "mezzanine stage." In this period of time, the company is in the process of preparing for a public offering in the near future: dealing with accountants, negotiating with underwriters, and promoting the firm to brokerage houses. Chapter 12, "Public Offerings," provides a detailed discussion of the activities that take place during this stage.

The financing activities are aimed at restructuring the ownership position of the major shareholders prior to the public sale of stock. Repayment of borrowed debt at this stage is built into the proceeds of the underwriting. Funding at this stage can take on many forms, with most formal investors interested in these opportunities. Everyone wants "to get in on the action" prior to the initial public offering of a successful operation.

Acquisition Stage

Acquisition can actually take place at any stage in the business life cycle. Entrepreneurs are motivated differently at various stages and the pressures and incentives to sell originate from different sources. During the early development stages, many companies never receive sufficient product recognition; as a result, they never develop an adequate enough customer base to remain viable. In such cases, the owner will discontinue operations when all sources of capital are exhausted and, if a purchaser can be identified, sell the business for the market value of the assets.

Selling a business at a later stage of the life cycle presents a much greater opportunity for a capital gain for the owner. Businesses of the "mom-and-pop" variety that are marginally profitable can usually be sold at a small loss. Most successful operations that have entered into the expansion stage can capitalize on their growth potential and sell at a profit.

Business Failure

Churchill and Lewis (1983) have demonstrated that the grow-or-fail approach used to study small business is seriously flawed. As we discussed earlier, it is not at all unusual for firms to plateau at any stage of the life cycle and remain profitable for many years. Why is it then that some firms reach endpoints in their development and either sell out, retrench, or fail? To more fully understand this issue, the focus must turn to the entrepreneur.

Businesses dissolve for various reasons. These include merger or acquisition, retirement or death of the owner, failure with no loss to creditors, or failure with loss to creditors (usually referred to as *bankruptcy*). There is little agreement as to the numbers or percentages of dissolutions that belong in each category. However, most analysts studying business failure statistics will agree that the majority of the dissolutions (80–90 percent) are voluntary or at least involve no loss to creditors.

A **business failure** is defined as a business closure that involves a loss to creditors. Not all business closures are failures. In fact, over 75 percent of all closures are voluntary dissolutions in which all debt obligations are paid. Business bankruptcies are included in the category of business failures, not all failures are classified as bankruptcies. A **bankruptcy** is an official petition to a federal court on behalf of a business that cannot meet its debt obligations. The petitioner is seeking either a reorganization of the debts of the business (Chapter 11) or the liquidation of its assets (Chapter 7).

Most discussions on business failure are flawed because of the lack of good data on the subject. Two of the major sources of data on business dissolutions are the Administrative Office of the United States Courts and *Business Failure Record* published by Dun and Bradstreet. However, these sources are not directly comparable because the Dun and Bradstreet data exclude certain key industries such as finance and mining and do not fully cover others such as service and agriculture.

There are many reasons offered for business failures, including: 1) inadequate sales, 2) undercapitalization, 3) stiff competition, 4) inventory and receivables problems, 5) high overhead, and 6) poor location. According to Dun and Bradstreet, however, very few failures (less then 10 percent) are caused by factors beyond the control of management. Most can be attributed to poor management, which manifests itself in the following ways:

1. The entrepreneur has inadequate knowledge of the particular business and industry.

2. The entrepreneur did a poor job of gathering and evaluating information on the business before undertaking the venture.

3. The entrepreneur has poor accounting skills and/or an inability or unwillingness to maintain adequate financial records on the business.

4. The entrepreneur is a poor cash manager. In addition, the skills of forecasting and budgeting are lacking.

5. The entrepreneur lacks a knowledge of the sources of additional capital once the need has been identified.

Regardless of its apparent causes, business failure is primarily the responsibility of the entrepreneur. A close examination of the previously cited reasons reveals that they all deal with the various aspects of information processing. A breakdown in information processing at any level can lead to serious problems for the business concern. Data gathering and recording is important for any business, but this is particularly true for the entrepreneurial venture. The entrepreneur must plan for growth and this means being able to analyze, synthesize, and disseminate information at each critical stage of the business life cycle.

Summary and Conclusions

This chapter has provided a brief overview of the financing problems faced by owners of entrepreneurial ventures. The information gap—the difference between what is requested by funding sources and what is provided by business owners—is a critical factor in the inability of many smaller firms to secure the capital needed to grow and prosper. A thorough understanding of the principles and practices of planning and financing is a major step toward new opportunities and greater rewards.

References

Birch, David L. and McCracken, Susan. *The Small Business Share of Job Creation, Lesson Learned from the Use of Longitudinal File*. Washington, D.C.: Small Business Administration, November, 1982.

Carland, James W.; Hoy, Francis; Boulton, William; and Carland, Joanne A. "Differentiating Entrepreneurs from Small Business Owners: A Conceptualization," *Academy of Management Review* (April, 1984), pp. 354–359.

Churchill, Neil C. and Lewis, Virginia L. "The Five Stages of Small Business Growth," *Harvard Business Review* (May/June, 1983), pp. 30–50.

The State of Small Business: A Report of the President. Washington, D.C.: Government Printing Office, May, 1985.

Part I
Planning and Analysis

2
The Business Plan

Good business managers are almost always good planners. The very nature of the planning process forces the entrepreneur to carefully analyze the economic events and conditions that are expected in the future and allows the orderly development of possible strategies to respond to them. The reasons for planning are very simple and straightforward. In addition to making one a better manager, planning 1) encourages a more efficient and effective means of coordinating activities, 2) provides a yardstick against which actual performance can be measured, and 3) enables the establishment of clear channels of communication with owners, employees, and funding sources.

The purpose of this chapter is to examine the business planning process. This will include an analysis of the benefits and objectives of business plan preparation. The actual content and format of the business plan is presented in great detail and is followed by a discussion of how the business plan is read and evaluated by prospective funding sources.

The Planning Process

The entire planning process encompasses the activities of strategy development and program implementation. The first step in effective planning is to determine the extent of the resources—human and financial—that are available for implementation of the firm's strategy.

The business plan documents all the events—past, present, and future—that will affect the operation of an enterprise. It is important to state explicitly all the assumptions on which the plan is based, giving details on the possible actions and reactions to the described events. The plan provides a description of the associated costs and revenues of each event. Final details are presented in a cash flow summary to show the results of the events on this important variable.

The emphasis of the plan should be implementation. The goal should not simply be the process of putting together the plan, but executing the plan and making sure that it comes to life. This underlines the importance of the entrepreneur's taking an active role in the preparation of the plan. A plan that is prepared by an outside consultant or a hired manager who has no implementation authority can turn out to be simply a time-consuming exercise.

Consultants that are closely directed by members of the entrepreneurial team can and do play a vital role in the preparation of the business plan. However, planning cannot take place in an ivory tower that is totally removed from the competitive business environment. Care must be taken to ensure that the consultant does not become the driving force behind the plan.

One of the best resources that a closely held business possesses in the planning process is its front-line managers. These managers have a vested interest in the results of the planning process because they will be expected to implement the plan.

Benefits from the Planning Process

Planning cannot occur in isolation from the day-to-day operations of the business, and neither can financing. Financing a company, especially one in the early growth stages, requires a well-conceived plan. However, financing is not the only benefit to be received from the planning process.

Benefits to the Entrepreneur

The planning process goes a long way in helping to make the entrepreneur a better manager. As we all know, one can only manage the future. Today's decisions have no impact on the past, and, since most decisions cannot be implemented instantaneously, they have very little impact on the present. Economic decision making has its impact in the long term—a period of time during which the decisions have an opportunity to bring about structural change. In other words, today's decisions determine the alternative operating strategies available in the future.

The business planning process gives the entrepreneur an opportunity to systematically analyze the economic, financial, and competitive prospects of the business venture. The planning process forces many entrepreneurs to realistically analyze the enterprise or venture for the first time. The discipline of a formal business plan can be summarized as follows:

1. It subjects the entrepreneur's best assumptions about the future to the close scrutiny of the prospective funding source.
2. It forces careful consideration of all pertinent aspects of the operation. Although there is no guarantee that important details will not be omitted,

the use of available business plan outlines and checklists ensures that all major areas will be covered.

3. It provides details about operating strategies and the results they are expected to achieve.

4. It quantifies goals and objectives, thus providing measurable targets and benchmarks against which forecasts can be compared with actual operating results.

The planning process is a tool of management that promotes a more efficient use of all company resources. By establishing a long-term course of action, the entrepreneur becomes a better manager. As the entrepreneur learns from the process, better and more accurate plans will result (which is important in developing a sound relationship with any financial intermediary, as we shall see later).

Benefits to the Funding Source

In addition to making the entire evaluation process much easier, a sound business plan will accrue many of the same benefits to the funding source that it does to the entrepreneur. By providing a complete overview of the entire operation—from goals and objectives to operating assumptions to measurable targets—the funding source has a clear, concise document that contains most of the information required to perform a complete business and financial analysis on the operation or venture.

The business plan identifies the important aspects of a firm's operations—marketing, management, facilities, and finance. It provides details of the market potential and plans for securing a share of that market. It also identifies capital equipment requirements. Through prospective financial statements, the business plan exhibits a company's ability to service debt or provide an adequate return on equity.

More importantly, it identifies critical events and gives management an opportunity to discuss the venture's potential for success or failure and any contingency plans that are being considered to handle either potentiality. For the funding source with no prior involvement with the entrepreneur, the business plan provides a useful guide to assessing the individual's ability to plan and manage an ongoing operation.

Objectives of the Business Plan

There are two reasons that can cause an entrepreneur to recognize the need for a business plan. One focus of a plan could be on the internal operations of a firm and would take the form of a strategic plan or feasibility study. The other objective could be to attract outside financing and would result in a funding proposal. Each of these will be examined in more detail.

The Operating Plan

The entire planning process offers the entrepreneur the opportunity to prepare a systematic analysis of a firm's complete operation. This includes an examination of the full range of variables—human, economic, and financial—that play a vital role in the long-term prospects of the business.

The main focus of the **operating plan** is to systematize corporate strategies and determine the impact of certain policies on profitability and the ability to generate cash. In this connection, the operating plan is merely an outgrowth of the overall strategic planning process that is implemented in many closely held businesses.

The process of strategic planning is essential in the planning process of all businesses. Although the planning activity is important for the smaller firm, recent empirical evidence presented by Sexton and Van Auken (1982) indicates that only a minimal level of strategic planning is used in most smaller firms. Despite the recognized importance of implementing a planning function, fewer than 25 percent of the sampled firms were classified as being oriented toward the principles of strategic planning. In other words, only one out of four entrepreneurs used a written plan of any kind to help in developing operating strategies for their businesses.

The focus of the strategic plan should be on implementation. Without a strong bias toward how the plan is to be implemented in the business operation, the planning process ends up as merely a ritualistic exercise that goes no further than the annual board meeting.

A functioning strategic plan takes time to implement. Many entrepreneurs are not patient enough to operationalize the planning process; it may take several years before significant tangible benefits are realized. The entire process is one of assessing where an operation stands in relation to the current competitive environment, predicting the possible changes in the market that may have an impact on the operation, and plotting strategies to deal with those changes.

A **feasibility study** is nothing more than a strategic plan dealing with a specific issue that has a potential impact on the business operation. Feasibility studies are commonly used to plot the impact of certain decisions on the profitability of an operation. This can include the introduction of a new product into an existing line of products, expansion into a new geographic market, or additions to plant facilities. In a sense, feasibility studies are much more limited in scope than a full-blown strategic plan; however, they are useful in examining the impact of business decisions on the profitability of an operation.

The Funding Proposal

A business plan intended for use as a funding proposal is a document that has obviously been prepared for external circulation. Its content is determined to a great extent by the evaluation requirements of the funding source being approached.

Much of the operational and technical information that is so vital to the implementation process in an operating plan is of secondary importance in a funding proposal. In many cases, the entrepreneur may be reluctant to share this specialized information in the initial presentation and, for the most part, it may not be necessary. The technical information referred to can vary widely in content from construction requirements to product design standards to engineering specification. In general, highly technical information need not be included in the initial presentation, but it should be made available upon request to sources requiring additional details on those aspects of the venture. Different funding sources will be particularly interested in certain aspects of the operation and relatively unconcerned about other aspects. These emphases will be discussed later in this chapter.

The business plan is more than a funding proposal, however, it is a guide to operating a business. As a funding proposal, it is a selling document designed to attract funds, not customers. In preparing the plan, the entrepreneur has the responsibility to fully state his or her case and should realize that the document being prepared is a commitment to act according to the plan. It is a document that provides the details about the individual's intentions and expectations regarding the future prospects of the venture.

The business plan should include all information that may prove pertinent to the funding source, especially if it might be construed as potentially damaging. It is much better to share all of this information early in the negotiations, especially if it might cause the funding source to lose interest in the project. By initially suppressing potentially relevant data, the entrepreneur runs the risk of casting a shadow of doubt on the credibility of the entire venture when the information surfaces. Have no doubts; all relevant data eventually surface.

Pitfalls in Developing Funding Proposals. For all of the obvious benefits of a sound business plan, there are several serious pitfalls that should be avoided when seeking funds from a financial institution.

Probably the most common mistake that is made by entrepreneurs is one of approaching a funding source either without a written proposal or with an incomplete or poorly written proposal. The very nature of many existing financial intermediaries requires written documentation on all loans and investments that are made. At a minimum, this means current and past financial statements and something in writing about the funding request, how the funds are going to be used, and how they will be paid back.

Even Little Things Mean a Lot

The experience of Andrew Johnson in his search for venture capital emphasizes the importance of maintaining credibility when dealing with funding sources. Andrew Johnson had been employed by a Fortune 500 firm for over eighteen years, the last four of which he had been division manager of a southwestern manufacturing facility. The firm was experiencing problems with the operation not being able to cover its fully allocated costs. In other words, the facility on its own was showing a profit; however, when the administrative overhead from the national office was added into the costs, it was no longer profitable.

This is a classic example of an operating division of a large firm being a prime target for a management buyout. Mr. Johnson recognized this and made a proposal to the national office to purchase the division and set it up as a closely held business. The process began to develop quite rapidly. A price was negotiated, a commercial bank was contacted, and a business plan was developed. The only problem was that Mr. Johnson needed some additional equity capital. This was not a critical issue because the bank knew of a venture capitalist that would be interested in this type of a venture.

It all seemed to be going perfectly. The management team was in place, all the funding sources were preparing to commit to the necessary capital, and customers were lining up to place orders with their new supplier. Then a problem emerged. As final negotiations with the venture capitalist were taking place, it was discovered that Mr. Johnson had misrepresented himself on his personal resume.

Over eighteen years ago, when he initially applied for a job at the Fortune 500 firm, he falsely claimed to be a graduate of a major university. Once the claim was made, it became difficult to retreat from that position. Now, eighteen years later and over three months into the negotiations with the venture capitalist, the facts emerged and the venture capitalist backed out of the venture. The misrepresentation did not materially affect the feasibility of the venture, but it did bring into question the credibility and character of the principal owner.

Mr. Johnson was able to salvage the project. Ten months later, with a new bank and a different venture capitalist, the acquisition was completed. The lesson to be learned is quite obvious. Be truthful in everything, even if it seems insignificant. If you cannot be trusted in the little things, how can you ever be trusted in the more important things?

A frequent problem with business funding proposals stems from a lack of substantive documentation. There is nothing more distracting from an otherwise well-prepared proposal than unsupported or unrealistic assumptions. This in turn results in unreliable prospective financial statements and significant latitude to doubt the ability of the venture to support the profit and cash flow projections.

Two final cautions. First, make sure that the appropriate funding source is being approached. An entrepreneur with a startup venture who presents an uncollateralized operating capital loan request to a bank is probably wasting both his and the banker's time. The important factors to take into consider-

Shopping for Dollars

A good example of justifiable loan shopping happened during the normal course of acquiring an existing broadcast license. Marvin Raley, owner of a successful FM radio station, was seeking to diversify his holdings by acquiring an AM facility in a nearby city. The only available facility was an AM–FM station that was being sold as a package. After studying the market, analyzing the sales potential, and realistically evaluating his financial leverage, it was obvious that the purchase price was much too high for his particular situation.

Several weeks later, Mr. Raley was contacted by the station owner and given the following proposition. A large, publicly held broadcasting company had made an offer on the FM license, but could not purchase the AM license because of Federal Communications Commission (FCC) regulations. If Mr. Raley could put together the proper financial package, he could buy the AM license separately. The only problem was that he would also have to abide by the timetable established by the FM buyer. Mr. Raley had less than forty-five days to put together a complete business plan, file the necessary application papers and supporting documents with the FCC, and secure the complete financing package. The dilemma was quite obvious. Given the time constraint, Mr. Raley could not afford even one rejection from a potential funding source and still hope to meet the externally imposed deadline.

This seemed to qualify as one of those times when "shopping" was justified. Multiple copies of the financing proposal were sent to banks in two cities and SBICs specializing in broadcasting from coast to coast. Some were reluctant to review a package simultaneously with other funding sources and refused the opportunity. However, several chose to look at the proposal and a financing plan was offered by more than one. This was one of those infrequent and uncontrollable situations in which an entrepreneur reluctantly accepted a deadline for completing a funding package and was forced to shop. It was a successful shopping expedition in this case, because Mr. Raley was open and honest with everyone he dealt with. It also helped that the acquisition was a sound financial opportunity: good market, good management, and a realistic purchase price. Just for the record, Mr. Raley owned and operated the station for less than five years, over which time it became the number one station in its market, and he sold it for four times the original acquisition price to an unsolicited buyer.

---

ation when determining the proper funding source will be discussed more thoroughly in Chapter 9, "Capital Procurement."

Finally, avoid shopping a proposal. The term *shopping* is used to describe the practice of simultaneously presenting the proposal to more than two or three funding sources. There are several reasons why an entrepreneur might even consider shopping a proposal; however, almost all have negative implications.

In most cases, a time deadline for securing the required funds is not a good reason to shop a proposal. It tends to be interpreted as an indicator of poor management and planning on the part of the entrepreneur. Shopping for terms is usually unnecessary because most institutional funding sources use the same evaluation criteria. In general, if you are making your presentation to the right source in the first place, terms will be fairly uniform across the industry. Given the amount of effort required to review a proposal, most sources do not like to be put in the position of devoting the considerable time required to evaluate a proposal only to find that the business has gone elsewhere. If you must shop the plan, make your intentions known at the outset of the negotiation.

Business Plan Preparation

Although there is no business plan outline that is appropriate for all possible business applications and funding sources, the following guidelines can easily be adapted to cover a number of venture opportunities.

Preparation of a business plan is a time-consuming activity. However, the task should never be delegated to outside consultants or company managers who have no implementation responsibilities. The business plan should reflect the entrepreneur's own personality, style, judgment, foresight, and pragmatism.

The entire process of preparing the plan should be monitored closely by the entrepreneur and other individuals who have the responsibility of carrying out its policy prescriptions. These individuals must participate in the process; otherwise, the plan reflects only the vision of the planner. Without this link, the responsibility of implementing the plan is required of individuals who do not know the plan, do not understand it, do not believe in it, and are not able to defend it. An effective business plan cannot be put together by someone who is removed from the daily operations of the company.

Content and Format

The preparation of a business plan is the first step in developing a systematic approach toward implementing business policy and achieving business goals and objectives. It provides both the entrepreneur and the firm's operating managers with a tool to evaluate actual performance and compare it with planned performance.

The business plan also provides valuable information to potential investors or creditors about the nature of the venture and its market environment, the extent of financial support requested, the benefits that will accrue to the firm as a result of the financial support, who will be using the resources and in what way, and what financial returns the venture will generate over time for both the firm and the investor.

Every book or journal article written on business planning contains a suggested business plan outline. One source for sample plans is available in

I. Table of Contents
II. Summary of Highlights
III. The Business and the Industry
    A. The Nature and History of the Business from Its Inception
    B. The Legal Form of the Business
    C. Goals and Objectives
    D. Unique Advantages and Opportunities
    E. Description of the Business Operation
IV. Products and/or Services
    A. Developing a Sales Forecast
V. Market Strategy
    A. Target Market
    B. Market Segmentation
    C. Promotion Strategy
    D. Sources of Information
VI. Management Team
VII. Financial Proposal
    A. Financial Summary
    B. Historical Financial Statement Analysis
    C. Prospective Financial Statements
    D. Assumptions to Financial Statements
    E. Analysis of Risk
VIII. Appendices

Figure 2–1. The Business Plan Format

most libraries that have good business listings—10K reports and annual reports published for all publicly held firms. In addition, most stockbrokers have offering circulars and prospectuses of companies going public that provide insight into the format of a good plan. Thus, the business plan format presented in Figure 2–1 is only one of many possible formats that could be used. It is presented because it is easily adapted to cover a wide range of possible applications.

Table of Contents. This may seem like a very minor item in the overall scheme of putting together a business plan, but the table of contents serves a valuable purpose in the venture evaluation process. The first reading of a business plan is done solely for the purpose of identifying key issues that are critical in determining whether or not the funding source is interested in a closer analysis of the proposal. The table of contents is in effect the road map for the reader, so it is important that it present information clearly, provide sufficient detail to identify all key aspects of the proposal, and include page numbers of all the major categories. A sample table of contents is presented in the appendix to this chapter.

Summary of Highlights. The plan should begin with a brief summary (two to three pages) of the entire document. This should begin with a statement of the purpose of the plan and a clear summary of the financial support being requested. The remainder of the summary should describe each major section of the plan, including a separate paragraph on each of the following: the business and industry, the product/service, the firm's market strategy, the management team, and the projected profitability and cash-generating ability.

The statement of purpose should focus on what is expected of the reader and whether the plan has been prepared as an internal operating plan or an external funding proposal. If the purpose of the plan is a funding proposal, the sources and uses of the requested capital should be presented in some detail. This will include an analysis of the benefits to both the firm and the investor. Other important considerations include details on the unique features of the firm, its product, and market niche.

The Business and the Industry. The most appropriate place to begin the formal presentation is a description of the history of the business and an analysis of its current operation within the context of the industry environment. The following points should be discussed.

The Nature and History of the Business from Its Inception. It is important to include a description of the operating history of the organization and its management. If the business plan is being prepared for a new venture, this section should provide a description of the emergence of the idea or concept and give details on the developmental stage of the operation at the current time.

The Legal Form of the Business. The organizational form that has been established for the business should be discussed. The reasons for choosing to establish the enterprise as a proprietorship, partnership, or a corporation should also be delineated. Special features such as a limited partnership arrangement, Subchapter S corporation, stock issues under section 1244 of the Internal Revenue Code, or other related information should be clarified. See Chapter 8, "Forms of Business Organization," for details on the types of organizational forms that can be used and the implications of each one.

Goals and Objectives. A written statement of the goals and objectives of the entrepreneur is a critical addition to the material that will be evaluated. Until a goal is verbalized and open for critical evaluation, it is only a dream. Goals and objectives should be divided into short-term and long-term goals. They should also be quantifiable. This is to ensure that they can be measured and a determination can be made at some future date as to whether or not they have been accomplished. The funding source uses the information in this section to determine the reality of the entrepreneur's vision for the operation.

Unique Advantages and Opportunities. This section gives the entrepreneur an opportunity to discuss the market niche of the venture. Product quality, cost advantages, or location may be the source of the advantage. Whatever its basis, the unique features of the business, its operation, and/or the market should be emphasized. The funding source is looking for an advantage on which to capitalize.

Description of the Business Operation. A description of the business operation identifies the venture according to the type of business: retail, wholesale, manufacturing, assembly, or service. It also identifies the development stage of the business as a startup, early growth, or expansion, or if the business is an acquisition or buyout.

The location of the business and a description of the facilities should also be included in this section. Every business has some distinct facilities or process requirements. The location of the business is usually much more important to those types of businesses whose success depends on high visibility and easy access to the public, such as retail operations or service firms. This requirement means that the area traffic patterns (foot and automobile) and the availability of public transportation and parking are important considerations that should be discussed. On the other hand, it is not as important for the owners of a manufacturing operation to be as concerned with these aspects of the actual location. More important for this type of operation are its proximity to suppliers, an adequate labor force, and possibly access to an interstate highway or a railway line.

Manufacturing and retail operations usually place a heavy emphasis on facilities, while service firms are more concerned with processes. If facilities are important, the following information should be included:

1. A description of the business location, including the availability of utilities, zoning requirements, and a diagram of the plant providing details on office space, storage, parking, and other relevant data.
2. A description of the machinery and equipment, listing all that is currently in use and all that is to be acquired with the proceeds of this plan.

For a service operation in which facilities are relatively unimportant, emphasis should be given to a discussion of the important processes that make the firm unique in delivering services to its customers. Examples include takeout and delivery services for a pizza restaurant, a scheduling procedure that reduces patient waiting time for a private practice dentist, or the national computer network used for house listings by a real estate broker.

After discussing the business operation, a brief description of the current situation and future prospects for the industry should be included. This includes an analysis of sales and product trends, key competitors, new product or market developments, key regulations, and other exogenous factors that can influence future patterns of growth or change at the industry- or economy-wide level.

Products and/or Services. The next section should focus on the nature of the specific product or service that the firm is providing. The description can include brochures or photographs, if they are appropriate.

The firm's comparative advantage or market niche should be analyzed. This includes the unique aspects of the product/service and addresses such issues as price, quality, technology, and location. The existence of copyrights, patents, franchises, or trade secrets should be described.

Any major problems or opportunities should be analyzed, along with contingency plans to be implemented in the event that they occur. This section should provide details on all exogenous factors such as legislation, competitors' actions, and other items outside the entrepreneur's control that could significantly affect the venture.

Estimates of the total market size and potential should be discussed by developing forecasts based on potential customers, recognized trends, and behavior of the competition. This includes a demographic classification of the firm's customers. The size and development of the market in terms of dollars and units should be estimated. Secondary source information includes government documents, trade publications, and other industry data.

The firm's major competition should be examined in terms of product policy, pricing, and planned actions. This includes details about their strengths and weaknesses and a discussion of the similarities and differences of their operations.

Based on a review of the information provided about the firm's customers, trends, and competition, a sales forecast should be constructed. This involves making a projection of the market share that can be realistically captured over the next three to five years. For startup ventures, the key to accurate forecasting is to secure verifiable purchase commitments from key customers.

Under certain circumstances, community service factors can play a vital role in an investment decision. This is particularly true if loans are to be guaranteed by a government agency or if the lender or investor is concerned about the delivery of products, services, or benefits to a particular area, segment of the population, or special interest group. Community service factors include such things as the effect on the community in terms of number and skill level of individuals employed, dollar size of the payroll, and the beneficial services and other advantages to the various segments to the community.

Developing a Sales Forecast. Forecasting sales or market share usually starts with a review of the past sales history of the operation. By examining the growth rate of sales over the past five to ten years, an estimate of the future sales growth can be made.

Of course, much more goes into a sales forecast than an examination of historical sales trends. The state of the industry, conditions in the national economy, and the competitive environment in the local market are of critical importance. The firm also has some control over product demand by decisions made in the areas of product pricing, advertising and promotion, credit policies, and new product development.

Most closely held businesses do not make their own forecasts of general economic activity, but rely on outside forecasts. Some of the more commonly used economic forecasts are published by Chase Econometrics, Data Resources, Inc., and Wharton Econometrics. Industry forecasts are published by Moody's and Standard and Poor's. Characteristics of the target market can be determined by analyzing data available through public sources such as the Department of Commerce or various direct survey techniques.

Market Strategy. This section of the business plan translates the market potential and sales forecast of the previous section into the actual methods and strategies by which they will be accomplished. The first task is to define the relevant target market and then a workable promotion strategy can be devised.

Target Market. Quite possibly the most important task of any entrepreneur is to identify the relevant population that is interested in buying the product/service being marketed. The first step in this regard is to classify individuals on the basis of the unique characteristics that affect their buying behavior. This exercise is referred to as "segmenting the market."

Market segmentation is the process of dividing the total market into the various submarkets that have different behavioral characteristics. Young married couples, for example, have different purchasing patterns than the elderly. The purchasing decisions of individuals who live in the Pacific Northwest will differ from those of individuals who live along the Texas Gulf Coast. College graduates tend to spend their income differently than high school dropouts.

To know the composition of the target market is to better understand the decision-making process that takes place in the minds of the consumer public. Not only can this information be used effectively to forecast sales, but it can also be used as a vital part of the promotion strategy to influence buyer behavior.

After the relevant submarket has been identified, the entrepreneur can map out a strategy to penetrate it. Only then can the rest of the market strategy be effectively developed and implemented—product pricing, distribution channels, advertising and promotion strategy, and branding, packaging, and labeling.

Market Segmentation. Before a market can be segmented, there are several prerequisites that must be satisfied. The first prerequisite is that the relevant submarket must be distinct from all other submarkets. The test of distinction lies in the ability to uniquely identify the distinguishing characteristics of the submarket and measure its size.

Secondly, the submarket must be significant from a merchandising perspective. It must be of sufficient size in terms of disposable income and discretionary spending to warrant the attention that it will be given. Finally, the submarket must be accessible; it must be sufficiently close in terms of geographic location or proximity to channels of distribution so the product can be promoted, sold, and distributed.

There are several factors that should be taken into account when actually segmenting a market:

1. *Demographics of the Market.* The market can be segmented according to the following demographic characteristics of its inhabitants: age, sex, marital status, ethnic background, number of children in the household and their composition, income, and home ownership. Certain characteristics of the head of the household are also commonly used, such as occupation and education.

2. *Geographic Characteristics.* In segmenting a market geographically, the actual concentration of the population can be identified by locale. Other factors that are important include access to the transportation network, availability of printed and electronic media, and prevailing climatic conditions.

3. *Buyer Behavior.* This approach to segmentation explores the process by which consumers make their purchasing decisions. The behavioral aspects to examine include motives for buying, amount of the product consumed, and degree of product loyalty. Purchasing patterns can also be explored—where the purchase is made, how often the item is purchased, the time of the year when the purchase is made, the quantities in which it is purchased, and consumer preferences for using cash or credit.

Promotion Strategy. The remainder of this section of the business plan should provide an analysis of the pricing strategy that the firm will use, along with a summary of the pricing patterns of the major competition in the target

market. The analysis includes list and discount prices, special non-price services, and strategy in terms of market penetration.

A description of the channels of distribution will also be included in this
section. This is simply a description of the mix of direct retail sales, whole-
salers, distributors, manufacturers' representatives, or other means chosen to
get the product/service to the consumer.

A brief discussion of the advertising and promotion strategy is also appropriate in this section of the plan. The actual marketing concept and media
channels that will be utilized should be analyzed. This includes details on all
media that will be used to transmit the promotion message: television, radio,
newspapers, handbills, billboards, trade journals, word-of-mouth, and special point-of-purchase promotions. The actual content of the advertising is
not as important as the reason for its inclusion in the overall strategy.

Particularly important for most consumer products is the branding,
packaging, and labeling that will be used. If the main product line is consumer oriented, this aspect should be discussed. Emphasis should be placed
on the unique or different features that may be relevant.

Sources of Information. Information to complete this section is available
through several sources. Much of the demographic data is available through
the Bureau of Census of the U.S. Department of Commerce, which publishes
these data all the way down to the neighborhood level. This so-called "tract"
data provides a wealth of information in a simple-to-use format. Table 2–1
provides information from two typical census tracts in Waco, Texas.

From the information given on these two tracts, it can be seen that the
two neighborhoods have quite different characteristics. Tract 9 is an older
area of town, while Tract 25.02 is a relatively new suburban area. The median
ages of the populations are significantly different, with 41.7 years in Tract 9
and 33.0 years in Tract 25.02. Over 23 percent of the population of Tract 9
is over 65 years of age, compared to only 5 percent of Tract 25.02.

Both neighborhoods are predominantly white, 83.8 and 97.4 percent for
Tracts 9 and 25.02, respectively. However, they differ in educational attainment, income, and percentage living in owner-occupied housing.

This is a classic case of two racially similar neighborhoods that differ
significantly in age distribution and, as a result, will have quite different needs
in terms of products and services. Differences in educational attainment result
in differences in tastes and preferences. Income differentials have a major
impact on the ability to purchase goods and services. These differences must
be identified and understood by the entrepreneur before embarking on any
venture that targets a specific type of consumer. A thorough understanding
of what the census data offers will play a key role in venture planning and
business formation.

Although census tract information has its limitations, it can be effectively

Table 2–1
General Population Characteristics, 1980
Census of Population, Waco, Texas

	Tract 9	Tract 25.02
Population	4,461	7,292
Males	1,958	3,645
Females	2,503	3,647
Age Distribution		
Under 5 years	365	471
5–19 years	811	2,119
20–24 years	420	298
25–44 years	994	2,291
45–64 years	820	1,744
65 years and over	1,051	369
Median age	41.7	33.0
Race		
White	3,739	7,104
Black	206	25
Hispanic	486	98
Indian	8	13
Asian	13	50
Other	9	2
Percent High School Graduates	59.0	85.5
Household Income		
Total households	1,855	2,370
Less than $5,000	291	69
$5,000 to $9,999	415	117
$10,000 to $19,999	708	399
$20,000 to $34,999	337	1,121
$35,000 to $49,999	64	493
$50,000 and over	40	171
Median income	$12,681	$27,404
Mean income	$15,453	$28,975
Percent Owner-Occupied Housing Units	69.9	89.2

Source: Bureau of the Census.

combined with the marketing research compiled by most local newspapers to gain rich insights into consumer buying behavior. The marketing departments of local newspapers in most metropolitan areas maintain ongoing research efforts in their area of coverage. The purpose of this research is to generate advertising revenue for the newspaper, and typically, the information is available to all potential advertisers.

The marketing research available from local newspapers is usually based on consumer surveys that are conducted regularly to determine area consumer purchasing patterns. The information found in Table 2–2 is excerpted from the Waco market survey published annually by the *Waco Tribune-*

Table 2–2
Sample Consumer Survey: Traffic

Department and Discount Store Traffic

Question: "At which of the following stores, if any, have you shopped during the last thirty days, whether or not you bought anything?"

	Current Shoppers (Past 30 days)	%	1981 Survey	%	Diff. + or −
Kmart	91,100	68%	78,000	62%	+ 6%
Sears	84,600	63%	69,000	55%	+ 8%
JCPenney	66,800	50%	54,000	43%	+ 7%
Montgomery Ward	66,500	50%	54,000	42%	+ 8%
Dillard's	61,000	46%	51,000	40%	+ 6%
Cox's	47,100	35%	48,000	38%	− 3%
Gibson's	42,900	32%	42,000	33%	− 1%
Goldstein-Migel	42,900	32%	38,000	30%	+ 2%
Bealls	27,500	21%	25,000	20%	+ 1%
Holt's	16,700	13%	13,000	10%	+ 3%
Target	67,000	50%	—	—	—
TG&Y	52,000	39%	—	—	—
Leon's Cinderella	8,800	7%	—	—	—
Base: Adults in Waco MSA	134,000	100%	126,000	100%	

Shopping Center Traffic

	Current Shoppers (Past 30 days)	%	1981 Survey	%	Diff. + or −
Richland Mall	109,000	81%	92,000	73%	+ 8%
Lake Air Mall	88,000	65%	81,000	64%	+ 1%
Westview Village	55,000	41%	49,000	39%	+ 2%
Southgate	45,000	33%	41,000	33%	—
Eastgate	32,000	24%	26,000	20%	+ 4%
Fairgate	35,000	26%	22,000	18%	+ 8%
Bosque Square	24,000	18%	—	—	—
Base: Adults in Waco MSA	134,000	100%	126,000	100%	

Source: *Waco Tribune-Herald, Waco Market Audience Analysis,* Belden Associates Continuing Market Survey, 1984. Reprinted with permission.

Table 2–3
Retail Sales

	Waco 1982	National Rank
Population (MSA)	178,900	200
Households	66,100	196
Effective Buying Income (EBI)	$1,504,531,000	206
Median household (EBI)	$18,722	264
Households with EBI of $50,000 & over	3,900	197
Retail sales	$992,933,000	184
Per HH retail sales	$15,022	64
Buying power index	.0771	196
Eating establishment sales	$82,952,000	197
Food sales	$239,310,000	185
General merchandise sales	$110,142,000	219
Furniture sales	$41,209,000	187
Auto sales	$215,119,000	141
Gasoline sales	$74,634,000	214
Apparel store sales	$47,453,000	171
Building supply sales	$29,169,000	280
Drug store sales	$29,077,000	197

Source: *Waco Tribune Herald, Waco Market and Audience Analysis*, Belden Associates Continuing Market Survey, 1984. Reprinted with permission.

Herald and is typical of the data available from most metropolitan daily newspapers. This information includes population updates, area demographics, retail sales information, consumer psychology, and shopping patterns.

Another important source of information is the annual *Sales and Marketing Management Survey of Buying Power*. Since the population census is conducted only once every ten years, the information in this publication is extremely valuable. It includes population updates, income estimates, and retail sales volume with breakdowns by type of establishment (restaurants, food stores, general merchandise, furniture, auto, gasoline, apparel, building supplies, and pharmacy). An example of the data available from this source is provided in Table 2–3.

Management Team. Management is the entity that takes all of the elements discussed in the strategic business plan and turns them into a successful business enterprise. The educational attainment, employment history, and skill level of the key management personnel are vital in the firm's ability to achieve its stated goals and objectives.

It is important to include in this section the names, stated responsibilities, and titles of the key personnel in the organization. This includes all operating managers, company officers, members of the board of directors, and individual owners of the business. Required information includes details on each individual's areas of expertise. The reader will be interested in the depth and breadth of the management team. Most of the details can be included in resumes listed at the end of this section or in an appendix at the end of the plan.

Management is a process, and it is important to understand how the individual managers fit into the entire organizational hierarchy. Their effectiveness in attaining established organizational goals depends critically on the structure of the organization. Thus, it is important to include an organizational chart that provides details on the functional divisions of the operation. These divisions are shown on the organizational chart by vertical separations of the various duties that are performed, such as sales, service, operations, accounting, production, and finance. If the firm is large enough, there will also be horizontal divisions according to the different levels of responsibility. The organizational chart itself will closely resemble the pyramid-shaped organizational structure that is so closely associated with the effective business operation.

An ownership plan should also be included in this section, the details of which will vary depending on the proposed financing. The information typically requested includes a list of owners, the distribution of ownership, the amount of capital invested, and the levels of compensation of all key personnel. This section of the plan should also provide details on any employment agreements that exist, deferred compensation plans, life insurance policies, loans to owners, and other legal or financial obligations of the firm at the time of the request.

Financial Proposal. The financial section of the business plan is where the whole plan comes together, a fact that makes it one of most important sections of the entire plan. This is where the funding strategy is given in detail and the projections for debt repayment or equity return are spelled out. This section must be precise in its presentation, clearly analyzing the financial requirements of the business and outlining all the relevant assumptions that may impact on the future operation.

The strategy for presenting a firm's financial condition includes a detailed analysis of the current financial position as depicted through historical financial statements and the feasibility of the proposed venture as shown in the financial projections.

Financial Summary. It is useful to begin the financial section of the business plan with a summary of the financial position of the firm and an analysis of how the proposed funding will benefit the operation. This will also include a statement of sources and uses of the proposed financing. Sources of funds include all proposed loans listed separately, institutional equity sources, and other equity sources such as personal and stockholders' equity. The statement of uses of funds provides a breakdown of how the total capitalization of the venture will be put to use. The breakdown includes details on the amounts to be spent on land, buildings, equipment, furniture and fixtures, organizational expenses, operating capital, and other items.

A brief discussion of the financial history of the firm, current profitability, and future prospects is a key element of this summary. The discussion may include an analysis of key financial ratios and their trends, along with comparisons to the relevant industry data. All important assumptions pertaining to the prospective financial statements should be discussed. This includes any potential problems that could arise and any contingency plans that are in place to deal with these problems.

Historical Financial Statement Analysis. The firm's historical financial statements include income statements and balance sheets from the three most recent fiscal years and current statements that are as up-to-date as possible (under no circumstances should they be more than ninety days old). These statements should be arranged in a format that is easy to read and follow, preferably the comparative format.

Ratio analysis should include relevant liquidity, asset utilization, leverage, coverage, and operating ratios. In addition, the statements should be arranged in common-size format and an analysis of the relevant cash flows should be conducted. See Chapter 5, "Tools of Financial Management," for a discussion of the techniques involved in a complete financial analysis.

Prospective Financial Statements. In many ways, this is the most critical section in the entire business plan. It is here that the entrepreneur's goals and objectives are translated into dollars and cents. This section shows how the marketing strategy and sales forecasts make their way to the "bottom line." Income statements, cash flow statements, and balance sheets for at least three years must be included. For the first year, the income and cash flow statements should be provided on a monthly basis. After that, annual statements are sufficient, unless the business has a strong seasonal component. Under those circumstances, quarterly statements are required. The prospective balance sheet should include one representing the operation at the beginning of the projection period and an ending balance sheet for each year of the projection period.

Assumptions to Financial Statements. An often overlooked, but critical aspect of the prospective financial statements is a summary of the major assumptions that are the basis of the calculations. In effect, this provides an explanation of the mathematical logic that goes into the generation of each number on the prospective statements. The assumptions are not an attempt to justify the sales and cost estimates; they simply enable the reader to check the calculations for accuracy.

Analysis of Risk. Under most circumstances, it is useful to provide the reader with an estimate of the degree of risk involved in the proposed venture. Especially for new ventures, this means a carefully constructed breakeven analysis and a series of projections under various sales and cost estimates—a "what if" analysis.

Breakeven analysis is discussed more thoroughly in the following chapter. The "what if" analysis is a tool used to show the degree of sensitivity of profitability and cash-generating ability to changes in certain sales and cost estimates. A discussion of the degree of operating leverage can also be included.

After the basic prospective financial statements have been generated, an analysis should be made of the major down-side risk involved in the venture. As is the case with almost any venture, certain events can take place that would cause the operating results to deviate considerably from the original estimates. The purpose of the "what if" analysis is to show the impact of such an event on the firm's expected operations. The most common circumstances examined under "what if" include changes in the sales and cost estimates or varying assumptions on the timing of certain critical events, such as the completion of leasehold improvements, the delivery and installation of manufacturing equipment, or the closing of a key contract.

This section should be closed with a brief statement analyzing the effects that changes in the timing of certain events can have on such factors as sales, profitability, cash flow, and especially financing requirements. The primary threats and opportunities facing the venture should be discussed, along with contingency plans that will be implemented in the event of their occurrence.

Appendices. There may be a need to include other documents as supporting information for the plan. These include signed contracts, market research data to support sales estimates, technical drawings, construction plans, or other details that do not seem to fit within the logical flow of the plan itself.

Other supporting documents that may be required include copies of the partnership agreement if the firm is a partnership or the articles of incorporation and bylaws if it is a corporation. If the business is operating under an assumed name, it may be necessary to include a copy of the assumed name registration. Other legal documents such as patents, copyrights, leases, appraisals, cost estimates, or other relevant information may be appropriate.

The rule of thumb to use in deciding what documents to include should be: Will the absence of this document leave unanswered questions in the mind of the reader? If the answer to that question is "yes," include the document.

Business Plan Evaluation

The entire exercise of business planning should be conducted with the ultimate objective being to provide the prospective reader with the necessary information required to evaluate the financing request. In all likelihood, the financial proposal will receive only a brief scanning. Most financing sources receive hundreds of proposals every year and must use a considerable degree of discretion in evaluating individual proposals.

This fact highlights the importance of the manner in which the proposal is brought to the attention of the prospective funding source. The ideal method of presentation is through personal contact or professional referrals. Personal acquaintance with a bank loan officer or venture capitalist does not guarantee financing, but it probably means that the individual will at least give the business plan a more careful reading. If you do not know these individuals personally, then referrals from attorneys, accountants, or business consultants are the second best means of ensuring that your proposal receives the attention you think it deserves.

As the business plan is being prepared, keep in mind the information that the prospective reader considers essential: 1) business and industry characteristics, 2) size of the funding request, 3) financial performance of the company, 4) quality of the management team, and 5) profitability of the investment.

Business and Industry Characteristics. Most financing sources specialize in certain types of investments. This is particularly true for venture capitalists and, to a certain extent, commercial banks. The business should be clearly classified within a certain business category and industry. The facts that will interest the source include types of products, geographic location, number of years the business has been in operation, and sales volume and profitability.

Size of the Funding Request. Most financial institutions have guidelines that they follow as far as size of financing is concerned. There is almost always a minimum based on the fixed costs of processing a request. For many types of institutions—commercial banks, SBA, and SBICs—there is a legal limit to the amount of funding that can be extended to any individual or enterprise. Somewhere between these extremes is a range of fundings that the institution prefers to make. It is important to be within this preferred range of fundings in order to receive adequate consideration from the individual reviewing the request for the financial institution.

Financial Performance of the Company. Regardless of the funding source, the area of historical performance will be carefully examined. In the first reading, the reviewer will be looking for some general indicators of performance. These indicators include the liquidity position of the operation as evidenced by key financial ratios: current and quick ratios, sales-to-receivables, and cost of sales-to-inventory. Profitability indicators are also critical—profit before taxes-to-tangible net worth. The firm's ability to generate cash as evidenced by cash flow from operations will also be examined.

Additional borrowing power is determined by examining the firm's leverage position as shown by the debt-to-equity ratio and a careful analysis of the available collateral in the form of unencumbered assets. The initial capitalization structure of the firm is of interest, as well as the current net worth position.

Quality of the Management Team. As stated earlier, the management team is of vital concern to the prospective funding source. The reader will be looking for information on the founders, current owners, and key managers of the operation. Each individual will be examined in terms of personal expertise and related work experience. The entire management team will be evaluated in terms of depth of expertise in each particular area, but more importantly in terms of breadth of coverage of each important area—production, marketing, personnel, and finance.

Profitability of the Investment. Because most private sector funding sources are in the business to make a profit for their owners, the determining factor in the funding decision is whether or not the investment is potentially profitable relative to the risk involved. Lenders take into consideration such things as the marginal cost of funds and compensating balances. Equity sources are more interested in the percentage of the company being offered, the valuation of the outstanding stock, and the terms of the investment—stock, convertible debentures, debt with options to buy stock, or straight debt.

The important issue to remember when putting together a business plan is to do everything possible to ensure that the reader is able to easily locate all of these points of interest. The plan must pass the initial screening test before it can move on to the more rigorous analysis, where final funding decisions are actually made.

Summary and Conclusions

This chapter presented an overview of the strategic planning process as it applies to the owner of an entrepreneurial venture. A systematic business planning procedure is extremely beneficial to the entrepreneur. It not only forces the entrepreneur to examine all aspects of his current operation, but it also provides a format to deal with and plan for the future.

Sound planning also provides benefits that extend beyond the daily operations of a business. When used as a financing proposal, the business plan serves as a means of bridging the information gap between what is required by funding sources to conduct a financial analysis and what is typically provided by the smaller business concern.

Business plans come in many different shapes and sizes. The length and format used will depend on its purpose and the objectives of the entrepreneur. Some plans are operating plans used to guide company management in the implementation of the goals and objectives of the firm. Others are financing proposals used for the purpose of capitalizing a new venture or business expansion.

Preparing a business plan is a time-consuming activity. It is not something that can typically be thrown together in a single afternoon. The information that goes into a business plan depends on the purpose of the plan. As long as three basic areas are covered adequately, the actual format of the business plan is unimportant. The three areas that must be covered are market, management, and finance. The market must include a description of the business and industry, the product/service, and the market strategy. Management encompasses the backgrounds of the owners and key managers. Finance includes historical and projected financial data.

Business plans should be written with the reader in mind. Whatever its purpose, the plan must provide the prospective reader with the relevant information needs to fulfill his/her responsibilities. Whether this is a manager or a bank loan officer will determine a great deal as far as content and format are concerned. Planning is a future-oriented process. The more we plan for the future, the fewer surprises we will face.

References

Jones, W. David. "Characteristics of Planning in Small Firms," *Journal of Small Business Management* 20(3) (July, 1982), pp. 15–19.

Mancuso, Joseph. *How to Start, Finance, and Manage Your Own Small Business,* Englewood Cliffs, NJ: Prentice-Hall, 1978.

Moyer, Reed. "Strategic Planning for the Small Firm," *Journal of Small Business Management* 20(3) (July, 1982), pp. 8–14.

Sexton, Donald L. and Van Auken, Philip M. "Prevalence of Strategic Planning in Small Business," *Journal of Small Business Management* 20(3) (July, 1982), pp. 20–26.

Van Kirk, John E. and Noonan, Kathleen. "Key Factors in Strategic Planning," *Journal of Small Business Management* 20(3) (July, 1982), pp. 1–7.

Appendix 2A
Sample Business Plan

Micro Systems
A Microcomputer Retail Store

Prepared by

Johnathan Ash
and
Darnell Greene

Submitted to

First National Bank
Austin, Texas
July 1986

Table of Contents

I. Summary of Highlights

This business plan is presented as a financing proposal. The principals, Johnathan Ash and Darnell Greene, are proposing to establish a computer retail specialty store at 3200 Guadalupe Street in Austin, Texas, approximately one mile north of the University of Texas campus. To begin operations, the principals will invest $90,000 cash and are seeking a bank loan of $200,000.

The business will be a corporation with three operating areas: sales, systems design and support, and administration. The sales area will be handled by Johnathan Ash. He has an MBA from Baylor University and six years' work experience in retail sales and sales management for the J. C. Penney Corporation. Systems design and support will be the task of a hired manager, Michael Moran. Mr. Moran has a graduate degree in computer science from Texas A&M University and has a working knowledge of four computer languages. His related work experience includes private consulting and four years teaching in the Austin community college system, during which time he was also manager of the Greenpoint Mall Computerland operation. Administration will be the direct responsibility of Darnell Greene, also a Baylor MBA. Mr. Greene has operated a small marketing firm and an income tax preparation firm and has worked as an auditor for the accounting firm Deloitte, Haskins and Sells for three and one-half years.

The firm will open in January 1988. Its initial focus will be on orientating the firm to its various publics. These will include the immediate community, the University of Texas and its neighboring professional districts, and the Austin market in general. Operations during the second through fifth years will concentrate on expanding market area and share and further adaptation to the immediate community needs. Expansion to sites near other major universities will be considered at this stage of the business.

The microcomputer industry has only been in existence since 1976. Since that time, it has expanded to a $6 billion per year industry. There are over 150 manufacturers participating in the industry, with over 3,200 retail outlets. The major manufacturers are IBM, DEC, Apple, Commodore, Tandy, and Hewlett-Packard. The market is segmented into three main areas: business, home, and transportable microcomputers.

The proposed store will carry the IBM and DEC product lines in the business class. Computers that have software and operating systems compatible with these two will be carried in the home and transportable segments. This will allow the software line to operate on all hardware carried in the store. Service will include all instruction, delivery and installation, seminars, systems design, and maintenance.

The target market consists of the business/professional and student communities of Austin. Specifically, market promotion will focus on the professional community in the immediate area of the store and the university community.

Estimated annual market size is 4,600 systems sold. First year sales are projected to be 2 percent of the total market. Sales volume for the first year of operation is estimated at approximately $594,000.

The principals will contribute $90,000 cash equity to the project and are seeking a line of credit of $200,000. Based on these conservative sales estimates, the operation will be able to cover administrative overhead expenses, variable expenses, and normal debt service and still be able to generate a moderate cash flow. The financial position in 1988 and 1989 is expected to be greatly improved as the market share expands and the systems design work increases.

II. Business Venture and Industry

A. THE PROPOSED BUSINESS VENTURE

1. Nature of the Business

The principals are proposing to open Micro Systems, a retail computer sales and service store to be located in Austin, Texas, in the vicinity of the University of Texas campus. The total estimated cost of opening a retail computer outlet is $250,000. Liquid capital of $90,000 and an additional $200,000 in the form of a loan or credit line is required to capitalize the operation. The principals will invest $90,000 in cash and are seeking a commercial bank interested in extending a term loan for the $200,000.

2. Structure of the Company

Micro Systems, Inc. will be as organized as a Subchapter S corporation and operate the retail store Micro Systems. Each shareholder will own one-half of the interest in the corporation, with profits and losses distributed accordingly.

3. Goals and Objectives

There are two major short-term goals for the venture. The first goal is to have the financing package completed by October and the retail store opened by January 1988. This will allow adequate time to complete leasehold improvements and initiate operating policies and procedures prior to the beginning of the spring semester at area universities. The second goal is to obtain an IBM authorized dealership. IBM is the leading hardware developer in the industry and it will be extremely important to secure those rights. Negotiations are now under way with IBM representatives to secure dealership rights. Approval of this funding proposal will remove the final obstacle that stands in the way of awarding of those rights.

The first year of operation will focus on orienting the business to the computer requirements of the local university communities and the nearby business and professional communities. The store operation will tailor its inventory, hours of operation, terms of sale, and services offered to support the needs of these customer categories.

Longer-term goals include the establishment of additional stores near other major university campuses. By this time, the organization will be incorporated and operating managers of each location will be offered a profit-sharing arrangement that will enable them to purchase up to 15 percent of the stock in the store they are managing.

4. Unique Advantages and Opportunities

a. *Concept.* The proposed venture will introduce an entirely new approach to computer retailing in the Austin market. Micro Systems will approach the market as a full-service retailer. In addition, it will operate a multifaceted vertical marketing program aimed at the business and professional community. The Micro Systems approach will focus on providing services to the customer, rather than simply hardware and software sales. These services will include professional systems consulting to assist customers in choosing a complete computer package uniquely designed for their needs. Also, a Micro Systems consultant will ensure that the system is performing properly and the customer has mastered the basic skills necessary to utilize it.

b. *Competition.* No major retailer has yet established a location in the vicinity of the university campus. Personal computers are now being sold through local department stores (Dillards and Sears) and a nearby Radio Shack. Thus, there is no specialist computer store in the market at this time.

c. *Location.* There is a high degree of customer turnover in and near a major college campus. Every year over 10,000 new students cycle in and out of the market. With a major segment of the market constantly renewing itself, the opportunities for continued customer support are promising.

d. *Target Market.* While the national pool of college students will decline through 1994, Texas is the only large state in which college enrollment is expected to increase. Because of net migration into the state and the relatively low tuition cost, the state's college enrollment is expected to increase by 10 percent by the year 2000 (*Wall Street Journal*, March 13, 1986).

With the location of the Microelectronics and Computer Technology Corp. (MCC) near the University of Texas campus, the opportunities for computer-related business growth in the Austin area will increase dramatically. Already the central Texas region is being referred to as the Silicon Prairie and a vast network of venture capitalists has developed. By remaining close to the cutting edge in computer research, Micro Systems will be able to service the expanding business and professional market in the area.

    e. *Computer Literacy.* The computer users of today are becoming literate at an earlier age, on the average, than those of a decade ago ("The Computer Age," *Time,* February 12, 1986). With this trend expected to continue into the future, each successive freshman class will have a higher degree of computer literacy than the preceding class. This will serve to increase the pool of potential student and faculty consumers at our campus computer store.

    f. *Convenience of Service.* Students and faculty will have access to service, software, and supplies within a mile of home, school, and office.

5. Business Operation

    Micro Systems will market microcomputers, peripherals, software, and services. All software sold will be supported through the typical industry warranties. Likewise, hardware will be maintained through an in-store authorized service center. Instructional seminars will be held for customers, potential customers, and other fee-paying individuals who wish to attend. A leasing program will be available both for individuals who wish to become familiar with operating a computer before purchasing one and those who may be unable to purchase outright, but wish to begin using a computer. Finally, a consignment program will be initiated to sell used computers for customers who wish to upgrade their systems.

B. THE INDUSTRY

1. General

    In 1975, Apple Computers introduced the first personal computer. Before 1974, the use of personal computers was confined primarily to hobbyists. In the past decade, computer usage has expanded dramatically. While the industry is not currently experiencing the 100 and 200 percent annual growth rates of the late 1970s and early 1980s, sales are expected to rise 28 percent in 1987.

    In conjunction with its annual Man of the Year selection in 1982, *Time Magazine* conducted a telephone survey of over 1,000 registered voters, polling them about their opinions on the microcomputer industry. Over 80 percent felt that in the very near future home computers would be as commonplace as television sets and automatic dishwashers. Two-thirds felt that the personal computer would ultimately increase productivity and raise living standards. The same percentage felt that the personal computer would improve the quality of their children's education.

    Of more immediate interest, industry experts forecast shipments of $2.77 billion during the 1987 Christmas season alone. The number of households owning computers has increased steadily to approximately 14 percent. Industry researchers predict that this figure will rise to 25 percent by the end of the decade ("Micro Computer Sales on the Rise," *Wall Street Journal*, June 13, 1986).

2. Manufacturing Industry

Since its beginning in 1976, literally hundreds of computer manufacturers have entered the marketplace. There are three major product types produced: the home-use computer, the small business computer, and the portable computer. The home-use computer usually has very limited capabilities. The market for these toylike units, which are capable of little more than video games, has virtually collapsed, with five major manufacturers dropping out of the market in 1984 alone.

Micro Systems will focus its attention on the small business computer system, more commonly called the *personal computer*. This segment of the market is the largest in terms of both dollars and varieties of models available. Prices range from around $1,000 for a system with one disk drive, black-and-white monitor, and dot-matrix printer to $10,000 for a system with hard disk, color graphics display, and letter-quality printer.

The portable computer is the most recent development in the industry. Osborne was introduced in 1981 as the first portable computer, and has since dropped out of the market. The leading portable producer, Compaq, has enlarged its share of the portable computer market by manufacturing a high quality unit that will run software designed for the IBM personal computer. The portables offer the same capabilities as the desk-top varieties and are priced between $700 and $4,500.

The major producers in the industry are IBM, Apple, DEC, Commodore, and Hewlett-Packard. Since IBM entered the industry in 1981, it has become the standard to emulate. The fastest growing portions of the market are the IBM compatible and IBM clone. Compatibles and clones offer the same capabilities as the IBM PC at much lower prices.

With the school system now producing more computer-literate individuals, the target market for more sophisticated models is likely to continue expanding. As this generation of students graduates into the business and professional world, new markets for the professional models in home use will open.

Development of computer programs on compact disks will provide the innovative thrust to take the industry into the 1990s. A compact disk, which resembles a palm-sized record album, can store about 1,000 times more information than the conventional floppy disk used today. The big advance in sales is likely to come when the industry begins to use the audio-visual capabilities of the compact disk in software design.

3. Retail Industry

The retail market is composed of independent stores, franchise operations, mass marketing, and OEM direct marketing. The first retail outlets were designed to serve the hobbyist. As the microcomputer received more attention as a home-use system, full-service speciality retail outlets began to spring up. Recently, franchises and OEM outlets have gained in popularity. The most noticeable trend has been the success of the franchises and the use of mass marketing of home and personal computers through discount stores.

As the microcomputer becomes more of a commodity item, distribution and sales methods will continue to be less specialized, with the emphasis away from OEM outlets to chain stores, such as Sears and Target. A notable exception to this trend is the market segment seeking business applications to the personal computer. Low prices are not the only criterion that this segment uses in its computer purchasing decision; service, both before and after the sale, is also highly important. It is this segment of the market that Micro Systems will focus on.

III. Product and Service

Micro Systems will provide a variety of products and services. The product line will be composed of the microcomputer hardware of several of the major computer manufacturers: IBM, Apple, Compaq, and DEC. The number of manufacturers included in the major line will be limited to maximize the exposure of each system, but provide a sufficient variety to offer the customer comparison and choice. One major concern will be compatibility among the product lines, such as desk-top to portable. Products will be selected according to operating systems, so that at least one product in each category will be compatible with one in every other category. This will enable customers to purchase compatible lines for each of their needs. Hardware selection will also revolve around the availability of software. The models chosen currently have the most software available.

Micro Systems will offer a full range of services to the customer and prospective customer. Full instruction will be given on the use of the hardware and software packages purchased in the store. In addition to these services, which are provided free of charge to customers, educational seminars will be offered to the fee-paying public.

Complete systems consulting will also be offered to prospective clients. Individual and business requirements will be evaluated and suggestions made for the hardware and software package that best services those requirements. To complete this aspect of the operation, full installation services will also be provided. A service representative will deliver and install the equipment if it is desired by the customer. This service is highly recommended to business customers and includes the installation of software packages, in-house instruction, and sample data operations. As a full-service retail outlet, we are seeking clients who require this total systems package.

Maintenance will be provided by qualified service technicians in our authorized service department. A consignment service will also be offered to customers to assist them in selling their used computers when they upgrade at Micro Systems.

IV. Market Strategy

A. AUSTIN PROFILE
The local market is Austin, Texas. The target market will be the students and faculties of the four local universities in the area and the business and professional people in northern Austin.

1. Trade Area
Austin is centrally located in the hill country of Texas. Approximately 2.5 million people live within 100 miles of the central city. The immediate trade area—Travis and its surrounding counties—has a population of over one million, with a disposable personal income of over $10 billion. Austin is considered the primary shopping area for most of these people.

2. Expanding Population
Austin has experienced a steady, stable growth over the past several decades. A 36 percent increase since 1972 now gives metropolitan Austin a population of approximately 450,000. This growth is expected to continue into the future, with the population of 1990 projected to exceed 550,000.

3. Balanced Economy
Austin is not dependent on one industry. As Austin is the capital of Texas, the state government is the largest single employer. However, over 600 manufacturing operations are represented in the area and provide a stable employment base to protect against major structural employment shifts.

4. Future Market
The area provides one of the most promising environments for the entrepreneur in the entire state of Texas. There is an expanding local population. The university enrollments are expanding and faculty and facilities in the important areas of computer science and electrical engineering are being emphasized at the University of Texas as a result of its commitment to MCC.

5. Expected Growth
Austin's rapid growth pattern provides a base for both prosperity and stability into the next decade. Its economy is secured on the base of the offices of the state government and student and faculty base at the University of Texas. In addition to the 60,000 students and faculty at this institution, there are also six other institutions of higher learning in the metropolitan area.

There are over 600 major manufacturing facilities in Travis, Williamson, and Hays counties, adding over $1.2 billion in value to products, with a payroll of over $440 million annually. In addition to the high technology base already in the area, including IBM, Motorola, Burroughs, Texas Instruments, Tracor, Data General, Lockheed Missile and Space, Continuum Software, and Tandem Computers, Austin has successfully attracted the Microelectronics and Computer Technology Corp. to locate next to the University of Texas campus. MCC has been described as an exercise in "technology venturing." **Technology venturing** is a term used to describe the process in which resources are brought together for the purpose of fostering the advancement of science, its conversion into useable technology, and its application to commercial ventures.

Twelve major high-tech companies headed by Control Data Corp. have agreed to pool their resources in an effort to advance the frontiers of computer science and artificial intelligence. This consortium will develop technology for application and commercialization to be licensed to the individual participants.

While MCC itself offers no general market product and directly employs only about 400 workers (mostly computer scientists and engineers), approximately sixty cities in twenty-seven states attempted to attract the cooperative research facility. Austin won the courtship in 1983 on the basis of a financial and institutional package known as "The Texas Incentive for Austin." The package included financial commitments of $41.75 million from the University of Texas and Texas A&M University and $20.5 million from the local Austin business community. The universities committed to establish additional faculty positions, including endowed, chaired professorships in electrical engineering and computer science and thirty faculty positions in microelectronics and computer science. Additional money was committed to fund research facilities at the two campuses and provide fellowship support for twenty-five graduate research assistants in the two areas and robotics.

Texas has long been considered the domain of the oil and gas industry and only an insignificant generator of new technology. However, the recruitment of MCC into the central Texas region has produced a welcome reaction from the venture capital community. In a market where money chases opportunities, Austin has become the fastest growing venture capital market in the country. The availability of venture capital has the effect of accelerating the formation of new business by fostering a high turnover of scientists and engineers who acquire expertise and depart to form new spinoff companies funded by the venture capital. These changes in the central Texas environment will help the area become a national leader in technology venturing and serve as a catalyst for growth in the business sector of the local community.

6. Labor Force

The labor force in the Austin metropolitan area is estimated by the Chamber of Commerce at 265,000. The labor force is well educated and highly skilled by national standards. Texas is a "right-to-work" state and wage scales are competitive. Labor union activity is minimal and labor friction is rare.

B. Local Market Area

Micro Systems will actively solicit customers from the entire Austin area. However, attention will be concentrated on the local universities and the business and professional communities in the northern Austin area. The following is a breakdown of the areas by census tract with general conclusions on market potential.

The prime target areas are the north central census tracts, including tracts 1 through 6, with portions of tracts 15 through 18. Secondary areas are those located north of M. L. King, Jr. Boulevard and west of Lamar Boulevard.

Tracts 1 through 6 are the older districts of Austin surrounding the University of Texas. Tracts 15 through 18 are newer developments. Both areas have significant business activity.

In addition to the 6,500 self-employed residents of the target tracts, there are over 20,000 additional self-employed individuals in the rest of the Austin metropolitan area. The area of northern Austin where Micro Systems will locate is highly concentrated with private medical practices, hospitals, and other professional groups, including attorneys, public accountants, and educators. There is also a high concentration of university students, as evidenced by the census data. There are also 20,000 individuals classified as executives or professional managers living in the target area.

With over 40,000 business and professional prospects in the Austin area plus 60,000 students, the market potential is encouraging. According to a study reported in *InfoWorld* (March 1985), nationwide, over 10 percent of the business and professional market buys a computer every year. This translates into 4,000 prospects in the Austin area, with 2,000 in northern Austin alone. Student purchases amount on the average to 1 percent of the relevant population, or approximately 600. These annual estimates are likely to increase with the growing popularity of computer technology in general and the positive environment in the Austin area.

Of the 4,600 immediate prospects, it is anticipated that Micro Systems will capture 2 percent of the market in the first year of operation, or approximately 90 unit sales. The standard unit price of a sale is estimated at $6,600, based on $4,000 for hardware, $1,500 for software, $700 for a printer, and $400 for peripherals and supplies. Naturally, some systems will cost more and some will cost less. This figure, however, will be used in all financial projections.

Second year market share goals will increase to 4 percent of the total volume, or 180 sales. The dollar value of this share is $1.12 million. This rapid increase is caused by achieving recognition in the Austin community and an aggressive sales and marketing campaign.

Third through fifth year market shares are projected to increase by one percentage point per year to 7 percent by the fifth year. This is approximately $2.1 million in current dollars, using a static estimate of the potential market. This estimate is fully attainable because of the business and professional focus of the operation, the prompt and aggressive nature of the promotion and marketing program, and the rapid and continuing growth of the Austin business community.

Service and consignment income have not been included in the earnings estimates. The typical computer store operation with a full-service repair shop can expect an additional 25 percent in income. Thus, market share estimates can be as much as 25 percent off and the projected sales will still be attainable.

C. LOCATION

Micro Systems will be located at 3200 Guadalupe in Austin, Texas. This location is one mile north of the University of Texas campus and two miles north of the central business district. The location has been chosen because of its nearness to the target market and the relative absence of nearby competitors.

The store is on a strip center, which has ample free parking, street access, and high traffic visibility. Large electric signs are already in place and will require only a change in face plates. Guadalupe is a highly traveled street and a major commuter thoroughfare. Traffic counts provided by the Austin Transit Authority show a daily flow of over 31,000 vehicles at an average speed of 28 miles per hour. There are major intersections two blocks north and three blocks south of the location. Signal lights at these intersections sufficiently break the flow of traffic to allow vehicles easy access to the store parking lot with little risk.

D. COMPETITION

Austin is a dynamic city of young executives and professionals. Accordingly, there are already a number of computer retail stores in operation in the city. Of the thirty stores in operation, only fifteen specialize in small business applications. Of these, only the two Computerland stores are authorized IBM dealers. The other operators are entertainment oriented and offer little in the way of systems design and consulting. The two Computerland stores have some expertise in these areas and thus represent the closest competitors to the Micro Systems operation.

ABC Computers is located five miles west of Micro Systems, Applied Computer Concepts is two miles north, and Data Standard is one and one-half miles south in the downtown area. These stores are likely to offer the most direct competition in the area of hardware sales. The three stores offer complete systems packages in the lines they carry; however, none carries IBM equipment. In addition, they have no systems design consulting to offer their clients, aside from the casual expertise of their sales representatives. Thus, the Micro Systems concept of a complete systems design capability will offer an operating and competitive edge over the three firms.

The two Computerland locations are eight and twelve miles away at regional shopping malls. These locations provide good customer access and if the computer were an impulse purchase, it might very well provide a significant competitive edge. Location does provide some exposure, but when the customer is ready to buy, service is the key. Price competition will not be a factor in this market. Thus, the systems design expertise and on-site service capability will give Micro Systems an edge even over these well-respected operations.

The other operations are functioning as computer shops. They sell to individuals who wish to buy computers, but provide little in the way of solutions to business or educational problems. A study by *PC World* (May 1985) on computer retailing indicates that the full-service stores are the most likely to be successful in a marketplace dominated by the more sophisticated, computer literate users of the future.

E. Promotion Strategy

1. Target Market

a. *Community.* The primary promotional strategy will focus on the professional and business community of the northern Austin area and the educational market of the Austin area universities, particularly the University of Texas. This also includes a significant number of medical practitioners and specialists, attorneys, and public accountants. There are several industrial parks in the immediate area, which contain numerous small- to medium-sized businesses.

The University of Texas has increased its commitment to computer and engineering sciences as a result of the location of MCC on the campus. With an increasing number of students and faculty in these areas, Micro Systems will carry the same systems and software installed at the university for those individuals looking to have a compatible system at home. While this segment of the market is currently small, indicators suggest that it will be one of the fastest growing in the area. Several of the smaller local universities require their incoming freshmen to purchase their own microcomputer and others, including the University of Texas, highly recommend it. Micro Systems intends to cultivate this potential and position itself to be the major local supplier for this market.

b. *Pricing.* Retail pricing will be at full list price as is the policy suggestion of the major suppliers: IBM, Apple, and DEC. The strategy behind this is that a full-service operation will draw customers who require these services and are willing to pay for them. These customers will include a vast portion of the small business and professional community. This strategy has proven to be successful in other similar operations around the country.

c. *Guarantees*. Micro Systems will honor all manufacturers' guarantees for products and additionally warrant the service function of the operation. This service warranty will include a return policy on equipment if back-up service provided by the manufacturer has been insufficient.

d. *Branding, Packaging, Labeling*. The store will be packaged and presented in a similar fashion to the successful franchise operations of Computerland and Entré. All products sold will be manufacturer-branded and displayed prominently. All personnel will be required to wear professional dress at all times. Because of a significant amount of off-premises sales calls, personnel will be viewed as part of the product and will be required to be professionally packaged themselves.

e. *Public Relations*. To attain the community recognition that is necessary for the business to grow at the anticipated rates, Micro Systems will be a member of the Austin Chamber of Commerce and the principals will join other local business and social organizations such as Lions and Rotary. In addition, Micro Systems will play an active role in the extracurricular activities of the area universities by sponsoring computer seminars, participating in fairs and expositions, and providing guest lecturers.

A newsletter targeting the business and professional community will be published bi-monthly. This newsletter will serve to inform the target group of the technological advances in the microcomputer field as originally reported in the leading microcomputer publications. Computer advances and applications in the various fields of business, such as electronic medicine, dentistry, architecture, and law will be stressed. This newsletter will be initiated in the second year of operation and will be paid out of the advertising budget.

f. *Advertising*. In addition to the specialized signs, point-of-purchase displays, and opening day promotions, Micro Systems will advertise in the local print and air media. The advertising budget is projected at 2 percent of gross sales plus an additional $21,500 for initial opening promotions. Advertising copy and presentations will be developed by Cross and Associates, a regional advertising firm that also handles southwestern advertising for several prominent businesses including Control Data and IBM. Advertising will be supplemented by our bi-monthly newsletter and specialized mailouts to cover the needs of the local community.

2. Justification of Market Share

Sales personnel will call directly on qualified prospects who have been identified by the use of response cards in brochures and other printed advertising. These prospects will be invited to attend seminars in which systems will be demonstrated and software applications explained. Customer referrals will also be solicited. A formal program of contact and follow-up will be initiated to ensure periodic exposure and an ever-expanding mailing list.

While the local market is large enough to support all current operations, Micro Systems' specialized systems approach will provide a significant market niche to support the modest market share projections. By providing services not offered by the competition, including demonstrations, seminars, and systems design, the market segment requiring these extras can be successfully penetrated.

Market research indicates a high interest for computer systems among university students. The successful approach to this group will include academic and recreational applications, in addition to an emphasis on the career potential of computer literacy.

Market share increases from 2 percent of the market to 4 percent of the market from year one to year two are readily attainable, given current market circumstances. Current market potential in the Austin area is 4,600 units per year and is growing at a rate of 2.5 percent annually. A two percentage point annual increase in market share may seem overly optimistic, so a more conservative growth rate was applied in the construction of the financial projections.

V. Management Organizational Structure

A. LEGAL ENTITY

The legal form of the business will be a corporation with Johnathan Ash and Darnell Greene each owning 50 percent interest in the company. Each will contribute one-half of the equity and profits will be shared according to that contribution.

B. ORGANIZATIONAL STRUCTURE

The functional operation of the business will be divided into three major areas, with the three individuals involved each being responsible for one area.

1. Sales

Mr. Johnathan Ash will be responsible for the sales department of the store. Mr. Ash will closely follow developments in the industry to ensure that the product line remains up to date. His duties will also include coordinating the efforts of the sales personnel and maintaining their level of competence in the systems offered.

2. Systems Design and Support

Mr. Michael Moran will be responsible for systems design and operation. This will include assembly, operation, training, and service for all units sold. The training room and authorized service shop will come under Mr. Moran's supervision.

3. Administration

Mr. Darnell Greene will be responsible for the daily operation of the business. It will be his duty to maintain the store front display, process all orders, and perform all accounting functions and other administrative duties essential to the operation. Advertising coordination, newsletter publication, and general follow-up activities will come under his direct supervision.

C. Background of Principals

Johnathan Ash is a graduate of Florida State University with a degree in International Business. After six years in retail sales and sales management with the J. C. Penney Corporation, he returned to Baylor University to earn an MBA in Entrepreneurship and Marketing. He is experienced in the use of the Commodore and IBM personal computers, has exposure on the IBM 4331 mainframe, and was a computer lab assistant for one year while at Baylor.

Darnell Greene has a BBA from the University of Wisconsin and an MBA from Baylor. His fields of study were accounting and management. After three and one-half years as an auditor for Deloitte, Haskins and Sells, Mr. Greene opened a small marketing firm in Michigan that is still being operated by members of his family. He has also operated a seasonal income tax preparation firm for the past several years. His various auditing assignments while with DH&S required the knowledge of computer systems. His duties included the supervision of staff and the familiarity of client requirements as related to data storage and retrieval. He is familiar with the Apple and IBM personal computers.

Michael Moran has a BBA in Accounting from Baylor University and an MS in Computer Science from Texas A&M University. He has been in systems design and consulting for four years since graduation. During the same period, he was the manager of one of the Austin Computerland stores and taught in Austin area community colleges. He is proficient in four computer languages: BASIC, FORTRAN, COBOL, and dBase. In addition, he has a working familiarity with many of the common software packages in use today.

VI. Financial Proposal

A. FINANCIAL SUMMARY

Micro Systems Inc. will open with a $200,000 bank loan and $90,000 in shareholder's equity. Total capitalization for the project will be as follows:

Inventory	$ 62,500
Leasehold Improvements	30,000
Furniture and Fixtures	25,000
Prepaid Rent	2,000
Working Capital	170,500
	$290,000

First year operations are projected to show the expected sales of $611,556. With breakeven sales at almost $640,000, the initial operating loss will be $18,696. Even during the startup phase of the business, cash flow from operations is showing signs of developing a favorable pattern. The negative $137,861 is almost exclusively caused by the aggressive build-up in inventory of $149,460 during this same period.

Breakeven sales levels are reached during the tenth month of operation and cash flow estimates show positive values beginning in the second quarter of year two. Second and third year estimates show steady improvement; net profit is projected at $50,101 and $91,230 for those two years, respectively.

Servicing the proposed loan is well within the capability of the operation as forecasted. However, to maintain an adequate cash cushion for operating purposes, it is projected that a short-term line of credit is necessary in year two. A credit line of approximately $100,000 would serve to smooth out the cash cycle and be adequate for the three projected years.

A close examination of the projected values for the firm's financial ratios show that they begin at acceptable levels and show improvement over the projection period. The current and quick ratios remain around 2.0 and 1.0 throughout the three-year projections and are both trending upward between the second and third year. Strong asset utilization ratios and an improving leverage position mark the entire period. Profitability moves quickly to acceptable levels after the initial startup.

B. ASSUMPTIONS TO FINANCIAL PROJECTIONS

1. Sales Revenue

Unit sales for the first year are projected at 2 percent of the estimated market of 4,600 potential customers. With the average selling price of a unit estimated at $6,600, gross sales are projected at $611,556.

Sales for the subsequent two years of operation are expected to grow by 100 and 30 percent, respectively. This is the result of capturing a market share of 4 and 5 percent in these two years.

2. Returns, Allowances, and Discounts

Returns, allowances, and discounts are projected at 3 percent of gross sales. As a result, net sales for year one is projected at $593,209.

3. Cost of Goods Sold

Cost of sales is estimated at 60 percent of net sales in year one, increasing to 62 percent in years two and three.

4. Operating Expenses

Operating expenses are projected according to the following schedule:

Advertising—$21,500 plus 3% of gross sales

Auto Expense—maximum of $400 or 1.3% of gross sales

Credit Card Expenses—5% of credit sales

Commissions—4% of net sales

Depreciation—ACRS schedule

Insurance—$6,000 annually

Accounting and Legal—$1,800 annually

Payroll Taxes—8% of salary expense

Phone—$500 initial cost, then 0.5% of gross sales

Rent—$2,000 per month

Salaries—$9,000 per month

Utilities—1% of gross sales

Operating expenses are projected to increase by 45 and 20 percent, respectively, during the second and third years.

5. Cash and Credit Sales

Sales breakdown is projected at 50 percent cash and 50 percent credit card sales.

6. Accounts Receivable

All credit card sales are projected to be collected in the month following the sale. Subsequent estimates are made assuming a constant sales/receivables ratio of 15.06.

7. Inventory
First year inventory levels remain at 25 percent of annual sales levels during each month. Years two and three levels are based on a cost of sales/inventory ratio of 2.75.

8. Debt Service
Debt service is based on a $200,000 loan for ten years at 16 percent.

C. ANALYSIS OF RISK
The major risk to be encountered is the area of sales volume. Unsuccessful market penetration could slow the speed at which the operation reaches the breakeven level of sales. Although this is potentially an issue, even if the estimated sales growth rates are one-half of the projected rates, breakeven sales at the operating level are achieved in the second year.

With a reduced sales estimate, cost estimates are also lower. Using a pessimistic scenario of cost escalation in which operating expenses grow at 60 and 80 percent of the rate of sales growth (instead of 45 and 67 percent in the most likely forecast), net losses of $17,220 and $2,258 are incurred in years two and three, respectively. However, this slower growth rate in sales and escalated cost schedule still does not hamper the operation's ability to service the debt and requires the same $100,000 line of credit as in the most likely case.

D. PROSPECTIVE FINANCIAL STATEMENTS
The relevant financial statements follow.

Micro Systems
Projected Opening Balance Sheet
January 1, 1988

Assets		Liabilities and Equity	
Current assets		Current liabilities	
Cash	170,500	Current portion—LTD	8,833
Inventory	62,500	Total current	8,833
Prepaid rent	2,000		
Total current	235,000	Long-term liabilities	
		Bank loan	191,167
Fixed assets		Total long-term	191,167
Leasehold impr.	30,000	Liabilities	200,000
Furn. and fixt.	25,000		
Total fixed	55,000	Owners' equity	90,000
Total assets	290,000	Total liab. and equity	290,000

Micro Systems
Projected Income Statement
For the Twelve Months Ending December 31, 1988

	Jan.	Feb.	March	April	May	June	July	Aug.	Sept.	Oct.	Nov.	Dec.	Total
Sales revenues													
Hardware	0	20,000	22,000	24,200	26,640	29,280	32,200	35,440	38,960	42,880	47,160	51,880	370,640
Software	0	7,500	8,250	9,075	9,990	10,980	12,075	13,290	14,610	16,080	17,685	19,455	138,990
Printers	0	3,500	3,850	4,235	4,662	5,124	5,635	6,202	6,818	7,504	8,253	9,079	64,862
Paper	0	500	550	605	666	732	805	886	974	1,072	1,179	1,297	9,266
Peripherals	0	1,500	1,650	1,815	1,998	2,196	2,415	2,658	2,922	3,216	3,537	3,891	27,798
Gross sales	0	33,000	36,300	39,930	43,956	48,312	53,130	58,476	64,284	70,752	77,814	85,602	611,556
Returns	0	990	1,089	1,198	1,319	1,449	1,594	1,754	1,929	2,123	2,334	2,568	18,347
Net sales	0	32,010	35,211	38,732	42,637	46,863	51,536	56,722	62,355	68,629	75,480	83,034	593,209
COGS	0	19,206	21,127	23,239	25,582	28,118	30,922	34,033	37,413	41,178	45,288	49,820	355,926
Gross profit	0	12,804	14,084	15,493	17,055	18,745	20,614	22,689	24,942	27,452	30,192	33,214	237,284

Operating expenses													
Advertising	1,792	2,782	2,881	2,990	3,111	3,241	3,386	3,546	3,721	3,915	4,126	4,360	39,851
Auto	400	429	472	519	571	628	691	760	836	920	1,012	1,113	8,350
Credit card	0	825	908	998	1,099	1,208	1,328	1,462	1,607	1,769	1,945	2,140	15,289
Commissions	0	1,280	1,408	1,549	1,705	1,875	2,061	2,269	2,494	2,745	3,019	3,321	23,728
Depreciation	688	688	688	688	688	688	688	688	688	688	688	688	8,250
Insurance	500	500	500	500	500	500	500	500	500	500	500	500	6,000
Acct. and legal	150	150	150	150	150	150	150	150	150	150	150	150	1,800
Payroll	720	822	833	844	856	870	885	902	920	940	962	986	10,538
Phone	500	165	182	200	220	242	266	292	321	354	389	428	3,558
Rent	2,000	2,000	2,000	2,000	2,000	2,000	2,000	2,000	2,000	2,000	2,000	2,000	24,000
Salaries	9,000	9,000	9,000	9,000	9,000	9,000	9,000	9,000	9,000	9,000	9,000	9,000	108,000
Utilities	500	330	363	399	440	483	531	585	643	708	778	856	6,616
Total	16,250	18,971	19,384	19,837	20,340	20,884	21,486	22,153	22,879	23,687	24,569	25,542	255,980
Oper. profit	−16,250	−6,167	−5,299	−4,344	−3,285	−2,139	−871	535	2,063	3,765	5,623	7,672	−18,696
Interest	2,667	2,658	2,648	2,639	2,629	2,620	2,610	2,600	2,590	2,580	2,570	2,559	31,370
Net profit	−18,917	−8,825	−7,947	−6,983	−5,914	−4,759	−3,481	−2,065	−527	1,185	3,053	5,113	−50,066

Micro Systems
Projected Cash Flow Statement
For the Twelve Months Ending December 31, 1988

	Jan.	Feb.	March	April	May	June	July	Aug.	Sept.	Oct.	Nov.	Dec.	Total
Receipts													
Cash sales	0	16,005	17,606	19,366	21,319	23,431	25,768	28,361	31,178	34,315	37,740	41,517	296,605
Credit sales	0	0	15,180	16,698	18,368	20,220	22,224	24,440	26,899	29,571	32,546	35,794	241,939
Equity	90,000	0	0	0	0	0	0	0	0	0	0	0	90,000
Loan	200,000	0	0	0	0	0	0	0	0	0	0	0	200,000
Total	290,000	16,005	32,786	36,064	39,686	43,651	47,992	52,801	58,077	63,885	70,286	77,311	828,544
Disbursements													
Inventory	62,500	0	14,324	26,888	29,577	32,612	35,723	39,334	43,367	47,554	52,471	57,618	441,968
Leasehold impr.	30,000	0	0	0	0	0	0	0	0	0	0	0	30,000
Furn. and fixt.	25,000												25,000
Advertising	21,500	990	1,089	1,198	1,319	1,449	1,594	1,754	1,929	2,123	2,334	2,568	39,847
Auto	400	429	472	519	571	628	691	760	836	920	1,012	1,113	8,350
Commissions	0	1,280	1,408	1,549	1,705	1,875	2,061	2,269	2,494	2,745	3,019	3,321	23,728
Insurance	500	500	500	500	500	500	500	500	500	500	500	500	6,000
Acct. and legal	150	150	150	150	150	150	150	150	150	150	150	150	1,800
Payroll	720	822	833	844	856	870	885	902	920	940	962	986	10,538
Phone	500	165	182	200	220	242	266	292	321	354	389	428	3,558
Rent	4,000	2,000	2,000	2,000	2,000	2,000	2,000	2,000	2,000	2,000	2,000	2,000	26,000
Salaries	9,000	9,000	9,000	9,000	9,000	9,000	9,000	9,000	9,000	9,000	9,000	9,000	108,000
Utilities	500	330	363	399	440	483	531	585	643	708	778	856	6,616
Debt service	3,350	3,350	3,350	3,350	3,350	3,350	3,350	3,350	3,350	3,350	3,350	3,350	40,200
Total	158,120	19,017	33,671	46,598	49,689	53,158	56,751	60,896	65,509	70,342	75,965	81,890	771,605
Cash flow	131,880	-3,012	-885	-10,534	-10,002	-9,507	-8,759	-8,095	-7,433	-6,457	-5,679	-4,579	56,938
Cumulative	131,880	128,868	127,983	117,450	107,447	97,940	89,181	81,086	73,653	56,196	61,517	56,938	

Micro Systems
Projected Balance Sheet
December 31, 1988

Assets

Current assets

Cash	56,938
Inventory	149,460
Accounts rec.	39,377
Prepaid rent	2,000
Total current	247,775

Fixed assets

Leasehold impr.	30,000
Furn. and fixt.	25,000
Less: depr.	8,250
Total fixed	46,750
Total assets	294,525

Liabilities and Equity

Current liabilities

Accounts payable	63,423
Current portion—LTD	10,354
Total current	73,777

Long-term liabilities

Bank loan	180,814
Total long-term	180,814
Liabilities	254,591
Owners' equity	90,000
Retained earnings	−50,066
Total liab. and equity	294,525

Micro Systems
Projected Income Statements

	1989	1990
Sales estimate	1,186,418	1,542,343
Cost of sales	735,579	956,253
Gross profit	450,839	586,090
Operating expenses (+ depr.)	332,659	397,540
Lease and rental expense	26,400	29,040
Operating profit	91,780	159,510
Interest expense	29,850	28,066
Profit before tax	61,930	131,444
Taxes	11,829	40,214
Net profit	50,101	91,230

Micro Systems
Projected Cash Flow Statements

	1988	1989	1990
Plus: Sales	593,209	1,186,418	1,542,343
Less: Change in accounts rec.	39,377	39,377	23,626
Less: Purchases	505,386	853,602	1,036,498
Plus: Change in payables	63,423	63,423	38,054
Less: Operating expenses	223,730	324,409	389,290
Less: Lease and rental	24,000	26,400	29,040
Less: Change in prepaids	2,000	0	0
Cash Flow from Operations	−137,861	6,053	101,943
Other expenses or income:			
Less: Taxes	0	11,829	40,214
Net Cash Flow from Operations	−137,861	−5,776	61,729
Costs of financing:			
Less: Interest expense	31,370	29,850	28,066
Net Cash Flow	−169,231	−35,626	33,663
Current debt amortization:			
Current maturities of long-term debt	0	0	12,137
Notes payable—short term	8,833	10,354	102,918
Cash Flow after Debt Amortization	−178,064	−45,980	−81,393
Financing requirements:			
Change in gross fixed assets	55,000	0	0
Cash Flow Requirements	−233,064	−45,980	−81,393
Other sources of funds:			
New notes payable—short term	10,354	102,918	115,555
New long-term borrowing	−10,354	0	0
Total Other Sources	0	102,918	115,555
Change in Cash Balance	−233,062	56,938	34,163
Cash Flow Analysis			
Days sales outstanding	24	24	24
Days COGS in inventory	153	133	133
Days purchases in payables	46	54	58
Cash conversion period	132	103	99
Break-even sales	639,952	944,891	1,122,579

Micro Systems
Projected Balance Sheets

	1989	1990
Assets		
Cash	113,876	148,039
Accounts and notes receivable	78,754	102,380
Inventory	267,483	347,728
Prepaid expenses	2,000	2,000
Total current	462,113	600,147
Gross fixed assets	55,000	55,000
Accumulated depreciation	16,500	24,750
Total assets	500,613	630,397
Liabilities and Net Worth		
Accounts and notes payable, trade ...	126,846	164,900
Notes payable—short term	102,918	115,555
Current maturities—LTD	12,137	14,228
Total current	241,901	294,683
Long-term debt	168,677	154,449
Total liabilities	410,578	449,132
Common stock	90,000	90,000
Earned surplus	35	91,265
Total liabilities and net worth	500,613	630,397

Micro Systems
Projected Ratios

	1988	1989	1990
Percentage of Total Assets			
Cash and equivalents	19.33	22.75	23.48
Accounts and notes rec.			
(trade)	13.37	15.73	16.24
Inventory	50.75	53.43	55.16
All other current	0.68	0.40	0.32
Total current assets	84.13	92.31	95.20
Fixed assets (net)	15.87	7.69	4.80
Total assets	100.00	100.00	100.00
Percentage of Total Liabilities and Net Worth			
Notes payable—short term	3.52	20.56	18.33
Current maturities—LTD	0.00	2.42	2.26
Accounts and notes payable (trade)	21.53	25.34	26.16
Total current liabilities	25.05	48.32	46.75
Long-term debt	61.39	33.69	24.50
Net worth	13.56	17.98	28.75
Total liabilities and net worth	100.00	100.00	100.00
Percentage of Sales			
Sales	100.00	100.00	100.00
Cost of sales	60.00	62.00	62.00
Gross profit	40.00	38.00	38.00
Operating expenses	43.15	30.26	27.66
Operating profit	−3.15	7.74	10.34
All other expenses	5.29	2.52	1.82
Profit before tax	−8.44	5.22	8.52
Ratios			
Current	3.36	1.91	2.04
Quick	1.31	0.80	0.85
Sales/Receivables	15.06	15.06	15.06
Cost of sales/Inventory	2.38	2.75	2.75
Sales/Working capital	3.41	5.39	5.05
EBIT/Interest	−0.60	3.07	5.68
Cash flow/Current Mat. LTD	NA	4.81	6.99
Fixed/Worth	1.17	0.43	0.17
Debt/Worth	6.38	4.56	2.48
Percent profit before taxes/Tangible net worth	−125.37	68.78	72.51
Percent profit before taxes/Total assets	−17.00	12.37	20.85
Sales/Net fixed assets	12.69	30.82	50.99
Sales/Total assets	2.01	2.37	2.45
Percent depr., depletion amort./Sales	1.39	0.70	0.53
Percent lease and rental exp./Sales	4.05	2.23	1.88
Percent officers' comp./Sales	15.17	NA	NA

3
Preparing Prospective
Financial Statements

I t should be quite obvious from the previous discussion of the business planning process that the preparation of financial forecasts and projections plays a very important role. The actual mechanics of preparing prospective financial statements are very simple, but the process itself is rather complex.

A prospective financial statement can take the form of either a financial forecast or a financial projection. In order to fully appreciate the process of preparing prospective financial statements, the distinction between the terms "forecast" and "projection" should be made clear.

In 1985, the Auditing Standards Board of the American Institute of Certified Public Accountants (AICPA) issued a *Statement on Standards for Accountants' Services on Prospective Financial Information* entitled "Financial Forecasts and Projections." The purpose of this statement was to provide guidance to accountants who prepare forecasts and projections for their clients. This statement clearly distinguishes the differences between a financial forecast and a financial projection.

A **financial forecast** is defined as a set of prospective financial statements, including balance sheet, income statement, and cash flow statement, which represents the expected financial position of a business entity at some point in the future. It is based on assumptions reflecting expected conditions and events and a course of action that will be taken by the firm's management. A financial forecast is expressed in monetary terms as a specific value or range of values.

A **financial projection** is also defined as a set of financial statements that includes the same reports and represents the expected financial position of a business entity at some point in the future. However, a financial projection is based on one or more hypothetical assumptions and presents one or more hypothetical courses of action for management's evaluation. A financial projection is prepared to answer the question "What if . . .?" It is based on management's assumptions of the conditions that are expected to exist if specific actions are taken in response to certain events that could occur.

The final products of a financial forecast and a financial projection are quite similar. Both include the required financial statements and all significant assumptions upon which they are based. Thus, the real distinction between the two lies in the nature of the assumptions. The financial forecast is based on assumptions that reflect the conditions and events that are reasonably expected, to the best of management's knowledge and beliefs. In contrast, the financial projection is based on hypothetical assumptions that reflect conditions and events that might occur and a course of action that is likely to result.

A prospective financial statement is no more realistic than the assumptions (reasonable or hypothetical) upon which it is based. Thus, one of the most important aspects of the process (and the most difficult to learn) is that of recognizing and evaluating the reliability of assumptions.

Based on a set of carefully developed goals and objectives, the prospective financial statement provides the profitability and cash flow distinctions of a comprehensive strategic plan. As such, it provides extremely useful information about the business operation in general and the probable impact of various proposed changes on the operation.

Even though the process of preparing prospective financial statements is time consuming, it is an integral part of the overall management process. Accurate financial statements serve as an operating guide for the entrepreneur. They provide information that will be useful in anticipating problems and will actually serve to encourage innovation within the enterprise. The information will help in developing contingency plans to deal with problems when they arise or, better yet, operating techniques to avoid the problems altogether.

Financial statement preparation is a skill that can be learned and improved upon through practice. It is nothing more than a means of anticipating events that are likely to take place in the future. This is not as mysterious as it may seem at first because much of what will happen in the near future is not subject to change. Many factors that are not fixed can be influenced if they are properly understood and anticipated. Examples of items that are known and not subject to rapid change are rent, debt service, property taxes, officers' salaries, unit labor costs, and raw materials costs (at least in the short run). Items that can be influenced include utility costs, commissions, bonuses, advertising expenses, and maintenance. Thus, the preparation of prospective financial statements is a skill that is to be refined within the framework of what is known and anticipated about the future.

The key to a successful business operation is an active management process. This type of operation has a management team that is intimately involved in the day-to-day operations and planning process. The successful manager is future oriented and realizes that the past cannot be managed; previous decisions have already had their impact and the results cannot be altered. Even though our vision looking back into the past is 20–20, the only reason to study previous decisions is to evaluate their results and attempt to emulate successes and avoid failures.

We manage for the future. The process of managing an operation is an attempt to establish certain procedures and bring about a specific sequence of events. The decisions that are made today will have little effect on today's operations. They will, however, help determine the conditions under which future decisions will be made. Current production capacity is determined by past decisions such as whether or not to build a new plant facility, how much office space to acquire, or when to order additional production equipment. The effects of a decision made today to increase capacity will not be realized immediately. It takes time to construct a new plant, add office capacity, or accept delivery of new machinery and equipment.

A well-defined and flexible management philosophy includes the preparation of prospective financial statements. This provides a way for managers to anticipate future events and plan for them. The individuals who do not include this ingredient in their management philosophy will find themselves spending a significant amount of their time reacting to events, "putting out fires," rather than actively charting a course for their operation.

In this chapter we will examine the mechanics of preparing prospective financial statements. The discussion will include an examination of the steps taken in putting together prospective financial statements, the various methods used in forecasting and projecting, and some suggestions for constructing reliable forecasts.

Steps in Preparing Prospective Financial Statements

The fundamentals of preparing prospective financial statements are the starting point for the planning, budgeting, and decision making in any venture. Although the process is essentially the same for either a startup or an existing venture, the actual mechanics can be quite different. We will begin by discussing the steps involved in preparing prospective financial statements for an existing business and then explore the unique problems encountered in the context of a new venture.

Preparing Prospective Financial Statements
for the Existing Business

This type of preparation is a straightforward task. It involves a close examination of the firm's sales and operating history, an estimation of the sales expected during the period under study, and an estimate of the financial requirements necessary to support the predicted level of sales.

Sales History. A sales forecast begins with a careful analysis of the firm's sales and operating history over the past several years. The purpose of this exercise is to identify key factors that affect the operation and develop assumptions that will provide the basis for the prospective financial statements. For many closely held businesses, this may mean only three to five years of operating data. For others, there may be ten or more years of sales data to analyze. Depending on the degree of sophistication of the sales estimation technique used, more than ten years of operating data is seldom needed for the analysis.

Figure 3–1 summarizes the sales history for the Rosedale Health and Fitness Centers. Since its inception in 1979, the business has expanded from one facility with thirty pieces of Nautilus equipment, a whirlpool, sauna, and steam room to the point where it is now preparing to open its fifth center complete with indoor swimming pool, aerobics classes, indoor running track, and gymnastics facilities.

Figure 3–1 shows the sales history for Rosedale from 1979 to 1986, with projections to 1989. Rosedale was the first fitness facility to introduce Nautilus equipment to this southwestern urban market. Since opening their first center, the management has aggressively pursued the marketplace through continuous upgrading of equipment and heavy promotion.

Sales in 1980, the first full year of operations, were $269,000. Since that time, they have increased to $3,919,000, which represents a 56.28 percent annual compound growth rate. Much of this growth occurred between 1984 and 1986, over which time sales increased from $1,055,000 to $3,919,000.

Rosedale has expanded facilities quite rapidly over the seven years of operations, adding a new club every other year. The fifth health center will be in full operation in 1987 and is expected to add $665,000 in sales, with the four existing centers increasing sales by an average of approximately 18 percent. This projects to an estimated sales of $5,290,000 in 1987, or a growth rate of 35 percent.

The firm's long-range plan is to concentrate on improving the current operation by adding tennis and racketball facilities at several of the locations. The sales growth projections for 1988 and 1989 are 35 and 20 percent, respectively.

Many of the preceding estimates are dependent on the economic conditions in the local marketplace and the firm's ability to aggressively promote its product. It is important for the sales forecast to be as accurate as possible. The possible consequences of a significant forecasting error can be quite serious. Thus, it is important that, as the operation becomes more complicated, more advanced techniques of estimating sales be used.

Procedures for Estimating Future Sales. There are numerous techniques available for the entrepreneur who wants to estimate future sales for the existing business. The actual procedure used will depend on the nature of the problem and the data that are available.

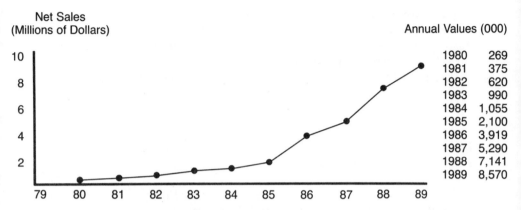

Net Sales
(Millions of Dollars)

Annual Values (000)

1980	269
1981	375
1982	620
1983	990
1984	1,055
1985	2,100
1986	3,919
1987	5,290
1988	7,141
1989	8,570

Figure 3–1. Sales History for Rosedale Health and Fitness Centers

Statistical Analysis. There is a wide range of statistical techniques that can be used for estimating future sales. The simplest method is the use of an adaptive mechanism. This technique takes into consideration only the most recent sales data to estimate future sales. The adaptive scheme is formulated as follows:

$$R_{t+1} = R_t + \lambda(R_t - R_{t-1})$$

where R_t is the level of sales in period t and λ is the partial adjustment coefficient representing the relative importance of the most recent period's absolute change (the expression in parentheses) in estimating next period's sales.

If $\lambda = 0$, the most recent period's change in sales is given no weight at all and $R_{t+1} = R_t$. This represents what is referred to as a "stationary state" estimate, where there is no change in sales. If $\lambda = 1$, the level of sales is expected to increase by the same absolute amount. That is to say, the expected change in sales is estimated to be equal to the most recent absolute change. Values of λ other than zero and one indicate that the change in sales is expected to be a fraction of the most recent absolute change. That fraction can of course be either greater than or less than one.

This formula can be used to estimate sales for Rosedale. To simplify the math, suppose the partial adjustment coefficient is assumed to be unity, indicating that we were expecting the same absolute increase in sales in the projection year as was experienced in the last historical year. R_t is equal to $3,919,000 and R_{t-1} is equal to $2,100,000 (sales in 1986 and 1985, respectively). Projected sales, R_{t+1}, are estimated using the preceding equation:

$$R_{t+1} = 3.919 + 1.0(3.919 - 2.1)$$
$$= 3.919 + 1.819 = 5.738$$

In other words, sales in 1987 are expected to be $5,738,000.

Another easy-to-use statistical technique is that of estimating future sales based on a relative change over time. The simplest approach is to assume that the sales will increase by the same percentage that it increased from period $t - 1$ to period t. The formulation for such an estimating scheme is:

$$R_{t+1} = R_t + [(R_t - R_{t-1})/R_{t-1}] \cdot R_t$$

If sales grew at a rate of 10 percent in the past period t relative to period $t - 1$, then future sales will be 10 percent greater in period $t + 1$ than sales of period t.

This technique can be easily illustrated using the Rosedale situation once again. If sales are expected to grow at the same percentage rate:

$$
\begin{aligned}
R_{t+1} &= 3.919 + [(3.919 - 2.1)/2.1] \cdot 3.919 \\
&= 3.919 + (1.819/2.1) \cdot 3.919 \\
&= 3.919 + 3.395 = 7.314
\end{aligned}
$$

In this case, sales are expected to be $7,314,000 in the projection year.

Each of the preceding methods is easy and inexpensive to use. However, they all share the same limitation: only information on past sales is taken into account in predicting future sales. Thus, strict reliance on these techniques limits one's ability to predict major turning points in the statistical series of data.

Regression analysis is a more sophisticated technique that overcomes many of the weaknesses of the previously discussed techniques. It is a general statistical technique through which one can formulate a causal relationship between a dependent variable and one or more independent variables. The procedure is used to estimate a functional relationship, and, given this relationship and estimated values of the independent variables, a value for the dependent variable can be estimated.

Simple regression is the estimation of a functional relationship between a dependent variable and one independent variable. The basic statistical relationship is one of fitting a least-squares regression line to the data. It can be shown graphically by the use of a scatter diagram.

A scatter diagram, as is implied by the name, is a graph showing the values of the two variables in relation to each other. Figure 3–2 shows the relationship between sales and advertising expenditures for the JLM Clothiers, a men's retail clothing store.

The graphical relationship is indicative of the actual statistical relationship between the two variables. The line drawn through the scatter diagram is the graphical representation of the least-squares line that best fits the ob-

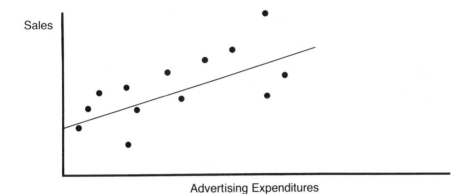

Figure 3–2. JLM Clothiers: Scatter Diagram of Sales and Advertising Expenditures

served data. Actually estimating the simple regression results in the following regression equation:

$$\text{Sales} = 141{,}215 + 15.75 \cdot (\text{Advertising Expenditures})$$
$$R^2 = .68$$

The equation predicts that for every one dollar increase in advertising, sales will increase by $15.75. Thus, if $10,000 is spent on advertising, sales are projected to be $298,715 [$141,215 + ($15.75 · $10,000)].

The coefficient of determination, R^2, can be interpreted as the percentage of the variation in the dependent variable that is explained by the variation in the independent variable. In the preceding example, 68 percent of the variation in sales is explained by the variation in advertising expenditures. The higher the value of R^2, the greater the level of confidence one has in the predictions based on the regression equation.

In most cases, there is more than one independent variable that is statistically related to the dependent variable. Under those circumstances, multiple regression analysis can be used to estimate the relationship. The multiple linear regression model provides a way to estimate the relationship between a dependent variable and several independent variables.

It is beyond the scope of this book to provide a detailed explanation of the use of linear regression. Most entrepreneurs who will be using this statistical technique as a forecasting tool will also be using a computer system for their data analysis. Thus, those interested in using multiple linear regression should study the appropriate chapter in the users' guide of the statistical package being used for estimation.

Two very popular packages are the Statistical Package for the Social Sciences (SPSS) and the Statistical Analysis System (SAS). With the increased popularity of personal computers, several statistical packages have also been developed for use with the microcomputer.

As long as the underlying structural relationships are fairly stable, the use of regression analysis in forecasting is quite reliable. In any case, assuming that the explained variance is relatively high, this systematic approach to forecasting is greatly preferred over the usual ad hoc procedures that many try to pass off as credible.

Estimating Financial Requirements. Once sales estimates are made, the next step in the process is to estimate the firm's future financial (asset) requirements. If sales growth is minimal, the only investment in assets may be for the purpose of replacing equipment that has worn out.

However, if sales are expected to grow appreciably, the firm can expect significant pressure to increase total assets. This can take the form of an incremental need for inventories to ensure appropriate delivery schedules or simply the proportionate increase in accounts receivable because of the simultaneous increase in credit sales. As a result, even a relatively moderate increase in expected sales can cause an increase in asset requirements and concurrently, a need for additional financing that might be beyond the firm's ability to generate the funds internally from operations.

The Percent-of-Sales Method. The percent-of-sales method is a simple technique used to estimate the financial requirements of a firm. The basic assumption underlying the calculation is that the firm's total asset base is a function of its sales volume. The first step in using this method is to express the various balance sheet and income statement categories as a percentage of sales. The prospective financial statements are then generated by multiplying these values by the expected future sales volume. Certain categories are likely to increase at roughly the same rate as sales, while others will not. The categories are referred to respectively as "spontaneous" and "nonspontaneous." Those asset and liability categories that increase more or less automatically are cash, accounts receivable, inventory, and accounts payable.

The categories that are not expected to vary proportionately with sales include balance sheet items such as gross fixed assets, accumulated depreciation, notes payable, common stock, and retained earnings. These items change either at the discretion of the managers of the firm or as a result of other operating factors. In addition, various expense categories can be considered fixed or quasi-fixed in nature. These include rental expense, depreciation expense, interest expense, and administrative salaries. As a result, these items must be estimated under a different set of assumptions.

The balance sheet and income statement for the Lake Brazos Catfish

Huts, Inc., a family-owned chain of restaurants, are given in Exhibit 3–1. Sales volume in 1986 was $1,526,600, with an after-tax profit margin of 11.2 percent. Shareholders of the corporation received 28.0 percent of the after-tax profit as dividends. Sales are expected to increase by 11 percent in 1987 to a level of $1,694,530.

The first step in preparing prospective financial statements using this method is to express each financial statement category as a percentage of sales. Under most circumstances, the percent-of-sales ratios used will be from the most recent fiscal year. However, it is not at all unusual to examine the trend on these forecasting ratios and project new values or use averages of past values. For purposes of this illustration, we will use figures from the

EXHIBIT 3–1

Lake Brazos Catfish Huts, Inc.
Balance Sheet for the Period Ending December 31, 1986

Assets

Cash	$ 21,810	1.43%
Cash equivalents	176,460	11.56
Accounts receivable	42,660	2.79
Inventory	87,590	5.74
Prepaid expenses	25,810	1.69
Total current assets	$ 354,330	
Gross fixed assets	$1,142,760	n.a.
Accumulated depreciation	184,400	n.a.
All other noncurrent	36,060	2.36
Total Assets	$1,348,750	

Liabilities and Net Worth

Accounts payable (trade)	$ 83,580	5.47
Short-term notes payable	40,700	n.a.
Accruals	54,270	3.55
Current maturities—LTD	10,450	n.a.
Total current liabilities	$ 189,000	
Long-term debt	$ 47,610	n.a.
Deferred income tax	12,160	0.80
Common stock	29,460	n.a.
Paid-in capital	96,690	n.a.
Retained earnings	973,830	n.a.
Total Liabilities and Net Worth	$1,348,750	

EXHIBIT 3–1 continued

Income Statement
For the Twelve Months Ending December 31, 1986

Net sales	$1,526,600	100.00%
Cost of sales	765,200	50.12
Gross profit	$ 761,400	49.88
Operating expenses (excluding depr.)	442,300	28.97
Depreciation expense	37,620	n.a.
Operating profit	$ 281,480	
Interest expense	10,260	n.a.
Before-tax profit	$ 271,280	
Taxes	105,180	n.a.
After-tax profit	$ 166,100	
Dividends	46,460	n.a.

most recent year. Thus, the percent-of-sales ratios are calculated using the 1986 sales volume of $1,526,600.

The analyst should use discretion to ensure that only those categories that change spontaneously with sales are estimated using these assumptions. The categories that do not vary directly with sales, such as Gross Fixed Assets, are given the designation "n.a.," or "not applicable." These categories will vary at the discretion of the manager or according to some other prescribed formula. These ratios are shown in the second column of Exhibit 3–1.

The next step is to multiply these percent-of-sales ratios by the estimated sales volume of $1,694,530 (estimated sales for 1987) as shown in Exhibit 3–2. At this point in the analysis, there are several categories that must be changed using additional information available only to the forecaster.

Any addition to Gross Fixed Assets depends on the capacity of the existing physical plant. Additions in the form of facilities expansion or equipment are usually "lumpy," that is, they are added in fixed increments. If a plant is operating at full capacity and sales are projected to increase by 10 percent, it would be purely coincidental for Gross Fixed Assets to also increase by 10 percent. Accumulated Depreciation will in general be calculated by adding Depreciation Expense from the current year's income statement to Accumulated Depreciation from last year's balance sheet.

Long-Term Debt and its Current Maturities will depend on the rate at which the existing notes are being amortized and any new debt that is being added. Likewise, any changes in Common Stock and Paid-In Capital will depend on decisions made by the current owners of the company. Retained

EXHIBIT 3–2

Lake Brazos Catfish Huts, Inc.
Proforma Balance Sheet for the Period Ending
December 31, 1987

Assets

Cash	$ 24,208
Cash equivalents	195,863
Accounts receivable	47,351
Inventory	97,221
Prepaid expenses	28,648
Total current assets	$ 393,292
Gross fixed assets	$1,442,760[a]
Accumulated depreciation	267,020[b]
All other noncurrent	40,025
Total Assets	$1,609,057

Liabilities and Net Worth

Accounts payable (trade)	$ 92,770
Short-term notes payable	0[c]
Accruals	60,237
Current maturities—LTD	10,450[d]
Total current liabilities	$ 163,458
Long-term debt	$ 37,160[e]
Other noncurrent liabilities	13,497
Common stock	29,460[f]
Paid-in capital	96,690[f]
Retained earnings	1,082,481[g]
Total Liabilites and Net Worth	$1,422,746
Financing requirement	186,311
	$1,609,057

Income Statement
For the Twelve Months Ending December 31, 1987

Net sales	$1,694,530
Cost of sales	849,341
Gross profit	$ 845,189
Operating expenses (excluding depr.)	490,935
Depreciation expense	82,620[h]
Operating profit	$ 271,635
Interest expense	29,800[i]

EXHIBIT 3–2 continued

Before-tax profit	$ 241,835
Taxes	90,994[j]
After-tax profit	$ 150,841
Dividends	$ 42,190[k]

---

[a]New kitchen equipment and furniture is added to Gross Fixed Assets—net addition of $300,000.

[b]Accumulated Depreciation equals 1986 Accumulated Depreciation plus 1987 Depreciation Expense.

[c]Short-Term Notes Payable are paid by the end of the year.

[d]Unless additional information is given, assume that Current Maturities are constant.

[e]Long-Term Debt equals 1986 Long-Term Debt minus 1986 Current Maturities on Long-Term Debt.

[f]Values for 1987 are the same as those for 1986.

[g]Retained Earnings equals 1986 Retained Earnings plus 1987 After-Tax Profit less 1987 Dividends paid.

[h]Depreciation equals 1986 Depreciation plus 15 percent of $300,000.

[i]Estimated interest rate on 1986 debt [$10,260/($40,700 + $10,450 + $47,610)] times 1987 Long-Term Debt ($47,610) plus 1987 Financing Requirement ($186,311) times the interest rate on that loan (assumed to be 13.35 percent).

[j]Income taxes are estimated using the following schedule: 15 percent on income up to $25,000; 18 percent on income between $25,000 and $50,000; 30 percent on income between $50,000 and $75,000; 40 percent on income between $75,000 and $100,000; and 46 percent on all income over $100,000.

[k]Dividends paid are estimated to remain the same percentage of After-Tax Profits as in the previous year.

Earnings will be incremented by the projected After-Tax Profit minus any Dividends paid.

Income statement categories are estimated in the same manner. Categories such as Depreciation Expense, Interest Expense, Taxes, and Dividends do not vary directly with sales. Depreciation Expense, for example, depends on the type of plant and equipment being utilized and the specific tax treatment given. Interest Expense depends on the terms of the various loans outstanding and Taxes depends on the type of organizational structure and level of After-Tax Profit. For this example, dividends will be calculated as a percentage of After-Tax Profit.

By multiplying these percent-of-sales figures by the estimated sales for 1987 ($1,694,530), the estimates for the 1987 financial statements are derived. These calculations are shown in Exhibit 3–2. The calculations for those categories marked "n.a." in Exhibit 3–1 were made using the alternative assumptions given in the footnotes to Exhibit 3–2. Whether these prospective financial statements are considered financial forecasts or financial projections depends on the nature of these assumptions. If they accurately reflect the conditions that are expected to exist and the events that are likely to take place, they are correctly referred to as "financial forecasts." If, however, they are based on hypothetical, "what if" assumptions, they should be called "financial projections."

The Additional Financing Requirement. The additional financing requirement for the operation is calculated by comparing the Total Assets with the Total Liabilities and Net Worth. If Total Assets is greater than Total Liabilities and Net Worth, the operation will need additional financing based on the forecasting ratios used.

This additional financing can come from either internal or external sources. Funds generated internally are those that stem from operating activities. These are the spontaneous sources shown on the balance sheet (accounts payable and accruals) and retained earnings. External sources will include the issuance of Common Stock or additions to Paid-In Capital and all forms of debt, whether short term or long term. The decision on how to finance this shortfall will be made presumably on the basis of the availability and cost of the various types of financing.

Minimizing Your Reliance on External Funding Sources, Or, How to Determine Manageable Growth

Owners of entrepreneurial ventures are often unprepared to deal with the cash flow pressures that accompany rapid growth. It is difficult to convince an entrepreneur who is struggling through the early stages of a business that unrestrained sales growth could present major operating problems. A firm that grows beyond its ability to generate cash internally will find itself in a constant struggle to find new cash sources to support growth.

If the operation is not providing the necessary funds to support the rate of sales growth, then outside sources such as creditors or new investors must be identified. Without additional borrowed funds or new equity, the firm will either be forced to violate established financial policies or resort to drastic steps to keep the operation going.

Most managers have financial policies that they try to follow. Knowing that future growth potential depends on a firm's total asset base, many entrepreneurs will establish a policy of maintaining a stable total asset turnover (sales-to-total asset ratio). In addition to self-imposed financial policies, many firms have restrictions imposed on them by creditors or shareholders. Creditors, especially commercial lenders, often include financial covenants in loan contracts that force the firm to maintain certain financial ratios, such as debt-to-equity. And shareholders place a high value on the maintenance of a constant dividend payout ratio (dividends-to-profit).

With all these restrictions, how then can a firm grow beyond the limits placed on it by internal resources without being forced to sell assets or take other serious measures? Robert C. Higgins (1977) has developed a formula to help determine the rate of sales growth that a firm can safely sustain without violating internal policy or external restraints. Higgins's sustainable growth rate can be written:

$$g = \frac{m \cdot b \cdot (1 + B/E)}{A/S - \{m \cdot b \cdot (1 + B/E)\}}$$

where g = sustainable growth
m = after-tax profit margin
b = earnings retention rate
B = total liabilities
E = total owners' equity
A = total asset
S = sales

Suppose that a firm has an established policy of maintaining an asset-to-sales ratio of 1.5; creditors require a minimum debt-to-equity ratio of 2.5; and shareholders expect a dividend payout rate of 20 percent (indicating an earnings retention rate of 80 percent). Sustainable growth for a firm with an after-tax profit margin of 10 percent is calculated as follows:

$$g = \frac{(.10)(.80)(1 + 2.5)}{(1.5) - \{(.10)(.80)(1 + 2.5)\}}$$
$$= \frac{0.28}{1.22} = 22.95 \text{ percent.}$$

More leverage, or a higher debt-to-equity ratio, results in a higher sustainable growth rate. Holding values for the other variables constant, a debt-to-equity ratio of 4.0 results in a value for g of 36.36 percent. A higher earnings retention rate and a higher net profit margin have similar effects. Growth rates cannot always be maintained at or near sustainable rates. But it will serve the entrepreneur well to understand the concept of sustainable growth and use it in financial planning and analysis.

If Total Liabilities and Net Worth is greater than Total Assets, the operation has actually generated excess cash and the managers must decide how to apply the excess funds. The simplest decision could be to add the excess to Cash or Cash Equivalents. Alternatively, the funds could be used to add to the various asset categories, retire additional debt, or increase dividend payments.

Restricting Operating Ratios. Any restrictions on the operating ratios should be taken into consideration when determining the source and use of the additional financing requirements. Agreements to maintain certain compensating cash balances in a checking account, a specified current ratio, a maximum debt-to-equity ratio, or a minimum dividend payout ratio can all be taken into account in the final calculations. Adjustments for a minimum current ratio and a maximum debt-to-equity ratio are shown in the following calculations:

1. A minimum Current Ratio of 2:1

Maximum Current Liabilities	= 0.5 · current assets
	= 0.5 · $393,292
	= $196,646
Projected Current Liabilities	163,458
Maximum Addition to Current Liabilities	$ 33,188

2. Maximum Debt-to-Equity Ratio of 1:4

Maximum Debt	= 0.25 · owners' equity
	= 0.25 · $1,208,631
	= $302,158
Projected Total Liabilities	214,115
Addition to Debt	$ 88,043

3. Additions to Owners' Equity

Financing Requirement (from Exhibit 3–2)	$186,311
Addition to Debt	88,043
Additional Requirement	$ 98,268
Debt Portion (0.20 · $98,268)	19,654
Equity Requirement	$ 78,614

4. Summary of External Funding Requirement

Additional Equity Requirement	$ 78,614
Additional Debt Requirement	107,697
Total Financing Requirement	$186,311

Of the additional financing requirement, a maximum of $107,697 can be funded through borrowed capital. The addition to debt of $88,043 in step 2 of the preceding calculation is the maximum allowable with an owners' equity of $1,208,631. The additional requirement of $98,268 is met by adding one dollar to debt for every four dollars that is added to owners' equity. Thus, 20 percent of the additional requirement can take the form of additional debt, but the remaining 80 percent must be owners' equity, $19,654 and $78,614, respectively.

Restrictions on income statement categories can be implemented in much the same manner. It is a very simple exercise to restrict such ratios as Cost of Sales-to-Sales, Operating Expenses-to-Sales, Cost of Sales-to-Inventory, or Sales-to-Receivables to specific values. The net result of restrictions on the operating ratios will be to change the additions to Retained Earnings—the internal source of funds. Restrictions on the liquidity ratios will affect the level of inventory and receivables; this in turn will affect the cash flow position of the operation. Such a hypothetical exercise can give valuable insights into strategies that should be considered as responses to certain events that may occur in the future.

Prospective Financial Statements. The prospective financial statements for the Lake Brazos Catfish Huts, Inc., are presented in Exhibit 3–3. Based on the preceding calculations, the additional financing requirement is divided as follows: $33,188 into Short-Term Notes Payable, $74,509 into Long-Term Debt, and $78,614 into Paid-In Capital. This could obviously be refined further by amortizing the Long-Term Debt and placing the portion payable within the year in Current Maturities—LT Debt. For our current purposes, however, this seems unnecessary.

One final word of caution about the percent-of-sales method of preparing prospective financial statements is necessary. The technique assumes a constant asset- and liability-to-sales relationship. Thus, the method is most accurate when it is used primarily for short-range estimates of one to three years.

Financing Requirements and the Growth Rate in Sales. It may be necessary to make an estimate of the additional financing requirements without going through the process of constructing a complete set of prospective financial statements. By making several simplifying assumptions, the following formula can be used to estimate the additional financing requirements:

$$\text{AFR} = [(A_s/S)_0 \, \Delta S + \Delta A_d + \text{CDA}] - [(L_s/S)_0 \, \Delta S + mS_1 (1 - d) + D_1]$$

where

AFR = additional financing requirement

A_s = assets that increase at the same rate that sales increase; the spontaneous assets

S_i = sales in the ith period. In this case, period 0 is the last historical year and period 1 is the projection year

EXHIBIT 3–3

Lake Brazos Catfish Huts, Inc.
Proforma Balance Sheet for the Period Ending
December 31, 1987

Assets

Cash	$ 24,208
Cash equivalents	195,863
Accounts receivable	47,351
Inventory	97,221
Prepaid expenses	28,648
Total current assets	$ 393,292
Gross fixed assets	$1,442,760
Accumulated depreciation	267,020
All other noncurrent	40,025
Total Assets	$1,609,057

Liabilities and Net Worth

Accounts payable (trade)	$ 92,770
Short-term notes payable	0
Accruals	60,237
Current maturities—LTD	10,450
Total current liabilities	$ 163,458
Long-term debt	$ 37,160
Other noncurrent liabilities	13,497
Common stock	29,460
Paid-in capital	96,690
Retained earnings	1,082,481
Total Liabilities and Net Worth	$1,422,746
Financing requirement	186,311
	$1,609,057

$\Delta S = (S_1 - S_0)$; the forecasted change in sales

$\Delta A_d = (A_{d1} - A_{d0})$; the forecasted change in discretionary assets

CDA = current debt amortization; short-term debt and current portion of long-term debt to be retired during the projection year

m = the after-tax profit margin; PAT/Sales

d = the percentage of after-tax profits paid out in dividends

D_1 = depreciation expense in the projection year

Note that the first bracketed expression represents cash flow requirements, while the second bracketed expression represents sources of cash. The values for the Lake Brazos Catfish Huts are:

$$(A_s/S)_0 = 25.57 \text{ percent}$$
$$\Delta S = \$167,870$$
$$\Delta A_d = \$300,000$$
$$CDA = \$51,150$$
$$(L_s/S)_0 = 9.82 \text{ percent}$$
$$m = 10.88 \text{ percent}$$
$$S_1 = \$1,694,530$$
$$d = 27.97 \text{ percent}$$
$$D_1 = \$82,620$$

The additional financing requirement for the Lake Brazos Catfish Huts, Inc., can be found by inserting the previously given values into the AFR equation. The calculations are:

$$AFR = [.2557(\$167,870) + \$300,000 + \$51,150] -$$
$$[.0982(\$167,870) + .1088(\$1,694,530)(1 - .2797) + \$82,620]$$
$$AFR = [\$42,924 + \$300,000 + \$51,150] -$$
$$[\$16,485 + \$132,798 + \$82,620]$$
$$AFR = \$394,074 - \$231,903 = \$162,171$$

It should be emphasized at this point that the formula method is only a rough approximation of the additional financing requirement for the projection year. The $24,140 difference between the two calculations ($186,311 − $162,171) can be attributed to the lower after-tax profit percentage in the projection year of 8.90 percent as opposed to 10.88 percent in the last historical year. The after-tax profit differential is caused by differences in percentage depreciation and interest expense and a different average tax rate. If the 1987 profit margin were used in the formula, the two methods would result in the same AFR estimate.

Preparing Prospective Financial Statements for the Startup Business

In many ways, preparing prospective financial statements for the startup business is more problematic than preparing them for the existing business. First, there is no track record to use as a guide for future operations. Second, the uncertainty associated with a new venture increases the likelihood of forecast error. In spite of these problems, the benefits of the process are dramatic.

Preparing financial forecasts and projections for the new venture is an invaluable exercise in helping the entrepreneur anticipate problems and, in many cases, prevent them from happening. If used in conjunction with a constructive review process, it will promote a better understanding of the business operation and improve the management skills that are critical for the success of a business.

The process of preparing projections for the new venture is much different than for the existing business. Although it is conceptually a simple task, it can be quite complicated in practice. Thus, it is important for the entrepreneur to carefully document all that is known about the expense and capital structure of the new venture, and follow this procedure:

1. Define the typical unit of transaction for the operation.
2. Construct a breakeven analysis.
3. Evaluate the feasibility of reaching breakeven and verify the reasonableness of the breakeven point through industry data.
4. Present a range of estimates for the prospective financial statements.

The Unit of Transaction. All business activities can be described by a series of transactions that take place during the everyday operations. The purpose of a set of prospective financial statements is to keep track of these activities by placing a dollar value on each of them. The primary source of revenue for the typical business operation is the number of units of the product/service that is sold. The number of units sold is the tangible entity upon which the sales estimate is based.

If a firm is a distributor of widgets for a major widget manufacturer, it is a simple task to identify a widget as the unit of transaction. There may even be several different kinds of widgets that are being distributed. In that case, the sales estimate might be based on several categories of widgets, each of which has a different price. In most business operations, it is simple to define a unit of transaction.

Conceptually, the unit of transaction is either the item sold or the smallest sequence of activities that must be completed that contractually obligates a customer to pay. Although every business situation is different, each type of business has its own unique sequence of transactions that can be identified and used in the forecasting process. For the residential real estate broker, this sequence of activities is culminated by the mortgage loan closing. In the case of many retail establishments, the sequence is summarized by the cash register receipt or the sales ticket. The importance of this step in the process of generating prospective financial statements will become more evident when examining the reasonableness of the breakeven analysis.

Construct a Breakeven Analysis. Breakeven analysis is a useful management tool in almost any situation where two alternative projects are being examined. It is an inexpensive and relatively simple tool to use in this situation, but it can also be extremely valuable as a method of preparing financial projections for the startup venture.

There are always uncertainties associated with estimating future demand for a product. Breakeven analysis focuses on the expense side of the operation, so the uncertainty with respect to the sales estimate can be avoided. There is usually much less uncertainty in determining the expenses of an operation or the level of profit required. (The level of profit required is determined by the individual's opportunity cost of starting the venture.) By using these known values, a minimum required level of sales or revenues can be determined.

Fixed versus Variable Costs. The first step in constructing a breakeven analysis is to categorize the known costs of the operation into fixed and variable costs. The distinction between fixed costs and variable costs is based on the relationship between the cost category and sales volume. If the cost varies as sales volume varies, it is a variable cost. If it does not vary, it is a fixed cost.

This classification may seem very straightforward, but it is not. In many cases, the actual distinction between fixed and variable costs is not at all clear. In those cases, the analyst must use considerable discretion in making the determination. Take, for example, the classification of direct labor. Under normal circumstances, it is usually considered a variable expense. However, if there is considerable slack time in a particular production process, an increase in output can be handled without the addition of any direct labor expense. Under these circumstances, direct labor is effectively a fixed expense until additional workers are hired or overtime wages paid to current jobholders. Another example is depreciation. Normally considered a fixed expense, depreciation can actually be increased if equipment is used beyond its normal capacity. The component being referred to, of course, is the actual wear and tear on equipment, which is known as *economic depreciation* or more simply, *user cost.* Increased utilization will increase maintenance costs and may even require additional equipment.

Certain costs have both a fixed and a variable component. Telephone expense is an example of this type of cost. There is a fixed monthly charge for basic service and a variable cost associated with the number of long-distance calls that are made. Compensation to sales staff and supervisory personnel is typically a fixed base salary plus a commission or bonus based on the level of sales.

Other expenses are "lumpy" in nature; they are fixed over a certain range of output and must be increased by a fixed amount when they are increased.

Equipment can be fixed until the desired output is greater than its production capacity. At that point, if output is to be increased to meet demand, additional equipment must be purchased.

Supervisory salaries are also an example of this type of expense. The number of supervisors will remain constant until management decides to add another supervisor. At that time supervisory salaries will increase by the amount of the new supervisor's salary and remain fixed at that level until additional supervisory personnel are added.

It is important to distinguish among other types of costs. There are certain costs that are fixed as long as the operations are ongoing. However, they can be eliminated in the event of a shutdown. Once again, supervisory salaries are an example. Other costs are inescapable in the event of a short-term shutdown, but can be avoided in the event of a liquidation. These so-called "standby fixed costs" include certain maintenance and security expenses and minimum utility costs to maintain service. Finally, some costs are purely discretionary costs. Often referred to as "programmed costs," they are costs incurred in an attempt to increase sales volume, and not as a result of increased sales. They include such costs as advertising expense, travel expense, research and development outlays, and consulting fees. These costs, which are fixed by management decision, are based on specific programs that are being undertaken. The distinction between programmed costs and fixed costs is not very clear and care should be taken in their classification.

Table 3–1 provides a suggested classification scheme for fixed and variable costs. Keep in mind that this breakdown is provided as a general guide-

Table 3–1
Cost Classification: Fixed versus Variable

Fixed Costs	*Variable Costs*
Administrative Expense	Cost of Goods Sold
Depreciation of Equipment and Machinery	Direct Labor
	Employee Wages
Note Payments	Sales Commissions
Rental Expense	Executive Bonuses
Supervisors' Salaries	Raw Materials
Overhead Expense	Freight Expense
Storage Expense	
Property Taxes	
Utilities	
Advertising Expenses	Advertising Expenses
Opportunity Cost of Time	

line and is not to be interpreted as a fixed rule. As we mentioned earlier, classifying costs as fixed or variable will depend on the specific circumstances under which the breakeven analysis is being conducted.

The Breakeven Analysis. After all costs have been classified as fixed or variable, the next step in the breakeven analysis is to develop the relationship between costs and output. The analysis itself is focused on calculating a sales volume (either in units sold or dollar revenue) that will be sufficient to cover all fixed and variable expenses and result in a zero accounting profit. As we will discover later in the discussion, a positive dollar profit or a profit percentage can be added to the analysis to take into consideration the important economic concept of opportunity cost.

These breakeven targets can be arrived at either by mathematical or graphical analysis. The mathematical approach to breakeven analysis is based on a simple formula that recognizes the relationship among sales volume, fixed costs, and contribution margin. The mathematical approach is the more precise of the two alternatives and is summarized by the following relationships:

$$TR = P \cdot Q$$
$$TC = TFC + AVC \cdot Q$$

where

$$TR = \text{total revenue for the period}$$
$$TC = \text{total cost for the period}$$
$$P = \text{unit price for the product}$$
$$Q = \text{unit output for the period}$$
$$TFC = \text{total fixed cost for the period}$$
$$AVC = \text{average variable cost (per-unit cost) for the period.}$$

Breakeven output for the period is determined by solving a simple mathematical relationship. Zero-profit output is determined by equating total revenue and total cost, as follows:

$$TR = TC$$
$$[P \cdot Q] = TFC + [AVC \cdot Q]$$
$$[P \cdot Q] - [AVC \cdot Q] = TFC$$
$$Q[P - AVC] = TFC$$
$$Q = \frac{TFC}{P - AVC}$$

In other words, breakeven volume is calculated by dividing total fixed cost by the per-unit contribution margin (the difference between price and average variable cost for each unit produced). The technique can be illustrated by a numerical example. Assume there is a fixed relationship between cost and output in the short run and the following values:

$$P = \$10.00 \text{ per unit}$$
$$\text{TFC} = \$150,000 \text{ per year}$$
$$\text{AVC} = \$7.00 \text{ per unit}$$

Substituting these values into the preceding formula:

$$Q = \frac{\$150,000}{\$10.00 - \$7.00}$$
$$Q = \frac{\$150,000}{\$3.00}$$
$$Q = 50,000 \text{ units}$$

For every unit that is sold, $7.00 goes to pay the variable expenses of bringing that unit to the market. The remaining $3.00, referred to as the *contribution margin*, is applied toward the fixed costs of the operation. It will take a sales volume of 50,000 units to completely cover fixed costs and reach the breakeven point. At a sales price $10.00 per unit, this means that breakeven revenue is $500,000 ($10.00/unit · 50,000 units).

Under certain circumstances, it may be more convenient because of data availability or other reasons to calculate the breakeven point using contribution margin percentages rather than per-unit cost data. This approach can be shown by a simple manipulation of the general breakeven formula:

$$Q = \frac{\text{TFC}}{P - \text{AVC}}$$

Multiply both sides of the expression by P and get

$$P \cdot Q = \frac{\text{TFC}}{(P - \text{AVC})/P}$$
$$\text{TR} = \frac{\text{TFC}}{1 - \text{AVC}/P}$$

where $(1 - \text{AVC}/P)$ is simply the contribution margin expressed in percentage terms. In our example, average variable costs are 70 percent of the selling price. Therefore, contribution margin is 30 percent (1 − .70), and breakeven revenue is once again $500,000 ($150,000/.30).

There are several modifications that can be made to the simple model just presented. Most relevant to this discussion is the addition of a fixed profit or a profit percentage to the calculation. This particular modification can be extremely useful in situations in which a specific profit goal is being considered or the opportunity cost of time and capital is formally incorporated into the analysis.

Consider the situation in which an entrepreneur, in order to start a business, must leave a job where he was earning $50,000 annually. In addition to the income lost, the business is going to require a $100,000 equity investment that will come from personal savings earning a 10 percent return. The opportunity cost of starting this venture is measured by the foregone earnings of the individual (salary plus interest). Thus, the fixed cost of the operation from an economic perspective is $210,000 ($150,000 given previously plus the $60,000 foregone earnings). The breakeven point can be recalculated by adding this fixed profit goal (π) to the numerator of the breakeven formula. The calculation is:

$$Q = \frac{TFC + \pi}{P - AVC}$$
$$Q = \frac{\$150,000 + \$60,000}{\$10.00 - \$7.00}$$
$$Q = \frac{\$210,000}{\$3.00}$$
$$Q = 70,000 \text{ units}$$

The addition of the fixed profit goal of $60,000 increases the breakeven point to 70,000 units, or $700,000.

If the profit goal is stated in terms of a percentage of sales, it can be added to the analysis by including it as simply another variable cost. Assume that the profit goal is 10 percent of sales. In other words, for every one dollar in sales, ten cents should go to profit. This can be stated more formally by adjusting the breakeven equation:

$$TR = \frac{TFC}{1 - AVC/Q - \pi/Q}$$
$$TR = \frac{\$150,000}{1 - .70 - .10}$$
$$TR = \frac{\$150,000}{.20}$$
$$TR = \$750,000$$

Considering the original problem, a requirement of a 10 percent profit margin will increase the breakeven volume to $750,000, or 75,000 units.

It is also important that the manager be able to visualize the cost-volume relationship in graphical form. The use of the breakeven chart is very helpful in this context. The typical breakeven chart is shown in Figure 3–3, with values on the horizontal axis representing output volume and values on the vertical axis representing revenues and costs.

The revenue and cost functions are all drawn as linear functions, based on the assumption of fixed relationships between these variables and output. Obviously, other relationships can be assumed. For example, the revenue function could be drawn curvilinear if it is assumed that the firm will have to lower prices to increase sales. The straight-line revenue function is appropriate, however, under conditions that approximate perfect competition over the relevant range of output. In other words, as long as a fixed market price is assumed for the output levels being considered, the straight-line revenue function is appropriate.

Fixed costs are drawn as a horizontal line, reflecting the assumption that they are fixed for the output range under consideration. Total cost, also drawn as a straight line, is the sum of total variable cost and total fixed cost.

The actual breakeven point is found by the intersection of the total revenue and total cost functions. Since the slope of the revenue function is greater than the slope of the cost function, they will eventually intersect. In other words, as output increases, revenues will increase faster than costs. Otherwise, a breakeven point is impossible.

The purpose of the breakeven chart is not solely to show the point where revenues and costs are equal. Although this is of interest to the manager, the graph will also show the relationship between profit (or loss) and output at the various sales volumes. The profit-output relationship is shown graphically in the lower portion of the diagram.

It is a straightforward exercise to change certain assumptions such as product price, average variable cost, or total fixed cost. This flexibility enables the manager to quickly estimate the effect of price or cost changes on the breakeven point and the resulting changes in the relationship between profit and volume.

Limitations of Breakeven Analysis. Because it is a simple technique, breakeven analysis has certain limitations.

1. Breakeven analysis is a static tool for analyzing information in one period. Many investment decisions that are unprofitable in one period may be profitable in subsequent periods.
2. The technique relies on cost-revenue relationships that are fixed. In cases

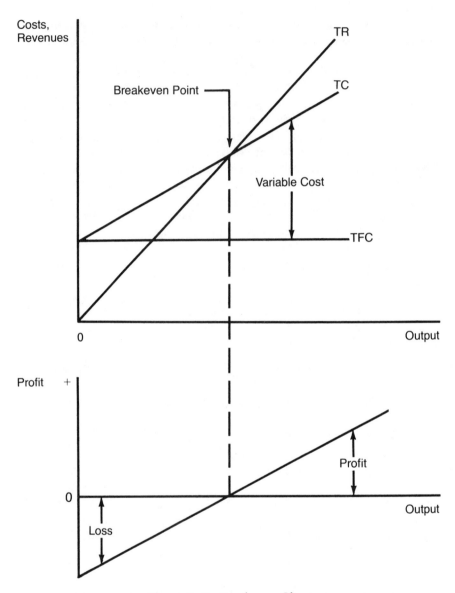

Figure 3–3. Breakeven Chart

The Cost-Lag Loop

One of the major limitations of the breakeven analysis is its fixed cost–revenue assumption. In a perfect world, fixed costs are fixed by management decision and variable costs change predictably with sales volume. Profits are maintained by keeping sales volume above a certain level, namely, the breakeven point. In the real world, however, fixed costs have a tendency to increase as sales volume increases and variable costs tend to be fixed as sales volume declines. The result is that costs rise more readily than they decline. This in turn produces what is called the **cost-lag loop**, in which the decline in costs lags behind the decline in sales volume.

The careful manager is aware that every business is susceptible to this phenomenon and plans for the inevitable downturn. The cost cycle has six distinct phases as shown in the figure [Kyd (1986)]:

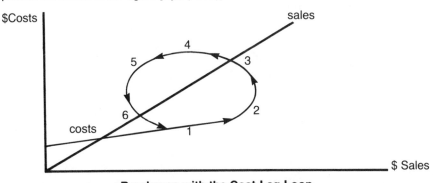

Breakeven with the Cost-Lag Loop

1. In the *profit-control phase,* sales and costs rise proportionately, roughly approximating the traditional breakeven chart.

2. In the *saturation phase,* costs rise faster than sales. An operation that functioned efficiently at a smaller sales volume often experiences inefficiencies as sales increase. Increased inventory costs, inefficient technology, new employees, overtime charges, and rising overhead contribute to this problem.

3. In the *spending-momentum phase,* the operation, geared up for a higher sales volume, continues to spend at previous levels even as sales start to decline. This stage occurs during the early stages of a sales downturn.

4. In the *unprofitable-control phase,* management recognizes the sales downturn and begins the process of belt tightening. Costs once again decline roughly in proportion to the sales decline. The difference between this phase and the profit-control phase is that overhead costs are much higher.

5. In the *desperation-cut phase,* management realizes that previous cost cutting measures have failed to return the operation to a profitable position. Lack of financial support from lenders and investors creates a situation in which fixed costs become variable and the operation is cut drastically.

6. In the *savings-momentum phase,* employees and management at all levels join in on the cost saving measures and voluntarily reevaluate, renegotiate, liquidate, and take other steps to save money.

    The key to surviving the cost-lag loop is to understand its dynamics and carefully track the operation's cost-revenue relationships. It is important to remember that no trend continues indefinitely. Controlling costs, even during periods of increasing sales, is the key to a successful operation.

---

in which significant economies of scale are present, costs will be a decreasing function of revenues.

3. In constructing a breakeven analysis, it is implicitly assumed that the output produced during the period is sold during the same period. Although this may be a valid assumption in the long run, it presents some difficulty in dealing with inventory fluctuations in the short run.

4. Breakeven analysis does not properly take into consideration the time value of money. It is a generally accepted investment strategy to accept or reject an investment based on the relationship between the discounted cash flow and the required investment outlay.

5. No investment opportunity exists in isolation. There are almost always alternative uses of funds, to which the value of an individual project must be compared before an investment decision is made. Making project comparisons based on breakeven points reveals little about their relative profitabilities.

Although it is easy to expand on the limitations of breakeven analysis, it should be remembered that it is quite useful. Breakeven analysis is a simple, inexpensive screening device. It is often the first step in the process, and usually serves to determine whether it is worthwhile to do a more intensive analysis.

As we have discovered, breakeven analysis can be an invaluable tool in the process of preparing prospective financial statements for the new venture startup. Since most expenses can be determined ex ante, there are only two variables left to determine—profit and demand. By simply specifying profit as any other cost, the breakeven point can be estimated and compared with total market demand to validate the believability of achieving that level of sales.

Feasibility and Reasonableness of Breakeven. The next step in the process of preparing prospective financial statements is to evaluate the probability of reaching the breakeven volume that has been estimated. There are two tests for evaluating the feasibility of the breakeven sales volume. The first is to compare the estimated breakeven point with the capacity of the operation and the second is to compare it with the size of the target market.

If the breakeven point is greater than the capacity of the operation or it represents an unreasonably large share of the target market, the likelihood of achieving that level of sales may come into question. Critical examination of the breakeven point relative to capacity and market size is an important step in the process of preparing prospective financial statements and should be carefully implemented.

At this point in the analysis, the use of comparative data from industry sources can also be a vital step in evaluating the component parts of the analysis. The industry sources available include trade publications that focus on specific types of businesses, such as *Nation's Restaurant News* or annual volumes of the *Radio Financial Report* published by the National Association of Broadcasters. Comparative and historical data on over 350 different industries listed by SIC code are published by Robert Morris Associates in *Annual Statement Studies*.

Other publications provide invaluable information for the entrepreneur in estimating revenues and expenses for the new venture. The *Small Business Reporter* series published by the Bank of America has issues on business operations, certain professional practices, and individual business profiles. The Accounting Corporation of America, in its *Barometer of Small Business*, publishes financial data on small business. This publication provides not only information on average operating expenses, but also includes details on the seasonal nature of sales in various industries. The U.S. Small Business Administration provides detailed operating data and descriptive information on many kinds of businesses in its *Urban Business Profile Series*. These publications are available at many university libraries.

Comparison data should only be used as a guideline for estimating cost and revenue relationships for new ventures. They should not be rigidly followed because differences between industry data and the firm's operating results are expected. The purpose of the comparison is to point out differences and explain the reasons for variations from industry norms.

Income and Cash Flow Estimates. The final step in the process is the actual construction of the prospective financial statements. All the information necessary to complete the forecasts has been compiled in the previous steps. The task at this stage of the analysis is to assemble the information into a format that can be actively used in the decision-making process.

Combining the sales estimate with the expense estimates from the breakeven analysis, the prospective income statement can be generated. A cash

Estimating Sales from Published Data

The following example will provide details on how to use comparison data to construct prospective financial statements for a startup venture. In this case, a group of female entrepreneurs are planning to open a women's apparel store in a large regional shopping mall. Operating data have been gathered from several sources and are summarized in the following table.

It is possible to prepare a sales estimate for the first year of operation from this information. Based on operating data furnished by the shopping mall management, sales are projected at $450,000, ($450/square foot · 1,000 square feet). RMA data indicate that with an inventory of $63,000, annual sales will be $315,000 [($63,000 · 3.0)/.60]. This works out to be only $315 per square foot of retail space, which is well under the shopping mall average. The best strategy in preparing prospective financial statements is to be conservative. Thus, the lower estimate will be used in the actual prospective income statement.

Using ACA data, the sales figures are spread over the year by multiplying the annual sales estimate by the monthly weights given in the table (for example, $315,000 · .073 = $22,995 for January). This results in the following monthly sales estimates:

January	$22,995	May	$24,885	September	$24,570
February	20,475	June	24,885	October	25,515
March	26,775	July	22,365	November	26,775
April	25,830	August	24,255	December	45,675

Women's Apparel Store
Operating Data

Source	Information
RMA *Annual Statement Studies*	Inventory Turnover = 3.0 Cost of Sales/Sales = .60
ACA *Small Business Barometer*	Seasonal Pattern for Sales

January	.073	July	.071
February	.065	August	.077
March	.085	September	.078
April	.082	October	.081
May	.079	November	.085
June	.079	December	.145

Source	Information
Shopping Mall Management	Average Sales per Square Foot of Retail Space = $450
Business Plan	Retail Space = 1000 square feet Inventory at Cost = $63,000

flow statement should also be constructed to delineate between both revenues and receipts and expenses and expenditures. This topic will be covered in greater depth in Chapter 4, "Basic Accounting Relationships."

Estimating Capitalization Requirements. It is critically important that the total capitalization requirements for a new venture be realistically estimated. One of the primary symptoms of a failing business is lack of capital. In many cases, this is the direct result of the entrepreneur beginning an operation "on a shoestring" without an adequate capital base.

In general, the capitalization requirements for a startup venture can be estimated by simply adding the venture's operating capital requirement to the one-time startup expenses. These expenses include: deposits, inventory, equipment, furniture and fixtures, land and building, leasehold improvements, licenses and permits, and organizational expense.

One rule-of-thumb method for estimating the operating capital requirement is to assume zero sales for three to six months and have in reserve enough capital to cover operating expenses for that period of time. A more precise way to estimate the operating capital requirement is to base it on the maximum cumulative cash flow deficit from the monthly cash flow projections.

In the case of the proposed women's apparel store, the one-time startup expenses for the store total $147,000. An operating capital requirement of $28,000 is added to this, to come up with the total capitalization requirement of $175,000. The owners have $100,000 available to them for equity purposes, leaving an additional external financing requirement of $75,000 to be secured from a commercial bank loan.

Financial Forecasting and the Microcomputer

Microcomputer technology has made tremendous progress in the past decade. Since the introduction of the Apple computer in 1978 and the IBM PC three years later, the microcomputer has become a standard piece of equipment in both home and office. Along with the progress that has been made in hardware development, such software packages as VisiCalc, Lotus 1-2-3, WordStar, MicroSoft Word, dBASE, and others have dramatically changed the way we conduct our daily lives.

The computer is designed to assist in analyzing large amounts of data quickly and efficiently. Although data manipulation and data analysis can be automated, there is nothing magical about computer output. One major pitfall to avoid is the misconception that computer output is always accurate.

An internal logic error in a model will result in inaccurate output, and analysis based on that output will be incorrect. The accuracy of a model should always be tested with a set of sample data.

How to Use an Electronic Worksheet

The first software program that the financial planner should become familiar with is the electronic spreadsheet or worksheet package. Popular worksheet packages include VisiCorp's VisiCalc and Lotus Development Corporation's Lotus 1-2-3.

A worksheet in one of these packages is simply a working space made up of a series of rows and columns on which a variety of mathematical, scientific, and accounting relationships can be specified. The worksheet in VisiCalc is 252 rows by 65 columns; the Lotus 1-2-3 worksheet is much larger, measuring 2,040 rows by 256 columns.

An electronic worksheet can be used in much the same way that a pencil and a columnar pad is used. The advantages of using the electronic worksheet are the speed and accuracy of the calculations and the fact that recalculations are possible with a single keystroke.

As the worksheet is developed, various functional relationships among variables and groups of variables can be defined. Changes in the values of certain variables affect the values of variables in other parts of the worksheet. When key values are changed, if the system is designed correctly, it will automatically recalculate the model and change the values of all variables that depend on the changed key values.

All of the mathematical operations available on most good calculators are available on the electronic worksheet. In addition, there are built-in functions that allow logical comparisons to determine values in the worksheet.

The worksheet application that should be learned is the technique of building a worksheet template. This timesaver is simply a worksheet that has been preprogrammed with all the relevant formulas for a specific application. It has a standard format containing all the titles and formulas that are used repetitively in the analysis. The template is saved separately and data are added only when the financial analysis is performed.

The purpose of a template is to save time when repetitive analyses are performed on different data sets. Each time a financial analysis is done, the task involves: 1) loading the software package, 2) loading the worksheet template, and 3) filling in the data. The program automatically calculates all the values.

It is beyond the scope of this book to make you an expert in the use of microcomputers and electronic worksheets. However, there are several excellent aids on the market today to assist you in the development of computer skills (see Cohen and Graff, 1984). The worksheet template is the financial analysis tool of the future. Streamlining this important planning function is the first step toward business success.

The CPA's Role in Preparing Prospective Financial Statements

Often a higher degree of reliability and credibility will be required of prospective financial statements than is normally expected of those that are generated for internal use. This is particularly true when the statements are used by individuals outside the firm who are making investment and loan decisions that affect the firm.

It is not that reliability and credibility are unimportant when the statements are used for internal planning purposes. They will, however, be held to a much higher set of standards when used, for example, in an offering statement for a stock sale or negotiations for a bank loan.

Under these circumstances, independent certified public accountants can provide a valuable service in assisting in the preparation of prospective financial statements. In "Financial Forecasts and Projections" (1985), the AICPA defined engagements for the purpose of preparing prospective financial statements in much the same way that it classified engagements to prepare historical financial statements. The services provided in the preparation of prospective financial statements are classified as an examination, a compilation, and an agreed-upon procedures engagement. These services roughly compare with an audit, a compilation, and a review, respectively. A discussion of the procedures used in classifying historical financial statements is deferred to Chapter 4, "Basic Accounting Relationships."

The examination of prospective financial statements is the most rigorous procedure offered by an independent accountant. It involves evaluating the preparation and presentation of the prospective financial statements and the supporting assumptions upon which they are based. The results are a set of prospective financial statements that are appropriate for general use.

Based on the work done during the examination, the accountant will express an opinion. This is not given to guarantee the results, but to verify that the information conforms with generally accepted accounting principles and assure the user that the underlying assumptions are reasonably supported.

Only limited procedures are performed in the compilation of prospective financial statements. The engagement primarily involves assembling statements based on information and assumptions provided by management. In contrast to the examination, the accountant provides no assurances about information provided, only that none of the assumptions or other aspects of the reports are obviously inappropriate.

During an agreed-upon procedures engagement, the independent accountant will perform procedures agreed upon by the individuals who will use the prospective financial statements. The resulting statements are appropriate for limited use that should be specified prior to the engagement.

Using an independent CPA in the preparation of prospective financial statements will enable an entrepreneur to put together a more convincing business plan. The increased reliability and credibility of prospective financial statements prepared by a CPA can mean that external funding sources place a much higher level of confidence in the forecasts and projections.

Summary and Conclusions

The preparation of prospective financial statements can take place in either a passive or an active management environment. In the passive environment, it is merely an indicator of the events and conditions that are expected to occur during some future time period. At the end of that period of time, it represents a comparison between what was expected to happen and what actually happened.

In an active environment, on the other hand, the preparation of prospective financial statements presents an outline of the necessary steps that must be followed to achieve the written goals of management. Within this framework, the entrepreneur has the opportunity to periodically review operating performance and take preventative action if the results prove negative. This is indicative of an active, as opposed to a reactive, management style.

A set of prospective financial statements should be an active and dynamic tool. In order to be properly implemented, they are a part of an expanded system that includes: 1) a carefully determined statement of goals, 2) a set of appropriate operating and financial strategies for achieving these goals, and 3) a management information system that functions to transmit results to the individuals responsible for goal setting and implementation.

As an integral part of the strategic planning process, the preparation and use of prospective financial statements help take decision making out of a crisis atmosphere and place it within the context of company goal setting. This is especially true for the closely held business, where systematic financial forecasts and projections actually facilitate the flow of information within the business. Instead of the typical situation where information flows haphazardly through an informal network, prospective financial statements help to formalize planning and reporting, thus improving management performance.

This is even more critical in smaller firms because they are already less likely to diversify products or markets to reduce risk. This dynamic process serves to reduce risks by emphasizing the importance of periodically reviewing progress and revising goals and procedures as new information is made available.

References

American Institute of Certified Public Accountants, "Financial Forecasts and Projections," *Statement on Standards for Accountants' Services on Prospective Financial Information,* October, 1985.

Attacking Business Decision Problems with Breakeven Analysis. Washington, D.C.: Small Business Administration, Management Aids Series No. MA 1.008.

Cohen, Neil, and Graff, Lois. *Financial Analysis with Lotus 1-2-3.* Bowie, MD: Brady Communications Company, Inc., 1984.

Higgins, Robert C. "How Much Growth Can a Firm Afford?" *Financial Management* (Fall, 1977), pp. 7–16.

Kyd, Charles W. "Controlling the Cost-Lag Loop," *Inc.* (July, 1986), pp. 110–112.

SAS User's Guide: 1979 Edition. Cary, NC: SAS Institute Inc., 1979.

User's Guide: SPSS^X. New York: McGraw-Hill Book Company, 1983.

Part II
Accounting and Finance Concepts

4

Basic Accounting Relationships

Generating a profit is the primary goal of every business enterprise. Every action and decision has an impact on whether that profit goal is realized. Keeping accurate financial records does not in itself make a person a better manager, but it is a good indicator of managerial effectiveness. The proper financial information in the correct format provides not only the confirmation of the relative success of past decisions, but also information that will assist the entrepreneur in making wise decisions in the future.

Accurate financial records provide details on the financial health of an operation—the level of sales volume, the trend in sales, the gross profit margin, and net profit margin. In addition, they can provide valuable information that can be used in the bidding process, in determining credit policies and collection procedures, and in evaluating the probable effect of a change in prices on sales volume.

Outside financing sources also have a need for detailed information about the business operation. These outside sources include suppliers who require financial statements before authorizing trade credit, commercial lenders who use the information to assess the likelihood of repayment of loans, equity investors who use the information to evaluate the potential return on an investment, and, of course, government agencies such as the Internal Revenue Service who use the information to determine federal income tax obligations.

The purpose of this chapter is to describe the fundamental relationships of financial accounting—not the principles of accounting. Our goal is to provide a broad overview of the basic accounting system and how the information is compiled to create the various financial statements. Distinctions among the various types of accounting methods will be emphasized and the various types of financial reports will be discussed.

The Accounting Equation

The basic task of financial record-keeping is the documentation of every business-related transaction. Every action that relates to the operation can be described by means of a transaction. Paying rent to a landlord for use of office space, purchasing office supplies, paying employees, buying machinery or equipment, securing a contract, and selling a product are all transactions that should be recorded.

The fundamental relationship used to keep track of transactions is defined in terms of the following categories: assets, liabilities, and capital. **Assets** are the economic resources of the business. **Liabilities** are the legally binding obligations of the owners and represent outside claims against the assets of the business. **Capital** consists of the amount that the owners have contributed to the operation and the cumulative income reinvested in the operation; it represents the residual claims of the owners against the assets of the business.

In order to be included as an asset, an item must have an expected economic benefit; it must be either a potential revenue generator or cost reducer. Other characteristics of assets are identifiability, separability, and measurability. Although it is important, separate marketability is not necessarily a criterion for inclusion as an asset. In fact, many assets that cannot be disposed of separately, but are expected to result in a future economic benefit, are identifiable and measurable and thus meet the definition for inclusion as an asset. Assets include such items as cash, marketable securities, inventory, property and equipment, and intangibles. Most of these items are readily identified, are easily separated from one another, and have a measurable value based on an expected economic benefit.

One asset category that presents some measurement problems is intangibles. Patents and trademarks are included in this category. Even though their market value is measured by the discounted cash flow they can generate for the firm, they are recorded for accounting purposes at their historical acquisition cost. The unexpired portion of a license or lease is also an economic resource. Purchased goodwill, although not a separable economic resource, is identifiable and measurable and, as such, is considered an asset. It actually represents the difference between the amount that a buyer is willing to pay for a resource and the market value of the separable assets comprising that resource.

Identification, separation, and measurement are also important criteria for defining liabilities. However, they are more easily measured and included because most are denominated in monetary terms and are closely associated with a legal obligation. Contractual liabilities, such as credit of all forms, and other binding agreements should always be regarded as liabilities for purposes of financial accounting.

Capital in a business enterprise represents the various claims to assets of the owners. It is alternatively referred to as *net worth* or *owners' equity*. Looking at the concept another way, it can be viewed as a "plug" figure, representing the residual value of an enterprise—the difference between the value of the economic resources based on generally accepted accounting principles and the legal claims of creditors against those resources.

The extent of the owners' claims against assets is an important concept for users of financial statements. The components of capital include the initial and any subsequent investments of the owners (the value of property contributed by the owners), and the net income reinvested in the operation (the value of what the business itself contributes by selling goods and services at a price greater than cost). These components include common stock, preferred stock, treasury stock, paid-in capital, and retained earnings.

The fundamental relationship is described by the accounting identity:

$$\text{Assets} = \text{Liabilities} + \text{Capital}$$
$$\text{Property} = \text{Claims to Property}$$

This identity is the foundational concept of the entire accounting process, and as such, every business transaction can be shown in terms of its impact on the three terms in this equation. Every transaction affects both property and, in turn, claims to property. Changes in property are recorded under assets. Changes in claims to property are recorded under liabilities and capital, depending on whether the claims of creditors or owners are affected.

Transactions are usually recorded in what is referred to as the "general ledger." A general ledger account exists for each asset, liability, and capital item. The peculiarity of the entire process lies in the method that has evolved over the years for recording increases and decreases for each category. Each category is identified by its own separate account, which usually occupies a separate page in the general ledger. Each account identifies the category being recorded and provides space for showing increases and decreases in the account.

Several hundred years ago, double-entry bookkeeping emerged as the best way to keep track of transactions. Since every transaction affects property and/or claims to property, double-entry accounting requires that every transaction be depicted by at least two entries—in order to show the change in property and/or the claims to property.

The practice has been established whereby increases in the various categories are shown on one side of a vertical line and decreases are shown on the other side. This accounting technique is referred to as the **T-account.** The left side of the T-account is called the *debit side* and the right side is called the *credit side*. Increases in an asset account are recorded on the left-hand

Assets		=	Liabilities		+	Capital	
+	−		−	+		−	+
Dr	Cr		Dr	Cr		Dr	Cr
Incr	Decr		Decr	Incr		Decr	Incr

Figure 4–1. General Ledger Accounts

side (debit side) of the T-account and decreases are recorded on the right-hand side (credit side).

As in any mathematical relationship, moving from one side of the equation to the other reverses the sign—a positive value on one side of the equation becomes negative when it is moved to the other side. The result is that increases in liability and capital accounts are recorded on the right-hand side (credit side) and decreases are recorded on the left-hand side (debit side). Thus, debit (Dr) means left-hand side and credit (Cr) means right-hand side. Another fundamental relationship emerges from this practice—the summation of all the debits is equal to the summation of all the credits. The convenience of this relationship lies in the fact that the mathematical accuracy of all bookkeeping entries can be verified by simple addition. Figure 4–1 provides an illustration of this.

The recording of transactions is seldom made directly to the general ledger accounts. Usually a record of transactions is made before they are "posted" to the general ledger. This record is called the **general journal** and it contains a listing of each transaction, the accounts to which it is debited and credited, the date of the transaction, and a brief explanation.

The general journal is the starting point for the entire bookkeeping process. It serves several useful purposes: 1) it provides an explanation of each transaction, 2) the chronological listing provides an easy-to-follow format, and 3) it expedites the final posting to the general ledger. A typical general journal listing is shown in Figure 4–2. In practice, transactions are first recorded in the general journal in the order in which they occur. In order to expedite the final posting to the general ledger, reference numbers are also recorded showing the accounts in which the item will appear and whether it represents an increase or a decrease in those accounts.

Note that the posting reference in the general journal refers to the general ledger account to which that item is posted. The cash account is number 101, retained earnings is number 301, and so on. The cross reference is given in the general ledger, showing the page number of the general journal on which the entry was originally recorded.

Information in this format is quite accessible and easy to follow, but it is not very helpful in analyzing changes in property or claims to property. It merely provides a detailed description of individual transactions, when they

Date	Description	Ref	Dr	Cr
7-26	Office Equipment	125	2,500	
	Notes Payable	215		2,500
	(purchase furniture from Nelms on installment)			
7-30	Retained Earnings	301	900	
	Cash	101		900
	(July secretarial salary)			
7-31	Cash	101	7,500	
	Retained Earnings	301		7,500
	(Cash sales to TGI)			

Figure 4–2. The General Journal

occurred, and whether they resulted in increases or decreases in various accounts.

In order for the information to be useful to the decision maker, it must be rearranged in order to show all transactions in each account separately. This task is accomplished by posting the chronological listings from the general journal to the accounts in the general ledger showing changes in property and rights to property.

As stated earlier, a characteristic of the double-entry bookkeeping system is that it is always in balance. This means that at any time during the posting process, the summation of all the debits must equal the summation of all the credits—the left-hand side of the accounts must add up to the same number as the right-hand side of the accounts. This device, which is called the **trial balance,** is used to determine the accuracy of the posting process.

General ledger accounts are typically categorized under the headings of assets, liabilities, and capital, which should come as no surprise. The assets accounts include cash, cash equivalents, accounts receivable, inventory, land and buildings, machinery and equipment, accumulated depreciation, prepaid expenses, and intangibles. Liability accounts include accounts payable, notes payable, and accruals. Capital items include ownership equity accounts such as common stock, preferred stock, treasury stock, paid-in capital, and retained earnings. Often, accounting systems show the retained earnings account as two separate categories: revenue and expenses. Since sales, rentals, and other revenues increase owners' rights, these transactions increase capital and show up as a credit in the retained earnings account. Expense items such as wages, rent, utilities, depreciation, and interest decrease ownership rights and are recorded as a debit to the retained earnings account.

Periodically, increases and decreases in the accounts are netted against one another to determine the balances in each account. This is typically done at the end of an accounting period (usually monthly), with the account balances displayed in an orderly fashion. This ordering of accounts is called the **balance sheet** or **statement of financial position.**

The number of accounts in the general ledger varies according to the size, nature, and requirements of the business operation. The accounts are ordered in the general ledger to correspond with the way they are listed on the balance sheet. The retained earnings account is a summary of the changes in ownership rights resulting from the operation itself. The detailed listing of these changes is called the **income statement.** The basic statements will be discussed in the following section.

Basic Financial Statements

The operation of any business enterprise is reflected in the basic financial statements: the balance sheet, the statement of operations or income statement, and the statement of changes in financial position or funds flow statement. Collectively, they give a summary of the firm's operations over the accounting periods under review and the firm's financial position at the end of each of those periods.

In addition to the quantitative information provided in the financial statements, most firms also provide qualitative information in the form of footnotes or disclosures. These notes are equally important in analyzing a company's operation. Although the statements provide details on what has happened during the accounting period, the footnotes provide additional details that are too cumbersome to include in the body of the statements, but are nevertheless important.

Income Statement

The income statement for The Sports Emporium for the year 1986 is shown in Exhibit 4–1. Notice that there are three major components of the income statement: operating revenues, expenses, and profit.

Operating Revenues. Operating revenues represent actual or expected cash inflows from the sale and delivery of goods and services during an accounting period (in this case, annually). In order to be recorded as an operating revenue, the transaction by definition must be the result of an activity that is central to the ongoing operation—goods delivered or services rendered.

Operating revenues are called by various names depending on the specific kind of business operation—sales, royalties, or rents. The main point to recognize is that only revenues generated as part of the major operation are recorded as operating revenues. Interest earned on a certificate of deposit,

EXHIBIT 4–1

The Sports Emporium
Income Statement
For the Year Ending December 31, 1986

Net sales	$1,350,060
Cost of sales	807,950
Gross profit	$ 542,110
Operating expenses:	
Advertising	$ 45,140
Depreciation	14,570
General and administrative	286,680
Rent	23,410
Repairs and maintenance	12,320
Total operating expenses	$ 382,120
Operating profit	$ 159,990
Interest expense	$ 15,600
Other expense (income)	(6,050)
Before-tax profit	$ 150,440
Income taxes	$ 48,952
After-tax profit	$ 101,488

---

proceeds from the sale of a fixed asset, or an insurance settlement, for example, would be recorded as a non-operating revenue.

Expenses. Expenses represent actual or expected cash outflows that result from the sale or delivery of goods and services during an accounting period. Recorded as either "cost of goods sold" or "operating expenses," they must result from an activity that is central to the ongoing operation.

Expenses are referred to by various names, depending on the specific type of business operation—wages, salaries, depreciation, or advertising. Non-operating expenses, such as a major casualty loss or other item that results in the reduction of assets, are listed in a separate section of the income statement.

Profit. Profit represents the difference between the revenues generated by the business operation and the corresponding expenses incurred. There are different measures of profit that should be highlighted, including gross profit, operating profit, before-tax profit, and after-tax profit.

Gross profit is a measure of how successful the operation is in turning merchandise inventories into profit. This measure of profitability is determined by the average mark-up on goods and services sold. The Sports Emporium, for example, has an average mark-up of 67 percent on its merchandise. This translates into a gross profit margin of 40 percent.

Operating profit is the difference between operating revenues and operating expenses. This measure examines the profitability of the business that is attributable solely to the activities that are central to the ongoing operation as described earlier. Note that operating profit does not take into consideration interest expense, which is determined by the way the firm is capitalized, or income taxes, which are determined by such things as organizational form and the peculiarities of the federal income tax codes.

Before-tax profit and after-tax profit are the two most widely used measures for determining the relative success of an operation. For all the emphasis placed on these two measures of profit, neither represents an addition to cash balances when the accounting records are kept on an accrual basis. The implications of cash-basis accounting versus accrual-basis accounting will be discussed more extensively in the next section.

Balance Sheet

The primary purpose of a balance sheet is to show the financial position of a business operation at a particular point in time. The balance sheets for The Sports Emporium for the years 1985 and 1986 are given in Exhibit 4–2. Note carefully that the statements show the firm's financial position as of the last day of each of those respective years. This point becomes important when the two balance sheets are viewed along with the 1986 income statement. The 1985 balance sheet gives a picture of the operation at the beginning of the year; the income statement provides a summary of the operation during the year; and the 1986 balance sheet shows the impact of the year's operation on the firm's financial position.

The balance sheet is broken down into the three main components of assets, liabilities, and capital. Each category is further broken down into subcategories and listed in order of liquidity. Assets are listed according to the ease of converting them into cash: current assets, fixed assets, intangibles, and other assets. Liabilities are listed in the order in which the obligations come due: current liabilities, long-term liabilities, and other liabilities. The capital accounts represent owners' claims against assets and are obligations that never come due.

The owners' equity account (capital account) is divided into two major areas: owners' investment and retained earnings. The **owners' investment** is composed of preferred stock, common stock, paid-in capital, and treasury stock. The two classes of stock, preferred and common, both represent own-

EXHIBIT 4–2

The Sports Emporium
Balance Sheets as of December 31

	1985	1986
Assets		
Cash	$ 71,824	$ 66,820
Accounts receivable	46,740	58,930
Inventory	299,040	316,300
Prepaid expenses	4,990	5,650
Total current assets	$422,594	$447,720
Gross fixed assets	$168,570	$206,500
Accumulated depreciation	(46,710)	(61,280)
Intangibles	8,370	7,880
Total Assets	$552,724	$600,820
Liabilities and Capital		
Accounts payable	$117,290	$ 79,890
Short-term notes payable	43,280	45,820
Accruals	28,150	28,930
Current maturities—LTD	7,450	10,960
Total current liabilities	$196,170	$165,600
Long-term debt	$ 92,180	$ 79,220
Deferred income tax	10,330	8,520
Total liabilities	$298,680	$253,340
Preferred stock	$ 4,760	$ 4,760
Common stock	45,000	45,000
Paid-in capital	7,770	8,668
Treasury stock	(5,000)	(5,000)
Retained earnings	201,514	294,052
Total Liabilities and Capital	$552,724	$600,820

ership in the firm. The main distinctions in this classification are that preferred stock pays a fixed dividend and the owners of preferred stock have a preferential position to common stock owners in the event of a business liquidation. Paid-in capital represents the owners' investment in the business in excess of the par value of the stock purchased. Treasury stock is common stock that has been repurchased by the company; in effect, it is negative equity.

Retained earnings is the portion of the net earnings of the firm that is not paid out in the form of dividends, but rather reinvested in the operation.

This represents the "residual equity" of the operation, the portion of the owners' claims against property that are not distributed outright. The total owners' equity will then be calculated by adding together preferred stock, common stock, paid-in capital, and retained earnings and subtracting treasury stock.

The major problem in preparing a balance sheet is a measurement problem. Items such as cash and cash equivalents do not really present a conceptual problem in their measurement. However, other asset categories such as plant, property, and equipment are more problematic. Standard accounting practice is to value these items on a historical-cost basis. In other words, they are valued on the books at their original cost rather than at their fair market value.

The measurement of liabilities does not present the same conceptual problem as the measurement of assets. This is because of the fact that liabilities are almost always associated with a legal obligation and thus are measured in monetary terms. The conceptual difficulties in measuring liabilities, such as how to record a capital lease obligation or how to handle debt that is convertible into equity, are beyond the scope of this discussion. These important issues are discussed in most intermediate accounting textbooks.

One final relationship that must be emphasized before leaving the balance sheet discussion is the reconciliation of the owners' equity account. Referred to as the "statement of retained earnings" or the "reconciliation of net worth," this relationship can either be presented in the capital account of the balance sheet or in a separate statement.

The statement is based on the relationship between the retained earnings as shown on one year's balance sheet and those of the previous year. Presented in the form of a formula, it can be seen that:

$$RE_1 = RE_0 + PAT_1 - DIV_1$$

In other words, retained earnings in year one (RE_1) is equal to retained earnings in year zero (RE_0) plus after-tax profit in year one (PAT_1) minus dividends paid in year one (DIV_1). Unless there has been a prior period adjustment to retained earnings because of changes in asset valuation or accounting errors, this relationship should hold true. Using data on The Sports Emporium, this relationship can be illustrated:

1985 Retained earnings (Exhibit 4–2)	$201,514
1986 After-tax profit (Exhibit 4–1)	+ 101,488
	$303,002
1986 Dividends paid (Exhibit 4–3)	− 8,950
1986 Retained earnings (Exhibit 4–2)	$294,052

Statement of Changes in Financial Position

In some ways, any discussion on the statement of changes in financial position is irrelevant. By the summer of 1987, the statement is scheduled to be replaced by the cash flow statement. In order to fully appreciate the significance of this change in accounting methodology, a few comments about the current practice are in order.

The statement of changes in financial position, or funds flow statement, is a required part of a complete set of financial statements provided by a firm. Even though no new information is presented beyond what is already shown on the income statement and the balance sheets, the format itself provides a uniquely different perspective of the firm's financial position.

. The problem with the current practice stems from the wide latitude that preparers have been given. There has been no clearly defined objective for the statement. Thus, there was no consensus on how concepts were to be defined or how data were to be presented. Without a clear statement of objectives, accountants were defining concepts and devising formats to suit individual objectives.

Over the past decade, the lack of uniformity in the preparation of this statement may have been counterproductive. Analysis of a study conducted by the Financial Executives Institute (Seed 1984) indicates that accountants were using different definitions of several key concepts, including "funds," "cash," and "cash flow from operations." In addition to the conceptual differences, the statements were being presented using a wide variety of formats. These practices detracted from the usefulness of the statement to individuals who wanted to evaluate the liquidity or solvency of an operation.

Currently, the Financial Accounting Standards Board allows the use of either a "working capital" or a "cash" definition of funds. Traditionally, the working capital concept has been used, but at best it is misleading. Increases in working capital do not necessarily indicate increases in liquidity, nor do decreases in working capital indicate decreases in liquidity. Defined as current assets minus current liabilities, **working capital** may increase for reasons totally unrelated to increases in cash (the true measure of liquidity). Increases in working capital caused by increases in inventory or accounts receivable actually use cash instead of generating cash.

For purposes of the following discussion, the traditional approach to the statement of changes will be used. There are two major implications of this approach: 1) a working capital definition of funds is used and 2) the format divides funds flow into the categories of sources and uses. The primary sources and uses are:

Sources of Funds

1. After-tax profit plus all noncash expenses such as depreciation and amortization.

2. Decreases in an asset account (except a component of working capital).

3. Increases in a liability account (except a component of working capital).

4. Increases in an equity account (except the retained earnings account).

Uses of Funds

1. Increases in an asset account (except a component of working capital).

2. Decreases in a liability account (except a component of working capital).

3. Payment of dividends.

4. Decreases in an equity account (except the retained earnings account).

Careful examination of this list provides insight into the construction of the funds flow statement. The bottom line on a funds flow statement using a working capital definition shows the increase or decrease in working capital from one year to the next. This is the reason for omitting changes in any component of working capital from the sources and uses.

The principal recurring source of working capital is after-tax profits. The actual accounting concept used is the change in the balance in the retained earnings account. Note that the funds flow statement begins with after-tax profits, emphasizing the importance of income and its components in assessing the performance of the business operation.

Other sources of working capital include decreases in an asset account (other than current assets). This occurs when fixed assets are sold. Unless a firm is in the business of selling machinery and equipment, any such transaction is considered to be nonrecurring and, in many cases, it will reduce the firm's ability to generate revenue in the future.

The increase in a noncurrent liability account often represents an increase in long-term bank borrowing (an increase in the notes payable balance). Increases in an equity account usually reflect additional ownership investment (an increase in common stock or paid-in capital). In any case, these represent an additional source of funds.

Other uses of cash include the purchase of additional machinery and equipment or an increase in another noncurrent asset account. Decreases in a noncurrent liability account, such as the repayment of a long-term loan, are also included as a use of funds. The payment of dividends to shareholders and a proprietorship or partnership draw also fall into this category.

Exhibit 4–3 presents the statement of changes in financial position for The Sports Emporium for the year 1986. The information used in creating this statement came from the 1986 income statement and the 1985 and 1986 balance sheets.

This traditional presentation nets working capital provided against working capital applied to get the increase or decrease in working capital.

EXHIBIT 4–3

The Sports Emporium
Statement of Changes in Financial Position
For the Year Ending December 31, 1986

Working Capital Provided:

After-tax profit	$101,488	
Plus: Depreciation	14,570	
Working capital from operations		$116,058
Plus: Decrease in intangibles		490
Increase in paid-in capital		898
Total working capital provided		$117,446

Working Capital Applied:

Increase in gross fixed assets	$ 38,030	
Decrease in long-term debt	12,960	
Decrease in deferred income tax	1,810	
Dividends paid	8,950	
Total working capital applied		61,750
Increase in working capital		$ 55,696

Net Change in Working Capital Consists of:

Increase (decrease) in current assets:

Cash	$ (4,984)	
Accounts receivable	12,190	
Inventory	17,260	
Prepaids	660	
		$ 25,126

Increase (decrease) in current liabilities:

Current maturities—LTD	$ 3,510	
Short-term notes payable	2,540	
Accounts payable	(37,400)	
Accruals	780	
		(30,570)
Increase in working capital		$ 55,696
Beginning working capital balance (year end 1985)		$226,424
Ending working capital balance (year end 1986)		$282,120

Additional details are also provided that show the breakdown in the net change in working capital. This is accomplished by delineating the net change in each working capital account to arrive at the net change in working capital.

The statement of changes in financial position is particularly helpful when used in conjunction with the other financial statements to show the liquidity and financial flexibility of a business enterprise. This method of presenting financial information offers a clear description of the actual sources of funds available to an enterprise and the manner in which they have been allocated over the last operating period.

Recognizing both the importance of the statement and the current conceptual problems, the Board has ruled that, effective June 30, 1987, all business entities must substitute a cash flow statement for the statement of changes in financial position. The FASB "Statement on Cash Flows" (1986) will also require a change in the format of the statement; it will be divided into the basic activities of operating, financing, and investing. The usefulness of the funds flow statement will be increased significantly by arranging the format according to type of activity instead of sources and uses. In this format, the operating, financing, and investing activities and their impact on funds flow can be delineated and understood. This issue will be discussed in more detail in Chapter 6, "Evaluating Cash Flow."

Basic Accounting Concepts

There are several basic accounting concepts that must be understood and recognized in order to thoroughly comprehend the way in which financial statements are prepared and how they fit together to provide a clear picture of the operation of a business.

Cash-Basis Accounting. Generally speaking, individuals are on a cash-basis accounting system for determining their income and expenses. Under such an arrangement, income is not considered earned until the cash is actually received and expenses are not considered incurred until payments are actually made.

This method of accounting is perfectly acceptable for an individual and may even be used for certain types of businesses. Using this format, certain items such as accounts receivable, prepaid expenses, accounts payable, and accruals do not show up on an operation's financial statement.

Accrual-Basis Accounting. For most businesses, accrual-basis accounting is the preferred method of keeping track of the transactions that affect property and rights to property. Under accrual-basis accounting, revenues are recorded in the time period in which they are earned, regardless of when the cash payment is received. In other words, when a sale is made, the balancing entry will be either to cash (if the customer pays cash) or to accounts receivable (if the customer receives trade credit).

Likewise, expenses are recorded at the time the obligation to pay is recognized as legally binding. If advertising space is purchased in the local newspaper, a decrease (debit) is recorded in the retained earnings account. The balancing entry will either be a decrease in the cash account (a credit if purchased with cash or check) or an increase in the accounts payable account (a credit if trade credit is used).

One interesting characteristic of the accrual-basis accounting system is the way prepaid expenses are treated. Expenses paid in advance are not treated as expenses until they are actually incurred in providing a product/service for sale. For example, only one-twelfth of an annual insurance premium shows up as an expense each month, even though the payment was made at the beginning of the fiscal year. This method of accounting does not consider an item to be an expense until it is actually used in the production process.

Thus, the goal of accrual accounting is to record revenues, expenses, gains, and losses during the time periods in which they affect company performance as measured by profits, rather than merely to list cash receipts and disbursements. Current cash receipts can actually result from business activity of earlier periods and current cash disbursements can actually relate primarily to expected future activity. Thus, the primary difference between accrual and cash accounting is in the recognition and matching of revenues, expenses, gains, and losses.

Types of Financial Statements

Lenders and investors must make difficult decisions on funding individual and business ventures. To aid them in their decision making, the funding source requires a business plan with a complete set of financial statements. Our discussion will now focus on the level of confidence that can be placed in the accuracy of the financial statements that are included in the business plan.

The size of the financing proposal and previous experience with the entrepreneurs making the request will determine the level of detail required in the financial statements. Smaller requests from long-standing clients will be evaluated on the basis of unaudited financial statements. Larger requests from prospective clients will require financial statements on which an independent accountant has expressed an "opinion" about the fairness with which they represent the financial condition of the firm. In these cases, the funding source is faced with a very difficult situation. Audited financial statements can be so expensive for the closely held firm that they are not used. The dilemma involves either making a funding decision with incomplete information or losing a potentially good customer by demanding more reliable, and thus more expensive, financial data.

Unaudited Financial Statements

Prior to 1979, the use of unaudited financial statements provided very little assurance to the funding source about the extent of the independent accountant's involvement in their preparation. The involvement could have been as minimal as transcribing data from the client's records to the appropriate financial statement—thus relying on the accuracy and validity of the data as it was prepared by the firm's in-house accounting staff. On the other hand, the independent accountant could have taken steps to verify certain information, such as the collectibility of accounts receivable, the method of valuing inventory, or other related data. In this case, the limited audit procedures went unnoticed because the casual reader had no idea of the extent of the independent accountant's involvement in the preparation of the financial statements.

The dangers of assuming too much (or too little) involvement places the funding source in the position of having a false sense of confidence (or caution) in the financial statements themselves. The dilemma is evident when the accountant's signed and dated disclosure statement for unaudited statements is examined:

> The accompanying financial statements were not audited by us and accordingly we do not express an opinion on them.

In 1979, the American Institute of Certified Public Accountants (AICPA) authorized a two-tiered approach to the preparation of unaudited financial statements. The two types of financial statements are referred to as 1) a compilation and 2) a review. It is important that lenders and investors understand both the difference between these financial statements and the extent of the independent accountant's involvement in their preparation.

Financial Statement Compilation. The **financial statement compilation** is a method of generating financial statements with a minimum level of assurance as to the fairness with which they represent the firm's financial condition. The compilation is, for all practical purposes, a reflection of the financial position of the operation based on data provided by the in-house accounting staff.

In order to compile financial statements, the accountant should be familiar with the "nature of the entity's business transactions, the form of its accounting records, the stated qualifications of its accounting personnel, the accounting basis on which the financial statements are to be presented, and the form and content of the financial statements" (*Statement on Standards for Accounting and Review Services No. 1*, p. 5).

An independent accountant is not required to undertake any action to verify or review the accuracy of the data supplied by management. However, if the accountant is aware of any information which, if disclosed, would appreciably alter the reported results, he should take steps to obtain additional information or correct any error.

The accountant's disclosure statement that accompanies the financial report provides information on the independent accountant's overall involvement in the process of generating the financial statements and some insight into the level of assurance provided by the reports. The following is an example of a disclosure statement that would accompany a compilation report.

> We have compiled the accompanying balance sheet of [company name] as of [date] and the related statements of income, retained earnings, and changes in financial position for the year then ended, in accordance with standards established by the American Institute of Certified Public Accountants.
>
> A compilation is limited to presenting in the form of financial statements information that is the representation of management (owners). We have not audited or reviewed the accompanying financial statements and, accordingly, do not express an opinion or any other form of assurance on them.

Under certain circumstances, the owners of a firm may request that all financial statement disclosures be omitted from the report. In this case, the accountant may do so, providing this is stated in the accountant's report as follows:

> Management has elected to omit substantially all of the disclosures required by generally accepted accounting principles. If the omitted disclosures were included in the financial statements, they might influence the user's conclusions about the company's financial position, results of operations, and changes in financial position. Accordingly, these financial statements are not designed for those who are not informed about such matters.

Financial Statement Review. In situations where the funding source requires more assurance on the validity of the financial information than is available with the compilation report, an alternative type of unaudited financial statement is the review report. A **financial statement review** provides the users of financial statements with limited assurance that the financial information has been gathered, recorded, and presented in accordance with generally accepted accounting principles.

Although the review procedures are more thorough than those used in the compilation report, they are not as rigorous as those performed as part of a financial statement audit. The basic prerequisite for performing a financial statement review is that the accountant have a thorough knowledge of the business and industry and any specific accounting practices unique to that business and industry.

Certain inquiries should be made to guarantee a complete understanding of the operation:

1. Investigate the accounting principles and practices followed.

2. Examine the procedures followed in recording transactions and accumulating financial information.

3. Determine whether any individual items or relationships appear unusual. Such a determination would be made by analyzing prior financial statements, comparing actual results with forecasted results, and examining the relationships in light of what would be expected based on past operating data.

4. Review actions taken at various policymaking meetings that affect the financial statements. These meetings include those attended by shareholders, the board of directors, and committees.

5. Determine whether generally accepted accounting practices and principles have been followed and whether there has been a significant change that appreciably affects the operating results shown on the financial statements.

6. Discuss events that have taken place since the date of the financial statements that may impact on the results in the financial statements.

Even though the accountant performing the review is required to be independent of the business operation, the review is a limited procedure and does not provide the same level of assurance as a complete financial audit. The most important difference between a review and an audit is the lack of any independent verification of financial information in the review process.

The accountant's disclosure statement for a review report is very revealing in distinguishing this type of financial statement from the compilation report. A typical disclosure will read as follows:

We have reviewed the accompanying balance sheet of [company name] as of [date] and the related statements of income, retained earnings, and changes in financial position for the year then ended, in accordance with standards established by the American Institute of Certified Public Accountants. All information included in these financial statements is the representation of the management (owners) of [company name].

A review consists principally of inquiries of company personnel and analytical procedures applied to financial data. It is substantially less in scope than an examination in accordance with generally accepted auditing standards, the objective of which is the expression of an opinion regarding the financial statements taken as a whole. Accordingly, we do not express such an opinion.

Based on our review, we are not aware of any material modifications that should be made to the accompanying financial statements in order for them to be in conformity with generally accepted accounting principles.

Audited Financial Statements

The objective of providing audited financial statements is to increase the user's confidence in the fairness of the financial information contained in the statements. An independent auditor ordinarily expresses an "opinion" on how fairly they represent the financial position and results of operations in conformity with generally accepted accounting principles.

An independent accountant conducting an audit will comply with the generally accepted auditing standards established by the AICPA. General auditing standards deal with the training and experience of the individuals actually responsible for performing and supervising the audit, the analytical review procedures followed, and other considerations that will materially affect the outcome of the audit.

The most important characteristic of audited financial statements is the fact that the accountant supports the amounts shown on the statements through independent verification. This includes taking a physical inventory, reviewing the amount and collectibility of accounts receivable, and determining the appropriateness of accounting for long-term investments.

The standard auditor's disclosure statement reads as follows:

We have examined the balance sheet of [company name] as of [date] and the related statement of income, retained earnings, and changes in financial position for the year then ended. Our examination was made in accordance with generally accepted auditing standards and, accordingly, included such tests of the accounting records and such other auditing procedures as we considered necessary in the circumstances.

In our opinion, the financial statements referred to above present fairly the financial position of [company name] as of [date] and the results of its operations and the changes in its financial position for the year then ended, in conformity with generally accepted accounting principles applied on a basis consistent with that of the preceding year.

The Big Eight Discover Small Business

A recent development among the so-called Big Eight accounting firms is their discovery of the small business sector. Small business advisory services have been set up in offices across the country to solicit and serve owner-managed companies. Touche Ross has its Private Companies Advisory Service; Price Waterhouse has its Small Business Services; and Deloitte, Haskins and Sells has its Emerging Business Services Group. Whatever they are called, each has been established to serve the unique needs of the entrepreneurial venture and enter into partnership with these emerging firms, helping them to grow and develop into full-fee paying clients.

Recognizing this as the market segment with the highest growth potential, the Big Eight are targeting privately held businesses that have sales of less than $100 million. Several are looking primarily at firms that have sales of less than $1 million.

The task of the small business specialist is to identify the smaller firms that have a growth-oriented philosophy and a highly marketable concept. These firms typically lack expertise in specific areas such as capital formation, computer systems, and financial management. Thus, it is this type of business that is likely to require an increasing range of business services as the operation expands.

The services are the same as those that have been offered by accounting firms for years. The difference is that the emerging business is now the target of an aggressive marketing effort to attract entrepreneurial firms in the early stages of growth. For those firms fitting the desired profile, the opportunity to establish a relationship with a Big Eight firm is a chance to enter the fast lane in the development process. The availability of resources and expertise is far beyond the reach of the typical owner-managed firm.

Use of Financial Statements

It is very important that the users of financial statements have a clear understanding of the types of procedures that accountants undertake to generate these reports. Financial statement users should recognize that audited statements are not always necessary. In every case, the benefit of requiring the increased involvement of an independent accountant must be weighed against the increased cost of that involvement.

The most important aspect of this discussion is familiarity with the different types of financial statements. Users of these statements should be aware of the level of involvement of the independent accountant and the degree of assurance that is placed on each type of report.

Summary and Conclusions

This chapter has provided an explanation of the process of recording financial data and compiling information into financial statements. The three types of financial statements discussed were income statements, balance sheets, and statements of changes in financial position.

Cash-basis accounting and accrual-basis accounting were contrasted, with an emphasis on the major differences between them. When using a cash-basis accounting system, revenues are not recognized until cash is actually received and expenses are not recorded until cash is actually paid out. In contrast, the accrual-basis accounting system attempts to match revenues with the expenses incurred in generating those revenues.

Finally, the three types of financial reports were discussed: compilation, review, and audit. Users of financial statements need to understand the differences among these reports and know the level of assurance that can be placed in the fairness of each type of report.

References

Seed, Allen H. "The Funds Statement: How Can It Be Improved?" *Financial Executive* (October 1984), pp. 52–55.

Statement on Standards for Accounting and Review Services No. 1. New York: American Institute of Certified Public Accountants, 1979.

5
Tools of Financial Management

Financial management is commonly defined as using financial information to make management decisions that have a direct impact on the financial position of a business operation. It is often thought that this includes only areas that are purely financial in nature such as profit forecasting and cash budgeting. However, the way the term will be used in this chapter will include activities such as analyzing financial statements, comparing company performance with industry standards, and making adjustments in the firm's operations based on the findings.

This chapter will examine the various tools that play a significant role in the entrepreneur's task of managing the finances of a business. The following section will explain the technique of financial statement analysis using the traditional ratio approach. This will entail calculating and comparing a set of indicators that measure the financial health of a firm in five key areas: liquidity, asset utilization, coverage, leverage, and profitability. The final section will examine other key financial concepts that aid the entrepreneur in analyzing the condition of the business: net present value and its applications and the concepts of risk and leverage.

The Traditional Approach to Financial Analysis

One of the critical tasks facing an entrepreneur is to examine the financial feasibility of a business decision. An important aspect of this task is to arrange the information from the financial statements in such a way that comparisons among the various aspects of the business can be made. The steps in analyzing a set of financial statements are:

1. Arrange the financial statements in a comparative format.
2. Calculate common-size financial statements.
3. Compute a set of financial ratios.
4. Examine trends in the ratios and compare them with industry standards.

Comparative Financial Statements

The first step in analyzing financial statements is to organize the financial data into a comparative format. Three years financial data for Richland Gifts, Inc. are presented in comparative format in Exhibit 5–1. The key feature of this method of presenting financial statements is that the data are arranged in such a way that changes and trends in the various categories can be spotted and analyzed quickly.

This method of arranging financial statements becomes even more important when analyzing the financial information from a closely held business. Smaller firms tend to change accounting practices and even accountants more frequently than larger firms. Use of the comparative format will minimize the problems encountered in presenting and understanding data from financial statements where categories are frequently added or deleted from year to year because of varying levels of activity.

Common-Size Financial Statements

The second step is to calculate common-size financial statements from the data. The format of the presentation is similar to that of the comparative financial statements. The difference is that the data entry for each balance sheet category is expressed as a percentage of total assets. The common-size income statement is generated by dividing each income statement category by total sales and expressing it as a percentage.

The common-size statements for Richland Gifts, Inc. are shown in Exhibit 5–2. The primary advantage of this method of presenting financial statements is that it facilitates comparisons with industry standards or other firms by normalizing the data. In other words, this method of presentation adjusts for differences in asset size or sales volume and makes the comparison of data across firms and over time more meaningful.

Traditional Ratio Analysis

One way to compare the various parts of a business is to calculate a set of financial ratios. Ratio analysis is an analytical technique used to establish relationships among income statement, balance sheet, and cash flow statement categories.

When using ratio analysis to examine a firm's financial statements, try to answer the following questions:

1. Does financial balance exist? This refers to the relationship among the essential areas of the firm's operations. Balance is an indicator of growth

EXHIBIT 5–1

Richland Gifts, Inc.
Comparative Financial Statements

Balance Sheet as of 12–31	1984	1985	1986
Assets			
Cash	$ 13,600	$ 18,075	$ 17,700
Accounts receivable	2,800	3,700	4,800
Inventory	48,600	51,700	68,250
Prepaid expenses	1,200	1,200	2,500
Current Assets	$ 66,200	$ 74,675	$ 93,250
Gross fixed assets	58,250	64,150	69,250
Accumulated depreciation	8,740	22,440	36,735
All other noncurrent	4,500	3,500	2,500
Total Assets	$120,210	$119,885	$128,265
Liabilities and Net Worth			
Accounts payable	$ 6,000	$ 7,500	$ 10,000
Short-term notes payable	12,000	10,000	16,000
Taxes payable	965	1,805	2,500
Current maturities—LTD	11,375	12,820	14,450
Current Liabilities	$ 30,340	$ 32,125	$ 42,950
Long-term debt	54,910	43,535	30,715
Common stock	30,000	30,000	30,000
Retained earnings	4,960	14,225	24,600
Total Liabilities and Net Worth	$120,210	$119,885	$128,265

Income Statement for Year	1984	1985	1986
Net sales	$124,500	$155,750	$187,250
Cost of sales	68,475	82,550	101,100
Gross profit	$ 56,025	$ 73,200	$ 86,150
Operating expenses	$ 31,750	$ 41,400	$ 53,150
Depreciation and amortization	8,740	13,700	14,295
Operating profit	$ 15,535	$ 18,100	$ 18,705
Interest expense	$ 9,700	$ 7,200	$ 6,500
Before-tax profit	$ 5,835	$ 10,900	$ 12,205
Income taxes	$ 875	$ 1,635	$ 1,830
After-tax profit	$ 4,960	$ 9,265	$ 10,375

EXHIBIT 5–2

Richland Gifts, Inc.
Common-Size Financial Statements

Balance Sheet as of 12–31	1984	1985	1986
Assets			
Cash	11.31	15.07	13.80
Accounts receivable	2.33	3.09	3.74
Inventory	40.43	43.12	53.21
Prepaid expenses	1.00	1.00	1.95
Current Assets	55.07	62.29	72.70
Fixed assets (net)	41.19	34.79	25.35
All other noncurrent	3.75	2.92	1.95
Total Assets	100.00	100.00	100.00
Liabilities and Net Worth			
Accounts payable	4.99	6.26	7.80
Short-term notes payable	9.98	8.34	12.47
Taxes payable	0.80	1.51	1.95
Current maturities—LTD	9.46	10.69	11.27
Current Liabilities	25.24	26.80	33.49
Long-term debt	45.68	36.31	23.95
Net worth	29.08	36.89	42.57
Total Liabilities and Net Worth	100.00	100.00	100.00

Income Statement for Year	1984	1985	1986
Net sales	100.00	100.00	100.00
Cost of sales	55.00	53.00	53.99
Gross profit	45.00	47.00	46.01
Operating expenses	25.50	26.58	28.38
Depreciation and amortization	7.02	8.80	7.63
Operating profit	12.48	11.62	9.99
Interest expense	7.79	4.62	3.47
Before-tax profit	4.69	7.00	6.52
Income taxes	0.71	1.05	0.98
After-tax profit	3.98	5.95	5.54

and stability. If balance exists, the essential ratios will be average or better.

2. What is the degree of risk involved in the operation?
3. Are there significant trends in the ratios over time?
4. How do the ratios compare with industry standards?
5. If the ratios vary significantly from period to period or from industry averages, what are the causes of the variation? Is the present situation serious? What resources are available to correct any problems?

The ratios we will discuss are grouped into five categories: liquidity, asset utilization, coverage, leverage, and profitability. There is one word of caution before we begin. There are many possible ratios that could be calculated. We will concentrate on a small number of ratios that will be used as general indicators of performance. The ones chosen to be calculated and discussed are those for which comparable industry data are available. Our comparative data is Robert Morris Associates (RMA) *Annual Statement Studies,* and we will use the same method of calculation as used by RMA.

Liquidity Ratios. Liquidity analysis serves as a quick indicator of the ability of the operation to meet its current obligations as they mature. The resources available to meet current obligations are cash and assets that are easily converted into cash, such as marketable securities, inventory, and accounts receivable. These assets are found in the Current Assets section of the balance sheet. The dollar amount of current obligations is found in the Current Liabilities section of the balance sheet. The liabilities include accounts payable, accruals, short-term notes payable, and current maturities of long-term debt—obligations that by definition are due within one year.

Current Ratio. The current ratio is one of the most widely used indicators of a firm's short-term solvency. It reflects the firm's ability to service its current liabilities out of current assets. The ratio is calculated by dividing current assets by current liabilities. The current ratio for Richland Gifts is:

$$\text{Current Ratio} = \frac{\text{Current Assets}}{\text{Current Liabilities}} = \frac{\$93,250}{\$42,950}$$
$$= 2.17 \text{ times.}$$
$$\text{Industry Average} = 1.70 \text{ times.}$$

The current ratio provides a general idea of the overall adequacy of current assets to meet current liabilities as they mature. It is also a measure of the margin of safety the business has in paying short-term obligations if the value of current assets fell for some reason. Richland Gifts' current ratio of 2.17 is slightly better than the average of 1.70 for other novelty and gift shops. Additionally, Richland could liquidate its current assets at 46 percent of their book value and still repay its short-term obligations in full (1/2.16 = .46, or 46 percent).

Quick Ratio or the Acid Test. The quick ratio examines the relationship between the most liquid of the current assets (cash, cash equivalents, and accounts and notes receivable) and total current liabilities. It represents a stricter measure of liquidity, focusing only on the most liquid of current assets. You will notice that inventories are excluded from the calculation. Thus, the resulting ratio is a more conservative measure of liquidity than the current ratio. Also called the "acid test" ratio, it is calculated by dividing the sum of cash and equivalents and trade receivables by total current liabilities.

$$\text{Quick Ratio} = \frac{\text{Cash \& Equivalents} + \text{Trade Receivables}}{\text{Total Current Liabilities}}$$
$$= \frac{\$22,500}{\$42,950}$$
$$= 0.52 \text{ times.}$$
$$\text{Industry Average} = 0.20 \text{ times.}$$

Richland's quick ratio is somewhat better than the industry average. However, the ratio is less than one, indicating that the company shows a dependency on inventories or other current assets to pay off short-term obligations. In the case of a company liquidation, current liabilities could be paid off at a rate of 52 cents on the dollar without relying on the sale of inventories. This is an important consideration, because inventories are the most illiquid of the short-term assets.

Asset Utilization Ratios. The second category of ratios is the asset utilization ratios, which are indicators of the ability to effectively manage the assets of the firm. These ratios are designed to show the relationship between an income statement category (usually Net Sales) and a balance sheet category.

Sales/Receivables. This ratio, often referred to as the receivables turnover ratio, indicates the number of times that accounts receivable turned over during the year. It is calculated by dividing net sales by trade receivables (accounts receivable and notes receivable as a result of trade).

$$\text{Sales/Receivables} = \frac{\text{Net Sales}}{\text{Trade Receivables}}$$
$$= \frac{\$187,250}{\$4,800}$$
$$= 39.01 \text{ times.}$$
$$\text{Industry Average} = 36.70 \text{ times.}$$

The fact that accounts receivable are turning over more rapidly than the industry average is a good indicator for the Richland management. However, in the case of this type of retail business, there are problems in interpreting this ratio that stem from the large percentage of cash sales. If all sales were cash sales, with no credit sales and no accounts receivable, then this ratio would have a value of infinity. When interpreted alone, the ratio says little about the quality of the receivables themselves.

Days Sales Outstanding. The average number of days that this accounts receivable balance remains outstanding indicates how long the average customer takes to pay for merchandise purchased. Often referred to as the *average collection period,* it is calculated by dividing 365 by the ratio of sales to receivables.

$$\text{Days Sales Outstanding} = \frac{365}{\text{Sales/Receivables}}$$
$$= \frac{365}{39.01}$$
$$= 9.36 \text{ days.}$$
$$\text{Industry Average} = 9.95 \text{ days.}$$

This value of this ratio should be consistent with the credit and collection policy of the company. Richland's performance in this area is once again quite consistent with the industry average. This ratio shares the same bias as the Sales/Receivable ratio. There is no distinction made between cash sales and credit sales, so the ratio has a definite downward bias (as the Sales/Receivable ratio has an upward bias). As long as the ratio of cash sales to credit sales is similar to that of the industry, the suggested method of calculation and interpretation is appropriate.

Cost of Sales/Inventory. The efficiency of inventory management is shown by the Cost of Sales/Inventory or inventory turnover ratio. It indicates the number of times the investment in inventory turns over in one year. It is calculated by dividing cost of sales by inventory.

$$\text{Cost of Sales/Inventory} = \frac{\text{Cost of Sales}}{\text{Inventory}}$$
$$= \frac{\$101,100}{\$68,250}$$
$$= 1.48 \text{ times.}$$
$$\text{Industry Average} = 2.20 \text{ times.}$$

The result of this calculation indicates that Richland Gifts' inventories are turning over at a slower rate than that of the average industry operation. The absolute difference between the two ratios is somewhat deceptive. The way to interpret this ratio is to examine it relative to the industry norm. Looking at it in this manner, the Richland inventories are turning over at a rate that is only 67 percent of that of the industry. This low turnover rate is an area of some concern.

There are two problems involved with this particular ratio. One is a problem in calculation and the other is a problem in analysis. In calculating this ratio, there is some question as to what is the proper value to use for inventory. Should you use year ending inventory or an average inventory (beginning plus ending divided by two or a monthly summation divided by 12)? Once again, the choice is somewhat dictated by the industry comparison data available. As long as inventory management procedures are similar, the ratio should be calculated in the same manner as the comparison figures.

The analysis problem is a bit more complex. There can be two possible interpretations for any single value of this ratio. A high value could mean a good choice of inventory stock resulting in a high degree of liquidity. On the other hand, it could be indicative of an inventory level that is too small relative to the level of sales, which often results in merchandise being out of stock.

A low value for this ratio could indicate inventory levels that are too high relative to the level of sales. It could also mean that inventory might be obsolete or in some other way unfit for sale. This low value might simply be the result of a conscious decision on the part of management to increase the level of inventories for some well-defined reason, such as projected shortages in raw materials or an increase in expected future demand.

Days Cost of Goods Sold in Inventory. This ratio, often shortened to *days inventory,* is a measure of the average length of time that an inventory item is in stock. Conceptually, it is the number of days from the time goods are received by the firm until they are sold to the customers. It is calculated by dividing 365 by the ratio of cost of sales to inventory.

$$\text{Days Inventory} = \frac{365}{\text{Cost of Sales/Inventory}}$$
$$= \frac{365}{1.48}$$
$$= 246 \text{ days.}$$
$$\text{Industry Average} = 166 \text{ days.}$$

The use of this ratio clarifies the effect of the slower inventory turnover of Richland Gifts. On average, merchandise is in inventory 80 days longer than in the typical store. Even though the operation seems to be doing relatively well, it would probably be a sound idea to study the inventory patterns and merchandising decisions to determine the reason for the slow inventory turnover.

Sales/Working Capital. The sales-to-working-capital ratio measures how effectively working capital is being used in financing current operations, or generating net sales. A relatively low ratio is indicative of underutilized current resources. On the other hand, a relatively high ratio often points to an overextension of resources. This type of current undercapitalization will leave short-term creditors unnecessarily exposed. The ratio is calculated by dividing net sales by net working capital (current assets minus current liabilities).

$$\text{Sales/Working Capital} = \frac{\text{Net Sales}}{\text{Net Working Capital}}$$
$$= \frac{\$187,250}{\$50,300}$$
$$= 3.72 \text{ times.}$$
$$\text{Industry Average} = 8.00 \text{ times.}$$

At only one-half the industry average, this ratio provides some additional evidence that the Richland management is not using its inventories and thus, its working capital effectively.

Sales/Net Fixed Assets. This ratio is a measure of how effectively fixed assets are being utilized. Fixed asset utilization or fixed asset turnover is the first of two ratios that measure the ability to manage a firm's long-term assets. Sales/Net Fixed Assets is calculated by dividing net sales by net fixed assets (plant and equipment minus accumulated depreciation).

$$\text{Sales/Net Fixed Assets} = \frac{\text{Net Sales}}{\text{Net Fixed Assets}}$$
$$= \frac{\$187,250}{\$32,515}$$
$$= 5.76 \text{ times.}$$
$$\text{Industry Average} = 12.20 \text{ times.}$$

The fact that Richland's fixed asset utilization ratio is significantly below industry average suggests an underutilization of fixed assets in generating sales. There are several conceptual problems in interpreting this ratio. Differences in accounting practices, use of leased equipment, or differences in the labor intensity of the operation can cause difficulty in comparing this ratio across firms. If the book value of fixed assets seriously understates their market value (caused by accelerated methods of depreciating equipment for tax purposes or inflation), significant differences in this ratio between new operations and older, more established operations will arise. Reliance on operating leases for capital equipment instead of actual ownership can artificially inflate this ratio. In addition, if the operation varies sharply from the industry in the degree of labor utilization, its asset turnover ratio is also likely to vary.

Sales/Total Assets. The last asset utilization ratio we will discuss is the Sales/Total Asset ratio. This ratio is a measure of total asset utilization or total asset turnover. It provides information on the effectiveness of the use of the firm's total assets in generating sales. It is calculated by dividing net sales by total assets.

$$\text{Sales/Total Assets} = \frac{\text{Net Sales}}{\text{Total Assets}}$$
$$= \frac{\$187,250}{\$128,265}$$
$$= 1.46 \text{ times.}$$
$$\text{Industry Average} = 2.20 \text{ times.}$$

The evidence that Richland Gifts is not making efficient use of its assets continues to grow. Turnover seems to be a problem with the operation. Of the five turnover ratios discussed, only receivables turnover compared favorably with the industry average. Management should make an effort to analyze this area carefully.

Coverage Ratios. This category of ratios measures the firm's ability to service its debt—interest charges plus principal amortization. The ratios indicate the number of times fixed debt charges are covered out of operations. The purpose of this category of ratios is to identify the firms that are relying too heavily on the use of debt to capitalize the operation.

EBIT/Interest. A firm's ability to meet its annual interest expense is measured by this ratio, often called "times interest earned." It is calculated by dividing earnings before interest and taxes by annual interest expense.

$$\text{EBIT/Interest} = \frac{\text{Earnings Before Interest and Taxes}}{\text{Annual Interest Expense}}$$
$$= \frac{\$18,705}{\$6,500}$$
$$= 2.88 \text{ times.}$$
$$\text{Industry Average} = 3.60 \text{ times.}$$

This ratio is slightly below the industry average, indicating that Richland, while still adequately covering interest charges, is less capable of taking on additional debt than the average firm.

Cash Flow/Current Maturities of Long-Term Debt. This ratio measures the extent to which the principal on debt is covered by the cash flow of the operation. Since cash flow from operations is the primary source of repayment of debt, this ratio is indicative of the firm's ability to service the current portion of its long-term debt obligations. It is calculated by dividing cash flow by current maturities of long-term debt (CMLTD). Following RMA's calculation of this ratio, cash flow will be defined as profit after taxes plus depreciation expense.

$$\text{Cash Flow/CMLTD} = \frac{\text{Cash Flow}}{\text{Current Maturities of Long-Term Debt}}$$
$$= \frac{\$24,670}{\$14,450}$$
$$= 1.71 \text{ times.}$$
$$\text{Industry Average} = 1.30 \text{ times.}$$

This ratio for Richland is slightly better than the industry average, indicating good coverage of maturing long-term debt.

Leverage Ratios. This category of ratios is closely related to the coverage ratios. They measure the extent to which the firm is capitalized through debt. Highly leveraged companies will, on average, have higher values for coverage ratios.

A heavy reliance on debt sources to finance a business is quite common for new ventures. Firms that are highly leveraged are much more vulnerable to downturns in business activity and have a higher degree of risk associated with their operations.

Debt Ratio. This ratio measures the percentage of the total capitalization being supplied by creditors. The higher this ratio is, the greater the risk to creditors will be in the event of a business downturn. The debt ratio is calculated by dividing total liabilities by total assets.

$$
\begin{aligned}
\text{Debt Ratio} &= \frac{\text{Total Liabilities}}{\text{Total Assets}} \\
&= \frac{\$73,665}{\$128,265} \\
&= 57.43 \text{ percent.} \\
\text{Industry Average} &= 78.90 \text{ percent.}
\end{aligned}
$$

The owner's position in the Richland Gift operation is a much greater percentage of the total capitalization than that of the typical industry operation. That is to say, the creditors have supplied a much smaller proportion of the financing for the operation than would be expected in this industry. Based on this ratio, the owners of Richland are in a good position to seek additional outside financing if they desire to do so.

Fixed/Worth. This ratio measures the relative degree to which the owners have invested their equity in fixed assets (plant and equipment). The higher this ratio is, the more vulnerable creditors will be in the event of a company liquidation. The lower the ratio is, the better the cushion will be in the case of such an event. The ratio is calculated by dividing net fixed assets (gross fixed assets minus accumulated depreciation) by tangible net worth (total net worth minus intangibles).

$$
\begin{aligned}
\text{Fixed/Worth} &= \frac{\text{Net Fixed Assets}}{\text{Tangible Net Worth}} \\
&= \frac{\$32,515}{\$54,600} \\
&= 0.60. \\
\text{Industry Average} &= 0.80.
\end{aligned}
$$

The owners of Richland have invested significantly less of their equity in fixed assets than the owners of the typical firm in the industry—60 percent and 80 percent, respectively. A heavy use of operating leases for capital equipment (not shown on the balance sheet) will tend to lower this ratio. The

Richland operation has no leased equipment, and the typical industry operation has a significant amount (as evidenced by the fact that 6.30 percent of sales goes to lease and rental expense for the average firm), so the cushion enjoyed by Richland is relatively better than the comparison indicates.

Sales/Worth. When the Fixed/Worth ratio is multiplied by the Sales/Net Fixed Asset ratio, the resulting ratio is commonly referred to as the "trading ratio." Sales/Worth measures the extent to which a firm's sales volume is supported by equity capital. A high value for this ratio is indicative of a heavy debt burden and an operation that is dependent on continued favorable internal and external conditions. A relatively low value for this ratio means either excess resources or inadequate sales for the level of invested capital. This ratio is calculated by dividing net sales by tangible net worth.

$$\text{Sales/Worth} = \frac{\text{Net Sales}}{\text{Tangible Net Worth}}$$
$$= \frac{\$187,250}{\$54,600}$$
$$= 3.43 \text{ times.}$$
$$\text{Industry Average} = 9.76 \text{ times.}$$

The trading ratio is 3.43 for Richland, compared to 9.76 for the average industry operation. This is additional evidence that the sales volume is inadequate relative to the equity capital investment.

Debt/Worth. The ratio of debt-to-worth shows the relative investment that creditors have in the business compared with that of the owners. A low value for this ratio is indicative of a company that has a low level of financial risk and a great degree of flexibility in future financing decisions. It is calculated by dividing total liabilities by tangible net worth.

$$\text{Debt/Worth} = \frac{\text{Total Liabilities}}{\text{Tangible Net Worth}}$$
$$= \frac{\$73,665}{\$54,600}$$
$$= 1.35 \text{ to one.}$$
$$\text{Industry Average} = 2.40 \text{ to one.}$$

The interpretation of this ratio is somewhat similar to that of the debt ratio. In fact, it should be noted that this ratio (D/E) is simply an algebraic transformation of the debt ratio (D/A).

$$\frac{D}{A} = \frac{D}{D + E} = \frac{D/E}{1 + D/E} \quad \text{and} \quad \frac{D}{E} = \frac{D}{A - D} = \frac{D/A}{1 - D/A}.$$

The Debt/Asset ratio will vary within its limits of zero to 100 percent, while the Debt/Worth ratio will vary between zero and infinity. In both cases, the larger the number is, the more vulnerable the position of the firm's creditors will be and the more limited the firm will be in securing additional external debt without first securing an additional equity injection.

Profitability Ratios. Profitability is often the measure that is used to evaluate overall management performance. Although all the ratios examined to this point are indicative of the type of job management is doing, the profitability ratios reflect two very important aspects of the firm's operations that have not been examined yet. First, they show whether the expense structure of the operation is appropriate for the level of sales generated. Second, they express the profitability of the operation relative to the level of resource investment.

Gross Profit Margin. This income statement ratio is calculated by dividing gross profit (net sales minus cost of sales) by net sales.

$$\begin{aligned} \text{Gross Profit Margin} &= \frac{\text{Gross Profit}}{\text{Net Sales}} \\ &= \frac{\$86,150}{\$187,250} \\ &= 46.01 \text{ percent.} \\ \text{Industry Average} &= 44.80 \text{ percent.} \end{aligned}$$

The closeness of the Gross Profit Margin to the industry average indicates that Richland's pricing practices are in line with those of the industry.

Net Profit Margin. This ratio measures the after-tax profits as a percentage of sales. It is calculated by dividing profit after tax by net sales.

$$\begin{aligned} \text{Net Profit Margin} &= \frac{\text{After-Tax Profit}}{\text{Net Sales}} \\ &= \frac{\$10,375}{\$187,250} \\ &= 5.54 \text{ percent.} \\ \text{Industry Average} &= \text{Not Available.} \end{aligned}$$

The *Annual Statement Studies* does not publish a comparison figure for Net Profit Margin; however, it does publish the before-tax profit margin.

Richland's before-tax profit margin is substantially higher than the industry average (6.52 percent compared to 4.60 percent), so the Net Profit Margin should also compare favorably.

EBIT/Total Assets. The ratio of Operating Profit to Total Assets, referred to as the basic earning power of assets, measures how effectively the firm is generating profit from its total assets. It is calculated by dividing earnings before interest and taxes (EBIT) by total assets.

$$\text{EBIT/Total Assets} = \frac{\text{Earnings Before Interest and Taxes}}{\text{Total Assets}}$$
$$= \frac{\$18,705}{\$128,265}$$
$$= 14.58 \text{ percent.}$$
$$\text{Industry Average} = 12.54 \text{ percent.}$$

This ratio is used to compare the effective use of assets in generating profit regardless of either the manner in which the operation is capitalized or the firm's specific tax situation. By using EBIT (operating profit), one is able to determine the basic ability of the operation to generate profit. Firms with the same basic earning power but different degrees of financial leverage will earn vastly different returns for their shareholders. The Richland operation is faring slightly better than the typical industry firm in this area, with a basic earning power ratio of 14.58 percent, as compared to 12.54 for the typical firm.

Return on Assets (ROA). This ratio measures the ability to generate after-tax profit out of a given total asset base. Return on assets is calculated by dividing after-tax profit by total assets.

$$\text{Return on Assets} = \frac{\text{After-Tax Profit}}{\text{Total Assets}}$$
$$= \frac{\$10,375}{\$128,265}$$
$$= 8.09 \text{ percent.}$$
$$\text{Industry Average} = \text{Not Available.}$$

RMA data does not provide tax information for comparisons. Thus, when using this data base for comparison purposes, there is no way to generate industry averages for after-tax ratios. However, an 8.09 percent ROA compares favorably to the opportunity cost of holding those assets in another form, such as U.S. Treasury Bills, which were earning around 8 percent at the time.

Return on Equity (ROE). The return on equity measures the amount that the operation has given back to the stockholders. This ratio is calculated by dividing after-tax profit by tangible net worth.

$$\begin{aligned} \text{Return on Equity} &= \frac{\text{After-Tax Profit}}{\text{Tangible Net Worth}} \\ &= \frac{\$10,375}{\$54,600} \\ &= 19.00 \text{ percent.} \\ \text{Industry Average} &= \text{Not Available.} \end{aligned}$$

No operation can hope to survive and adequately provide for future growth without generating a return for its stockholders. The 19 percent ROE is probably sufficient to keep the owners of the Richland operation satisfied with their investment. One word of caution: extreme care should be exercised when interpreting this ratio. A high return could be the result of an under-capitalized firm coupled with a substandard profit (measured by the net profit margin), rather than an efficiently run operation.

A Closer Look at Profitability Analysis. The ability to generate a return on assets and a return on equity is a function of the ability to control the relevant categories on both the income statement and the balance sheet. This fact is made clear by establishing the relationship among all the categories of the ratios just discussed. Figure 5–1 depicts the entire system of ratios that goes into calculating return on equity (ROE), which is referred to as the *duPont System.*

The major components that establish the relationship we call *return on equity* are net profit margin, total asset turnover, and the debt ratio. Analyzing the figure in general, it is evident that the return on equity ultimately depends on the ability to manage the income statement categories that go into the calculation of net profit margin, in addition to total asset turnover.

Concentrating on the left-hand side of the figure, we begin with net sales of $187,250 and go through a series of subtractions (expenses, interest, and taxes), ending up with an after-tax profit of $10,375. Dividing after-tax profit by net sales yields a net profit margin of 5.54 percent. This is interpreted to mean that stockholders as residual claimants receive a return of 5.54 cents from every dollar of sales.

The right-hand side of the figure shows the breakdown of total assets into current and noncurrent assets. Dividing net sales by this value yields the total asset turnover of 1.46. In other words, each dollar of assets is used to generate $1.46 in net sales during the year.

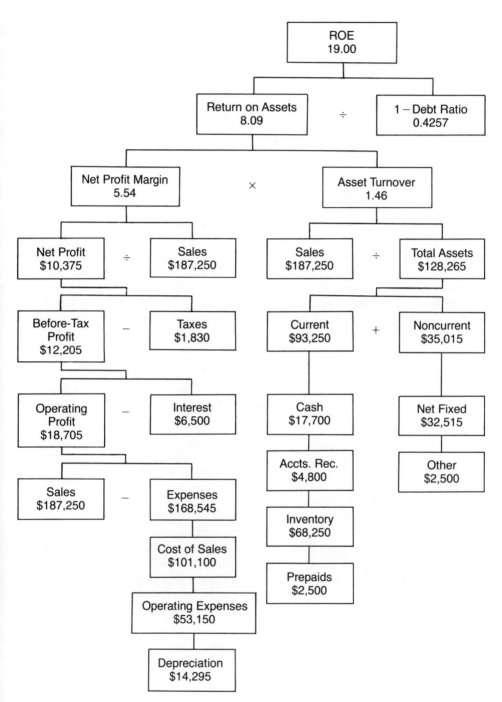

Figure 5–1. **Return on Equity (ROE) Ratio System Applied to Richland Gifts, Inc.**

To get return on assets, simply multiply the net profit margin by total asset turnover.

$$\text{Return on Assets} = \text{Net Profit Margin} \cdot \text{Total Asset Turnover}$$
$$= \frac{\text{After-Tax Profit}}{\text{Net Sales}} \cdot \frac{\text{Net Sales}}{\text{Total Assets}}$$
$$= 5.54 \text{ percent} \cdot 1.46 = 8.09 \text{ percent.}$$

Assets turned over 1.46 times during the year, so the net profit margin of 5.54 percent yields a return on assets of 8.09 percent. If total asset turnover is less than one, ROA will be less than net profit margin and vice versa. Note that a below average net profit margin can be enhanced by an above average total asset turnover to maintain an adequate return on assets.

Return on equity depends on ROA and the debt ratio. Thus, firms with the same ROA can have quite different ROE, depending on the use of financial leverage. Highly leveraged firms will have, other things being equal, higher values for ROE and higher risk. The return on equity can be calculated by dividing return on assets by one minus the debt ratio (referred to as the equity ratio).

$$\text{Return on Equity} = \frac{\text{Return on Assets}}{\text{Equity Ratio}} = \frac{8.09 \text{ percent}}{1 - .5743}$$
$$= \frac{8.09 \text{ percent}}{.4257} = 19.00 \text{ percent.}$$

By using a greater degree of financial leverage, firms can turn a mediocre ROA into an attractive ROE. The ability to keep stockholders content depends on the ability to generate a return for their invested capital. An increase in the return on equity can come about by increased profitability, better asset utilization, or increased leverage. Note that only increased leverage results in more risk. The other two result in increased return without increased risk. Thus, it is important to consider these three key areas when analyzing a firm's financial condition. Ignoring any one area can give a distorted view of the operation, or even more critically, cause one to overlook details that are important in the overall analysis.

Analyzing Trends in Financial Ratios. Ratios are general indicators of business performance and only one of the tools that should be used in evaluating an operation. The value of ratio analysis can be enhanced in several ways. In addition to the industry comparisons that we have already incorporated into the analysis, it is important to view the ratios within the context of their historical trends. In fact, trend analysis may be a more significant indicator

EXHIBIT 5–3

Richland Gifts, Inc.
Three-Year Ratios Summary with Comparisons

	Period Ending December 31			
	1984	**1985**	**1986**	**RMA**
Liquidity				
Current ratio	2.18	2.32	2.17	1.70
Quick ratio	0.54	0.68	0.52	0.20
Asset Utilization				
Sales/Receivables	44.46	42.09	39.01	36.70
Days sales outstanding	8.21	8.67	9.36	9.95
Cost of sales/Inventory	1.41	1.60	1.48	2.20
Days inventory	259	228	246	166
Sales/Working capital	3.47	3.66	3.72	8.00
Sales/Net fixed assets	2.51	3.73	5.76	12.20
Sales/Total assets	1.04	1.30	1.46	2.20
Coverage				
EBIT/Interest	1.60	2.51	2.88	3.60
Cash flow/CMLTD	1.20	1.79	1.71	1.30
Leverage				
Debt ratio	70.92	63.11	57.43	78.90
Fixed/Worth	1.42	0.94	0.60	0.80
Sales/Worth	3.56	3.52	3.43	9.76
Debt/Worth	2.44	1.71	1.35	2.40
Profitability				
Gross profit margin	45.00	47.00	46.01	44.80
Net profit margin	3.98	5.95	5.54	NA
EBIT/Total assets	12.98	15.10	14.58	12.54
Return on assets	4.14	7.73	8.09	NA
Return on equity	14.19	20.95	19.00	NA

of operating performance than comparing a ratio from a given point in time with an industry average. Through this technique, it can be established whether the ratios are improving or getting worse. This aspect of the analysis can either be presented in tabular or graphical form. Exhibit 5–3 presents the calculated values of the ratios for the three years of financial data available for Richland Gifts, Inc.

It is important to carefully distinguish between trends that are significant and those that are not. From data presented in Exhibit 5–3, we can see that the liquidity ratios have remained steady at levels above the industry standard. Although asset utilization ratios are worse than industry averages, they are steadily improving, with the possible exception of the Cost of Sales/

Inventory ratio. Coverage is improving and does not seem to be a problem. Less debt than the average firm is indicated by the lower than average leverage ratios. In addition, there seems to be a downward trend in these ratios, which is indicative of a conservatively run operation. Finally, over the past three years, there has been a significant improvement in the profitability ratios.

A Final Look at Ratio Analysis. Ratio analysis is used for many different purposes. Of importance to our discussion is the tendency for creditors to use ratios in assessing the creditworthiness of a potential borrower. In order for a manager to stay one step ahead in the lending process, it is important to understand the objective measures used by creditors in the lending decision. This understanding is critical to the long-term viability of a business operation.

Ratios are only as good as the financial data from which they are calculated. Unusual cost items, heavily depreciated equipment, or other specific accounting practices can have a significant effect on financial statement values, which in turn will affect the calculated ratios.

Ratio analysis has traditionally been used as the primary tool of financial managers in evaluating the performance of a business operation. A complete analysis includes the calculation of a series of ratios that indicate how well a business is performing in five different areas: 1) liquidity, 2) asset utilization, 3) coverage, 4) leverage, and 5) profitability. In order to enhance the value of this management tool, the ratios should be compared with those of other firms in the same line of business (cross-section analysis), and over time with ratios of the same firm from previous time periods (trend analysis).

Other Key Financial Concepts

There are a number of other financial concepts that could be appropriately included in a discussion of the tools of financial management. For the purposes of this presentation, we will focus on the concepts that are particularly useful to the entrepreneur in planning and evaluating venture opportunities.

Net Present Value

Almost everyone has used the expression, "Time is money." It is obvious that, literally speaking, time is not the medium of exchange used to expedite our daily transactions. What concept, then, is this expression actually trying to convey? It is actually referring to the idea that every activity has an opportunity cost. The very fact that we choose to undertake one activity means that we are foregoing the opportunity to engage in some other activity.

Think of time as you would any other resource. The specific reference to money indicates that the opportunity cost of a particular block of time can be measured by the foregone monetary return that could have been earned in our next best use of that time.

Rational decision makers take time into consideration when evaluating opportunities. They are deeply concerned with the timing of benefits and costs and attempt to speed up benefits and postpone costs. The concept of net present value is central to the issue of comparing alternative opportunities whose benefit and cost streams vary across time. It is also a principle that has other applications. Our understanding of these issues will begin with a discussion of the concept of time preference.

The Concept of Time Preference. Generally speaking, when an individual is given a choice of either consuming a particular good now or consuming the same amount at some future date, the individual will choose to consume now. Most people place a higher subjective value on immediate consumption than on future consumption. That is to say, most people have a positive rate of time preference. This does not mean that people are irrational and short-sighted and have no thought for the future. Given the reality of mortality and all the other uncertainties related to the choice itself, it is no wonder that an individual will choose a dollar today rather than a dollar a year from now. In much the same way, time preference is a characteristic of investment decisions.

The Discounting Process. The concept that is actually the core of economic decision making is the process of discounting. Suppose that $1,000 can be invested today in a twelve-month certificate of deposit earning a 10 percent annual return. One year from now that investment will have grown to $1,100, or ($1,000 · 1.1). This can be stated generally by the following formula:

$$FV_1 = PV \cdot (1 + r)$$

where

FV_1 = the future value of the investment in one year
PV = the present value of the investment
r = the interest rate.

Considering that same $1,000 investment, if the interest rates were 12.5 and 15 percent, the amount would have increased to $1,125 and $1,150, respectively. If the initial investment were $2,000 and $3,000 at the 10 percent interest rate, the amount would have increased to $2,200 and $3,300, respectively.

Looking at the same investment opportunity from a different perspective, if an individual wishes to have $1,100 in one year, he would have to invest $1,000 at an interest rate of 10 percent. In order to have $1,125 or $1,150 in one year, that same $1,000 would have to be invested at 12.5 percent and 15 percent, respectively. This problem is simply the reverse of the preceding one. Instead of solving for FV_1, the equation is written in such a way that PV is the unknown value. The result is as follows:

$$PV = \frac{FV_1}{(1 + r)}$$

The expression $1/(1 + r)$ is referred to as the **discount factor**, whereas $1 + r$ in the previous equation is referred to as the **compound factor**. Thus, discounting and compounding are two different ways to look at the same question. Current values are compounded forward through time by using a growth rate called the *rate of interest*. Future values are discounted back to the present using this same rate, which is called the *rate of discount*.

Multi-Period Discounting. Expanding the number of time periods under consideration complicates the mathematics slightly, but does not change the basic nature of the problem. The problem can be conceptualized by setting up a sequence of investments in consecutive one-year certificates of deposit (CD). Assume that the original $1,000 investment plus interest earned is to be reinvested in a second certificate of deposit. At the end of the second year, the value of the investment will be $1,210 [($1,000 · 1.1) · 1.1]. Likewise, if a third CD is purchased, the value of the investment at the end of the third year will be $1,331. The formula that depicts this type of compounding is:

$$FV_n = PV(1 + r)^n$$

That is to say, an initial investment of PV will grow to FV_n in n years at an annual interest rate of r percent.

The discounting process is simply the reverse of the compounding process, so it follows that the general formula for discounting can be written:

$$PV = \frac{FV_n}{(1 + r)^n}$$

Using the logic presented in the formula, it can be deduced that if $1,000 can grow to $1,331 in three years at an annual percentage rate of 10 percent,

Table 5–1
Compound Factors for Determining the Future Value of $1
at Various Interest Rates for Different Time Periods

Year	2%	4%	6%	8%	10%	12%	14%	16%	18%
1	1.020	1.040	1.060	1.080	1.100	1.120	1.140	1.160	1.180
2	1.040	1.082	1.124	1.166	1.210	1.254	1.300	1.346	1.392
3	1.061	1.125	1.191	1.260	1.331	1.405	1.482	1.561	1.643
4	1.082	1.170	1.262	1.360	1.464	1.574	1.689	1.811	1.939
5	1.104	1.217	1.338	1.469	1.611	1.762	1.925	2.100	2.288
6	1.126	1.265	1.419	1.587	1.772	1.974	2.195	2.436	2.700
7	1.149	1.316	1.504	1.714	1.949	2.211	2.502	2.826	3.185
8	1.172	1.369	1.594	1.851	2.144	2.476	2.853	3.278	3.759
9	1.195	1.423	1.689	1.999	2.358	2.773	3.252	3.803	4.435
10	1.219	1.480	1.791	2.159	2.594	3.106	3.707	4.411	5.234

Table 5–2
Discount Factors for Determining the Present Value of $1
at Various Discount Rates for Different Time Periods

Years	2%	4%	6%	8%	10%	12%	14%	16%	18%
1	.980	.962	.943	.926	.909	.893	.877	.862	.847
2	.961	.925	.890	.857	.826	.797	.769	.743	.718
3	.942	.889	.840	.794	.751	.712	.675	.641	.609
4	.924	.855	.792	.735	.683	.636	.592	.552	.516
5	.906	.822	.747	.681	.621	.567	.519	.476	.437
6	.888	.790	.705	.630	.564	.507	.456	.410	.370
7	.871	.760	.665	.583	.513	.452	.400	.354	.314
8	.853	.731	.627	.540	.467	.404	.351	.305	.266
9	.837	.703	.592	.500	.424	.361	.308	.263	.225
10	.820	.676	.558	.463	.386	.322	.270	.227	.191

then the present value of $1,331 to be received three years from now, discounted at 10 percent, is $1,000.

Even though the mathematical calculations are really quite simple, it will often be much more efficient to use conversion factors such as those given in Tables 5–1 and 5–2. These tables present the compound factors and discount factors for various values of r and n.

Using these tables is really quite simple. First, examine how the tables are constructed. The various interest/discount rates are given by the column headings and the various time periods are indicated in the first column. The body of the tables is composed of the precalculated compound/discount factors. To illustrate the use of the compounding process, find the future value of $1 invested at 12 percent for five years. Using Table 5–1, you would find the column headed "12%," move down to period 5, and note that the initial dollar investment will have grown to $1.762.

Investments of various amounts can be evaluated by simply multiplying the compound factor by the initial value of the investment. For example, if the initial investment in the preceding case were $500, the future value would be $881 ($500 · 1.762).

Problems in discounting are equally as simple to solve. What if you were interested in knowing the present value of $1 to be received five years from today, discounted at 12 percent? Using Table 5–2, under the column headed "12%," the relevant discount factor for five years is 0.567. That is to say, $0.567 invested at 12 percent will grow to $1.00 in five years; the present value of $1.00 to be received in five years is 56.7 cents, using a discount rate of 12 percent. To adjust for different size payments, simply multiply the discount factor by the amount of the payment.

Applications to Decision Making. There are, of course, many applications of the net present value concept in the area of financial decision making. As we stated earlier, it is one of the single most important concepts in financial management. Our discussion will focus on two of these applications.

Net Present Value of Investment Alternatives. The concept of net present value can be applied in situations in which an entrepreneur is faced with a variety of investment alternatives that differ in cost and benefit streams. A typical situation has some of the following characteristics. Usually the entrepreneur is faced with making an initial investment outlay to initiate the project. In the early years, the costs often exceed the returns. If the project is to be successful, this pattern must be reversed in later years so that a profit is earned.

The concept of net present value can be applied to calculate the residual value of the cost and benefit flows that will accrue at various future time periods. These costs and benefits are usually discounted at a rate equal to the opportunity cost of funds. One of the most difficult decisions to make in the entire investment analysis is the choice of the discount rate. Because of the nature of the discounting process, it can be observed that the net present value of a project varies inversely with the discount rate chosen. Thus, any project will look better if a low discount rate is chosen. Although a risk-adjusted weighted average cost of capital may be the best rate to use for the discounting process, the following rule-of-thumb should provide a good starting point for choosing a discount rate.

If the project is to be financed out of equity funds, pick a rate that is

Calculating Present and Future Values with a Hand-Held Calculator

With the increased availability of inexpensive electronic calculators, the speed and accuracy of the compounding and discounting process has been dramatically improved. On most financial analyst-type calculators, the keystroke sequence for finding the future value of an investment will be as follows. Each bracketed expression (i.e., {PV}) represents a single keystroke.

1. Enter the number of periods [{number of periods}, {N}].
2. Enter the periodic interest rate [{interest rate}, {%i}].
3. Enter the amount of the investment [{investment}, {PV}].
4. Compute the future value of the investment [{2nd}, {FV}].

Alternatively, this problem can be solved by using the exponential function of the calculator. In this case, the keystroke sequence will be as follows: [{compound factor}, {2nd}, {y^x}, {number of periods}, {=}, {x}, {investment}, {=}].

The keystroke sequence for finding the present value of a sum to be received at some future date involves basically the same steps, with one very important change.

1. Enter the number of periods [{number of periods}, {N}].
2. Enter the periodic interest rate [{interest rate}, {%i}].
3. Enter the future value [{future value}, {FV}].
4. Compute the present value [{2nd}, {PV}].

Likewise, the discounting problem can be solved using the exponential function. In this case, the keystroke sequence is as follows: [{discount factor}, {2nd}, {y^x}, {number of periods}, {=}, {x}, {future value}, {=}].

Because of rounding errors, the infinite number of possibilities for the compound/discount factors, and the number of periods, the use of an electronic calculator is far superior to the practice of looking up the values in the tables. However, extreme caution should be taken when keying in values. What may seem to be an insignificant keystroke error can be compounded into a major mistake in the decision-making process. In order to reduce the likelihood of computational error, those unfamiliar with the use of calculators might do well to take advantage of expanded tables available for most professional work.

---

representative of the rate of return that can be earned in the best money market alternative available. If the project is to be funded from borrowed capital, use a rate equal to the interest rate on the debt. If a combination of debt and equity is to be used, use a weighted average of the two rates. Ultimately, the rate used should reflect the desired rate of return on the investment being evaluated, whatever rate is used.

The net present value of a project (NPV) can be calculated using the following formula:

$$NPV = (R_0 - C_0) + \frac{(R_1 - C_1)}{(1 + r)} + \frac{(R_2 - C_2)}{(1 + r)^2} + \ldots + \frac{(R_n - C_n)}{(1 + r)^n}$$

The first term in the expression is the initial net cost of the project. The initial return (R_0) is probably equal to zero, so the first term is almost always negative. No discount factor is applied to this term because it is incurred at the current period. The other terms are simply a period-by-period application of the discounting process, using the net of returns in excess of costs in the numerator each time. If the project has any residual value at the end of the investment period, then a final term should be added to the calculation, $S/(1 + r)^n$, where S is the residual or salvage value of the project.

Suppose that the desired return on a project under consideration is 10 percent. The initial cost of the project will be $100,000. The net benefit stream is projected to last for three years, and the values are expected to be $50,000, $88,000, and $120,000. The residual value of the investment is $30,000. What is the net present value to the prospective investor? The solution is:

$$\begin{aligned}
NPV &= -\$100,000 + \frac{\$50,000}{(1.10)^1} + \frac{\$88,000}{(1.10)^2} \\
&\quad + \frac{\$120,000}{(1.10)^3} + \frac{\$30,000}{(1.10)^3} \\
&= -\$100,000 + \$45,454.55 + \$72,727.27 \\
&\quad + \$90,157.78 + \$22,539.04 \\
&= \$130,879.04
\end{aligned}$$

The decision to accept or reject a project depends on whether the project is being evaluated in isolation of other projects or it is being compared to other projects. If the project is the only one under consideration, its acceptance or rejection will be based on whether the net present value is positive or negative. A positive net present value indicates that the project is feasible and should be accepted; a negative net present value indicates the opposite.

In this example, we are in effect comparing the isolated project with our next best investment alternative, as measured by the discount rate chosen. A positive net present value indicates that the rate of return on the project is greater than the best alternative rate of return, whose value depends on whether the funds are equity or debt.

If two similar projects are being considered, each of which requires the same initial investment, the one with the greatest net present value should be chosen, assuming, of course, that they are mutually exclusive. This particular investment rule is not always valid, however, because investment alternatives are rarely the same. Initial investments differ, risks differ, and investment periods differ. Thus, it is necessary to look at the rate of return per dollar invested instead of merely net present value.

Internal Rate of Return. The choice of the discount rate is absolutely critical in determining the net present value of an investment alternative. In fact, when comparing two projects that have significantly different net benefit flows, even a small change in the discount rate can lead to a reordering of the projects. What is needed then is a criterion for making investments that is insensitive to interest rates. This fact has contributed to the use of the concept of the internal rate of return for these purposes.

The **internal rate of return** (IRR) on an investment alternative is actually the yield on a project and is defined as the rate of discount that forces the net present value to equal zero. The method for calculating the internal rate of return is to take the preceding formula for net present value, set it equal to zero, and solve for r, which becomes the IRR. In other words, the internal rate of return is the discount rate that equates the present value of the net benefit stream to the initial net cost of the project.

The actual solution to the equation involves the process of trial and error. Without the use of an electronic calculator, the process involves choosing a value for IRR and solving for the NPV. If the result is greater than zero, the IRR used in the calculation was too low and a larger value should be tried. Likewise, a negative NPV indicates that the value of IRR used was too high and a smaller value should be tried.

If a project is being evaluated in isolation, the decision to accept or reject it is based on a comparison between the internal rate of return and the market rate of interest. If the internal rate of return is greater than the market interest rate, the project is accepted. Assuming that the market interest rate is the relevant borrowing rate for the entrepreneur evaluating the project, a given rate of return greater than the market interest rate indicates that investing in the project will result in borrowed capital growing faster than its opportunity cost.

If multiple projects are being evaluated simultaneously, they should be ranked in order of their internal rates of return. All projects that have an internal rate of return greater than the market interest rate are feasible. However, investment should begin with the project that has the highest internal rate of return and continue until all available capital resources are exhausted or all feasible projects have been undertaken.

Two precautionary notes should be addressed before we conclude the discussion on the internal rate of return criterion. First, the calculation implicitly assumes that the net benefit stream generated in the early years of the

Calculating Internal Rates of Return

The process of iterating toward a value for the internal rate of return can be a tedious procedure. Many financial calculators are programmed to calculate internal rates of return. If the net benefit stream is constant in each period, the keystroke sequence will be as follows.

1. Enter the number of periods [{number of periods}, {*N*}].
2. Enter the periodic net benefit [{net benefit}, {*PMT*}].
3. Enter the initial net cost [{initial net cost}, {*PV*}].
4. Compute the internal rate of return [{2nd}, {%*i*}].

Even if the net benefit stream is not constant in each period, the basic steps involved in the calculation are the same. The net benefit stream is entered, the initial cost is entered, and the internal rate of return is computed. With a non-constant benefit stream, the first step of this process is more complicated. The typical keystroke sequence is as follows.

1. Enter the net return for period one [{1}, {*N*}, {net return}, {*FV*}, {2nd}, {*PV*}, {*STO*}].
2. Enter the net return for period two [{2}, {*N*}, {net return}, {*FV*}, {2nd}, {*PV*}, {*SUM*}].
3. Continue step two until the net returns for each period have been entered.
4. Enter the residual value of the project [{*n*}, {*N*}, {residual value}, {*FV*}, {2nd}, {*PV*}, {*SUM*}].
5. Recall and store the net return stream [{*RCL*}, {*STO*}].
6. Enter the initial net cost [{net cost}, {*PV*}].
7. Compute the internal rate of return [{2nd}, {%*i*}].

---

project will be reinvested at the same market rate of return. If these opportunities to reinvest do not exist, then the internal rate of return actually overstates the true return that can be earned on the project because the benefit stream must be reinvested at a lower rate of return. A second assumption implicit in the calculation is that there is only one sign change in the net return stream—negative in the early years and positive in the later years. If there is more than one sign change in the net return stream, there will be more than one solution to the internal rate of return. This will involve solving a quadratic formula with multiple roots. Although this sort of net benefit stream is possible, the typical flow involves only one sign change—negative to positive—during the investment period under consideration.

Amortizing a Loan. One of the more useful applications of the net present value concept involves the process of amortizing an installment loan. Most business loans are repaid by making equal periodic payments, which usually occur every month, to the funding source. There are two steps in the process of loan amortization: 1) calculating the monthly installment payment and 2) generating an amortization schedule.

The monthly installment on a note is the equal monthly payment that will retire both principal and interest over the term. It is calculated from an adaptation of the net present value formula. Applying what we already know about calculating the net present value of project, we can adapt the NPV formula to the equal monthly retirement of installment debt as follows:

$$LOAN = \sum_{t=1}^{n} \frac{PMT}{(1 + r)^t}$$

where LOAN is the initial loan principal to be repaid, PMT is the equal monthly installment, and the summation term $\sum_{t=1,n} [1/(1 + r)^t]$ is the present value interest factor of an annuity (PVIFA), which can be rewritten:

$$PVIFA = \frac{1 - \dfrac{1}{(1 + r)^t}}{r}$$

Thus, the formula for calculating the periodic payment necessary to amortize an installment loan can be written:

$$PMT = \frac{LOAN}{PVIFA}$$

Suppose an entrepreneur has an opportunity to borrow $100,000 at 14 percent annual interest for a period of seven years. What will the monthly installment be on this loan? The first step in the calculation will be to solve for the PVIFA. Solving the previously given PVIFA formula results in a value of 53.35. Note that this calculation is for a monthly installment. As a result, $t = 84$ (12 months times 7) and $r = 0.01167$ (14 percent divided by 12). Completing the calculation results in a monthly payment of approximately $1,874.

Each installment payment consists of the interest payment on the outstanding principal balance, with the residual going to retire a portion of the loan itself. The actual breakdown of the portions of the installment payment that go to pay interest and principal is referred to as an **amortization sched-**

Calculating an Installment Payment

Using a calculator, the periodic payment on an installment loan can be calculated by entering the following keystrokes:

1. Enter the number of periods [{number of periods}, {*N*}].
2. Enter the periodic interest rate [{interest rate}, {%*i*}].
3. Enter the loan principal [{loan principal}, {*PV*}].
4. Compute the periodic payment [{2nd}, {*PMT*}].

Make sure that the number of periods and the periodic interest rate are keyed in correctly. If it is a monthly installment, the number of periods is number of years in the loan times twelve and the interest rate in the annual rate divided by twelve. A quarterly installment will use four instead of twelve to adjust the number of periods and the interest rate.

ule. Table 5–3 presents the amortization schedule for a $1,000 loan at 12 percent for one year. The interest expense for the first month is $10.00. The rest of the monthly payment, $78.85, goes toward retiring the principal, leaving a loan balance of $921.15 at the end of month one. As interest expense accrues only on the outstanding loan balance, the second month's interest expense is only $9.21 and a larger portion of the payment goes toward retiring the principal. Thus, monthly interest expense declines and monthly principal payments increase over the life of the loan.

Table 5–3 can be used to generate amortization schedules for 12 percent, one-year loans of any dollar amount. Expanding the schedule to represent a $100,000 loan requires that each entry be multiplied by 100. If the loan amount desired is $122,250, the entries are simply multiplied by 122.25.

Types of Risk

In reference to a business opportunity, **risk** is typically defined as the chance of injury or loss, indicating that there is some degree of probability of the occurrence taking place. Thus, the concepts of risk and variation are naturally linked to each other.

The process of evaluating the riskiness of a business venture involves attaching an expected probability to each of the identifiable possible outcomes. The larger the variance or dispersion of those outcomes is, the greater the risk involved will be. The greater the risk is, the higher the return necessary before the rational investor is willing to assume that risk.

The financial management literature includes the extensive use and discussion of several different types of risk. We will briefly discuss four of the

Table 5–3
Loan Amortization Schedule

Loan = $1,000
Interest rate = 12%

Terms = 1 year
Monthly payment = $88.85

Month	Interest	Principal	Balance
1	$10.00	$ 78.85	$921.15
2	9.21	79.64	841.51
3	8.42	80.43	761.08
4	7.61	81.24	679.84
5	6.80	82.05	597.79
6	5.98	82.87	514.92
7	5.15	83.70	431.22
8	4.31	84.54	346.68
9	3.47	85.38	261.30
10	2.61	86.24	175.06
11	1.75	87.10	87.96
12	0.89	87.96	0
Total	$66.20	$1000.00	

more common types: 1) beta risk, 2) corporate risk, 3) business risk, and 4) financial risk. Those that are interested in doing further reading on this subject are encouraged to pick up any good financial management textbook, such as Brigham and Gapenski (1987) and Maness (1988).

Beta Risk. This aspect of risk is based on the concept of the beta coefficient from the Capital Asset Pricing Model. It measures risk from the viewpoint of the individual investor who holds a highly diversified portfolio of financial assets. When used in its usual sense, beta risk affects the value of a stock to an individual shareholder.

It is possible to use this definition of risk in the process of evaluating a single venture investment opportunity. However, it is fairly impractical and difficult to calculate a beta coefficient for a single project. In fact, it may even be unmeaningful to do so.

Corporate Risk. This type of risk refers to the probability that a company will incur a significant enough loss on a capital expansion project that the overall operation will be jeopardized. A **significant loss** can be defined as anything from a serious reduction in company earnings to financial bankruptcy.

The concept of corporate risk focuses specifically on the operational stability of a firm and, as such, is of much greater importance to the owners of a closely held business than beta risk. Likewise, the stability of an operation is important to a number of different groups in addition to the owners. Creditors, suppliers, employees, and even the local community have a stake in the long-term viability of an operation.

Larger corporations typically use computer simulation models to estimate corporate risk as part of their capital budgeting procedure. Computer simulation models range anywhere from highly sophisticated econometric models on mainframe computers to electronic spreadsheet models on personal computers. Entrepreneurs are more likely to have access to a microcomputer and one of the many spreadsheet software programs, so our discussion will focus on techniques that can be easily adapted to the microcomputer.

One commonly used measurement technique is referred to as **sensitivity analysis**. This approach involves compiling an earnings forecast that is "most likely" to occur and estimating the net present value of the capital project based on these projections. This base forecast is then adjusted using different possible values for sales volume, unit price, cost of sales, operating expenses, capital expenditures, or any other key variable. After each change in a variable, the forecast is revised and the net present value recalculated.

The purpose of the entire process is to examine the sensitivity of the net present value, or how much the NPV changes, when other aspects of the project change. Other things being equal, the greater the change in net present value is when one of the other variables changes, the more sensitive it is and the greater the risk will be.

This method of estimating corporate risk is often called "what if" analysis because of the fact that its purpose is to answer such questions as: "What if poor weather conditions cause delays in completing the project and we lose one month's sales?" and "What if cost of sales is 35 percent of sales instead of 32 percent of sales?"

The entrepreneur who truly understands his operation will be able to develop the various scenarios that are likely to have the greatest impact on the outcome of a capital expansion project and attach the appropriate probabilities on each one. By developing "optimistic" and "pessimistic" forecasts to go along with the "most likely" forecast, the entrepreneur will be able to develop a systematic approach to capital budgeting that will compare favorably with the more expensive and sophisticated techniques used by larger corporations.

Business Risk. Another commonly used aspect of risk is the notion of business risk. **Business risk** is defined as the risk that is associated with an operation using no debt. This form of risk exists in all business operations because no one can predict the future with 100 percent accuracy.

The uncertainty of the future is the primary source of business risk. It manifests itself in the fact that forecasters rarely make predictions with any reliability. There are many identifiable reasons for this inconsistency: fluctuating economic conditions, changing competitive factors, labor problems, and acts of God. These phenomena have occurred in the past and are likely to occur in the future. Thus, in the world of business, there is no sure thing. No sector of the economy is free from this type of risk. It varies across sectors and across firms within the same sector, but nevertheless it does exist.

The actual level of business risk within an operation is determined by factors affecting the firm's market and will vary across operations. These influences include proximity to suppliers, climatic conditions, labor availability, and local government policy. These are all factors that influence the firm's decision to locate in a particular area.

There are additional factors affecting business risk that are to varying degrees under the control of the management. These include:

1. The variability of demand for the product or service.
2. The variability of pricing.
3. The variability of input prices and operating expenses.
4. The price elasticity of demand for the product; that is, the ability of the firm to pass on cost increases to customers in the form of price increases without negatively affecting sales revenue.
5. The proportion of fixed expenses to total expenses that affects the firm's ability to reduce costs when sales volume declines.

Since business risk is a phenomenon in every business operation, it is important for us to be able to measure it with some reliability. Although there is no single measure that will incorporate all the various sources of business risk, a widely used partial indicator is the concept of operating leverage.

Operating Leverage. **Operating leverage** is defined as the importance of fixed operating costs in a firm's operations. It specifically examines the change in operating profit brought about by a change in sales volume. As the degree of operating leverage (DOL) increases, a given percentage change in sales volume will result in increasingly larger percentage changes in operating profit. The **degree of operating leverage** can be defined as the percentage change in operating profit divided by the percentage change in sales volume.

As sales volume rises and falls, the profitability of an operation will behave similarly. The relative magnitude of this responsiveness varies from firm to firm depending on the percentage of fixed costs to total costs. The more significance that fixed costs have to an operation, the greater the responsiveness of operating profit will be, and thus, the use of operating leverage will be greater.

As an illustration of the use of operating leverage in evaluating business risk, consider the following situation. There are two companies in the same industry, Company A and Company B. Suppose Company A is a relatively capital intensive operation with a high percentage of fixed costs-to-total costs and Company B is a labor intensive operation with no fixed costs. Company A has fixed costs of $300,000 and variable costs of 40 percent of sales. Company B has no fixed costs and variable costs of 70 percent of sales. What is the degree of operating leverage for each operation?

One important characteristic to carefully note is that DOL is not constant for various levels of sales. In fact, it increases as the level of sales nears the breakeven point. The actual calculation of DOL can be accomplished by using the following formula.

$$\text{DOL} = \frac{Q(P - V)}{Q(P - V) - F} = \frac{\text{TR} - \text{TVC}}{\text{TR} - \text{TVC} - \text{TFC}}$$

where

$$
\begin{aligned}
Q &= \text{sales volume} \\
P &= \text{per unit sales price} \\
\text{TR} &= \text{total revenue } (P \cdot Q) \\
V &= \text{per unit variable operating cost} \\
\text{TVC} &= \text{total variable operating cost } (V \cdot Q) \\
F &= \text{total fixed costs (TFC).}
\end{aligned}
$$

Calculating the degree of operating leverage at $1,000,000 in sales results in the following values. Company A has a DOL equal to 2.0 ($600,000/$300,000) and Company B has a DOL equal to 1.0 ($600,000/$600,000). In fact, it should be noted that a firm that has no fixed costs is not using any operating leverage and will always have a DOL equal to 1.0.

Interpreting these values generated for DOL is rather straightforward. Using Company A, for example, a 1 percent decrease in sales results in a 2 percent decrease in operating profit. For Company B, the same 1 percent sales decrease results in only a 1 percent change in operating profit. We know that as fixed costs increase, the breakeven point for an operation increases. Likewise, operating leverage increases and the vulnerability of the operation to a business downturn increases.

Conceptually, all that is being measured is the slope of the operating profit function. Figure 5–2 provides a graphical look at the profit function against sales. Notice that the operating profit function for Company A is much steeper than that of Company B. Thus, it can be stated that, other things being equal, the steeper the operating profit function, the greater the level of business risk.

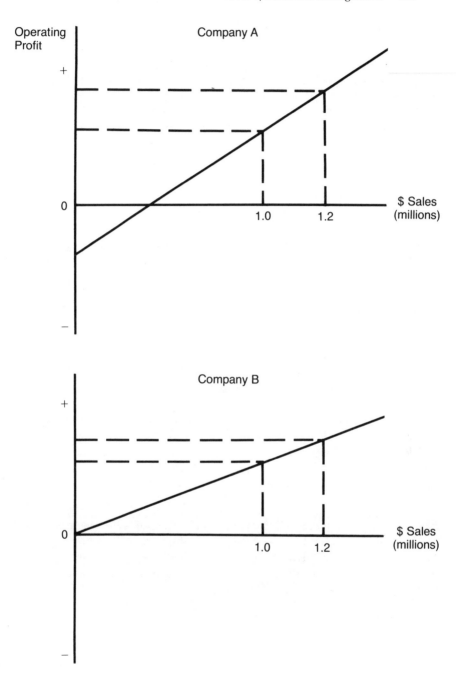

Figure 5–2. Profit Functions

Several of the factors that affect business risk can be controlled within a range of values. Sales volume can be influenced by the level of advertising expenditures. Product loyalty, brand name identification, and other related factors can also be affected by managers' decisions. However, the one area of decision making that can have the greatest impact is the choice of technology and its resulting impact on the percentage of fixed costs. Perhaps even more important are the related decisions on how capital improvements will be financed and the risk associated with those decisions.

Financial Risk. Financial risk is the additional risk placed on an operation by the use of debt or preferred stock. The common characteristic shared by these instruments is that both have fixed charges associated with them.

One of the interesting questions that perplexes owners and managers of businesses of all sizes is: "What percentage of the total capitalization should be in the form of debt?" Or more simply, "What is the optimal debt ratio for my particular operation?" The general rule is: As the debt ratio increases, the value of the firm to the entrepreneur increases, reaches a maximum, and then decreases. Thus, the optimal value for the debt ratio is the level that maximizes the value of the firm to its owners.

As we shall see in Chapter 13, the value of a business is determined in large measure by the net present value of the future earnings stream over which the owners have control. Thus, if the debt ratio is to affect the value of a business to its owners, it must do so by affecting the future earnings stream.

Careful consideration of the preceding statements results in the realization that increased debt leads to increased fixed obligations. Increased obligations affect profitability, which is typically examined through the traditional ratios such as return on equity. Measurement of financial risk is accomplished by using the concept of financial leverage.

Financial Leverage. Financial leverage actually measures the change in after-tax profit brought about by a change in operating profit. It can be defined as the percentage change in after-tax profit divided by the percentage change in operating profit. A firm that has no outstanding debt is not using financial leverage and thus has no financial risk.

The degree of financial leverage (DFL) can be calculated by using the following formula:

$$\text{DFL} = \frac{Q(P - V) - F}{Q(P - V) - F - I} = \frac{TR - TVC - TFC}{TR - TVC - TFC - I}$$
$$= \frac{\pi}{\pi - I}$$

where I is the fixed interest obligation and π is operating profit. All other symbols were defined previously.

Firms that do not use financial leverage have a DFL equal to 1.0 (because $I = 0$). With the addition of fixed interest obligations, the value for DFL rises, indicating increased financial risk. Suppose Company A in the previous example had to finance its capital expansion by borrowing from a bank, and the fixed interest obligation on its outstanding debt is $50,000 per year. Using the same information, the firm will have a DFL equal to 1.2 ($300,000/$250,000).

In order to use this concept to answer the question of the optimal debt ratio, earnings projections using various debt levels would have to be constructed. As you might imagine, in many cases, higher debt ratios lead to greater earnings. However, the increased earnings are accompanied by higher levels of risk. Eventually, the level of risk will be such that additional debt will only be available at increasingly higher interest rates, which will have a depressing effect on profitability.

In contrast, in publicly held companies, the debt ratio that maximizes earnings may not be the optimal debt ratio. In such cases, the optimal debt ratio is one that maximizes the stock's market price. Since the focus of this discussion is on the privately held business, the interested reader is referred to the additional readings mentioned earlier.

The Relationship Between Financial and Operating Leverage. The total leverage used by a firm can be estimated by the concept known as the degree of total leverage (DTL). By definition, the **degree of total leverage** is the percentage change in after-tax profit divided by the percentage change in sales volume. It can also be calculated by the following formula.

$$DTL = DOL \cdot DFL = \frac{Q(P - V)}{Q(P - V) - F - I}$$
$$= \frac{TR - TVC}{TR - TVC - F - I}$$

All variables were defined previously. Using the data given earlier for Company A, the DTL is 2.4. That is to say, a one percentage point increase in sales from its current level of $1,000,000 will result in a 2.4 percent increase in after-tax profit.

Summary and Conclusions

This chapter has provided a broad overview of the specific financial management concepts that are important in planning a new venture and determining the financial health of an existing operation. The primary focus was the calculation and use of traditional ratio techniques. Other important tools of financial management were also presented and their usefulness was explained.

Much more could have been included in this chapter and omission is not intended to imply that those concepts are not important. The purpose of this chapter was to highlight several of the more useful tools of analysis and not the entire tool kit. Such an objective would have required an entire manuscript and not a single chapter.

References

Brigham, Eugene F. and Gapenski, Louis C. *Intermediate Financial Management*. Second edition. Hinsdale, IL: The Dryden Press, 1987.

Kreps, Clifton H., Jr. and Wacht, Richard F. *Financial Administration*. Hinsdale, IL: The Dryden Press, 1975.

Maness, Terry S. *Introduction to Corporate Finance*. New York: McGraw-Hill Book Company, 1988.

Patrone, F. L. and duBois, Donald. "Financial Ratio Analysis for the Small Firm," *Journal of Small Business Management* (January, 1981), pp. 35–40.

RMA Annual Statement Studies. Philadelphia, PA: Robert Morris Associates, various years.

Van Voorhis, Kenneth R. "The duPont Model Revisited: A Simplified Approach to Small Business," *Journal of Small Business Management* (April, 1981), pp. 45–51.

6
Evaluating Cash Flow

The ratios discussed in the previous chapter are intended to assist the user of financial statements in evaluating the financial strength of a business enterprise. However, one should not fall into the trap of using them solely as one-dimensional indicators of financial health, namely, profitability. Although profitability analysis is an important ingredient in a complete financial evaluation, it is by no means the only one and it may not be the most important ingredient.

A critical aspect of financial health that is not adequately measured by financial ratios is liquidity. Although a category of liquidity ratios is available for analysis, including current and quick ratios, they use a working capital approach to define liquidity. By focusing on current assets and current liabilities, this practice completely ignores the true measure of liquidity—the ability to generate cash.

Johnson, Campbell, and Wittenback (1980) surveyed corporate treasurers about the relative importance they placed on cash flow analysis and liquidity analysis as measured by the traditional liquidity ratios. The respondents overwhelmingly placed more emphasis on cash flow in their task of maintaining corporate liquidity. In addition, their use of traditional ratios to analyze liquidity focused on two asset utilization ratios—accounts receivable and inventory turnover.

Thus, there are ways to arrive at measures of liquidity using traditional analysis and accrual-based financial statements. This chapter is not a criticism of the traditional approach to analyzing liquidity and solvency. Its purpose is to carefully outline the cash flow approach and offer suggestions for its use in supplementing the traditional approach.

The Cash Flow Approach

The cash flow approach has gained considerable attention in accounting and finance literature in recent years. As a part of the task of developing a complete conceptual framework for financial accounting and reporting, the Financial Accounting Standards Board (FASB) has published several concept statements on various aspects of the overall framework.

In Concept Statement No. 1, *Objectives of Financial Reporting by Business Enterprises,* the FASB states that "financial reporting should provide information to help investors, creditors, and others assess the amounts, timing, and uncertainty of prospective net cash inflows to the related enterprise." Even though this statement does not require that cash flow information be included in financial reporting, it recognizes that "information about cash flows or other funds flows may be useful in understanding the operations of an enterprise, evaluating its financing activities, assessing its liquidity or solvency, or interpreting earnings information provided." (FASB 1983, pp. 17, 21).

In Concept Statement No. 5, issued in December 1984, the FASB recognized the importance of the cash flow statement and concluded that conceptually "the cash flow statement should be part of a full set of financial statements." In 1985, the Board began to look at actually requiring the cash flow statement in place of the statement of changes in financial position. Before the cash flow statement became mandatory, it was determined that objectives for the statement should first be established and certain major cash flow concepts be defined.

Finally, in July 1986 the Board issued a *Statement of Cash Flows* requiring that the cash flow statement replace the statement of changes in financial position for all fiscal periods ending after June 30, 1987. The proposal also establishes objectives for the cash flow statement and definitions of key cash concepts. This policy change can be viewed simply as a reaction to current industry practices. Fully two-thirds of the financial statements generated in the corporate United States today already use cash instead of working capital for purposes of the statement of changes in financial position.

Defining Cash Flow

The simplest way to conceptualize cash flow is to think of it as a process in which cash actually flows into and out of a business operation. In summarizing the current cash receipts and cash outlays, the cash flow statement provides information on liquidity, financial flexibility, profitability, and risk. Once its importance is recognized, the next task is to define *cash flow.*

It is incorrect to assume that similar conclusions can be reached about liquidity, flexibility, and risk using any measure of cash flow (Gombola and Ketz 1981). The commonly used definitions of cash flow are after-tax profit plus depreciation and the change in cash balances on the firm's balance sheet. Although there is nothing inherently incorrect in using these definitions, they cannot be used interchangeably with the concept of operating cash flow

Cash Flow and the Business Cycle

Cash flow problems are easily identified in a small business environment. They usually take the form of a slower than normal turnover of inventory, gradual aging of accounts receivable, and increased difficulties in collecting from larger customers. As sales volume increases, it is not unusual for firms to spend at a faster rate than they get paid.

To a degree, these problems can be traced back to the influences of the economic business cycle. During expansions in economic activity, inventories and receivables are expanding "spontaneously" to keep pace with the increased sales. Individual firms usually adjust to downturns in business activity with a lag. Purchasing and spending decisions geared toward a higher level of sales take time to adjust to lower rates of growth. Thus, inventory turnover slows while at the same time operating expense as a percentage of sales increases, resulting in a cash flow problem.

Commercial banks respond to downturns in business activity by tightening credit. Unable to expand their credit lines, large firms respond by delaying payment to their suppliers. The combined response of the banks and big business has a ripple effect on the rest of the economy, creating acute cash flow problems for the small supplier.

Preparing for the next downturn is an important part of managing a business. Cash flow must be monitored carefully, especially during the latter stages of a business expansion. Remember, when it comes to the business cycle, what goes up will eventually come down.

(OCF). Only OCF adequately separates the operating activities of the firm from the investing and financing activities. Ultimately, OCF determines whether an entity is capable of generating cash to repay debt, distribute dividends, or reinvest in plant and equipment to maintain or expand operations.

The most useful concept of funds is cash. For the purposes of the cash flow statement, **funds** are defined as cash and cash equivalents. This definition takes into consideration the common practice of investing excess cash in highly liquid, short-term instruments such as certificates of deposit and commercial paper. This practice is not formally considered an investing activity, but rather a cash management activity. As such it is included in the definition of cash flow. When assessing the cash flow of an operation, it is of minor consequence if the cash is on hand, on deposit, or invested in highly liquid, short-term instruments.

Managing Cash Flow

The actual process of managing cash flow is more than a matter of preparing cash flow statements; it is one of managing the timing of receipts and expenditures. In the long run, cash inflows and cash outflows must at minimum be in balance in order for the firm to survive. That is not to say that an occasional period of negative cash flow will not be tolerated under any circumstances. The phenomenon may be caused by seasonal factors outside the control of management. It may even be encouraged if, for example, inventories can be purchased at bulk rates at a considerable savings to the firm.

Cash flow management requires an understanding of the relationships involved and a systematic means of planning and control. The key to such a mechanism is the availability of information and the ability to process and use that information. This points out the importance of an accounting system that will provide the necessary information. In some operations, the key element in such a system is the cash receipts and disbursements journal; in others, it may only be the checking account register. In either case, it is the information flow that is important because without the proper information, it is impossible to anticipate and plan for the timing of the cash flows.

The Cash Flow Cycle

An adequate cash flow is critically important to a business operation. This is especially true for startup and high growth business ventures which, on average, have inadequate cash reserves to begin with. It could be said that cash flow is the life blood of a business operation; without an adequate cash flow, a business will die in much the same way that a living organism dies without an adequate blood supply.

The Simple Cash Flow Cycle. It is essential that the cash flow relationship be thoroughly understood to enable the entrepreneur to initiate a cash planning and cash control procedure within the operation. The cash flow process is illustrated in Figure 6–1. The purpose of this discussion is to focus on the short-term cycle; we will not discuss long-term decisions such as capital expenditures, long-term debt, and equity. In Figure 6–1, each box depicts one of the stock concepts in the simple short-term cash flow cycle. The flows leading into and out of the boxes depict the productive activities that serve to sustain the operation.

Examining Figure 6–1, we can see that cash is used to purchase inventories. These inventories are sold, based on the market demand for the final product. Sales are made on a cash or credit basis. Cash sales flow directly into the cash account; credit sales initiate an accounts receivable account. The cash account is not directly incremented as a result of credit sales until the accounts receivable are ultimately collected.

Given the nature of the cash flow system, the process depends critically on the relative rates of the inflows and the outflows pertaining to each account. If purchases exceed sales, inventory levels increase and the accounts receivable and cash levels tend to decrease. A slowdown in collections results

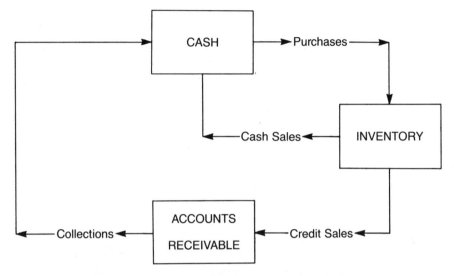

Figure 6–1. The Simple Short-Term Cash Flow Cycle

in a build-up in receivables and a reduction in cash. This illustrates the point that a change in one area of the system has potential repercussions in all the other areas of the operation.

The simple cash flow cycle depicted in Figure 6–1 would have to be refined and expanded to accurately reflect the cash flow process for a manufacturing operation. Instead of simply considering inventories, it would be necessary to extend the model to include raw materials, work-in-process, and finished goods inventories. Rather than discuss this in any detail, the interested reader should examine the presentation in Kreps and Wacht (1978).

The Complete Cash Flow Cycle. In order to complete the cash flow system, it is necessary to incorporate the various aspects of long-term decision making, including decisions regarding the acquisition of fixed assets and the means of financing those assets—long-term debt and ownership equity.

Figure 6–2 presents the complete cash flow system. In addition to the three stock items dealing with long-term decisions, a fourth stock account has been included—accounts payable—to distinguish between cash and credit purchases. The respective cash flows associated with these stock accounts are also indicated in the diagram.

Cash and credit purchases both flow directly into the inventory account. The inclusion of an accounts payable account results in the addition of a distinct outflow, representing the repayment of trade credit. For clarification, an outflow representing operating expenses has been added to this diagram. Most operations will have wages and salaries, utilities, rental charges, and other similar expenses incurred in connection with making the product ready for the market.

The primary focus of this diagram, however, is the stock and flow concepts associated with the long-term decision making process. The purchase and sale of fixed assets are the respective outflow and inflow associated with the fixed asset account. We will not discuss depreciation in this presentation. If it were included in the diagram, it would be shown as a flow from the fixed asset account to the inventory account.

In most cases, external financing is required to initiate an operation and ensure that it is able to satisfy market demand for its product. The addition of separate accounts representing creditors' funds and owners' funds will complete the system. Their respective cash inflows are shown as borrowings and equity; cash outflows are debt service and dividends (or owners' draw if the business is a proprietorship or partnership).

The principles of managing this particular cash flow system are identical to those of managing the simple system. The addition of the various activities merely complicates the tasks of keeping the stock accounts at their optimal levels and the rates of inflows and outflows balanced.

Not all cash outflows have been considered in this diagrammatical representation of the cash flow system. Many leakages from the system can also be incorporated into the analysis. These include inventory losses, bad debt losses, losses from the sale of assets, and taxes. We will not discuss these leakages in this presentation. Keep in mind, however, that they do exist and play a significant role in the complete cash flow planning model.

The Cash Conversion Period

The cash flow system given previously provides an invaluable tool in understanding the nature of the cash flow process. Now that the system is more clearly defined, it is time to move to the next step in the analysis. That step involves an examination of the length of time involved in actually completing the cash cycle; this is referred to as the cash conversion period.

The **cash conversion period** measures the length of the cash cycle in days and refers to the elapsed time from when payment is made for inventories until payment is received for finished products. The concept can be explained in terms of two ratios that were previously introduced in the discussion of ratio analysis—days sales outstanding and days inventory—and a similar ratio, days payable.

Days payable is calculated in much the same way as the other two ratios:

$$\text{Days Payable} = \frac{365}{\text{Purchases/Payables}}$$

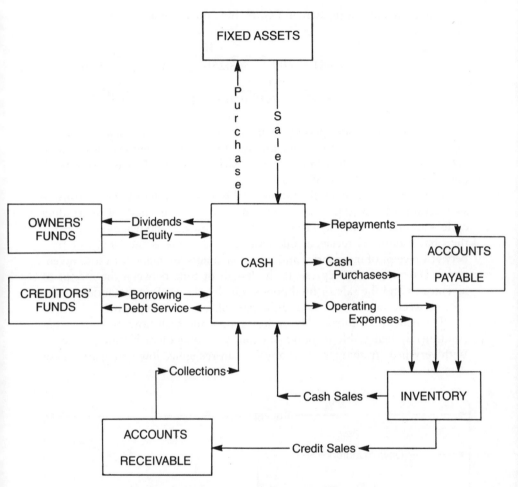

Figure 6–2. The Complete Cash Flow Cycle

The method of calculating purchases may not be immediately obvious to you. However, a typical set of financial statements contains all the information necessary to calculate its value. Since

Cost of Sales = Beginning Inventory + Purchases − Ending Inventory,

it follows that

Purchases = Cost of Sales + Ending Inventory − Beginning Inventory.

Using the data from Richland Gifts, Inc., the calculation is:

$$\text{Days Payable} = \frac{365}{(\$101{,}100 + \$68{,}250 - \$51{,}700)/\$10{,}000}$$

$$= \frac{365}{\$117{,}650/\$10{,}000} = \frac{365}{11.77} = 31.01 \text{ days.}$$

The cash conversion period is calculated by adding days sales outstanding to days inventory (a concept referred to as the trading cycle) and then subtracting days payable. In the case of Richland Gifts, the cash conversion period is 224 days (9 + 246 − 31).

Figure 6–3 provides a diagrammatical representation of the cash conversion period. The diagram uses a time line to depict the length of the trading cycle—the elapsed time between receipt of inventories and when payment for the final product is received. Likewise, days payable is the length of time between receipt of inventories and when payments are made for those inventories. Days inventory represents the length of time between the receipt of inventories and the sale of final goods. Finally, days sales outstanding is the time between the date of sale and the date of receipt of payment.

The benefits of thoroughly understanding the cash flow process go beyond merely being able to point out the symptoms of cash flow problems. With very little training, almost anyone can recognize low or negative cash

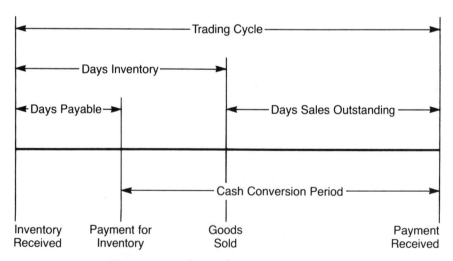

Figure 6–3. The Cash Conversion Period

balances, poor accounts receivable collections, failure to take advantage of discounts, high inventory turnover, and excessive reliance on short-term credit (bank financing and factoring). A working knowledge of the cash flow process helps the entrepreneur focus on a system of cash management and control. This is accomplished by comparing each stage of the cash cycle with industry averages and examining historical data for trends.

More on Timing

It should be clear by now that the source of most cash flow problems experienced by the typical firm is in the area of turnover—inventory and receivables. Because of the nature of most business operations, days inventory is typically greater than days payable. This results in a financing gap. That is to say, the firm must pay its suppliers for inventories before the goods are sold to customers and payment is received.

The implications of this are far-reaching. Of primary importance to the emerging small firm is the impact on its ability to sustain even a modest rate of sales growth. It is because of this gap that sales growth often exceeds the firm's ability to generate funds internally from operations. In this case, sales growth can be a problem unless it is carefully monitored and externally financed.

The aging of accounts receivable report shown in Exhibit 6–1 is a good way to identify the slow-paying customer. Invoices are grouped as follows: 0–30 days, 31–60 days, 61–90 days, and over 90 days. Improving collections while maintaining good customer relations depends on the correct strategy. Thus, it is important that problem customers be properly identified and the collection procedure be tailored to the individual. The strategy for collecting from a chronically slow-paying customer should be different from that designed to collect from a customer who is occasionally late in paying. The accounts receivable aging report can be an invaluable tool in systematically

EXHIBIT 6–1

Aging of Accounts Receivable Report				
Customer	0–30 days	31–60 days	61–90 days	Over 90 days
Concepts Plus	817.50	623.05		
JTP, Inc.	1,270.75	1,415.27	245.07	
Innovations			412.82	785.65
Mary Forth Assoc.	88.95	127.65		
CWS Enterprises	2,716.12	1,045.85		
Micro Systems	1,405.20			
Total	6,298.52	3,211.82	657.89	785.65

examining the efficiency of the entire credit and collections process.

The other aspect of this problem is inventory turnover. Although an extremely low rate of inventory turnover is a matter of concern, an extremely high rate tends to present the most critical problems because of the timing of cash inflows and outflows. This phenomenon, referred to as *overtrading,* is a characteristic of an undercapitalized operation. A relatively small inventory can easily result in an inability to meet customer demand for certain items. The result is lost sales and a reduced cash flow, which makes the firm vulnerable to a slowdown in the collections of accounts receivable.

The Cash Flow Statement

The presentation of the cash flow statement that is most meaningful to prospective users identifies three categories of activities: operating activities, investing activities, and financing activities. This is in sharp contrast to the traditional presentation in which only two categories, sources and uses, are used. If financial statements are to be used as a management tool, they must have a high degree of predictive value. Cash flow information grouped into these meaningful categories is more valuable in this regard than if it is grouped with dissimilar activities.

The currently popular sources and uses format for the cash flow statement fails to provide the kinds of information that many investors and creditors find useful. By aggregating in this fashion, the statement simply summarizes gross balance sheet category changes and says little about the ability of the entity to service debt or pay dividends.

Grouping the activities of the firm into the categories of operating, financing, and investing enables the user to easily examine similarities and differences among cash flows and identify relationships within and among the three activities. Since strict classification of all transactions into one of the three activities would be arbitrary, the Board has provided only general guidelines for this purpose. The definition of certain items depends critically on the specific nature of the individual business operation.

There are two principal approaches for reporting cash flows allowed: the indirect method and the direct method. The most widely used approach is the **indirect method.** A cash flow statement prepared in this manner begins with operating profit and adjusts it for items that were included in this calculation, but did not result in current period cash transactions. Examples of these adjustments are depreciation and amortization, deferred taxes, accruals, and gains or losses from the sale of assets.

The alternative approach is the **direct method.** This method of presentation shows the major components of operating cash receipts and operating cash disbursements. A cash flow statement prepared in this manner will begin with cash received from customers and subtract cash paid out to suppliers

Tracking Payment Patterns: Converting Receivables into Cash

Effective cash management depends critically on the ability to convert accounts receivable into cash. Many managers use traditional tools—including the accounts receivable aging schedule—to evaluate the effectiveness of a firm's credit and collection policies. The problem in using the traditional measures is that they can give misleading signals for reasons that are unrelated to a firm's collection experience.

The accounts receivable aging schedule is a biased measure of the sales collection experience of a firm. The source of the bias is in the fact that recent sales trends affect the calculations and can provide misleading results. In the situation where sales fluctuate because of seasonal factors, such as the Christmas holidays, the aging schedule often indicates a relative increase in older accounts for reasons that have nothing to do with the pattern of collections.

The table below presents the accounts receivable aging information in the familiar format. Each entry shows the percentage of the outstanding accounts receivable that are one, two, and three months old. The October accounts receivable balance for ABC Corporation is $2,124. The data indicate that 69.7 percent of that balance is less than 30 days old, 24.0 percent is 30–60 days old, and 6.3 percent is 60–90 days old.

Accounts Receivable Aging Schedule
ABC Corporation

Month	A/R	0–30	30–60	60–90
Oct	$2,124	69.7%	24.0%	6.3%
Nov	2,792	76.2	18.6	5.2
Dec	3,260	68.1	25.8	6.1
Jan	2,822	59.2	30.8	10.0
Feb	2,190	54.8	30.1	15.1
Mar	1,784	62.2	24.2	13.6

Based on information in this schedule, it appears that between November and February accounts receivable collections have slowed considerably. Current accounts (those less than 30 days old) as a percentage of total end-of-month receivables has fallen from 76.2 percent in November to 54.8 percent in February. Likewise, those accounts over 60 days old have increased from 5.2 percent to 15.1 percent. With the percentage of current receivables falling and the percentage of older receivables increasing, it would not be unusual to interpret that collections are slowing and a potential problem for the firm is at hand.

Fortunately for the ABC Corporation, tracking payment patterns is not a matter of recording the percentages of end-of-month accounts receivable that are 30, 60, and 90 days old. The proper way of examining collections is to measure the percentage of each month's sales that are collected in the month of the sale and the percentages collected in each of the subsequent months. Monthly sales is the only additional information that is needed to correctly monitor payments.

Each entry in the payment pattern schedule presented below is calculated from information given in the accounts receivable aging schedule. It is merely presented in a different format. October entries in the schedule are calculated as follows:

October sales	2,000
− October receivables 0–30 days old	− (.697 · 2,124)
= October sales collected in October	= 520

October receivables 0–30 days old	(.697 · 2,124)
− November receivables 30–60 days old	− (.186 · 2,792)
= October sales collected in November	= 961

November receivables 30–60 days old	(.186 · 2,792)
− December receivables 60–90 days old	− (.061 · 3,260)
= October sales collected in December	= 320

December receivables 60–90 days old	(.061 · 3,260)
− January receivables 90–120 days old	− 0
= October sales collected in January	= 199

Dividing each of these amounts by October sales results in the percentages in the table. Entries for the other months are calculated in a similar manner.

Payment Pattern Schedule
BC Corporation

Month	Sales	0–30	30–60	60–90	90+
Oct	$2,000	26.0%	48.0%	22.0%	10.0%
Nov	2,800	24.0	46.0	20.0	10.0
Dec	3,000	26.0	45.0	18.0	11.0
Jan	2,200	24.0	46.0	19.0	—
Feb	1,600	25.0	48.0	—	—
Mar	1,500	26.0	—	—	—

Data from this schedule are to be interpreted in the following manner. Of October sales of $2,000, 26 percent were collected in October, 48 percent in November, 22 percent in December, and 10 percent in January. The subsequent months show a similar pattern. In fact, collections vary little over the period under consideration.

A working understanding of the cash flow process is critical for the entrepreneur managing a growing business. The ability to forecast future cash requirements is particularly important if cash shortages are to be avoided. Likewise, the ability to forecast receivables collections is important in predicting cash requirements. The payments pattern approach to tracking accounts receivable is an invaluable tool that should be learned and used. Readers interested in a more complete discussion of this approach should see Lewellen and Johnson (1972) and Kyd (1986).

and employees. By focusing on the major recurring operating cash receipts and payments, this method provides historical insight into the operation of the business.

Cash Flows from Operating Activities: The Indirect Approach

The indirect approach to the calculation of operating cash flow provides insight into the quality of net earnings by focusing on the difference between income and operating cash flow. This approach starts with net income and adjusts it for items that did not result in current-period cash transactions.

Exhibit 6–2 illustrates a cash flow statement using the indirect method. Financial data are from the Richland Gifts case presented in the previous chapter. The format presented in Exhibit 6–2 starts with net income and adjusts for transactions that did not result in current period cash receipts or outlays. The first step is to add back depreciation and amortization. The next adjustment requires subtracting the increase in current asset accounts: accounts receivable, inventory, and prepaids. If the balances in the accounts decreased, the amounts would be added instead of subtracted. Next, any increases in current liability accounts—accounts payable and accruals—are added (decreases are subtracted). The resulting value will be called "cash flow from operations."

In order to arrive at the Board's concept of "net cash flow from operations," adjustments for taxes must be taken into consideration. The first adjustments must be to subtract taxes paid. Second, increases in taxes payable and deferred taxes are added, resulting in net cash flow from operations.

An explanation for the different treatment of taxes in the given format is necessary at this time. Taxes depend on the manner in which the firm is capitalized and organized. These decisions affect performance, but are not operating activities as typically defined. This further disaggregation, while still in compliance with the requirements of the FASB, provides additional information to help improve our understanding of cash flows.

Cash Flows from Operating Activities: The Direct Approach

The direct approach to the calculation of net cash flow from operations is shown in Exhibit 6–3. It begins with the derivation of operating cash receipts. This is done by adjusting sales for changes in the accounts receivable balance (subtracting increases or adding decreases). A sale will not add to the firm's cash balances unless funds are actually collected. Net cash inflows result from cash sales in the current period and collections of credit sales from prior periods. Current period sales are greater than actual cash inflows to the ex-

EXHIBIT 6–2

Richland Gifts, Inc.
Cash Flow Statements: Indirect Method

	Period Ending December 31	
	1985	1986
Cash Flows from Operating Activities:		
Net income	$ 10,900	$ 12,205
Noncash items included in operating profit:		
Plus: Depreciation and amortization	13,700	14,295
Less: Increase in accounts receivable	900	1,100
Plus: Increase in accounts payable	1,500	2,500
Less: Increase in inventories	3,100	16,550
Plus: Increase in accruals	0	0
Less: Increase in prepaids	0	1,300
Cash Flow from Operations	$ 22,100	$ 10,050
Adjustments for interest and taxes:		
Less: Taxes	$ 1,635	$ 1,830
Plus: Increase in taxes payable	840	695
Plus: Increase in deferred taxes	0	0
Net Cash Flow from Operations	$ 21,305	$ 8,915
Cash Flows from Investing Activities:		
Plus: All other income	$ 0	$ 0
Less: All other expenses	0	0
Increase (decrease) in gross fixed assets	5,900	5,100
Increase (decrease) in intangibles	0	0
Increase (decrease) in other noncurr. assets	−1,000	−1,000
Increase in treasury stock	0	0
Gain (loss) from sale of fixed assets	0	0
Cash Flow Requirements from Investing Activities	$ 4,900	$ 4,100
Cash Flows from Financing Activities:		
New notes payable—short term	$ 10,000	$ 16,000
Less: Notes payable—short term	−12,000	−10,000
Change in other current liabilities	0	0
New long-term borrowing	1,445	1,630
Less: Current maturities—LTD	−11,375	−12,820
Change in preferred stock	0	0
Change in common stock	0	0
Change in paid-in capital and other	0	0
Less: Dividends paid	0	0
Cash Flow Provided by Financing Activities	$ −11,930	$ −5,190
Change in Cash and Equivalents	$ 4,475	$ −375

EXHIBIT 6–3

Richland Gifts, Inc.
Cash Flow Statements: Direct Method

	Period Ending December 31	
	1985	**1986**
Cash Flows from Operating Activities:		
Net sales	$ 155,750	$ 187,250
Less: Increase in accounts receivable	900	1,100
Cash provided by operating activities	$ 154,850	$ 186,150
Purchases	$ 85,650	$ 117,650
Less: Increase in payables	1,500	2,500
Operating expenses plus interest	$ 48,600	$ 59,650
Plus: Increase in prepaids	0	1,300
Less: Increase in accruals	0	0
Cash disbursed for operating activities	$ 132,750	$ 176,100
Cash Flow from Operations	$ 22,100	$ 10,050
Adjustments for interest and taxes:		
Less: Taxes	$ 1,635	$ 1,830
Plus: Increase in taxes payable	840	695
Plus: Increase in deferred taxes	0	0
Net Cash Flow from Operations	$ 21,305	$ 8,915
Cash Flows from Investing Activities:		
Plus: All other income	$ 0	$ 0
Less: All other expenses	0	0
Increase (decrease) in gross fixed assets	5,900	5,100
Increase (decrease) in intangibles	0	0
Increase (decrease) in other noncurr. assets	−1,000	−1,000
Increase in treasury stock	0	0
Gain (loss) from sale of fixed assets	0	0
Cash Flow Requirements from Investing Activities	$ 4,900	$ 4,100
Cash Flows from Financing Activities:		
New notes payable—short term	$ 10,000	$ 16,000
Less: Notes payable—short term	−12,000	−10,000
Change in other current liabilities	0	0
New long-term borrowing	1,445	1,630
Less: current maturities—LTD	−11,375	−12,820
Change in preferred stock	0	0
Change in common stock	0	0
Change in paid-in capital and other	0	0
Less: Dividends paid	0	0
Cash Flow Provided by Financing Activities	$ −11,930	$ −5,190
Change in Cash Balance	$ 4,475	$ −375

tent that accounts receivable balances increase. This is the rationale behind the receivables adjustment in the calculation of operating cash receipts.

Cash disbursed for operating activities is calculated by adjusting purchases for changes in accounts payable (subtracting increases or adding decreases) and adding to that total operating expenses adjusted for changes in prepaids and accruals (adding increases in prepaids and subtracting increases in accruals). Purchases and other operating expenses that are not paid for do not result in cash outflows. Thus, adjustments for increases in accounts payable, prepaids, and accruals are made to arrive at the correct value for operating cash disbursed.

Cash flow from operations is then operating cash receipts minus operating cash disbursements. From this point on, cash flow calculations are identical using either the indirect or the direct method.

The accrual-based counterpart of cash flow from operations (OCF) is operating profit. A comparison of the two concepts is very revealing. Note that the basic components of OCF and operating profit are the same: sales, cost of sales, and operating expenses. The difference lies in the adjustments that are made to generate OCF: sales are adjusted by the change in accounts receivable, cost of sales are adjusted by the changes in inventories and accounts payable, and operating expenses are adjusted by depreciation expense and the changes in accruals and prepaids. Although Richland Gifts was generating a relatively stable net profit of $10,900 in 1985 and $12,205 in 1986, net cash flow from operations fell from $21,305 to $8,915.

The difference between the two concepts is obvious when the components of each are compared. Sales and cash receipts are not the same when there is a significant variation in accounts receivable. Expenses and cash disbursements are not the same when inventory levels, accounts payable, or accruals fluctuate to any degree. Thus, from a liquidity standpoint, operating profit is not an adequate measure of the firm's short-term ability to generate operating cash flow.

Cash Flows from Investing Activities

Certain activities that take place in a business are considered investing activities. These include net revenues generated from activities that are not central to the operation itself: interest and dividends on securities held, the purchase and sale of fixed assets, and purchases of treasury stock. Cash flow requirements from investing activities is the sum of non-operating revenues (net of non-operating expenses) plus any balance sheet account increases for fixed assets, intangibles, other noncurrent assets, and treasury stock.

Cash flow requirements from investing activities for the Richland Gifts, Inc., were $4,900 and $4,100 for the years 1985 and 1986, respectively.

There are two adjustments that may be required to ensure that the cash flow calculation balances with the change in the cash accounts. If the change in accumulated depreciation on the balance sheet does not equal the annual depreciation expense, the difference must be subtracted. This difference could be caused by the sale of fixed assets at other than book value (a gain or loss on the sale of the asset) or a change in its basis. Also, if financial statements from previous years were adjusted in any way, an adjustment to retained earnings must be made. To determine whether this is necessary, simply construct a net worth reconciliation statement as discussed in the previous chapter. If the statement does not balance, an adjustment to cash flow equal to the discrepancy will be required.

Cash Flows from Financing Activities

This component of cash flow measures the amount of funds provided by external financing. It is calculated by netting new borrowings and equities against current debt amortization and dividends paid.

New borrowings include both short-term notes and long-term debt. New equities include increases in preferred and common stock and additions to paid-in capital. Current debt amortization includes current maturities of long-term debt, and short-term notes payable. New borrowings netted against current debt amortization results in a cash outflow through financial activities for both years, <$11,930> in 1985 and <$5,190> in 1986. Although there was no change in equities and no dividends were paid for either of the two years being examined, these items are shown on the cash flow statement for clarification.

Change in Cash Balance

The change in cash balance (cash and cash equivalents) is calculated by subtracting the new cash flow requirements from investing activities from net cash flow from operations and adding the cash flow provided by financing activities. This is the actual change in the cash and cash equivalents accounts on the balance sheet between two consecutive years. Cash balances at Richland Gifts increased by $4,475 in 1985 and decreased by $375 in 1986.

Summary and Conclusions

The preceding discussion is not intended in any way to indicate that cash flow analysis should be substituted for traditional ratio analysis. The conclusion to be drawn from the discussion is that cash flow analysis should be used to supplement traditional ratio analysis and that these two tools of analysis should not be used in isolation from one another.

Although the basic components of the cash flow statement are the same as those found in the statement of changes in financial position using a cash definition of funds, the organization is quite different. This may not seem like a very significant difference; however, in terms of enhancing our ability to analyze the liquidity position of a business operation, it makes a great deal of difference. Instead of two major divisions in the statement, there are three. By providing for various definitions of cash flow, this organizational structure enables us to isolate liquidity problems. For purposes of management and control, it is much more productive to state that a firm is having cash flow problems because of its operations, an excessive debt service, or an overly ambitious capital expansion program than it is to merely state that it is having cash flow problems.

Cash flow analysis focuses on true liquidity, a concept that is not adequately measured by traditional ratio techniques. In the rapidly changing business and financial environment that we live in today, it is increasingly important for us to pay closer attention to this measure of a company's financial health and performance.

References

Financial Accounting Standards Board. *Accounting Standards: Statement of Financial Accounting Concepts 1–4*. New York: McGraw-Hill Book Company, 1983.

Gombola, Michael J. and Ketz, J. Edward. "Alternative Measures of Cash Flow—Part Two," *Cashflow* (November, 1981), pp. 39–42.

Johnson, James M.; Campbell, David R.; and Wittenback, James. L. "Problems in Corporate Liquidity," *Financial Executive* (March, 1980), pp. 44–53.

Kreps, Clifton H. and Wacht, Richard F. *Analyzing Financial Statements*. Fifth edition. Washington, D.C.: American Institute of Banking, American Bankers Association, 1978.

Kyd, Charles W. "Formula For Disaster?" *Inc.* (November, 1986), pp. 123–126.

Lewellen, Wilbur G. and Johnson, Robert W. "Better Way to Monitor Accounts Receivable," *Harvard Business Review* (May–June, 1972), pp. 101–109.

Maness, Terry S. *Introduction to Corporate Finance*. New York: McGraw-Hill Book Company, 1987.

Maness, Terry S. and Henderson, James W. "Check the Corporate Pulse by Administering Cash Flow Analysis," *Cashflow* (May, 1985), pp. 38–40.

7

Fundamentals of Credit Analysis

E very entrepreneur is at one time or another faced with the necessity of seeking financing from external sources such as relatives, commercial banks, and government sources. Regardless of the source, it is essential that entrepreneurs understand lending criteria as a guide to the preparation of business plans.

This chapter will provide information on the process of evaluating venture proposals from the perspective of funding sources. In order to really appreciate the reasoning behind the business plan outline and its accompanying discussion, entrepreneurs should be familiar with the elements of credit analysis. We will examine the general principles of evaluating creditworthiness, the loan-making process, the legal aspects considered in the lending process, and the use of bankruptcy prediction as a tool for credit analysis. While the focus of this chapter is on examining the credit decision, much of the discussion is applicable to investment decisions of equity sources.

Evaluating Creditworthiness

The process of credit evaluation is well-established in its practice within the financial community. The principles, which have been developed and refined over the years, should be understood and observed by anyone who wishes to use the institutionalized market as a source of financing. Often the practical implications of the loan-making process are misunderstood because the observer is ignorant of the theoretical aspects of the process.

Within the context of borrowing and lending, the term **credit** refers to the practice of giving an individual a sum of money and, in return, receiving a promise to pay it back at some future date. The entire credit evaluation process is geared toward evaluating the likelihood that the "promise to pay" will be honored. Our attempt to understand the process from the commercial lenders' perspective—banks, savings and loan associations, and insurance companies—will focus on evaluating the probability that the borrower will default on that promise.

Commercial lenders are by their very nature more conservative in their lending practices than the typical investor. These financial institutions have a fiduciary responsibility to their depositors because it is borrowed funds such as customer deposits and premiums that are being used in the lending process. The commercial lender is faced with the dilemma of earning an attractive rate of return for its shareholders while still providing a margin of safety for its depositors and taking into consideration the needs of the community it serves.

The Process of Credit Analysis

Commercial lending policy tends to dominate the operations of most financial institutions. Since the loan portfolio is usually the largest single asset on the balance sheet, this lending policy must be compatible with the overall objectives of the operation. A typical lending policy could include a high rate of growth in the loan portfolio or a reduction in the level of loan losses. But whatever the stated policy, its purpose is designed to maximize overall bank profitability subject to an acceptable level of risk.

The first step in understanding the credit analysis process is to examine the typical organizational structure of a commercial lender. The commercial loan officer is the most visible member of the loan division of a banking operation. The loan officer is usually an experienced analyst who has an extensive knowledge and understanding of financial and credit matters. It is the responsibility of the loan officer to interact with loan customers and stay abreast of important developments in their business operations in order to protect the bank's interests.

In many of the larger banking operations, the commercial loan officer does not perform the mechanical work involved in credit decision making. This task is the responsibility of the credit analyst, who gathers, compiles, analyzes, and interprets financial and credit information. The credit department of the bank both provides a valuable service to the lending department and serves as a training program for future loan officers.

The credit analyst, who is often a recent college graduate with a degree in business administration, will work closely with a lending officer in the preparation of the documents required for the loan presentation. Depending on bank policy and the loan officer's personal expertise and experience, loans over a certain dollar limit must be presented to a loan committee for final approval. In small community banks, this committee may consist of the bank president, while in larger banks it will include the senior loan officers. In any event, the recommendations of the presenting loan officer will have a significant influence on the committee's final decision.

Steps in Information Gathering. Many entrepreneurs have the mistaken impression that a loan officer should have the ability to take a set of financial statements, look at them briefly, and make a binding commitment to lend thousands of dollars on the spot. What is not understood about the process is that the loan officer must know something about the history and background of the borrower and his operation before even looking at a financial statement. Any financial analysis is meaningless without this knowledge.

The first step in the process of information gathering is a personal interview. The purpose of this general conference is to allow the entrepreneur an opportunity to formally present his business plan and discuss business goals and objectives with the loan officer. The banker will use this time to clarify various aspects of the business plan and collect some basic information for the customer's credit file.

Assuming that the bank has a continued interest in pursuing the lending opportunity, the credit file is turned over to the credit department for analysis. A credit analyst will be assigned the task of preparing a written evaluation for presentation to the loan officer. This evaluation will include a discussion of the financial condition of the firm. The report will also contain an analysis of the industry in which the firm operates, including a discussion of the market and the level of competition.

The credit departments of most large banks are organized to provide the credit analyst with the necessary resource materials to complete the evaluation report. The analyst's investigation requires access to a considerable amount of outside information. The sources for this information include:

1. *Other Financial Institutions.* The credit department frequently contacts other banks with which the loan customer does business. The information typically shared includes a history of the customer's account and background information on past loans.

2. *Suppliers.* Trade creditors of a business are often a valuable source of information to a commercial bank. Since most firms are very careful about the way they conduct their banking relationships, often the first indication of trouble shows up in the manner in which the firm deals with its trade creditors.

3. *Public Records.* A great deal of information is available through the county courthouse or records building. Although information on legal judgments, pending litigation, and similar data are available, the bank's investigation does not typically involve such data. The records that are most often accessed are those involving filings under the Uniform Commercial Code (UCC) at the state level. UCC filings provide the legal documentation required to establish the ownership, pledge, and transfer of real property, including data on mortgages and liens. Other data that is

frequently collected from public sources include corporate charters, assumed name registrations, and bankruptcy proceedings.

4. *Business Periodicals.* Most commercial loan departments either have a business library or easy access to a library facility. This library contains newspapers, trade publications, financial journals, and other reference materials to provide the credit department with current information for use in preparing loan evaluations. Trade directories and investment manuals provided by Dun & Bradstreet, Moody's Investors Services, and Standard & Poor's are typical of those held and used by most financial institutions.

5. *Credit Reporting Services.* A standard part of the credit investigation involves inquiring into the personal and business credit history of the loan applicant. An individual's personal credit history is usually available through a local credit reporting service. This report includes all consumer credit transactions with local merchants and national credit card services. Business-to-business credit transactions are reported by Dun & Bradstreet Credit Services. A typical D&B report (shown in Figure 7–1, pp. 188-189) provides summary historical, financial, public filing, operational, and banking information on the identified company. Also included in the report is a summary credit rating.

At some point during the investigation process, a representative of the bank will schedule a site visit to the place of business. The purpose of this visit is to carefully inspect the physical plant, examine the machinery and equipment, and possibly perform a physical inventory. The loan officer or other bank representative will use this time to acquire any additional information or verify details needed for the loan presentation.

Once the information is gathered and included in the final loan presentation, all that remains is for the loan officer or loan committee to make a final decision and determine the structure of the loan. In order to really understand the entire procedure, we will now discuss the important factors that are analyzed in the decision-making process.

Important Factors in the Credit Decision

In order to understand the process of credit analysis, one should realize that the credit decision is based on factors that are simply indicators of the probability that the borrower's "promise to pay" will be honored. Credit analysis is a judgment on the part of the evaluator of the probability that the borrower will honor this promise. Thus, the central focus of the process is to assess the borrower's ability and willingness to pay.

Before we begin our assessment of the capacity to repay, we will briefly

Don't Fall Victim to Credit Reporting Services

Unfortunately, many entrepreneurs do not become familiar with the workings of the credit reporting industry until they have been turned down for a loan. One of the steps in the loan review process is the request for a credit report from one of several computerized databases operated by TRW, Trans Union, Credit Bureau Inc., Associated Credit Services Inc., or Chilton Corporation.

Borrowers familiar with these services typically gain their knowledge as the result of being turned down for credit because of erroneous data on their reports. For example, a borrower may be reported to have bad debts that actually belong to an individual with a similar name, and favorable settlements of legal judgments or tax liens are not recorded and files amended. As a result, individuals see the credit reporting services as some sort of CIA or KGB of the lending process.

In order to avoid these unpleasantries, the entrepreneur should become familiar with credit reporting services before applying for a loan. If there are any problems with the accuracy of the information, they can be cleared up without slowing down the credit decision. Credit bureaus are required by the Fair Credit Reporting Act to make credit files available upon request. A copy of the report usually costs around $10. However, if the individual has been denied credit within the past 30 days based on information in the report, it is free of charge.

It is particularly important for married female entrepreneurs to inquire into the accuracy of their credit histories as reported by these services. Many women whose credit files were opened prior to 1977 may find that they have no individual credit identity. Before the Equal Credit Opportunity Act became law, many credit bureaus combined a married woman's credit history with that of her husband. Women seeking to secure credit on their own may find it difficult if they share accounts with their husbands.

In any case, it is important to investigate and challenge items that are in error. Bureaus are required to review any item challenged by an individual. If the item is not changed, the individual can write a statement explaining the situation, which will be incorporated into the report. Negative items, such as bad debts and bankruptcies, remain on the report for seven and ten years, respectively.

---

examine the concept of judging risk in the loan decision. The risk that the loan officer is trying to measure is often referred to as **default risk** and is defined as a borrower's inability or unwillingness to repay a loan according to the agreed upon terms.

There are two major aspects of default risk. The first is called **cash inadequacy** and refers to the inability of cash inflows to cover the required cash outflows according to a predetermined schedule. Consequently, a borrower that suffers from cash inadequacy will habitually be late in making required loan payments and other scheduled obligations. The second aspect is called **cash insolvency** and refers to the inability of cash inflows to cover the required cash outflows. The consequences of this problem are much more serious. Cash insolvency typically results in the failure of the borrower to repay

Summary: For quick appraisal and an overview of the company—the D&B Rating, company history and operation performance.

Special Events: Your decisions about a firm may be affected by the late-breaking events that could appear: criminal proceedings, bankruptcies, burglaries, fires, changes in ownership or acquisition.

Payments: A brief review of the company's payments including high credit extended, amounts owed and past due, and time period since last sale so you can evaluate how *you* will be paid.

Changes: Alerts you to shifts in management, business expansion or changes to legal structure, such as the incorporation of a proprietorship. Or changes in location or business name, so you can keep your records current.

Update: Provides you with recent changes in operation since the report was last revised.

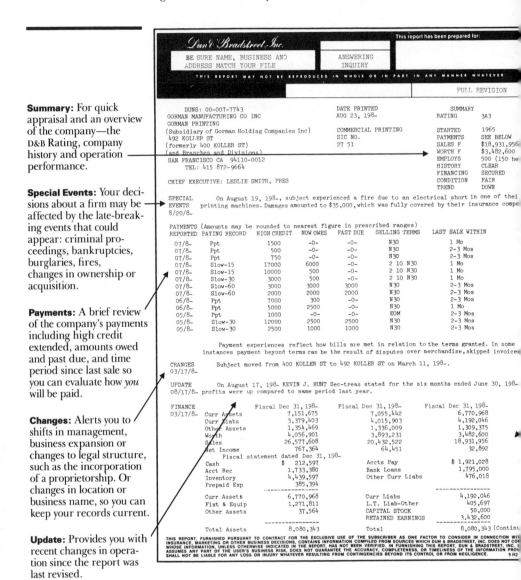

Figure 7–1. **Dun and Bradstreet Credit Report**

Dun & Bradstreet, Inc.

This report has been prepared for:

GORMAN MANUFACTURING CO INC
SAN FRANCISCO CA

AUG 23 198-

PAGE 2
CONSOLIDATED REPORT

THIS REPORT MAY NOT BE REPRODUCED IN WHOLE OR IN PART IN ANY MANNER WHATEVER

FULL REVISION

Annual sales $18,931,956; cost of goods sold $16,777,064. Gross profit $2,154,892; net income $32,892; dividends $29,640; monthly rent $2,500. Lease expires 1999.
Fire insurance on mdse & fixt $6,000,000.
Submitted by Kevin J. Hunt, Sec-Treas. Prepared from statement(s) by Accountant: Fred Mitchel, San Francisco, CA. Prepared from books without audit.
Other assets are tangible, composed of miscellaneous deposits and deferred items. Other current liabilities and long term liabilities are notes due on equipment.
On Mar 15, 198- Kevin J. Hunt, Sec-Treas, referred to the above figures as still representative.
He stated that sales for the 12 months ended Dec 31, 198- were down compared to the same period last year. Profit for the period was down but is expected to increase. Kevin J. Hunt stated that the net worth decreased at 12/31/8-, attributed to the purchase and retirement to treasury of a portion of the capital stock.
Current debt is in excess of net worth. Inventory is large in relation to sales and working capital is light compared to volume transacted.

On Mar 25, 198-, a suit in the amount of $500 was filed against Gorman Manufacturing Co Inc. by Z Henric Assoc.(Docket #27511) in San Francisco, CA. Cause of action was Goods sold and delivered.
Financing statement dated Jan 28, 198- against Gorman Manufacturing Co Inc. in favor of Swinger Corp., Malibu, CA. Amount $2,000. File #741170. State CA. Assignee: San Francisco, CA. Collateral: equipment.
On March 17, 198- Kevin J. Hunt reported action filed by Z Henric Associates was due to damages caused by faulty printer and has been settled. Count records reveal suit was withdrawn.

Balances average moderate six figures. Account open over three years. Loans extended to low seven figures, now owes low seven figures, secured by accounts receivable and inventory, and relation satisfactory.

LESLIE SMITH, PRES   KEVIN J. HUNT, SEC-TREAS
DIRECTOR(s): THE OFFICER(s)
Incorporated California May 21, 1965. Authorized capital consists of 200 shares common stock, no par value.
Business started 1965 by principals. 100% of capital stock is owned by parent.
LESLIE SMITH born 1926 married. Graduated from the University of California, Los Angeles, June 1947. 1947-1965 was the general manager for Raymor Printing Co.San Francisco, CA. 1965 formed subject with Kevin J. Hunt.
KEVIN J. HUNT born 1925 married. Graduated from Northwestern University, Evanston, IL, in June 1946. 1946-1965 was the production manager for Raymor Printing Co., San Francisco, CA. 1965 formed subject with Leslie Smith.
Related Companies: Through the financial interest of Gorman Holding Companies Inc., the Gorman Manufacturing Co Inc. is related to two other sister companies (Smith Lettershop Inc, San Diego, CA and Gorman Suppliers Inc., Los Angeles, CA). These sister companies are also engaged in commercial printing. There are no intercompany relations.

Subsidiary of Gorman Holding Companies Inc.,Los Angeles, CA, which operates as a holding company for its underlying subsidiaries. Parent company has two other subsidiaries.
There are no intercompany relations between parent and subject. A consolidated financial statement on the parent company, dated Dec 31, 198- showed a net worth of $7,842,226, with a fair financial condition indicated.
Commercial printing, engaged in letterpress and screen printing. Sells for cash 30% balance net 30 days. Has 1,000 accounts. Sells to commercial concerns. Territory: Nationwide. Nonseasonal.
EMPLOYEES: 500 including officers. 150 employed here.
FACILITIES: Rents 40,000 sq. ft. in 1 story concrete block building in good condition. Premises neat.
LOCATION: Industrial section on side street.
BRANCHES: Subject maintains a branch at 1073 Boyden Road, Los Angeles, CA.
07-23)9D9 /5)0039/02 00000   052

Finance: The essential components of the company—assets, sales, liabilities and profits—are revealed to you including comments that sum up the figures and trends.

Public Filings: Identifies specific dates of suits, judgments, tax liens and filings.

Banking: Loan experience and banking relationships are presented, giving you further insights into a company's purchasing power and liquidity.

History: The company's principals or owners are identified. You can easily determine whether their past business experiences and expertise complement the company's operations.

Operation: Completes your overall picture of a company—what it does, where it is located and the size of its floor space.

All information may not be available on every company.

the debt under any circumstances; the ensuing loss to the creditor is called *bankruptcy.*

Both of these problems should be avoided. Short of not lending at all, if a bank is to minimize default risk in commercial lending, its loan officers must be skilled at judging the probability that a loan customer will default on his promise to pay.

There are well-established procedures that are followed in making the credit decision. The financial analysis techniques that are used focus on measuring the customer's ability to pay. They examine the tangible aspects of the credit decision and have the advantage of decades of financial theory serving as a basis for their inclusion.

In many ways, the intangible variables that go into assessing the willingness of a person to fulfill an obligation are the most difficult to predict. Since they are so difficult to measure, the human factors must take precedence over other variables in making the credit decision. Even if the ability to pay is present, an unwillingness to do so will result in a worthless promise to pay.

Human Factors. Human action has been and continues to be the focus of the research efforts of the behavioral and social science communities. It is quite possibly one of the most studied and least understood topics in academia today. We expect people to behave in a particular way under a given set of circumstances, but we are often disappointed when our expectations are not met and people behave in a manner that we consider inappropriate. It is because of this fact that the elements in the credit decision dealing with human action take on such importance.

In the context of the closely held business, there are two main areas of human action that are to be examined: 1) the owner/managers and 2) the hired employees. In evaluating creditworthiness, the loan officer will examine past business successes and attempt to measure an individual's attitudes toward the repayment of a loan. Past success is relatively easy to determine and tends to be one of the best indicators of future success. The difficulty arises in trying to determine an individual's determination to fulfill an obligation under all circumstances. This aspect of an individual's personality is sometimes referred to as *character* or *integrity* and should not be confused with a person's reputation. Character is what a person is and does, not what others think about him.

Another consideration deals with the characteristics of the labor force. Although employee characteristics may seem out of the sphere of influence of the owner/managers, they are often a limiting factor in the ability of a firm to initiate certain projects. The loan officer should be aware of the labor force requirements of prospective borrowers relative to the availability of workers, their level of skill, productivity, and union status.

Financial Factors. The financial aspects of the credit decision are much more tangible in nature and thus are easier to measure than the human factors. Much of the previous two chapters was devoted to explaining the techniques of financial analysis, so the current discussion will be brief.

The financial element in the process of risk evaluation can be viewed as the ability of the operation to generate sufficient cash inflows to cover all obligations. Cash can be generated from operating sources and non-operating sources. The primary source of cash for the repayment of loans is the operation itself. In addition to this focus on cash flow from operations, the loan officer is also concerned with the availability and use of other sources of cash.

The experienced loan officer looks at the purpose of the loan as the secondary source of cash for repayment of the loan. If the additional cash for the repayment of a loan is not forthcoming from the operation, the next logical place to look for the cash is from the sale of an asset. The pledge of specific assets required by most banks is a secondary repayment source to insure against default. Collateral is almost always a significant consideration in all loans to closely held businesses.

If cash from operations and collateral are both insufficient to cover the obligation, the loan officer will turn to other non-operating sources of cash. The specific sources depend on the individual circumstances and can include the sale of unpledged assets or possibly the injection of additional capital into the operation by its owners. This third source of cash for loan repayment is so important that the bank often requires the inclusion of all unpledged assets as collateral for a loan in addition to a personal guarantee from the owners that the loan will be repaid.

Economic Factors. The general business climate prevailing in the target market, the industry in which the firm operates, and the overall economy play a critical role in determining the level of business risk involved in a particular venture. The environment in which the firm operates is the primary source of risk exogenous to the firm.

At the firm level the environmental risk manifests itself in man-made and physical disasters. Occurrences such as a fire, flood, tornado, theft, or death will almost always result in a business disruption. An entrepreneur can take certain precautions to minimize the risk, but it cannot be totally eliminated. However, it is possible to insure against losses that result from these disasters. Loan officers require adequate insurance coverage to prevent any losses to the bank.

The competitive environment in the local market is another important consideration. This includes the level of product demand, the number of firms and their success, and relative market shares. The industry environment is also important. This includes such issues as the nature of the product, the number and quality of close substitutes, and overall industry trends.

General business conditions, including the overall economic and political framework, determine the framework within which the management of the firm will operate. Interest rate trends, money supply forecasts, personal income growth, and legislative changes can all have significant influence on the ability of an operation to meet its financial obligations.

The Five Cs of Credit

The careful reader will have recognized that the previous discussion included a listing of the five Cs of credit: character, capacity, collateral, capital, and conditions. The relative importance of each of these aspects in the credit decision varies depending on the situation. There is no handy way to weight each aspect and develop a foolproof means of scoring for commercial lending as is often done in consumer lending.

Character. This aspect deals with the inner qualities of the individual that determine his or her personal commitment to the promise to repay the loan. In many cases, reputation accurately reflects an individual's ethics and moral standards, but sometimes it does not. As a result, the loan officer will have to carefully consider information on style of living, business and professional associations, church memberships, and personal habits to aid with this evaluation. This intangible aspect in the credit decision is quite often the most important. In most cases, any doubts about the character of an individual will result in a negative response from the bank.

Capacity. An examination of character is an attempt to discern an individual's willingness to repay, whereas capacity is a measure of one aspect of the ability to repay. Capacity is reflected in a firm's financial statements and is defined by its ability to generate cash flow from operations.

Collateral. In order to ensure repayment in the event that cash flow is insufficient to meet the obligation, many loans are secured by assets that are specifically pledged as collateral. Although this secondary source of repayment is essential, it should not be misunderstood. The concept of a "fully secured" loan can be deceptive unless the borrower realizes that the value of the asset as collateral depends on its marketability. This is the reason that very few assets are acquired with 100 percent financing.

Capital. The final margin of safety to ensure repayment can be viewed as the general credit of the firm as measured by capital or ownership equity. This is either determined by the market value of unpledged assets or the personal net worth of the major shareholders. Owners of closely held businesses, especially new ventures or those with limited track records, should plan on providing a personal guarantee for all commercial loans.

Conditions. The external environment in which the firm operates, or *condition,* is the final aspect analyzed in the credit decision. This includes conditions in the local market, the industry in which the firm operates, and the general economy.

The Loan-Making Process

The commercial lending process is only one aspect of the organizational structure of a typical financial institution. If the overall operation is to function efficiently, each area must be integrated into a well-defined system. The first step in this process is to establish a clear set of goals, policies, and strategies for the organization and to structure the operation to achieve them.

The typical bank may have stated goals that include a desired rate of return on invested capital or a target growth rate for commercial loans and deposits. In order to successfully achieve these goals, bank management establishes certain policies that all employees must follow. These policies usually include geographic and industry constraints. However, when dealing with a regional or large money-center bank, these constraints are not usually significant. This is because of the fact that these banks also have an established policy to promote diversification of their loan portfolios.

Most banks have established guidelines for operating ratios such as loans-to-assets and loans-to-deposits. Even though these target ratios do not directly affect the average loan customer, they determine to some extent the degree to which the bank is actively seeking new business.

Policies about the lending limits of individual loan officers have a much more direct impact on loan customers. Lending limits vary depending on the size of the bank and the experience and position of the loan officer. Generally speaking, the larger the bank is, the larger the lending limits will be. An executive vice-president has the authority to approve larger loans than a senior vice-president, who in turn has a higher lending limit than a vice-president.

Loans that are larger than the lending limit of the servicing loan officer must go to loan review committee for approval. Most banks have a loan review committee. This committee is composed of senior loan officers who meet frequently to review major loan proposals. The purpose of the committee is not only to review loan proposals, but also to evaluate and control the performance of loan personnel. As a result, most loan officers do not submit to the committee loan requests that have little chance of approval.

Steps in Lending

Our discussion thus far has touched on many of the steps in the lending process—from the loan proposal and application to the process of credit analysis and evaluation, to the final decision to accept or reject a loan request. The final steps in the process that have a direct impact on the loan customer involve the structuring of the loan and the loan review process.

Structuring a Loan. After the decision has been made to approve a loan, the structure of the loan must be specified. A loan's structure, which is sometimes referred to as the **terms of the loan,** encompasses such items as repayment schedule, pricing, compensating balances, and collateral.

Pricing a Loan. The practice of loan pricing involves equating the incremental costs and revenues associated with a particular loan customer to determine the interest rate that the bank will charge on a commercial loan. There are many complex issues involved in pricing a loan and as a result, there are probably as many ways to price a loan as there are banks involved in loan pricing. The purpose of the following discussion is to examine the conceptual framework and apply these principles and concepts to develop a general model for loan pricing.

The profitability of a loan to a commercial bank depends on the incremental contribution to the bank's net earnings. This contribution is calculated by summing all revenues generated directly from the customer in the form of fees, interest, and earnings on compensating balances. From that value is subtracted the total cost of providing the services, which includes the cost of funds, the administrative costs associated with the loan, activity costs on the customer's deposit accounts, and a risk premium based on the creditworthiness of the customer. The result is the net contribution to profit resulting from the addition of the loan to the bank's portfolio.

A thorough understanding of the loan pricing process helps an entrepreneur gain an appreciation for the complexities faced in structuring a loan agreement. It also goes a long way in diffusing a great deal of the hostility that emerges during the final negotiations. Exhibit 7–1 contains an example of the general loan pricing model that underlies the rate schedule used for commercial loans. Although it is seldom applied to individual loans, it does outline the considerations used by commercial banks in determining their lending rate schedule.

The first step in pricing a loan is to calculate the cost of the funds used to provide the loan. The principal concept in this calculation is "net borrowed funds." The average loan balance for the period is first calculated. The $100,000 in our example, however, may not be the actual amount of funds available for the borrower to use. If there is a compensating account balance

EXHIBIT 7–1

Loan Pricing Model

Cost of funds:

Average loan balance		$100,000
Less: Compensating balances	10%	10,000
Effective loan balance		$ 90,000
Plus: Reserves	10%	1,000
Net borrowed funds		$ 91,000
Times: Interest rate on borrowed funds		.10
Cost of borrowed funds		$ 9,100

Other costs:

Administrative costs	0.5%	500
Costs of services		600
Risk premium	1.5%	1,500
Total costs		$ 11,700
Plus: Bank's profit goal	2.0%	2,000
Total revenue required		$ 13,700
Less: Fees from services		500
Less: Value of compensating balances		900
Interest income required		$ 12,300
Interest rate		12.3%

---

required, this reduces the net amount available and it must be subtracted. In the example, the compensating balance requirement is 10 percent.

Since all banks are required to hold a certain percentage of their deposit balances in non-interest-earning reserve accounts, a portion of the compensating balance is not available to the bank either. In the example, the reserve requirement is 10 percent of deposit balances, so $1,000 is added to obtain the value for net borrowed funds. The cost of borrowed funds ($9,100) is calculated by multiplying the value for net borrowed funds ($91,000) by the interest rate the bank has to pay to secure the funds (10%).

Although the cost of borrowed funds is the largest single item in the total cost to the bank, there are other cost items that must also be taken into account. There are administrative costs that are the overhead expenses associated with servicing the loan account. These overhead expenses, which include salaries, facilities costs, and the cost of operating the loan and credit departments, are allocated to each individual loan based on a percentage of the loan amount. This percentage is calculated by dividing total overhead expenses by the average dollar amount of loans outstanding. In our example, this percentage is 0.5%.

The costs of services are the bank's costs of providing deposit accounts to the customer. These costs are based on the projected activity in the account; in our example they are estimated to be $50 per month.

Risk in commercial lending is based on the credit risk of the individual customer and the interest rate risk, or the probability that interest rates will increase during the term of the loan. Credit risk is based on the bank's provision for loan losses, which is a percentage of average total loans outstanding. It is allocated to each loan made by the bank based on this percentage. On the other hand, interest rate risk is often handled by writing variable-rate loans, rather than fixed-rate loans.

Assume that the provision for loan losses in the example is 0.75 percent of average total commercial loans outstanding. In the case of the loan being priced, the risk associated with the borrower is viewed as higher than the average risk on commercial loans. As a result the risk premium assigned to this loan is 1.5 percent.

The bank's profit goal is added to the total cost to reach a figure for the total revenue required to cover costs and return the desired profit. This profit goal is determined by top-level management within the bank and is strongly influenced by the competitive environment within the local marketplace. The primary factor in determining the profit goal is the difference between the interest rate the bank must pay on borrowed funds and the rate paid on risk-free investments, such as short-term U.S. government securities and other money market instruments. In our example, the profit goal is 2.0 percent, resulting in a total revenue requirement of $13,700.

An important source of income for the bank is the fees that are generated from the services offered. They include items such as loan origination fees, account service charges, commitment fees, and credit card fees. The compensating balance, net of the reserve requirement, has a value to the bank that is estimated by multiplying it by the interest rate on borrowed funds ($9,000 · 10% = $900).

Interest income required is the difference between the total revenue required and these two sources of revenue. The simple interest rate that must be charged on the loan (12.3 percent) is the interest income required divided by the average loan balance ($12,300/$100,000).

Admittedly, the loan pricing example in Exhibit 7–1 is a simple one. However, the basic structure presented is sound and forms the general model for all loan pricing decisions. The added complexities of loan pricing are simply beyond the scope of this book.

Compensating Balances. The concept of the compensating balance was referred to several times in the preceding discussion. It is a practice that is quite common in the U.S. banking community. As part of the loan agreement, the firm agrees to keep a certain percentage of the outstanding loan (usually 10–20 percent) in a non-interest-earning demand deposit. The purpose of this requirement is to permit the bank to earn a higher net return on the funds outstanding. Since the loan customer actually has access to less than the full amount of the loan, the net cost of the usable funds is higher.

Loan Review. The loan review process is a procedure that the loan officer follows to audit each item in his loan portfolio. The process is established to stay abreast of the condition of each loan customer and the way the loan is being serviced. The purpose of this periodic review is to reduce overall loan losses and detect problem loans as early as possible.

In addition to the data generated by the bank regarding the loan, the entrepreneur is required to provide periodic financial statements to aid the loan officer in this task. One of the major benefits to the borrower is the opportunity to take advantage of the expertise of the loan officer in spotting potential problem areas. Then the entrepreneur can take the necessary action to avoid the problem entirely.

A frequent result of the review process is the identification of a problem loan. This may eventually involve a loss to the bank, but more often it results in a restructuring of the loan agreement. The restructuring often includes either a new repayment schedule or an additional collateral requirement. In all cases, however, the purpose is to give the borrower a chance to work out of a problem situation and avoid losses to everyone involved.

Types of Loans

Bank credit is actually secured through many different types of financial instruments. The following discussion looks at several of the more common types of commercial loans available, including term loans, revolving lines of credit, and letters of credit.

Term Loans. Approximately half of all commercial and industrial loans are term loans. The term loan has several unique characteristics that make it distinct from other types of credit instruments. Maturities on term loans usually vary from one year to ten years, with the majority being less than five. As its name implies, a term loan is paid off over the life of the loan. The payments include principal and interest and are usually made in equal periodic installments, either monthly, quarterly, semi-annually, or annually. Most term loans are used to purchase real estate, machinery, and equipment, or to refinance existing debt.

Revolving Lines of Credit. This is a frequently used device to assist a customer with a seasonal credit demand. Often, firms in their early growth stages of development have not diversified sufficiently to generate a positive cash flow over the trading cycle. Once inventory is purchased, it is necessary to ride out the cycle until accounts receivable are collected. Without sufficient working capital, even a short delay can result in a severe cash flow problem.

The usual procedure is for the bank to commit a specified maximum amount of funds from which the customer is allowed to draw as needed. The customer is generally given the right to repay and reborrow during the term of the agreement, which is usually one year.

Repayment usually comes from the sale of the asset that is being financed with the loan—inventory or accounts receivable. Since the loan is often secured by these assets, the loan officer will examine them carefully to determine their value before making the credit decision. Inventory will be evaluated on such factors as amount, turnover, mix, and obsolescence. Accounts receivable will be valued by looking at turnover and aging to identify delinquent accounts and significant concentrations. A credit check will be conducted on any customer who has more than 10 percent of the total as outstanding receivables to estimate the vulnerability of the borrower to customer default.

Letters of Credit. A letter of credit is a financial instrument issued by a bank on behalf of its customer that obligates the bank to make a payment to a third party (usually a supplier of the customer) at a future date. The letter of credit is usually irrevocable and guarantees the purchase contract by the fact that it will be paid after certain conditions are met. Letters of credit are commonly used to effect transactions between importers and exporters.

The best way to explain the use of a letter of credit is by using an example. Suppose that Company A wishes to import merchandise from a foreign supplier, Company J. The merchandise is to be shipped by boat and is payable upon delivery. Before Company J agrees to begin the shipping process, an assurance of payment from Company A is required.

To effect the transaction, Company A has its bank issue a letter of credit in favor of Company J. The bank, while not a direct party to the transaction, promises to pay Company J for the merchandise upon receipt of documents stating that Company A has accepted delivery. The letter of credit is considered "self-liquidating." Resale of the merchandise will in theory generate the funds necessary to repay the loan.

Once the letter of credit is confirmed by a prime U.S. bank, the seller is protected against insolvency of the buyer and breach of contract. All letters of credit used for this type of transaction are subject to the provisions of the

Uniform Customs and Practice for Documentary Credits—International Chamber of Commerce Publication No. 290 available through the U.S. Council of the International Chamber of Commerce (1975). Any entrepreneur involved in the importing and exporting of merchandise is urged to become familiar with the provisions and implications of this document.

Legal Aspects in Lending

Given the scope of this book, it is not feasible to cover all the legal aspects that apply to every credit instrument used by the financial community. There are some basic legal principles, however, that govern the extension of credit and are fundamental to understanding the manner in which credit is granted.

The motivation for the banker to understand and follow these legal principles is to ensure that the bank has an enforceable claim against the borrower. Likewise, the borrower should be motivated to understand the implications of the legal contract that is being signed. The terms and conditions of a loan are easily misunderstood, so a banker will seldom lend money on the borrower's oral promise to pay. Thus, in most cases, the credit agreement will be in the form of a written note.

The borrower must be careful to read and understand the contents of the loan document because the law assumes that the borrower understands the contents of the document he has signed. The only usable defenses are ambiguities in the writing and fraud or misrepresentation at the time of the signing of the loan agreement.

Before initiating a loan agreement, a banker will take steps to determine whether the prospective borrower can legally borrow the money. In the case of a sole proprietor, the relevant issues are whether the individual is of legal age and mentally competent to enter into a contract.

In the case of a partnership, the same tests apply; in addition, the loan agreement will specify whether the individuals signing the agreement are jointly or individually liable. If the document is a negotiable instrument, that is, if the bank has the authority to sell it on the secondary market, provisions in the Uniform Commercial Code [Section 3-118(c) adopted in all 50 states] specify that the signers are jointly and individually liable.

Since a corporation is treated as an individual citizen of the state in which it was incorporated, it also has the right to borrow money. In actual practice, an authorized representative of the corporation can sign any loan agreement. Before this takes place, the bank will require evidence that the individual has this authority; this is usually given in the form of a resolution by the corporation's board of directors.

The Loan Document

The loan document is a written agreement between the borrower and the lender that sets out the terms and conditions under which the loan is made. Although the wording of the agreement differs from bank to bank, the basic format is the same. The typical loan document has four principal sections: 1) description of the loan, 2) representations and warranties, 3) financial covenants, and 4) provisions for default.

Description of the Loan. This section of the loan document provides the basic information on the amount of the loan, its maturity, the rate of interest, required fees, prepayment provisions, and collateral requirements. Recently, many banks have begun writing variable-rate loans to shift a portion of the interest rate risk to the borrower. If the loan is of the variable-rate variety, this section stipulates the nature of this variability: 1) the standard upon which the rate is based, 2) how it will adjust, and 3) how often and when it will be adjusted. The bank's formula for adjusting its lending rate is usually based on the national prime lending rate or some other published standard. Rates are usually set at prime plus a certain number of points (such as prime plus two points) and are adjusted periodically (such as at the end of each month). In addition, there are usually limits on the maximum adjustment that can be made over a period of time.

Representations and Warranties. During the period of evaluation and negotiation, the loan officer has based his judgment on the financial and personal information provided by the borrower. At the time of the execution of the loan agreement, the borrower is required to certify that the information provided is true and accurate. This section often lists specific documents such as the financial statements, the resolution of the board of directors authorizing the loan, outstanding debts and liens, pending litigation, subsidiaries, previous indictments, and bankruptcy filings.

Financial Covenants. The section that provides the details of the financial covenants is perhaps the most important aspect of the entire document. If the borrower violates one of the covenants, the lender has the legal right to accelerate the due date of the note. Section 1-208 of the Uniform Commercial Code specifically gives the bank this right if the financial situation of the borrower changes dramatically. The typical provisions include: 1) purpose of the loan, 2) proper maintenance of the facilities owned by the company, 3) submission of periodic financial statements, 4) maintenance of minimum values for key financial ratios such as working capital, current ratio, and debt ratio, and 5) restrictions on the further pledge of assets, additional borrowing, dividend payments, owners' compensation, mergers and acquisitions, sale or purchase of assets, or any other transaction that is not defined as falling within the normal operation of the business.

Provisions for Default. Other provisions are also included in the document which, if violated, will result in default on the part of the borrower. These provisions typically include: 1) failure to make payment within a certain period of time, 2) bankruptcy, and 3) misrepresentations of any of the information provided.

The Subordination Agreement

When credit is granted to a corporation, the loan officer usually requires that all corporate obligations to shareholders, officers, and members of the board of directors be subordinated to the bank loan. This is done by executing a standard subordination agreement.

State and Federal Regulations

In addition to the basic principles that apply to all credit documents, lenders are required to comply with certain state and federal regulations governing lending. The major consideration the bank must follow is based on the chartering provisions under which the institution was granted operating authority. Whether it operates under a state or a federal charter, the bank has a limitation on the amount of credit that it can extend to a single borrower. This limitation is usually stipulated in terms of a percentage of the bank's capital (10–15 percent depending on the charter).

In spite of this limitation, a bank can enter into a syndication with several other banks to participate in a loan that is more than its limit. The customer signs a loan agreement with the "lead" bank, which in turn sells a portion of the loan to "participating" banks. This arrangement is evidenced by an agreement between the banks and has no direct effect on the borrower. The sole purpose of the participating agreement is to define the responsibilities and payment and collection procedures among the banks.

Equal Credit Opportunity Act. Before 1974, credit could be denied for any reason that the loan officer considered relevant, including reasons not based on credit information. The Equal Credit Opportunity Act applies to all types of credit and prohibits "discriminating against an applicant for credit on the basis of race, color, religion, national origin, sex, marital status, or age" (Stephens 1981 p. 316).

This does not mean that a bank must lend money to anyone who requests a loan. It only means that the decision to extend credit must be based solely on the borrower's assets and ability to repay. A bank can have an established policy against making a certain type of loan, such as loans to cocktail lounges and liquor stores. As long as it can be established that the policy is followed in all cases, then the restriction is appropriate and defensible.

The provisions of this act have been implemented through Regulation B by the Federal Reserve Board. As a result, many traditional bank practices have been drastically altered, benefiting many smaller customers.

Community Reinvestment Act. This act was passed to make sure that commercial banks are sensitive to the credit requirements of all segments of their local communities. Prior to 1978, a bank could collect deposits within its designated market area and make its loans outside that area. The passage of this act ensures that this practice is not commonplace.

Women and Credit

Although female-owned businesses are the fastest growing segment of the small business community, their net incomes lag far behind those of male-owned enterprises. Smaller size, more vigorous competition, and a preponderance of part-time enterprises have kept the female average at around 30 percent of the male average for the past decade.

The differences do not end with income. Many female entrepreneurs at least perceive they are being discriminated against in the commercial loan process. The National Association of Women Business Owners found that more than half of the survey respondents who had been denied credit felt they had been treated unfairly. Eleven years after the passage of the Equal Credit Opportunity Act that prohibits such actions, discrimination is still an issue (Mitchell 1986).

A more recent study by the Small Business Administration on discrimination in commercial lending does not support this contention. Research conducted by Faith Ando (1986) suggests that female business owners are not discriminated against in their search for business loans.

The issue may not be one of discrimination against women as much as it is one of female industry preference. Most female-owned businesses are in the service sector where there are few tangible assets that can be pledged as collateral. Commercial banks in general are asset-based lenders and do not aggressively seek loan customers in the service sector, male- or female-owned.

Commercial banking is an industry that has yet to adjust to the soft-asset, knowledge-based economy of the 1980s. With over 70 percent of the U.S. economy now in the service sector, commercial lenders may be missing a tremendous opportunity to grow and expand along with this sector of the economy.

Truth-In-Lending Act. The adoption of the Consumer Credit Protection Act in 1969 marked a major breakthrough in consumer protection legislation. Later amended in 1982, the act requires that a lender must inform the borrower about the annual percentage interest rate being charged and the total amount of interest scheduled to be paid. In addition to these two major disclosures, the borrower is to be informed about any default provisions, prepayment penalties, collateral requirements, and insurance requirements. The Federal Reserve Board has implemented the provisions of this act through Regulation Z.

Usury Laws. Until the passage of the Depository Institutions Deregulation and Monetary Control Act of 1980 (DIDMC), many states had restrictions on the amount of interest that could be charged to various types of borrowers. As a result of DIDMC, however, all restrictions on interest rates that can be charged have been removed.

The preceding regulations are just a few of the many that could legitimately be included in the discussion. Many states limit certain practices, such as redlining, and all have adopted the provisions of the Uniform Commercial Code. The issues discussed provide a representative picture of the basic legal principles and regulations governing the extension of credit in the marketplace today.

Bankruptcy Prediction as an Analysis Tool

Commercial loan officers have been trying to predict business failure for decades. Outstanding loans to financially distressed firms will probably result in an increase in defaults. As we have seen as a result of the recent energy crisis, a concentration of loans to financially distressed firms can lead to bankruptcy on the part of the lender.

Even though bankruptcy prediction models have been presented in academic journals since the 1930s, they did not gain too much credibility until the research of William H. Beaver was published in the 1960s [see Beaver (1966, 1968)]. The results of Beaver's work indicated that certain financial ratios differed significantly among the seventy-nine failed and seventy-nine nonfailed firms in his sample. In addition, several ratios, especially cash flow to total debt, were good predictors of financial distress.

Probably the most widely quoted research in this area was conducted by Edward I. Altman (1968) in which he used a statistical technique called "discriminant analysis." **Discriminant analysis** is a method of finding a number of predictive variables and assigning specific weights to them so that their sum equals a single overall indicator (a Z-score).

Altman classified a group of ratios into the five standard categories: liquidity, asset utilization, coverage, leverage, and profitability. With the use of discriminant analysis he developed a model made up of five ratios that maximized the ability to predict bankruptcy. The original model states:

$$Z = 1.2X_1 + 1.4X_2 + 3.3X_3 + 0.6X_4 + 1.0X_5$$

where

X_1 = working capital/total assets
X_2 = retained earnings/total assets
X_3 = earnings before interest and taxes/total assets
X_4 = market value of equity/book value of total liabilities
X_5 = sales/total assets.

The statistical technique enabled Altman to classify firms as bankrupt and nonbankrupt solely on the basis of the Z-score. The critical value for Z that best differentiates between bankrupt and nonbankrupt firms is 2.675. A Z-score less than this will result in the firm's being classified as bankrupt; one greater than this will result in a nonbankrupt classification. Altman did, however, recommend the following classification scheme to improve the predictive power of the model:

Z < 1.81: bankrupt firm
Z ⩾ 2.99: nonbankrupt firm
Z > 1.81 but < 2.99: zone of ignorance.

This "zone of ignorance" is given this name because of the high degree of error involved in classifying firms with Z-scores in this range. The model correctly classified firms with Z-scores outside this range 95 percent of the time one year prior to bankruptcy and 72 percent of the time two years prior to bankruptcy.

It should be emphasized that a Z-score below 1.81 is no guarantee that a firm will be bankrupt within one year. It turned out that there was a 6 percent chance of classifying a nonbankrupt firm as bankrupt (Type I error). Likewise, a Z-score of 2.99 or above is no guarantee that a firm will not go bankrupt. There was a 3 percent chance of classifying a bankrupt firm as nonbankrupt (Type II error).

The major problem in using Altman's original model as a predictive tool is that it was designed to be used only for publicly traded firms. The model can be modified for use in predicting bankruptcy with a privately held firm simply by substituting book value of equity for market value of equity in the fourth ratio and re-estimating the weights. The model is less robust, but it still performs quite well (see Altman 1983).

Another interesting study in this area was conducted by Fulmer, Moon, Gavin, and Erwin (1984). The purpose of this study was to develop a model that would have direct application to assist financial institutions in incorporating bankruptcy classification models in their analysis of the creditworthiness of prospective loan customers. In order for a model to be relevant in this market, it had to be estimated with data that were representative of the smaller firm, which comprises 90 percent of the loan customers at commercial banks.

The model was estimated using data from sixty firms that had average total assets of $454,700, including firms in manufacturing, retail stores, and service. The results of their study estimating an "*H*-score" are presented in Table 7–1.

A negative *H*-score indicates that a firm has a high probability that it will fail; a positive *H*-score indicates a high probability of nonfailure. Notice that the ratios used in this model for small firms are quite different from those used by Altman to classify large firms. Only two ratios, retained earnings to total assets and sales to total assets, are used in both models. This points out that the ratios that best classify firms as failed and nonfailed can vary with the size of the firm.

The procedure for using either of these models to classify firms is very simple. The data for the following example is from the financial statements of Richland Gifts that was presented in Exhibit 5–1. The values for the ratios are multiplied by the coefficients of the respective models and then added.

Using the Altman model, the calculation is as follows:

$$Z = 1.2(.3922) + 1.4(.1918) + 3.3(.1458) \\ + 0.6(.7412) + 1.0(1.460) = 3.1249$$

This value is greater than 2.99, so Richland Gifts would be classified as a nonbankrupt firm.

Using the Fulmer, Moon, Gavin, Erwin model, the calculation is as follows:

$$H = -6.075 + 5.528(.1918) + 0.212(1.460) + 0.073(.2235) \\ + 1.270(.3349) - 0.120(.5743) + 2.335(.3349) \\ + 0.575(5.108) + 1.083(.6828) + 0.894(.4590) \\ = +0.5364$$

This is a positive value, so once again Richland is classified as a nonbankrupt firm.

This discussion is in no way intended to indicate that the bankruptcy

Table 7–1
Small Firm Bankruptcy Classification Model

Variables	Coefficient
Retained Earnings/Total Assets	5.528
Sales/Total Assets	0.212
Before-Tax Earnings/Book Value Equity	0.073
Cash Flow/Total Debt	1.270
Total Debt/Total Assets	−0.120
Current Liabilities/Total Assets	2.335
Logarithm of Total Tangible Assets	0.575
Working Capital/Total Debt	1.083
Logarithm of EBIT/Interest	0.894
Constant	−6.075
R^2	.767

Source: Fulmer, Moon, Gavin, Erwin (1984 p. 31).

classification procedure can serve as a substitute for a careful financial analysis. However, the methodology does provide the creditor with a tool that has been used successfully to predict with a high degree of accuracy whether a firm is likely to experience financial problems within one to two years. The main point of the discussion is to show that with a few exceptions, the classification models can be used to supplement the credit evaluation procedure used by many commercial lenders.

Summary and Conclusions

In this chapter we have taken a close look at the credit evaluation process from the perspective of the commercial lender. The typical organizational structure of a commercial bank was presented to provide a background to the steps in the credit analysis procedure. Important factors in the credit decision were also presented to give the entrepreneur a sound basis for the reasoning behind the business planning process presented in Chapter 2.

The methodology used to structure a loan was then discussed, along with the various types of loans that are typically used in commercial lending. The basic loan document was examined from a legal perspective, along with several of the more important state and federal regulations that are directly relevant to the procedures followed in commercial lending.

The chapter concluded with a discussion of two of the more popular bankruptcy classification models that have been developed over recent years.

References

Altman, Edward I. *Corporate Financial Distress: A Complete Guide to Predicting, Avoiding, and Dealing with Bankruptcy.* New York: John Wiley and Sons, 1983.

Altman, Edward I. "Financial Ratios, Discriminant Analysis and the Prediction of Corporate Bankruptcy," *Journal of Finance* (September, 1968), pp. 589–609.

Altman, Edward I. "Managing the Commercial Lending Process." In *Handbook for Banking Strategy,* edited by Richard C. Aspinwall and Robert A. Eisenbeis. New York: John Wiley and Sons, 1985, pp. 473–510.

Ando, Faith. "Access to Capital by Subcategories of Small Business." Paper presented at Eastern Finance Association meetings, Nashville, TN, April 1986.

Beaver, William H. "Financial Ratios as Predicators of Failure." In *Empirical Research and Accounting: Selected Studies, Supplement to Journal of Accounting Research* (May, 1966), pp. 71–127.

Beaver, William H. "Market Prices, Financial Ratios, and the Prediction of Failure," *Journal of Accounting Research* (Autumn, 1968), pp. 179–192.

Bettinger, Cass. "Bankruptcy Prediction as a Tool for Commercial Lenders," *Journal of Commercial Bank Lending* (July, 1981), pp. 18–28.

Eisenreich, Dennis C. "Credit Analysis: Tying It All Together—Part I," *Journal of Commercial Bank Lending* (December, 1981), pp. 2–13.

Eisenreich, Dennis C. "Credit Analysis: Tying It All Together—Part II," *Journal of Commercial Bank Lending* (January, 1982), pp. 2–16.

Fulmer, John G. Jr.; Moon, James E.; Gavin, Thomas A.; and Erwin, J. Michael. "A Bankruptcy Classification Model for Small Firms," *Journal of Commercial Bank Lending* (July, 1984), pp. 25–37.

Mitchell, Constance. "Businesswomen Say Credit Firms Still Discriminate on Basis of Sex," *Wall Street Journal* (June 26, 1986), p. 27.

Santomero, Anthony M. "Pricing Business Credit." In *Handbook for Banking Strategy,* edited by Richard C. Aspinwall and Robert A. Eisenbeis. New York: John Wiley and Sons, 1985, pp. 589–605.

Stephens, Harvey B. "The Legal Aspects of Bank Loans." In *Bank Credit,* edited by Herbert V. Prochnow. New York: Harper and Row, 1981, pp. 301–321.

Uniform Customs and Practices for Documentary Credits, I.C.C. Publication No. 290. New York: U.S. Council of the International Chamber of Commerce, October 1, 1975.

8
Forms of Business Organization

The choice of organizational form for a business enterprise is not a one-dimensional issue. Many entrepreneurs are mistakenly led to believe that the major consideration in choosing a legal structure is taxation. Although taxation is an important issue, there are many other considerations that must also be examined and understood before the decision is made.

The first step in choosing an organizational form is to have a clear picture of the purpose and ultimate goals of the business enterprise and a knowledge of how the legal structure can best contribute to accomplishing those goals. There are other considerations that are relevant to the decision, including: 1) the degree of financial risk and personal liability involved in the venture, 2) the influence of applicable laws, especially the federal income tax code, 3) the need and ability to attract additional professional and management expertise, and 4) the ability and capacity to attract the capital required to finance the venture.

The purpose of the following discussion is to provide a broad overview of the most common legal forms of organization available to the entrepreneur—sole proprietorship, partnership, and corporation. It is not meant to serve as a complete guide to the choice of organizational form. In this regard, there is no substitute for a competent attorney to avoid any misunderstanding of the complicated technical and legal issues and the added cost of an incorrect decision. The discussion will focus on the characteristics of the major forms of organization, highlighting the effects on the financial activities of the firm. Although some characteristics may not impact on the financial aspects of a firm directly, most have at least an indirect effect.

The owners and managers of large firms spend relatively little time and energy in this discussion. Large businesses are usually organized as corporations for compelling reasons, as we will see more clearly later in the discussion. The owners of smaller firms, however, must understand the implications of the various organizational structures because the relative benefits and costs of the choice may not be as obvious.

Characteristics of Organizational Forms

All businesses do not operate in the same industry; they vary in size; and their owners have different goals and objectives. Therefore, it is not unusual that they are organized differently. Some firms are small "mom-and-pop" businesses in which a single individual or couple manages the entire operation from production to sales to distribution to accounting and finance. Approximately 60 percent of the firms operating in the United States today have gross annual receipts of less than $25,000 and the vast majority of these are organized as sole proprietorships. (See Table 8–1.)

At the other end of the spectrum are the giant multinational companies such as Exxon, IBM, and Chrysler. These firms have thousands of shareholders, employ thousands of workers, and control billions of dollars in assets. Only about 4 percent of U.S. firms have annual receipts greater than $1 million and 85 percent of these are organized as corporations.

In between these extremes lie the majority of the businesses that touch our lives on a daily basis. For the "mom-and-pop" operation or the multi-

Table 8–1
Distribution of Firms According to Organizational Form in the
United States, 1982

Firms, by Gross Annual Receipts	Number of Firms (000)		
	Proprietorship	Partnership	Corporation
Total	10,106	1,514	2,926
Less than $25,000	7,203	759	620
$25,000 to $50,000	.1,117	178	218
$50,000 to $100,000	844	191	325
$100,000 to $500,000	838	293	1,021
$500,000 to $1,000,000	68	52	296
Over $1,000,000	36	42	446
	Receipts (billions)		
Total	$433.7	$251.6	$6,157.0
Less than $25,000	45.0	1.7	2.9
$25,000 to $50,000	39.9	3.3	6.6
$50,000 to $100,000	59.2	7.8	21.5
$100,000 to $500,000	166.4	41.5	242.1
$500,000 to $1,000,000	47.0	23.6	203.3
Over $1,000,000	76.2	173.7	5,680.6

Source: *Statistical Abstracts of the United States*, 106th edition, U.S. Department of Commerce, Bureau of Census, 1986, Tables No. 875 and 876.

Table 8–2
Forms of Business Organization

Topic	Sole Proprietorship	Partnership	Corporation
Liability to Owners	Full personal liability for business obligations	Joint liability for each partner	Liability limited to investment
Control	Full control vested in owner	Shared authority	Centralized management
Continuity	Dissolution when owner dies	Dissolution when any one partner dies	Permanent life
Capital Requirements	Limited availability; based on owner's credit	Expanded credit limit because of extra owners	Best access to capital markets
Cost and Convenience	Informal with no restrictions; little or no cost	Agreements recommended; low cost	Formed via charter; substantial fees required
Taxation	Net earnings taxed at owner's marginal rates	Net earnings taxed on partners' personal returns	Subject to corporate tax rates

national, the choice of organizational structure is easy. The former will be organized as a sole proprietorship and the latter will be a corporation. In situations where the choice is not that obvious, the following discussion should prove helpful. (See Table 8–2.)

Sole Proprietorship

The **sole proprietorship** is a business owned and managed by a single individual. Since this business form has no legal status in and of itself, the proprietor personally owns and holds title to all the assets used in the operation. Thus, business and personal assets are indistinguishable from a legal viewpoint which, as we shall see later, is an important issue in the choice of legal structure. With very few exceptions, sole proprietorships are small, local enterprises. Only about 10 percent have annual receipts over $100,000. Although the sole proprietorship often takes the form of a "mom-and-pop" operation, there is no legal limit to the scope and complexity of a business organized in this manner. The distinctive characteristic of this type of operation is that it seldom generates employment opportunities for anyone beyond the immediate family of the owner.

Advantages. The primary advantage of the sole proprietorship stems from the legal nature of the organizational form. Since the proprietor personally owns all the assets, he or she has sole rights to all the profits earned by the operation.

The sole proprietor does not share management responsibility and decision-making authority with anyone else. Thus, the individual has absolute control over the operation and can make decisions promptly and without consultation with other owners or partners. Highly motivated individuals can derive a great deal of satisfaction from this sort of management situation, knowing that the success or failure of the venture rests almost exclusively on themselves.

Another important reason that the sole proprietorship is so widely used is that there are very few legal restrictions placed on the organizer. As a result, it is easy to organize and there is little or no cost involved in the process. There are no formal agreements necessary and no separate fees or taxes to pay, so almost anyone with an idea and the initiative can go into business using this organizational form. There is one minor qualification that should be made; that is, if the proprietor is going to do business under an assumed name (any name other than his or her legal name), it must be registered with the governmental body that has jurisdiction over commerce in the area of operation. Usually this means that the name of the business must be filed at the records office of the county in which the business is located. The cost of this registration is minimal.

In the same sense that the sole proprietorship is easy to organize, it is also easy to dissolve. If circumstances should arise in which the proprietor wishes to discontinue operations, the process simply involves selling assets, paying debts, and closing the doors.

Disadvantages. The greatest single disadvantage of the sole proprietorship is that the owner is individually and personally liable for the full amount of all business obligations—operating losses, physical damages, and personal injury claims. This means that in the event of a bankruptcy, the proprietor may be required to use personal assets to pay business obligations.

Limited access to capital markets is another serious disadvantage to this form of organization. Thus, the ability of the operation to expand is based almost exclusively on the firm's ability to generate funds internally and the owner's ability to contribute capital personally. In many cases, loans are treated as personal loans rather than as commercial loans. This means that it is not unusual for personal assets to be used as security for business loans. Major capital expansions are limited because of the relative difficulty of the proprietorship to attract long-term funds. Thus, the ability to attract capital is determined to a large extent by the individual proprietor's personal ability and desire to do so.

The simplicity of the management structure of the sole proprietorship can also work to the disadvantage of the operation. It is one thing to have the ability to make decisions quickly and easily; it is quite another thing to have the management expertise to make the correct decisions. Limited size and growth potential make it difficult for the sole proprietorship to attract employees with the management capability to help in this aspect of the operation.

Given the lack of expansion potential resulting from the inability to attract capital and management expertise, this organizational form does not work well in situations where significant growth is projected. Organizational structure does not guarantee growth, but it can be a limiting factor.

Finally, since the sole proprietorship has no legal status apart from the proprietor, it ceases to exist upon the death, disability, or personal bankruptcy of the owner. This lack of continuity of ownership does not have to be a major problem if a little advance planning is done. Assets can be transferred in the event of death or extreme disability. Personal bankruptcy, however, is quite another matter, with the legal aspects of the situation determining the disposition of the property.

Partnership

A **partnership** is defined in Section 6 of the Uniform Partnership Act as a voluntary "association of two or more persons to carry on as co-owners a business for profit." The major implication of this arrangement is that the partners have joint control over the business operation. That is to say, they own all the assets, they are jointly responsible for all the liabilities, and each has an equity position in the business that carries with it the right to share in the profits.

Advantages. The partnership shares many of the same advantages of the sole proprietorship. It is easy to organize and has very few legal restrictions placed on it.

Access to capital is typically better than with the sole proprietorship. In many cases the firm is organized because of this fact, with several individuals combining their resources and talents to take advantage of a market opportunity.

Disadvantages. Like the proprietorship, it is not a legal entity. Unlike the proprietorship, there is shared authority and responsibility among two or more individuals. This distinction makes some form of agreement highly desirable. The agreement may be implied, oral, or written. In the absence of a formal agreement written by the partners, the Uniform Partnership Act can serve to settle any problems or disagreements. The governing act has been adopted in forty-seven states; the only exceptions are Louisiana, Georgia, and Mississippi. The drafting of an agreement usually raises the organizational costs of a partnership above those of a proprietorship.

The typical partnership agreement, referred to as the articles of partnership, addresses the following issues:

1. The character of the partnership—general or limited.

2. The name, purpose, and location of the business to be operated by the partnership.

3. The names of the partners.

4. The amount and type of capital to be invested by each partner.

5. The duties and authorities of the various partners, including required and prohibited actions.

6. The duration of the partnership.

7. Any applicable salaries and drawing accounts of the partners.

8. The formula for dividing profits and losses.

9. The bookkeeping and accounting methods to be used and the access rights to the financial records.

10. The rights of continuance for the surviving partners in the event of death, disability, or absence of a partner.

11. The rules governing the sale of partnership shares.

12. The understanding relating to the settlement of disputes.

Although the shared authority and responsibility of the partners implies a greater level of management expertise, it also leads to the major disadvantages of this organizational form. Each individual in the partnership is jointly liable for all the obligations of the business. This can result in one partner repaying all the debts of the firm, not just a proportion based on ownership share. The partner's liability to third parties is the only aspect of the association that cannot be varied from the rules set forth by the Uniform Partnership Act.

Shared responsibility also limits a partner's ability to withdraw from the association without the consent of the other partners. This is evidenced by the fact that the sale of partnership shares is likely to be governed by the terms of the written partnership agreement.

Finally, the partnership is more vulnerable to interruptions because there are more owners involved. Since the partnership is a voluntary association, if something were to happen to one of the partners—either death, extreme disability, withdrawal, or bankruptcy—the partnership would cease to exist. This automatic dissolution does not have to be a major problem, however, because insurance can be used to protect against business interruption caused by these factors.

Corporation

The one characteristic of the **corporation** that makes it distinct from the other two organizational forms is that it is a legal entity in and of itself. The corporation is treated as a citizen of the state in which it is incorporated. It can sue and be sued, own property, commit crimes, and pay taxes. This feature is quite important because it means that individuals doing business with a corporation are dealing directly with the corporation and not its owners.

Ownership of a corporation is divided into equal parts called *shares of stock*. Shareholders ultimately establish the direction of the corporation by electing a board of directors, who in turn hire a team of professional managers. The ownership of a majority of the shares of stock of a corporation means that the individual has "control" of the company.

Advantages. By far the most significant advantage of the corporate form is the fact that the shareholders have only limited financial liability. This means, of course, that individuals with claims against the corporation must deal directly with the corporation in settling those claims. If the assets of the corporation are not sufficient to satisfy the obligations, the individual shareholders are not liable for the difference. Thus, losses to owners are limited to the value of their investment.

There are some misconceptions about the implications of this feature of corporate structure. Many entrepreneurs feel that the corporate form will completely protect them from all the risks of operating a business. In some ways, it does serve as a buffer between the business and the owner, especially in the case of most property damage and personal injury suits. Piercing the corporate veil under these circumstances can be quite difficult for the plaintiff, unless individual negligence or fraudulent behavior can be proven.

Using the corporate structure to limit financial liability is quite another matter. In theory, the shareholders of a corporation have limited financial liability. However, in practice, the owners of a closely held corporation will almost always be asked to sign a personal guarantee for all corporate indebtedness.

Although this advantage is of limited practical value to the owners of a closely held corporation, there are other features that make this form preferred in many cases. The corporate structure adds to the continuity of the operation. Since ownership shares are easily transferred among individuals, the legal status of the business is not jeopardized by the death, disability, or bankruptcy of a shareholder. Under any of these circumstances, ownership rights are simply passed on to someone else who chooses to purchase them at their fair-market price.

The corporate form offers the opportunity to attract capital more easily and in many different ways than other organizational structures. In the first place, it is typically easier to find twenty investors that will put up $10,000 each than it is to find one investor to come up with $200,000. In addition to issuing shares of stock, the corporation can sell bonds and commercial paper to generate funds. In general, corporations have much better access to the long-term capital market than either the proprietorship or the partnership.

Disadvantages. Organizing a corporation is much more complicated and costly than organizing either a sole proprietorship or a partnership. In order to attain full legal status under the governing statutes, the organizers must follow certain procedural mechanics. These steps are referred to as "incorporating a business" and, while they differ slightly from state to state, the basic outline is the same.

The first step in the incorporation process is the preparation of the "articles of incorporation." This is a legal document that serves as an application for a corporate charter. It is drafted by an attorney, signed by the incorporators, and filed with the appropriate state official. The articles include the following information:

1. The unique name of the corporation. It cannot be the same as or similar to that of any other corporation doing business within the state.

2. The duration of the corporation. Most states allow corporations to have a perpetual life. In those that place a limit on the life of a corporation, the renewal procedure is quite simple.

3. The nature and purpose of the corporation. Most states allow a business to incorporate for any legal purpose. A general purpose clause can often be used to state the intended nature of the business enterprise in more general terms.

4. The address of the principal office of the corporation. The purpose of registering an office and an agent is to ensure that the state authorities have a means of contacting the incorporators should it become necessary to do so.

5. The financial structure of the corporation. The method of capitalizing the corporation must be established and specified. This includes information on the type and number of shares of stock that are authorized, whether or not it has a par value, and a designation of the voting rights of each class of stock. In addition, details on the initial issue are required—number of shares issued and price per share. Most states require that a minimum of $1,000 be raised or 10 percent of the authorized stock be issued.

6. The names and addresses of incorporators and directors. There is wide variation in the state statutes regarding the extent to which incorporators and directors must be identified. Most require that their names and addresses be included.

After the articles of incorporation are filed and all fees are paid, the state issues a corporate charter or certificate of incorporation. The charter evidences that the state has given the incorporators permission to conduct business as a corporation.

The first requirement for the incorporators after receiving the articles of incorporation and corporate charter from the state is to hold an organizational meeting. The main purpose of this meeting is to adopt bylaws governing the internal affairs of the corporation. The bylaws may be very simple, providing details on the location and time of shareholders' meetings, voting rights, quorum requirements, and procedures for electing directors. In contrast, they may be very complicated and provide rules governing the internal management of the corporation. At the first meeting, the board of directors is required to approve all actions of the incorporators. The directors are also required to elect the officers of the corporation, establish committees, select a bank, issue stock, approve a corporate seal, and conduct any other pertinent business at this meeting.

After this process is completed, the corporation may still not be ready to conduct business. If the corporation is to be involved in interstate commerce, it must receive a "certificate of authority" to conduct transactions in each state in which it plans to do business. In most cases, it is a mere formality to receive permission to do business in another state. However, there are penalties for violating this requirement, so steps should be taken to apply for and receive this certificate.

These requirements add to the time and cost involved in organizing under this form. In addition, the separate legal status of the corporation makes it directly subject to taxation apart from its incorporators.

Basic Tax Considerations

The preceding advantages and disadvantages must be considered on an individual basis in light of the tax consequences of each situation. The subject of business taxation is an extremely complex issue that is well beyond the scope of this discussion. However, a few of the basic principles will be noted here as they apply to the different forms of business organization.

Sole proprietorships and partnerships are taxed differently than corporations. Since neither is a legal entity, the net earnings of each are treated as the personal income of the owners and taxed directly based on individual ownership shares. Income tax rates are based on the graduated rates applicable to individuals. Under the old tax system, there were fourteen individual rates ranging from 11–50 percent. Under the new tax structure that becomes fully effective in 1988, there will only be two rates, 15 and 28 percent. The 28 percent rate will be effective on that portion of taxable income over $29,750 for taxpayers filing a joint return ($17,850 for individuals). For those families with adjusted gross incomes over $71,900 ($43,150 for single individuals), there will be an additional 5 percent surcharge, resulting in an effective top marginal rate of 33 percent. For 1987, the rate structure will consist of five brackets, ranging from 11 to 38.5 percent.

The corporation is a separate entity for tax purposes. Under the old tax structure, the rates applicable to corporate earnings were 15, 18, 30, and 40 percent for each income increment of $25,000 up to $100,000 and 46 percent on all earnings over $100,000. Under the new tax system, smaller corporations that have earnings of $50,000 and below will be taxed at a rate of 15 percent. Income between $50,000 and $75,000 will be taxed at a marginal rate of 25 percent. A graduated structure is then phased in on earnings up to $335,000. The effective marginal rate over this income range is 39 percent. Finally, corporations that have incomes over $335,000 will pay a flat rate of 34 percent.

When dividend distributions are made to shareholders, they are treated as personal income and a second tax is paid based on the recipient's personal tax rate. This result is often referred to as "double taxation" of corporate income. Individuals who own closely held corporations can avoid this double taxation by using several different techniques. A large portion of the net earnings can be paid to the owners in the form of tax-deductible salaries. Care should be taken to ensure that the distributions are "reasonable," based on IRS standards. Otherwise, excess salaries will be treated as dividends and taxed a second time.

The "accumulated earnings tax," which is levied on unreasonable accumulations of income in excess of $250,000, should also be avoided. The IRS defines *unreasonable* as the idle use of earnings, such as reinvestment in high-grade securities, substantial loans to shareholders, or corporate ownership of assets that personally benefit major shareholders. Reasonable accumulations can made for specific purposes such as major facilities expansion, retirement of debt, or planned acquisitions. This provision imposes a penalty tax of either 27.5 or 38.5 percent on unreasonable accumulations. Thus, the effective rate on excess accumulations can be as high as 72.5 percent, which is well in excess of either the maximum corporate or individual rate (34 and 28 percent, respectively).

Fringe Benefit Considerations

One of the advantages of the corporate form is the superior fringe benefit package that a corporation can offer its employees. The corporation can provide a benefits package that includes group insurance plans, sick pay benefits, and health and accident insurance benefits. Not only are these benefits tax deductible to the corporation, but they are also tax-free to the employee.

There are many other examples of fringe benefits that qualify for this favorable tax treatment. Qualified employees may be available for employee discounts on store merchandise. If working conditions warrant, the use of a company car or plane for business purposes may also qualify. Travel and entertainment expenses receive the same treatment under the proper circumstances as do health club memberships, domestic travel, and sporting event tickets.

One of the most important benefits is the qualified pension and profit-sharing plan, in which employer contributions are tax-deductible and employee benefits are tax-deferred until distribution. Owners of unincorporated businesses have also been given the opportunity to establish personal retirement plans. The Keogh plan allows the self-employed individual to make pre-tax contributions of up to a maximum of $30,000 or 25 percent of earned income, whichever is smaller. Accumulated interest and dividends are allowed to grow tax-free in the fund until the individual begins withdrawals at retirement (any withdrawals prior to age 59½ are subject to severe penalties). Individual Retirement Accounts (IRAs) provide individuals with essentially the same benefits. The major difference is the maximum contribution is only $2,000 for an IRA. Contributions to an IRA are not allowed for certain moderate to high income individuals who are covered by another qualified plan. For married individuals, the $2,000 maximum contribution is phased out completely over taxable incomes of $40,000 to $50,000 ($25,000 to $35,000 for single taxpayers).

Other Organizational Forms

There are several other popular ways to organize a business that should also be considered. These forms are often utilized for financial liability and tax considerations.

Limited Partnership

A **limited partnership** is a partnership that includes one or more general partners and one or more limited partners. From a legal perspective, a general partner in a limited partnership is no different from a partner in an ordinary partnership. In contrast, a limited partner is treated as an investor, and is allowed to contribute only capital and not management expertise.

The primary obstacle in the formation of an ordinary partnership is the unlimited personal liability that each partner accepts. This aspect tends to negate one of the major advantages that this organizational form enjoys over the sole proprietorship, which is greater access to capital. The limited partnership provides an attractive organizational alternative, with the favorable tax treatment of a partnership and the limited liability of a corporation.

The most significant characteristic of a limited partnership is the limited liability of its investors. This organizational form was established to enable investors to contribute capital to an enterprise and share in the profits without sharing in financial liabilities to creditors.

The limited partnership has characteristics of both an ordinary partnership and a corporation. Like a corporation, a limited partnership exists only if it is allowed by statute. Either the Uniform Limited Partnership Act or the Uniform Revised Limited Partnership Act is recognized as the governing statute in forty-eight states.

Forming a Limited Partnership. In order to form a limited partnership, a certificate of limited partnership must be filed with the proper authorities. In those states that have adopted the Uniform Limited Partnership Act, this document is filed in the county where the partnership is formed. States in which the Revised Uniform Limited Partnership Act (RULPA) has been adopted allow centralized filing in the office of the Secretary of State. Section 201 in the RULPA outlines the major requirements of the certificate of limited partnership:

1. The name of the limited partnership. In most cases, the surname of a limited partner cannot appear in the name of the business.

2. The general character of its business.

3. The address of the office and the name and address of the authorized agent to whom legal and other official documents can be sent. Under the RULPA, a limited partnership formed in one state simply has to register with the office of the Secretary of State in other states where it wishes to do business.

4. The name and the business address of each partner (specifying separately the general partners and the limited partners).

5. The amount of cash and a description and statement of the agreed upon value of the other property or services that have been or will be contributed by each partner.

6. The timing of any future contributions agreed to be made by each partner.

7. The conditions under which a limited partner has the right to assign any part of his financial interest to another individual.

8. The agreed upon terms and conditions pertaining to a limited partner's rights to withdraw from the partnership.

9. The rights of any partner to receive cash or property distributions.

10. The rights of a limited partner to have all or part of his investment returned in the event of his withdrawal from the partnership.

11. The timing and events leading to the dissolution of the limited partnership.

12. The rights of a general partner to continue the business in the event of the withdrawal of a general partner.

13. Any other matters the partners wish to include.

Financing a Limited Partnership. A limited partnership provides better access to capital than an ordinary partnership. Since investors are protected from general financial and legal liability, they are more likely to participate in a limited partnership. Also, unlike the investor in an ordinary partnership, the limited partner can have no active management responsibility. Thus, there is no practical limitation to the number of limited partners that can participate in the venture. Under the RULPA, capital contributions can take the form of cash, property, or services performed.

Partnership Responsibilities. General partners have basically the same rights and responsibilities as partners in an ordinary partnership. They manage the operation and have the authority to make all business decisions. In return, they can share in the profits, but they must accept full financial and legal liability for all business obligations.

Limited partners have no such rights and responsibilities. As investors, they cannot actively engage in the management of the business. Failure to comply with this requirement can mean the loss of limited partnership status. Limited partners have the right to a complete financial disclosure from the general partners, including the right to inspect any records that pertain to the investment.

Other Considerations. The sale of shares in a limited partnership is considered a sale of securities and must comply with state and federal regulations concerning such an offering. As with any other securities transaction, it can be organized as either a public offering or a private placement. If it is a public offering, the issue must be registered with both the Securities and Exchange Commission and the states in which the shares will be sold. A private placement exemption can be attained if no public advertising and soliciting is made and less than thirty-five investors are involved in the venture.

Another attraction of the limited partnership form is the favorable tax treatment it receives. As in an ordinary partnership, profits and losses bypass the legal business entity and are taxed directly to the individual partners. This works especially well in situations in which significant tax credits are involved or book losses are made because of allowances for depletion, depreciation, and amortization. These credits and losses are passed on to the individual partners who can use them to directly offset passive income earned in other pursuits.

Another advantage of the limited partnership form is its ability to generate profits quickly. This is primarily caused by a significantly reduced debt burden. As a result of the lower debt ratio, the business can operate profitably at utilization rates well below industry averages. This lower fixed cost burden is translated into a lower breakeven point for sales and an enhanced ability to access traditional debt sources such as commercial banks.

Subchapter S Corporation

In 1958, Congress enacted legislation to establish the Subchapter S corporation. This organizational form was set up to eliminate some of the tax disadvantages of the corporate form—double taxation of dividends and the tax treatment of losses. The Subchapter S designation allows a corporation that fulfills certain requirements and has filed for special treatment to be taxed as a partnership. In other words, the Subchapter S corporation is not a taxable entity as far as the Internal Revenue Service is concerned. Each shareholder pays income taxes based on his pro rata share of the corporation's earnings.

To qualify for Subchapter S treatment the following conditions must be met:

1. The corporation must be incorporated in the United States and be independent with no subsidiaries or affiliates.
2. There must be thirty-five or fewer shareholders.
3. There must be only one class of stock.
4. Shareholders must be individuals (U.S. citizens or resident aliens), estates of deceased persons, or certain types of trusts. Another corporation or partnership cannot be a shareholder.

Individuals forming a Subchapter S corporation enjoy the limited liability of corporate shareholders and the income tax treatment of owners of unincorporated businesses.

Section 1244 Stock

Federal tax law requires that losses on stock by sale, liquidation, or worthlessness be treated as long-term capital losses for income tax purposes. The major implications of this treatment are:

1. The losses can be used only to offset capital gains.
2. The losses can be used to offset ordinary income of only $3,000 per year.

If the business is a sole proprietorship or partnership, all operating losses can be deducted from the individual owners' income tax liabilities. Losses resulting from the sale of business assets can be deducted from ordinary income. In contrast, a corporation has the $3,000 maximum write-off against ordinary income; any excess can be carried back three years and forward five years to offset any capital gain. The excess is automatically treated as a short-term loss.

Section 1244 was added to the Internal Revenue Code in 1958 to encourage the flow of equity into small business. This revision allows the original investors of a corporation organized under Section 1244 to treat losses on either the disposition or worthlessness of stock as ordinary losses rather than capital losses. The following conditions must be met to qualify:

1. Shareholders must be individuals.
2. Shareholders must be original investors. If stock is sold, it reverts to regular treatment as a capital asset.
3. The stock must be common stock, issued for cash or property (shares issued for services rendered are ineligible).
4. No part of a prior issue can be outstanding at the time of the issue under Section 1244.
5. There must be no preferences or convertible features.
6. The corporation must qualify as a "small business corporation" and issue the stock under an acceptable plan. The plan must be in writing, specifying the number of shares to be issued. A maximum of $1 million can be raised for a corporation that derives at least one-half of its gross receipts from an active trade or business.
7. The amount of the ordinary loss deducted in any one tax year cannot exceed $50,000 per taxpayer.

The majority of closely held corporations should consider issuing stock under Section 1244. Considering the high incidence of failure in the first several years of a business's existence, this exception provides a good opportunity to take advantage of a favorable tax treatment in the event of a failure. Under all circumstances, however, an attorney should be consulted before a final decision is made.

The Franchising Alternative

A **franchise** is a situation in which the owner of a product, service, or concept, known as the "franchisor," contracts with an independent entrepreneur, known as the "franchisee," to sell or distribute the owner's product or service at a specific location. As a result, the franchisee is not directly involved in determining such items as promotion and advertising, trademarks, design of the facilities, sources of supply, and many of the other aspects of the operation that concern the independent entrepreneur. It is not that the franchisee is unconcerned about these details; the responsibility of setting up the business falls solely on the franchisor.

Although franchising is not a business organizational form in the traditional sense of the term, it is an alternative way of getting into business. In fact, franchising is nothing more than a distribution and marketing relationship between the franchisor and the franchisee. In this context, it is clear that the most successful franchise opportunities are those in which the franchisor has excellent advertising and marketing capabilities and a commitment to helping the franchisee develop the local market.

Franchising provides a means of allowing individuals to step directly into a business operation without all the usual problems associated with starting an independent operation. The individual franchisee's success is a function of finding the right franchise partner. In turn, the successful franchisor is faced with the same dilemma of finding suitable franchisees to build a strong organization.

There are basically two types of franchises available in the market today. Even though both are defined as franchises, each functions quite differently. The most familiar type of franchise is one in which the franchisor offers a complete system of doing business—including a name, an established image, and a standardized method of operations. Examples of this type of franchise include fast food restaurants, real estate agencies, housekeeping services, hotels, and health spas. A second type of franchise is one in which a manufacturer uses a franchise to distribute its products. This dealership arrangement is a very popular way for automobile manufacturers to market their products.

A *dealership* may or may not be considered a franchise. The two things to look for are exclusive selling rights within a specifically defined territory and ongoing advice in various functional areas such as accounting, personnel, quality control, purchasing, and advertising. In some situations, the dealer only has to meet certain minimum standards of operation; he can use the manufacturer's name in the business; and he does not pay royalty fees. Without a guarantee of territorial integrity, the manufacturer is free to set up another dealership in the same area or even next door. In these situations, the manufacturer does not pretend to be a franchise. The only ongoing interest that the manufacturer has in the arrangement is that of resupplying its dealers.

Another situation that appears to be a franchise on the surface but is not is the *pyramid business*. Originators of the operation place themselves at the top of the pyramid and spend most of their time selling dealerships. In turn, new dealers sell both products and more dealerships. Since each dealer receives a percentage of the business that is generated by the dealers below him on the pyramid, more time is spent selling dealerships and less time is spent selling products.

Franchising has become a very popular way for the owner of a successful business concept to expand into regional or national markets. There are currently over 1,500 companies offering franchises in the United States. Over 4 million workers are employed by the 500,000 individual franchisees, generating over one-third of the total retail sales in the country. (See Table 8–3.)

Owning a franchise is not the same thing as owning an independent business. Successful franchisors require standardized products/services and a uniform way of operating the business. This offers them more control of the overall operation and lends itself more readily to national advertising and referrals.

Owning a franchise is not a guarantee of success. It is important that an investigation for the right opportunity be carried out in a careful and systematic manner. Remember that entering into a franchise agreement is like taking on a business partner who has a significant amount of authority in determining the way the business is operated. Franchises should be evaluated according to the following criteria:

1. Profitability.
2. Future prospects.
3. Products and services.
4. Training programs.
5. Continuing assistance.
6. Historical track record.
7. Nature of the franchise arrangement.

There are several excellent sources of information available for individuals interested in learning either more about franchising in general or certain franchises in particular. The Small Business Administration publishes a checklist to guide individuals in their investigation of franchise opportunities. The Department of Commerce publishes the *Franchise Opportunities Handbook*, which is an excellent place to begin an investigation. The handbook contains basic information on all franchises available in the United States. Periodicals such as *Money* magazine and the *Wall Street Journal* regularly list current information on franchise opportunities.

Other sources include conventions and trade shows organized by national franchise organizations such as the International Franchise Association (IFA) and the National Franchise Coalition (NFC). The IFA established standards of ethical franchise operation and publishes a guide to franchises and

Table 8–3
Franchising in the U.S. Economy, by Type of Business

	1975	1985
Total Establishments		
Number (000)	434.5	481.2
Sales (billions)	$190.9	$529.3
Auto and Truck Dealers[1]		
Number (000)	31.8	27.0
Sales (billions)	$ 94.5	$257.6
Restaurants (all types)		
Number (000)	43.0	78.7
Sales (billions)	$ 12.3	$ 48.9
Gasoline Service Stations[1]		
Number (000)	189.5	130.0
Sales (billions)	$ 47.4	$111.3
Retailing (nonfood)		
Number (000)	37.2	44.8
Sales (billions)	$ 9.0	$ 18.8
Auto, Truck Rental Services		
Number (000)	6.5	12.2
Sales (billions)	$ 1.5	$ 5.3
Automotive Products & Services[2]		
Number (000)	47.5	38.0
Sales (billions)	$ 5.0	$ 10.6
Business Aids and Services		
Number (000)	22.2	57.3
Sales (billions)	$ 1.4	$ 12.1
Construction, Home Improvement, Maintenance & Cleaning		
Number (000)	10.8	21.5
Sales (billions)	$ 0.6	$ 3.7
Convenience Stores		
Number (000)	13.5	16.0
Sales (billions)	$ 3.9	$ 12.3
Education Products & Services		
Number (000)	1.3	8.0
Sales (billions)	$ 0.2	$ 0.8
Equipment Rental		
Number (000)	1.4	2.7
Sales (billions)	$ 0.2	$ 0.7
Food Retailing[3]		
Number (000)	11.8	19.2
Sales (billions)	$ 1.4	$ 10.4
Hotels and Motels[4]		
Number (000)	6.4	7.7
Sales (billions)	$ 4.6	$ 14.6
Laundry & Dry Cleaning Services		
Number (000)	3.2	3.3
Sales (billions)	$ 0.2	$ 0.3

Table 8–3 continued

	1975	1985
Recreation, Entertainment & Travel		
Number (000)	3.4	7.7
Sales (billions)	$ 0.2	$ 1.8
Soft Drink Bottlers[1,5]		
Number (000)	2.4	1.5
Sales (billions)	$ 8.2	$ 19.1
Miscellaneous		
Number (000)	2.7	5.7
Sales (billions)	$ 0.4	$ 0.9

Source: *Statistical Abstracts of the United States,* 106th edition, U.S. Department of Commerce, Bureau of Census, 1986, Tables No. 1398 and 1399.

1. Estimated by the International Trade Administration using Bureau of Census and ITA data.

2. Includes some establishments with significant sales of nonautomotive products such as household appliances and garden supplies.

3. Excludes convenience stores.

4. Includes campgrounds.

5. Includes soft drinks, fruit drinks and ades, syrups, flavoring agents, and bases. Excludes independent private label and contract-filler bottling companies, which accounted for 22 percent of the value of shipments of the total industry in recent years.

the NFC is a support organization for franchisees. Both organizations have a great deal of information available on franchise operations.

The prospective franchisee can obtain more detailed information on the company's operations through offering circulars and disclosure information. The Federal Trade Commission (FTC) has a requirement that franchisors provide all prospective franchisees with disclosure information, including details on the franchisor's business experience and financial position. The FTC does not guarantee the accuracy of this information. Verification is the responsibility of the prospective franchisee.

One major advantage of owning a franchise is the fact that the franchisor typically provides information on virtually all financial aspects of the operation, from franchise fees and royalties to projected revenues and expenses. The established franchisor is not only a good source of information, but also serves as a good bank reference for the franchisee seeking a loan.

Purchasing a franchise typically involves direct payments to the franchisor in addition to the other out-of-pocket expenses involved in any business venture. These payments include:

1. *A franchise fee.* This is a fixed, lump-sum charge for the rights to use the name, trademarks, and business operating procedure of the franchisor.

Franchising: A Strategy for Growth

A popular strategy used by many small companies to finance growth in the expansion stage of the business life cycle is franchising. The prospective franchisor can reap numerous benefits through a well-organized franchise program. One obvious benefit is the money generated through franchise fees and royalty payments. These payments, however, are not the only advantage. The introduction of an extensive distribution network operated by a motivated group of owner/managers establishes a potential for significant growth.

Franchising an idea is no guarantee of success. It is a time-consuming and expensive process. The minimum capital requirement to pay legal fees and finance the initial marketing effort is $250,000. Government regulations are burdensome. The Federal Trade Commission requires that franchisors provide an offering circular with a financial history of the franchisor to each prospective franchisee. The cost of preparing the offering circular and franchise agreement alone can run as high as $80,000.

Coming up with the necessary capital is only the beginning of the challenge. Perhaps the most important aspect of the program is identifying qualified individuals who have the expertise and capital and are interested in becoming franchisees. With the number of franchise opportunities available in the market today, the search for top-notch franchisees can be quite expensive.

In order to successfully introduce a franchise into today's market, several prerequisites are essential. The most important ingredient is an extensive support system for franchisees, including a formal training program, an integrated promotional effort, and a computer-based information system.

The franchisor must enter the market with a proven concept and no major operational problems. A solid financial and managerial resource base is also essential. The final consideration is profitability. The opportunity must provide an acceptable return on invested capital to both franchisor and franchisee. A franchising plan that has franchise fees as its primary revenue source is doomed to failure. Royalty payments based on franchisee sales should be the primary revenue source. Ultimately, the success of a franchise program is based on the success of the individual franchise operations.

Franchising offers a proven way of rapidly expanding into a market. With the right concept and the proper support in a controlled environment, it can be a sensible alternative to the traditional way of expanding an enterprise.

---

2. *Other franchise charges.* In an effort to standardize all franchise operations, franchisors require that certain inventories, supplies, construction materials, and architectural designs be used. These may be more elaborate and expensive than those that would be chosen by the independent entrepreneur.

3. *Services.* Franchises differ considerably with respect to the services that are offered to franchisees. These services include initial assistance such as site selection, employee selection, and training. Most established franchises also offer continuing assistance in the areas of accounting, advertising, and research and development.

4. *Equipment, furniture, and fixtures.* In order to present a consistent image, the franchisee will have a very narrow range of choices in furnishing the facilities. The franchisor will decide how much flexibility the franchisee has in making these decisions.

5. *Franchise royalties.* The franchisee will make periodic royalty payments based on a percentage of gross sales. The size of these payments usually depends on the nature of the continuing assistance offered by the franchisor.

It is interesting to note one important fact about the franchisor's revenues. Most good franchisors derive the majority of their revenues from royalty fees. This means that their success depends on the success of their operating franchisees. Franchisors who generate the bulk of their revenues from franchise fees are basing their success on selling additional franchises, and not building successful franchisees.

As stated earlier, owning an established franchise is no guarantee of success. However, with the higher risks of independent startup, the prospect of a proven business format, field support, computer systems, and training programs often makes a lot of sense. In addition, borrowing money to purchase an established franchise may be easier than borrowing money for an independent startup. The franchisee is automatically equipped with the records and operating histories of all the existing franchise locations. The banker does not have to rely solely on the capabilities of the entrepreneur because he has the operating histories of the entire franchise organization as a means of verifying data.

Franchising may not be suitable for everyone, but it is a proven way to get into business and shows great promise in a wide variety of venture opportunities. Whether the individual franchisee organizes as a sole proprietorship, a partnership, or a corporation will depend on the goals and objectives of the entrepreneur in the particular situation.

Summary and Conclusions

The choice of organizational structure plays a crucial role in a firm's ability to attract and retain capital. It is more than a matter of taxation, however, and should be given careful consideration by the owners of small firms. In the small firm environment, the choice of organizational form is not clear and should not be taken lightly.

The characteristics of the three major organizational forms were presented in this chapter. Although there is technically no legal limit to the scope and complexity of a business organized as a sole proprietorship, most growth-oriented entrepreneurial ventures will be organized as corporations to increase their ability to attract capital.

After examining the advantages and disadvantages of the sole proprietorship, the partnership, and the corporation, we discussed basic tax and fringe benefit considerations. In addition, other organizational forms were considered for their specific tax and financial liability implications. The limited partnership and the Subchapter S corporation are popular organizational forms used to take advantage of the tax benefits of a partnership and the liability protection of a corporation. Formation of a corporation under Section 1244 of the Internal Revenue Code can provide special tax advantages to firms in the early stages of the business life cycle.

The franchising arrangement that has become an extremely popular way of organizing a business concept was also discussed. Although a franchise is not an organizational form in the traditional sense of the term, when closely examined, it can be viewed as a partnership without joint financial and legal liability. Thus, an individual considering the purchase of a franchise should carefully analyze the franchise opportunity and understand the terms of the franchise agreement before entering into a contract.

Part III
Sources of Capital

9
Capital Procurement

A systematic examination of the financing alternatives available to entrepreneurial ventures must be done within an acceptable analytical framework. The primary emphasis of the next four chapters will be the careful analysis of the capital sources available to the typical entrepreneurial venture.

The traditional approach to this subject identifies sources by the length of time the capital remains with the firm before it is returned to its source. This technique is well-documented in the financial literature. Most introductory corporate finance textbooks are organized in this manner, having sections on short-, intermediate-, and long-term financial management. Today's financial managers have been trained to use these well-established techniques; generally accepted accounting practices identify assets and liabilities in this manner.

However, this approach to the study of financial management and capital procurement has one serious drawback. It is difficult to make clear distinctions among the various categories of capital. For example, the distinction between the intermediate term and the long term is not at all clear. The definitions are arbitrary and have evolved out of convenience rather than function. This lack of clarity makes it difficult to clearly distinguish among the various funding sources.

In order to overcome this major disadvantage, the material in the next few chapters will be organized according to whether the capital source is primarily a debt or an equity source. Before embarking on that discussion, however, we will examine briefly the traditional approach to capital procurement—the short-term versus long-term capital decision. In addition, we will make some observations about the relationship between the stages of the business life cycle and capital source alternatives.

The Traditional Approach to Capital Procurement

Within the traditional analytical framework of capital budgeting, acquisition and financing decisions are made with an attempt to match the term structure of the financing with the economic life of the asset. The uncertainty with respect to the actual useful life of the asset makes it virtually impossible to exactly match the maturity structure of a firm's assets and liabilities. This approach gives rise to a fairly strict distinction in the financial literature between short-term operating decisions, or working capital management, and long-term strategic decision making.

Working Capital Management

The term **working capital management** refers to administration and control of current assets and current liabilities. A complete discussion of the concept would include an examination of all current assets—cash and securities management and accounts receivable and inventory control. However, our approach will focus on how the firm finances its current assets through the use of short-term credit.

There is a tendency for small firms to rely more heavily than larger firms on the use of short-term credit. The primary reason for this tendency is that most small firms are effectively shut out of the long-term capital market. Because of the high-risk perception of the small, and in many cases undercapitalized, firm, most long-term sources have found investments in this area inappropriate. As a result, the small firm has had to rely on suppliers and the commercial banking industry as its two main sources of externally generated operating capital.

Small firms' greater reliance on short-term financing can be seen in Table 9–1. In 1975, firms with assets of less than $500,000 had short-term notes payable and trade credit amounting to 30.5 percent of total assets. In contrast to this, all firms had only 20.1 percent of their total assets in this form. Indeed, in almost every industry, the smaller firms show a heavier reliance on short-term debt than the larger firms.

Trade Credit. The primary categories of short-term credit are trade credit from suppliers and short-term loans from commercial banks. Even though trade credit is not associated with any type of financial institution, it is a significant source of financing for closely held businesses. Within the manufacturing industries listed in Table 9–1, approximately 68.5 percent of the small firms' current liabilities are in the form of trade credit, while only 50.9 percent of all firms' current liabilities take that form.

Table 9–1
Short-Term Financing in
Non-Financial Corporations and Manufacturing Firms
(percentage of total assets)

	All Firms	Small Firms
Non-Financial Corporations		
Accounts and Notes Payable	20.1%	30.5%
Manufacturing Firms		
Short-Term Loans	3.3%	7.5%
Trade Payables	8.5	16.0
Total	11.8%	23.5%
Total Current Liabilities	23.2%	34.3%

Source: Victor L. Andrews and Peter C. Eisemann, "Who Finances Small Business Circa 1980?" *Economic Review,* Federal Reserve Bank of Atlanta, August 1981.

Characteristics of Trade Credit. There are several important differences that distinguish credit and other types of short-term debt. The most important characteristic of trade credit is that, in most cases, it is granted on a relatively informal basis. There are usually no formal agreements negotiated and signed. Typically, the only evidence of the extension of credit is a bookkeeping entry in the accounts receivable ledger of the supplier. This is in sharp contrast to the noımally extensive closing documents that evidence the lending of capital at a commercial bank.

Trade credit is often referred to as a "spontaneous" source of financing. Since trade credit is normally used to finance the purchase of inventories and purchases expand as sales expand, the use of trade credit naturally expands as sales volume expands. In addition, a lengthening of the credit period also spontaneously generates additional financing.

Cost of Trade Credit. The use of trade credit is by no means costless. There is evidence that product prices are higher in an environment in which credit is used extensively. In addition, the practice of offering discounts for cash purchases is used regularly. Unless a discount is offered as part of the terms of the credit purchase, however, there is no direct way to compute the cost of trade credit. A supplier who sells on credit will have a credit policy that typically includes certain terms. For example, these terms might be listed as 2/10, net 30, meaning that a 2 percent discount is given if the invoice is paid in full within ten days of the invoice date. If the discount is not taken, the full amount is due and payable in thirty days. Under these circumstances, the cost of not taking the discount can be determined by the discount percentage and the length of time between the end of the discount period and the final due date of the invoice.

Suppose a firm were to buy $10,000 of inventory on terms of 2/10, net 30. If the invoice is paid in full within ten days of the invoice date, a 2 percent discount (or $200) is taken. Failure to pay within the discount period will mean that the full $10,000 must be paid by day thirty. The net effect is to pay $200 for the use of $10,000 for twenty days. Translated into an annual interest rate, the cost of not taking the discount is over 37 percent. If the firm has funds available to it from other sources for less than 37 percent, it would be wise to use those funds to take advantage of the discount opportunity. The formula used to calculate the approximate annual cost of not taking a discount is:

$$\text{Cost} = \frac{\text{Discount percent}}{100 - \text{Discount percent}} \cdot \frac{365}{\text{Due date} - \text{Discount period}}$$

(This formula gives the cost in terms of simple interest, where interest is compounded annually. In the case of continuous compounding, the cost will be substantially higher.) To illustrate the calculation, suppose the credit terms available to a firm were 1/10, net 30. The calculation would be:

$$\text{Cost} = [1/(100 - 1)] \cdot [365/(30 - 10)] = .01 \cdot 18.25 = 18.25\%$$

A smart money manager will take advantage of trade credit whenever it is available, providing the terms are reasonable. Trade credit is an important source of spontaneous financing, but it can be costly. Wise use will mean that payments are made on the last day of the discount period or on the final due date in order to take advantage of the full benefits of the extension of funds. Such use can play an important role in helping the money manager to synchronize cash outflows with cash inflows.

Short-Term Loans. Short-term loans represent the second most important source of short-term credit available to business firms (the commercial banking system has traditionally been the major source). This type of lending is also important to the banking system itself. Loans to businesses constitute approximately two-thirds of the total bank investment outstanding at any given time.

Characteristics of Short-Term Debt. The major difference between short-term debt and trade credit is that debt is a "nonspontaneous" source of financing. As a need for additional financing arises because of an expansion of the business operation, debt does not increase automatically. Each time financing is required, the short-term credit source must be approached and a formal request for funds must be made. Thus, there tends to be much more discretion on the part of the lender as to whether funds are made available.

Short-term loans by definition have listed maturities of less than one year. A common practice in short-term lending is to extend a loan for a period of time such as ninety days. Interest payments are then made at the end of each month and a specified principal reduction is made at maturity. Assuming the loan is handled according to the agreed-upon terms and the condition of the business remains satisfactory, the loan is typically renewed for another ninety-day period. This practice shifts the interest rate risk of long-term lending from the lender to the borrower.

Short-term loans are always evidenced by the signing of a promissory note. This note specifies the amount of the loan, the interest rate to be charged, the terms of repayment, and the collateral offered as security. Often there are other conditions to which the borrower must agree in order to get the loan. These include maintaining certain levels for key financial ratios, refraining from additional borrowing without lender permission, and maintaining compensating checking account balances of 10 to 20 percent of the outstanding principal balance of the loan.

In many cases, lenders use a line of credit as a means of short-term lending. The lender agrees to make a maximum amount of capital available to a borrower for a specified time period (usually one year). The borrower is able to make draws on the credit line up to the specified maximum before any of the principal is repaid.

Cost of Short-Term Debt. The cost of short-term debt varies depending on both the general economic conditions in the loanable funds market and the creditworthiness of the borrower. Most loans to closely held businesses are pegged to the prime lending rate (lending rates are quoted at prime plus points). Interest rates on short-term loans are usually calculated either as "simple" interest, "discount" interest, or "add-on" interest.

Simple Interest. This method is the simplest and probably the least used way to calculate interest costs. If you were to borrow $10,000 at 15 percent simple interest for one year, the lending institution would credit your account for $10,000 and in one year you would repay $11,500 (principal plus $1,500 interest cost). For loan terms of less than one year, the interest charge can be calculated by reducing the interest rate from an annual rate to a daily rate. The following formula will apply in any case:

$$\text{Interest cost} = \frac{\text{Annual interest rate}}{365} \cdot \text{Loan period in days} \cdot \text{Loan principal}$$

If the preceding loan had been for ninety days instead of one year, the interest cost would be calculated as follows:

$$\text{Interest cost} = (.15/365)(90)(\$10,000)$$
$$= (.000411)(90)(\$10,000)$$
$$= \$369.86.$$

Discount Interest. Under this method, the lender deducts the interest charge in advance. When a loan is discounted in this manner, the effective rate of interest is somewhat higher than the stated rate. Using the preceding example, the discount on a $10,000 loan at 15 percent will be $1,500. Thus, the borrower will have use of only $8,500 during the loan period and must repay the full $10,000 at maturity. The effective interest rate can be calculated as follows:

$$\text{Interest rate} = \frac{\text{Stated rate}}{100 - \text{Stated rate}}$$

In this case, the effective interest rate will be 17.65 percent [15/(100 − 15)].

Add-On Interest. Many small business loans are handled in the same fashion as consumer installment loans. The $10,000 loan is made and the interest cost is added on to the loan principal to determine the final face value of the note to be repaid. At 15 percent add-on interest, the note to be repaid would be $11,500. Assuming the funds are borrowed for one year, the monthly installment payments will be $958.33 ($11,500/12). Since the borrower only has full use of the $10,000 in the first month, the effective interest rate is substantially higher than 15 percent. In fact, the borrower has the use of approximately $5,000 on average during the course of the term of the loan. The effective interest rate can be approximated as follows:

$$\text{Interest rate} = \frac{2 \cdot \text{Payments/year} \cdot \text{Interest cost}}{\text{Loan principal} \cdot (\text{Total payments} + 1)}$$

In the preceding case, the effective interest rate is approximately 27.7 percent {(2 · 12 · 1,500)/[10,000 · (12 + 1)]}. With the passage of the Truth-In-Lending legislation in 1979, the use of this type of interest calculation has decreased substantially.

Effect of Compensating Balances on Interest Rates. Minimum balance requirements that are a stated part of the terms of a loan will add to the cost of borrowing only if the balances are larger than the firm would otherwise keep on deposit. If the minimum balance is larger than the borrower would normally maintain, the effect is to reduce the amount of the loan available for use and raise the effective interest on the borrowed funds. The following formula can be used to calculate the effective interest rate when compensating balances force the borrower to maintain larger balances:

$$\text{Interest rate} = \frac{\text{Interest cost}}{\text{Loan funds available}}$$

If the borrower normally keeps a minimum balance of $2,000 and the loan terms call for a $4,000 minimum, then only $8,000 of the borrowed funds are actually available for use. The simple interest of 15 percent is effectively 18.75 percent.

Long-Term Financing

Trade credit and short-term debt are used primarily to finance current assets, but longer-term funds are sought to finance investments in plant and equipment and other fixed assets. Intermediate- and long-term funds are available in the form of either equity or debt. Funds secured through the sale of stock or retained earnings are permanently available to the company, but borrowed funds must be repaid over a specified period of time.

Owners' Equity. Virtually every business enterprise has at least a portion of its financing from equity sources. The term **equity** refers to the investment of the owners of a company. The investment can take the form of either common or preferred equity. Common stock, whose equivalent for the unincorporated business firm is proprietorship or partnership equity, represents the ownership interest in the assets of the firm. As a common equity investor in a firm, the shareholder/owner is treated as a residual claimant. This status carries with it two major implications: 1) only after all expenses and interest obligations have been paid does the equity owner share in the earnings of the business, and 2) in the event of liquidation, it is only after all prior claims have been paid that the owner has any claim on the remaining assets.

The preferred equity holder has an interest in the business that is similar in some ways to that of the common equity holder and in other ways to the holder of bonds. Preferred stock increases the net worth of the firm. However, dividends on preferred stock represent a fixed charge to the firm and are not considered a deductible expense for the purpose of income tax calculations. Preferred equity holders are paid dividends before common equity holders. If the firm is unable to pay preferred dividends, they simply accumulate for payment at a later date before common dividends can be paid. In the event of liquidation of the company, the interests of preferred shareholders are subordinated to those of bondholders, but precede those of the owners of common stock.

Cost of Equity. A phrase often quoted when the funding of public sector projects is being discussed is: "There is no such thing as a free lunch." This statement is equally true when the funding of private projects is at issue. It is obvious that borrowed capital is available only at a price. What may not be so obvious is that capital from equity sources is not costless either. Although the cost of equity is not explicitly accounted for in a firm's financial statements, it is implicit in the opportunity cost of the equity funds themselves. **Opportunity cost** in this case can be defined as the earnings foregone by not using the funds in their best alternative use. There are three major components of equity capital to evaluate: 1) common stock, 2) preferred stock, and 3) retained earnings.

Common Stock. The cost of a common stock is more than just the cost of underwriting the new issue. The generally accepted method of calculating the cost of externally generated common equity is:

Cost of External Equity =
$$\frac{\text{Expected dividends paid/share}}{\text{Net price received/share}} + \text{Growth rate in earnings}$$

As is evident in the formula, estimating the cost of a new common stock issue is an inexact science. However, if the firm has experienced a relatively stable earnings and dividend pattern over the past few years, the calculation is rather straightforward. The results of this calculation can be interpreted as the percent earnings on the investment that must be generated to maintain the earnings, dividend yields, and growth to keep stock values at their projected levels. If no dividends are paid, this return is approximately equal to the growth rate in earnings.

Preferred Stock. The cost of preferred stock is calculated by relating the annual preferred dividend requirement to the net amount the issuer will receive:

$$\text{Cost of Preferred Stock} = \frac{\text{Preferred dividend/share}}{\text{Net price received/share}}$$

The calculation assumes that there is no requirement to retire the stock over time. In addition, there is no adjustment for tax obligations because dividend payments are not fixed expenses in the same sense as bond indebtedness and are therefore not a tax-deductible expense.

Retained Earnings. Current earnings that are retained and reinvested in the business have an implicit cost of capital assigned to them based on the principle of opportunity cost. From the owners' perspective, retained earnings should generate at minimum the same return that could have been earned in the best alternative investment opportunity.

Estimating the component cost of equity capital is a task that requires both a careful analysis and some subjective judgments on the part of the analyst. There are several approaches that have been used for this purpose in varying circumstances.

If all the underlying assumptions are satisfied, the Capital Asset Pricing Model (CAPM) can be used to estimate the implicit cost of equity. However, for many privately held businesses, the firm's ownership is not diversified enough and, as a result, the stock is not traded often enough to accurately estimate a stock's beta coefficient for use as an index of the riskiness of the stock. If a company's growth has been relatively stable, the required return on common stock can be calculated in much the same fashion as is the cost of external equity. Nonconstant growth rates into the future will require additional calculations to take this into consideration.

The subjective nature of the preceding calculations for the type of business being considered warrants that the method suggested for determining the cost of equity be simple and straightforward. Adding a two to four point risk premium to the interest rate on the firm's debt with the longest maturity is for all practical purposes as accurate as the more sophisticated techniques. The underlying premise is that a firm's equity is riskier and has a higher cost associated with it than its debt. Even though the risk premium is nothing but a judgment call, with proper analysis this method can be just as accurate as the more complicated approaches and infinitely more simple to estimate.

Intermediate- and Long-Term Debt. In a closely held business, most financing arrangements are made through direct negotiations with a lender for an intermediate term (something less than ten years). Loans of this type are often referred to as *term* loans. The distinctive feature of a term loan is that it is amortized—regular installments of principal and interest are made over the term of the loan. Loans of this type are usually made to purchase specific fixed assets. In this case, the loan term is matched with the economic life of the asset, which is pledged as collateral, and repayment is made from the cash flow generated by its use.

Cost of Debt. The cost of debt can be estimated by adjusting the firm's borrowing rate downward to reflect the fact that interest cost is a tax-deductible expense. This adjustment is made according to the following formula:

Cost of Debt = Interest rate on debt · (1 − firm's marginal tax rate)

Note that the interest rate on debt is the cost of new debt and not the cost of existing debt. Only marginal costs are relevant for economic decision making. Historical rates on debt are irrelevant in this context.

The Leasing Alternative. The main purpose of obtaining a term loan is to acquire the services of a fixed asset. Since machinery and equipment are not usually owned with the intention of reselling them for a profit, there may be no reason to actually hold title to the asset. Thus, leasing can be considered as a viable alternative to owning an asset. In fact, leasing can be viewed as a type of debt in which a fixed obligation to a creditor (the lessor) is incurred that must be met or the services of the asset will be lost.

There are several different types of leases available in the market today. Typically, leases are either arranged under a sale and leaseback agreement or as an operating lease. The common characteristic shared by these forms of lease agreements is that they are considered to be "off balance sheet" financing. This designation is appropriate because, under certain circumstances, neither the leased asset nor the lease obligation shows up on the firm's balance sheet, except possibly in a footnote or disclosure statement.

A firm entering into a financial (or capital) lease, on the other hand, must "capitalize the lease"; it must restate the firm's balance sheet to reflect the impact of the obligation on its financial position by reporting the leased asset under fixed assets and the present value of the future lease payments under current and long-term liabilities. Under the designation issued by the Financial Accounting Standard Board in FASB No. 13 (1976), a lease is classified as a capital lease when ownership of the property has been transferred from lessor to lessee because of noncancelable lease terms and at least one of the following conditions is true:

1. The lease transfers ownership of the property to the lessee.
2. Actual title to the asset can be obtained by the lessee at the conclusion of the agreement by purchasing the asset at less than expected fair market value at the option date.
3. The terms of the lease extend for a time period equal to at least 75 percent of the asset's useful economic life.
4. The present value of the future lease payments, discounted at a rate equal to the interest rate the lessee would have to pay on a new debt of similar maturity, is equal to at least 90 percent of the current asset value minus all applicable investment tax credits.

Leasing is frequently more expensive than long-term borrowing. However, there are certain advantages to leasing rather than buying an asset. In certain situations, leasing provides more financial leverage than the use of straight debt and it is a convenient way to finance assets in a piecemeal fashion. In today's financial market, leasing is frequently used for the purpose of transferring the tax credit for the investment to the lessor, who is in a higher marginal tax bracket; this increases the overall benefits of the arrangement to both parties.

Financial Planning and the Stages of the Business Life Cycle

Lenders and investors have similar goals in mind when they evaluate a business. Lenders are concerned with the ability of the firm to generate a sufficient cash flow to repay the debt obligation. Equity investors are interested in either the prospective rate of return on their investment or the capital gain that can be expected through the eventual sale of their ownership interest.

Even though the logic behind financing the closely held business is simple, it is often difficult for the entrepreneur to understand and accept the decisions that are made by potential lenders and investors. The source of frustration usually centers on misunderstandings about the financing process itself. The way to minimize this frustration is to enter into the negotiations with a well-conceived plan. This enables the entrepreneur to avoid the most common pitfalls of financing that lead to unnecessary delays in the process. These pitfalls include seeking the wrong kinds of funding, asking for inappropriate amounts, and approaching the wrong sources.

Understanding Financing Needs

A well-organized plan that clearly explains the goals and objectives of the entrepreneur and operation is a key ingredient in securing needed funds. Possibly the most critical step in securing financing is simply determining the capital needs of the business. One of the most common errors made in financing a business venture is designing a business plan around a certain amount of money. The wrong way to proceed in developing a financing plan is to begin by asking the question: "If we can borrow $250,000 (or some other amount), what can we do with it?" Instead, the entrepreneur should systematically: 1) determine how much capital is needed, 2) estimate the financing capacity of the operation, 3) determine if the plan can be modified to accommodate the financing capacity of the operation if needs are greater than capacity, and 4) identify potential sources.

Estimating Capital Requirements

There are several proven methods of determining the funding requirements of a business venture. The percent-of-sales method is probably the most widely used method of estimating the capital requirement for an existing business. For a new venture, the best way to determine the financing needs is to list the capital asset requirements (at cost) and add to that any organizational expenses and operating capital requirements.

Although the amount of the capital requirement is important, it is equally important to know specifically when it will be needed and for how long. These basic issues—how much, when, and how long—are fundamentally related and equally important in identifying the needs of a business.

For both an existing business and a new venture, the first step in estimating the funding requirement is to determine the probable range of the proposed financing. This is accomplished by generating cost projections for an "unlimited" budget and a "bare-bones" budget. These figures should then be matched with a pessimistic and an optimistic sales projection, respectively, to reflect the upper and lower bounds for the needed funds.

Calculating the additional funding requirement is simply an exercise in matching the expected capital asset costs (fixtures, equipment, supplies, and inventories) with the estimated operating capital requirement. It is more important to estimate the operating requirement accurately when planning a new venture startup than when planning an expansion for an existing business. The risk of undercapitalization, which is a function of the variability in net sales, is greater with a new venture than with an existing business.

Careful estimation of the operating capital requirement for a venture (new or expansion) requires the completion of a cash breakeven projection for the period of time necessary to generate a positive cash flow. Whether the funding request is based on the unlimited budget or the bare-bones budget will in large measure determine the margin of safety (the operating capital reserve) that is available. The principal point to recognize is that accelerated growth in sales is not a substitute for a small operating capital reserve.

The rapid-growth stage of an operation tends to be the phase in which operating capital requirements are the greatest. Sales growth leads to increased inventory needs and a mushrooming accounts receivables balance, which in turn leads to an increased need for operating capital. One of the fastest ways to experience difficulties in a "thriving" business is to enter into the stage of accelerated growth without either an adequate operating capital reserve or access to a reliable funding source.

This particular approach to identifying funding needs enables the entrepreneur to stay abreast of the financing requirements of the operation. The major benefit of a periodically updated cash flow projection is that it identifies well in advance the onset of a funding requirement—how much is going to be needed, when, and how long it will be needed. By removing the guess-work, the entrepreneur is able to project the needs of the operation more accurately and provide ample time to pursue and cultivate appropriate financing relationships.

The ability of the entrepreneur to satisfactorily secure the needed financing depends critically on the funding capacity of the operation. There is no general rule of thumb that can be used to determine funding capacity. The guidelines used depend on several factors, but primarily growth potential and type of business. High-growth operations in certain high-profile industries such as technology and computer-related areas will be evaluated differently than businesses in industries with low growth potential.

The main point to remember is that funding capacity is a function of many different variables, not the least of which is the source of capital. Approaching the appropriate source is in many ways as important as the financing plan itself.

Life-Cycle Stages and Sources of Funds

The more familiar, traditional approach to identifying sources of capital relies on matching the term structure of the funding request with the estimated useful life of the asset being financed. For example, inventory and accounts receivable are financed through revolving lines of credit; automobile loans are written for three to four year terms; and real estate is financed for up to thirty years. However, strict reliance on the traditional approach to venture financing is of limited value in the identification of funding sources for the entrepreneurial venture. Although it is true that many formal lenders are often thought to prefer either short-term or long-term loans, when the actual lending decision is made, short-term lenders will lend long term and vice versa.

A more productive way to classify funding sources is to recognize the varying degrees of risk associated with financing ventures at the different stages of the business life cycle—from the extremely high risk of a startup venture to the more moderate risk associated with a business expansion or buyout. Each stage in the life cycle offers a different risk/reward opportunity and, as a result, attracts only those funding sources that have the same risk/reward propensity. Even though most funding sources are interested in ventures at various stages of the business life cycle, they have a propensity to concentrate their activities in more narrowly defined categories. Thus, the likelihood of attracting a particular investor or lender will depend as much on the stage of the business life cycle as the term nature of the funding request.

Venture financing can be profitably categorized into stages that correspond to stages of the business life cycle: 1) development financing, 2) expansion financing, and 3) acquisition financing. There are several stages of financing within each of these categories, and there may be several components within each stage.

Development Financing. Because of the high risk involved in the early developmental stage of a new business venture, much of the financing available in this category takes the form of equity capital. There are three stages of financing within this category: seed, startup, and early growth.

Seed Financing. Seed financing represents the initial capital injected into a new venture to investigate and research a concept or prove an idea. Funding at this stage takes place prior to the actual startup of a venture, and as such, is often referred to as "pre-startup seed capital."

Although venture capital sources for this type of financing exist, fewer than one out of ten venture capitalists actively pursues seed capital investments. Those that are interested at this early stage compensate for the high risk they are absorbing by taking large ownership shares in the venture, often as high as 70–90 percent. As a result, most investments at this stage either come from personal savings or are secured through informal sources (friends and relatives, or the so-called "adventure capitalists").

Research and development activities are very costly and provide no guarantee of success. Thus, the entrepreneur has very few formal funding sources to explore. It is not until the basic research has proven itself that the formal venture capital community becomes a reliable source of funds.

Startup Financing. Startup financing is provided to companies that have progressed beyond the research and development stage and are ready to develop and market a product/service. Although the professional venture capitalist has an increased interest at this stage, the cost to the entrepreneur in terms of the percentage of ownership given up is still extremely high (50–70 percent) because of the level of risk. Thus, informal funding sources are still the most feasible at this stage of the life cycle.

For more modest investments, various government sources, such as the Small Business Administration or one of a number of different agencies, have special programs for small businesses in which the risk of loss to the creditor is reduced through guarantees or other inducements.

Early-Growth Financing. Early-growth or "first-stage" financing still relies heavily on equity sources as the best available option. Since the informal market is usually too small to meet the expanding capital needs of the firm, the formal venture capital industry becomes the primary source of capital at this stage. In addition, the reduced risk of the venture enables the entrepreneur to emerge from the negotiations with a majority of the stock under his control. Typically, the venture capitalist requires only 30–50 percent ownership to generate the desired rate of return on the investment.

At this point also, it is marginally feasible to consider commercial lenders as a source of capital. Commercial banks, especially those dealing in government-guaranteed lending, always have a small portion of their commercial loan portfolio in businesses at this early stage. Results from this author's study of commercial bank loan activity in Texas indicate that less than 15 percent of the total commercial and industrial loan portfolio is with firms in the early stages of the business life cycle.

Small Business Investment Companies and commercial finance companies occasionally become involved in ventures at this early stage. In any case, the specific circumstances of the opportunity determine their level of involvement. In actual practice, this means a careful assessment of the strengths and weaknesses of the management team, their success in previous ventures, and the amount of security that is offered in the form of collateral and personal guarantees.

Expansion Financing. After a company has been in operation for at least one year (in addition to the time it took to conceptualize the venture), the expansion phase of the business life cycle typically begins. In order to progress successfully beyond the development stage, the entrepreneur must secure the necessary expansion capital. Expansion capital can take the forms of retained earnings, additional equity, or debt capital. The specific form that it takes depends on the success of the firm and the specific purpose of capital injection.

Rapid-Growth Financing. Whether profitable or not, firms at this stage are experiencing accelerating sales growth and expanding capital requirements because of increased inventory levels and growing accounts receivable. Without external sources of cash, the firm's rate of growth is limited by its ability to generate funds internally through retained earnings. Rapid-growth financing usually takes the form of an operating capital loan from a commercial bank or other asset-based lender, such as a savings and loan association, business finance company, or business factoring company. Over one-quarter of the commercial and industrial loan portfolio of Texas banks is with firms at this stage of the business life cycle.

Sustained-Growth Financing. Businesses that successfully reach this stage of the life cycle have been in existence for a number of years and are almost always making a profit. Firms at this stage have many more options of alternative funding sources available to them. The entrepreneur has the choice of funding an expansion either with debt or equity, based on the relative cost of funds.

Over half of the commercial and industrial loans made by Texas banks are to businesses at this stage of the life cycle. Even though the venture capital industry is typically thought of as an early-stage investor, intense competition within the industry has forced many venture capitalists to look for investment opportunities at this later stage. In a recent study of its members, the National Venture Capital Association found that early-stage investments dropped from 44 percent to 37 percent between 1981 and 1984. During the same period of time, later-stage investments increased from 25 to 30 percent.

Bridge Financing. Financing at this stage is often referred to as "mezzanine financing." This can be defined as funding provided to a company that is in the process of preparing for a public offering in the near future. In most cases, the purpose of bridge financing is to fund the restructuring of the company, and repayment of the bridge loan is built into the proceeds of the underwriting. Most formal investors are interested in opportunities at this stage of the business life cycle. As in the previous stage, funding can take the form of either debt or equity.

Acquisition Financing. Acquisition financing can take the form of either a straightforward business acquisition or a leveraged buyout. The former represents a situation in which an individual or firm is simply seeking funds to acquire or merge with another company. In the latter situation, funds are provided to enable the existing management to secure ownership control of a business or an operating division of a major corporation. Interest in this type of investment opportunity is often quite high. A buyout usually means additional ownership equity and a fresh, new approach to a business that may have lost its operating efficiency or marketing appeal.

The specific circumstances surrounding the acquisition opportunity determine the financing alternatives. Acquisition can actually take place at any stage in the business life cycle; thus, the previous discussion will help determine the best source of funds. In general, however, sources of acquisition financing are available in both the debt and equity markets.

Summary and Conclusions

The funding should fit the purpose. In other words, the term structure of the obligation should be matched with the economic life of the asset being financed. In general, current liabilities should be used to finance current assets and long-term liabilities and owners' equity should be used to finance long-term assets.

However, it is extremely difficult to classify funding sources as strictly short term or strictly long term. A much more productive way to classify funding sources is by their risk/reward propensities. Matching the risk/reward structure of the opportunity with the risk/reward propensity of the funding source is made easier if one understands the relationship between risk and reward during the different stages of the business life cycle.

In the early stages of a business life cycle when risk is high, only those funding sources that have the flexibility to tap into the long-term growth potential of the venture will have a genuine interest in the opportunity. High risk is associated with high reward. The source of the reward is typically in the potential capital gains from the sale of an equity interest. The only other alternative is to significantly reduce the risk to the funding source through the use of a guarantee of repayment from a reliable outside party, such as the federal government.

Sources occasionally make mistakes in their financing decisions by taking on too much risk relative to the reward potential. However, the entrepreneur should not count on the low risk/low reward source (for example, the commercial bank) to make such a mistake and fund a high risk venture.

10
Equity Sources

Acommon characteristic of almost all businesses in the development stage of the business life cycle is a negative cash flow from operations. The major implication of this characteristic is that there is no excess cash being generated by the business operation from the sale of products/services to service debt. If the entrepreneur is to be successful in funding a new business, a thorough knowledge of the sources of equity capital is crucial.

This chapter will present a discussion of the main sources of equity capital available to entrepreneurs involved with firms that are in the early stages of the business life cycle, including informal investors, venture capitalists, and R&D partnerships. We will also examine stock placement alternatives that are not subject to the full registration requirements of the Securities and Exchange Commission.

Informal Investors

The term **informal investors** encompasses all sources of risk capital other than the institutionalized sources such as professional venture capitalists and the public equity markets. Although most startup ventures are funded either through the accumulated savings of the individual or those of close friends and relatives, nonrelated informal investors—adventure capitalists, as they are often called—represent a significant source of equity funds for new business enterprises.

Friends and Relatives

Because of the inefficiency of the informal market, most development stage financings are done through personal savings or investments from close friends and relatives. However, the high risk involved makes most entrepreneurs reluctant to ask personal acquaintances for substantial sums of money, thus limiting the equity position available for friends and relatives. In addition, the very nature of personal relationships and the general lack of sophistication on the part of investors result in a tendency to view the investment as a personal favor rather than a means of acquiring a financial return.

There are advantages and disadvantages to funding a venture in this manner. The primary advantage to the entrepreneur is the ability to secure capital at a very low cost in terms of the percentage of equity given up. A major disadvantage lies in the fact that, in all probability, close friends and relatives lack the kind of business experience and expertise necessary to evaluate the venture opportunity or benefit the operation in any tangible way. One should also be aware that, in the event of business failure, both the relationship and the venture are likely to be bankrupted.

Before entering into such a financial arrangement with a close friend or relative, the entrepreneur should consider the following points:

1. Assess the skills and financial resources that each individual brings into the relationship.
2. Take careful steps to ensure that each person understands his or her duties and responsibilities.
3. Identify each partner's long-term expectations for the business enterprise.
4. Insist upon a formal agreement identifying the vital areas of concern with respect to financial shares, management responsibility, profit distributions, and buyout options.

Adventure Capitalists

The second segment of the informal market is made up of a loose network of working investors who are actively seeking investment opportunities. Referred to as "adventure capitalists" or "angels," they will usually invest at the seed or startup stage of a venture which, for various reasons, is too small or too risky even for the traditional venture capitalist.

There are no data on the informal investment market, so any effort to describe the typical investor must be based on rough generalizations. A 1978 study by the Whittemore School of Business and Economics at the University of New Hampshire identifies informal investors as private individuals who have significant personal wealth and entrepreneurial experience (see Wetzel and Seymour 1981). They are quite often retirees, resignees, or executives in successful ventures who have experienced the problems and pitfalls of dealing with the formal venture capital market.

There are several distinct differences between the traditional venture capitalist and the adventure capitalist. In the first place, the adventure capitalist usually takes an active role in the management of the emerging firm. Although the venture capitalist is also typically thought of as an active investor, the typical venture capital portfolio includes dozens of companies. This is altogether too many for a small staff to actively manage. Thus, it would be highly unusual for the venture capitalist to become intimately familiar with the issues that confront the business on a day-to-day basis. In contrast, the adventure capitalist is involved in only a few ventures at any given time. Thus, they are able to deliver needed business and technical expertise quickly. Secondly, unlike the venture capitalist, the active informal investor expects to make money on every investment. With less capital and fewer investments, the adventure capitalist simply cannot afford to lose money on any deal. As a result, the level of interest in individual investments is quite high.

Networking in the Venture Capital Industry

Networking is a widely used and often misunderstood concept. It is simply a formal means of establishing relationships and participating in the flow of information. In other words, networking is a systematic way for individuals sharing a common interest to match ideas and opportunities.

As the formal venture capital market has grown and developed over the past decade, certain inefficiencies have become evident. Although the industry has functioned quite well in providing for the capital needs of emerging companies, it is clear that there is a serious shortage of equity options for the entrepreneur looking for less than $500,000.

This financing gap is being filled by the informal market. Accurate data is scarce, but William Wetzel and Craig Seymour (1981) estimate that private investors may finance over five times as many ventures as the formal public equity and venture capital markets combined. The major problem in the informal market is the inefficient information network. Identification of interested investors by entrepreneurs and venture opportunities by individuals who have capital is hit-or-miss at best.

In an effort to improve the workings of the informal market, the University of New Hampshire established the first venture capital network (VCN) in 1985. The goal of the VCN is to organize a system that matches entrepreneurs with private investors. Since the establishment of the first VCN, networks have been started at the University of Tulsa, Case Western Reserve University, St. Louis University, and the Indiana Institute for New Business Ventures. Others have been proposed in the states of Georgia, New York, and Illinois.

The typical VCN is not an investment advisor or broker/dealer. It is merely a listing service provided to facilitate the flow of information. Information on venture opportunities and investor preferences is placed in two separate data bases. As new information is added to the data bases, they are compared in an effort to match venture opportunities and investor preferences. When matches are found, investors are provided summary information on the venture. If additional details are desired, the entrepreneur and the investor are introduced to one another and carry on independently from then on.

In their short history, venture capital networks have seen only limited success. The concept is sound and the improved flow of information can only enhance the success of the informal market in financing new venture startups.

This segment of the informal market represents a potential source of seed and startup capital of the same magnitude as that available through the SBIC industry (discussed in the next section). These individuals are difficult to find and there is little formal guidance in identifying their whereabouts. Most are located strictly by word-of-mouth through contacts with other investors or professionals in related fields such as bankers, attorneys, or accountants.

The Venture Capital Industry

Historically, the main thrust of the venture capital industry has been in providing startup and other development-stage financing for small and emerging companies that have high growth potential. Today, however, the industry encompasses a much broader range of investment situations, including seed, expansion, and acquisition financing. The primary function of the industry has been the provision of equity capital to high-risk ventures.

The American College Dictionary defines **venture** as "a hazardous or daring undertaking; a business enterprise on which risk is taken." The relationship between Queen Isabella of Spain and Christopher Columbus can be accurately described as venture capital investment. The arrangement between the two was quite different from a typical trading voyage. It was more of a partnership than a debtor/creditor relationship.

The scope of the industry can be described by a set of operating characteristics. The organized venture capital industry:

1. provides capital for businesses in the development stage of the business life cycle.
2. invests in firms that are unable to attract capital from conventional institutional sources—public equity markets or credit-oriented financial institutions.
3. provides bridge financing for firms that are restructuring their equity positions in anticipation of a public stock offering.
4. provides funds for acquisitions and leveraged buyouts.

The venture capitalist largely fills the role of entrepreneur in the formal capital market. That is, the task of the venture capitalist is to discover information that has been overlooked by others. By exploring new business opportunities and taking risks, the industry is able to take advantage of unexploited profit opportunities.

Venture capital should not be confused with expansion capital. The differences between the two can be broken down into differences in function, risk, and reward. As seen in Table 10–1, the primary function of expansion

Table 10–1
Distinguishing between Expansion and Venture Capital

Type of Capital	Function	Risk	Reward
Expansion Capital	Facilities	Capital Market Criteria	Interest, Dividends
Venture Capital	Business Development	High	Capital Gains

capital is to expand existing operations. The need to expand may arise from demand increases that exceed the plant's production capacity or the desire to add new product lines or enter new markets. In contrast, venture capital exists to find and prove new business opportunities. The success of the industry rests in its ability to find investment opportunities that the capital market would otherwise overlook.

In order for an opportunity to attract expansion capital, it must meet the risk/reward criteria established in the formal capital market. The result of this formalized investment criteria is that market values closely approximate book values in most cases; new capital creation has not taken place. Venture capital is often referred to as "risk capital." By exploiting imperfections in the capital markets such as lack of information about the business opportunity, the venture capitalist is willing to accept risks that exceed those the expansion market will accept. The end result of this willingness to accept higher risks is a higher return on invested funds.

The return on expansion capital takes the form of interest yields on debt and dividends on common stock. To the extent that capital gains are realized on the sale of common stock, they result solely from accumulated dividends foregone on that stock. The venture capitalist receives returns on investment exclusively in the form of capital gains. The business development function of the venture capital industry results in the creation of firms that have market values in excess of the value of invested capital.

Historical Development of the Venture Capital Industry

Prior to World War II venture capital investment was carried out on an informal basis by wealthy individuals, syndicates of investors, or family organizations employing professional investment managers. The founding of the American Research and Development Corporation of Boston in 1946 marks the beginning of the industry as a formal institutionalized investor. However, it was not until 1958 that the industry took its first major step toward formal industry status. It was in that year that the Federal Reserve System completed its study on the availability of financing for small business (U.S. Federal Reserve System 1958).

The results of that study indicated that, while private commercial banks and the Small Business Administration were providing the short-term and working capital demands of the small business community, there continued to be an unmet demand for longer-term loans and especially equity financing. As a result, the Small Business Investment Act was passed into law, creating the Small Business Investment Company—private, for-profit corporations regulated by the SBA. In order to further encourage private investment in the industry, the federal government offered certain tax advantages and direct loans to leverage private capital.

By 1962, almost 600 SBICs had been licensed. The idea seemed to be a tremendous success. However, the success was short-lived because of the fact that industry managers and analysts did not really understand the mechanics of the new industry. Many of the firms were undercapitalized and a number went out of business; there were fewer than 300 SBICs in existence in the late 1960s.

Although the SBIC industry has not had the success that was originally anticipated, it was a major factor in the development of the venture capital industry. Recognizing the mistakes of the SBIC investors, a number of privately owned venture capital firms were formed to take advantage of an untapped segment of the capital market. Avoiding the early mistakes of the SBICs, particularly their short-term investment orientation, and free from much government regulation, these private venture capitalists began to experience a substantial degree of success by the late 1960s.

The venture capital industry has experienced phenomenal growth in the past decade, both in new capital commitments and funds disbursed to the business community. In 1983, over $4 billion in new capital was added to the venture capital pool and the industry actually invested $2.8 billion in over 1,000 companies. As recently as 1978, new commitments were only $570 million, with $550 million going to new investments.

Private Venture Capital Firms

The largest source of institutional equity capital comes from the privately owned, independent venture capital firm. Constituting some 68 percent of the total capital available at the end of 1983, these private firms have adopted a wide range of investment strategies. Some firms prefer development-stage financing, while others would rather invest in more mature companies or leveraged buyouts.

There are approximately 233 such firms in operation in the United States today. They range in capital size from under $10 million to over $200 million. The average investment for these firms is typically between $500,000 and $800,000. Most investments are syndicated to reduce the exposure of individual firms, so the total amount invested in one deal averages over $2.3

million (*Venture Capital Journal* May 1984). Private capitalization for the industry comes from several main sources: family trusts, pension funds, major corporations, endowments and foundations, insurance companies, and foreign investors.

Small Business Investment Companies

As of December, 1985, there were 518 SBICs operating in the United States. Of this number, 146 were 301(d) license holders or Minority Enterprise Small Business Investment Companies (MESBICs). Initial capitalization for an SBIC is secured through private sources. After organizing, the private investors are able to leverage their capital through government loans or government-guaranteed loans up to three times the firm's paid-in capital and paid-in surplus.

The operating characteristics of a MESBIC are similar to those of a regular SBIC, with two major exceptions: (1) MESBIC investors are eligible for SBA leverage of up to four times the amount of private capital and (2) investments can be made only in businesses whose majority ownership is considered "disadvantaged." Membership in a minority racial or ethnic group does not automatically qualify an individual as "disadvantaged" for purposes of this program, although it is a consideration.

Classification. SBICs are classified as either captive or noncaptive. A **captive SBIC** is one whose management and investment philosophy are determined by the objectives of a parent organization. The parent organization can be a single bank, a bank holding company, or any other type of organization, financial or non-financial. A **noncaptive SBIC** is one that is individually owned and independently operated. Table 10–2 provides a detailed breakdown of the SBIC industry by type of ownership.

Table 10–2
SBICs Classified by Type of Ownership, 1985

Type of Ownership	SBIC	MESBIC	Total
Bank Dominated	97	6	103
Bank Associated	15	6	21
Financial Organization	21	2	23
Non-Financial Organization	37	26	63
Individually Owned	185	105	290
40 Act Company	17	1	18
Total	372	146	518

Table 10–3
Capital Availability by Type of SBIC, 1985
(in millions of dollars)

Type of SBIC	Private Capital	SBA Obligations	Total Capital
Regular SBICs	$1,158,289	$1,018,526	$2,176,815
MESBICs	163,294	243,300	406,594
Total	$1,321,583	$1,261,826	$2,583,409

Fewer than one out of five SBICs are directly controlled or affiliated with a bank or bank holding company. Bank dominated SBICs (over 50 percent bank ownership) make up only 19.9 percent of the total, and bank associated SBICs (10–50 percent bank ownership) comprise only 4.1 percent. Other financial organizations own 4.4 percent of the total SBICs in operation and non-financial organizations own 12.2 percent. The predominant form of ownership is the individually owned SBIC, comprising 60.0 percent of the total.

Financing Characteristics. Because of the nature of the capital base of the typical SBIC, the financing available is often very limited. An SBIC may be paying interest on up to 80 percent of its capital, so cash flow considerations are critical to the fund manager. For the industry as a whole, approximately 48.8 percent of the total capital base is composed of loans and loan guarantees from the SBA. Table 10–3 gives a breakdown of the capital under SBIC control.

Because of the industry's leveraged financial position and the interest obligations that go along with SBA loans, most SBICs must generate current cash income on the funds that are invested in business ventures. There are two major implications that emerge. First, the typical SBIC investment comes at a later stage in the business life cycle than that of other venture capitalists. The major reason for this different investment strategy is that firms receiving assistance from an SBIC must be developed to the point where the operation is able to absorb a fixed debt service. In most cases, this occurs at a point late in the development stage or early in the expansion stage. Second, the typical financial instrument used by the industry involves some type of loan rather than straight equity interest. Table 10–4 shows the 1981 investment activity of the industry broken down into straight debt and equity-type investments. Only about one-third of the $388 million invested in 1981 was in the form of straight-equity participations. Straight debt accounted for 37 percent of the financings and the remainder was in the form of convertible debentures or debt with the option to buy stock.

Table 10–4
**Investment Activity by Type of Instrument,
SBICs and MESBICs, 1981**
(in millions of dollars)

Type	Straight Debt	Debt with Equity	Equity Only	Total
Regular SBIC	$109.18	$105.52	$118.21	$332.91
MESBIC	33.80	15.27	5.98	55.05
Total	$142.98	$120.79	$124.19	$387.96

The interest rates charged typically run from two to three points above the cost of funds from the SBA. The total cost will depend on the total capitalization package and the perceived risk involved.

The evaluation criteria used within the industry is similar to that of the venture capitalist. The most critical aspect in the evaluation of the venture is the credibility of the management team. Although this criterion is subjective, it can be displayed and enhanced through proper presentation of the business plan. In preparing the plan, the entrepreneur should emphasize the qualifications of the management team directly in the drafting of that particular section and indirectly in the quality of the marketing and financial plan.

Funding Uncertainty Slows SBIC Growth

Small business investment companies have traditionally been able to leverage their private capital by borrowing from the Federal Financing Bank at favorable interest rates. In 1986, Congress provided a new funding mechanism whereby the SBA would assist SBICs in funding loans in private capital markets.

The Federal Financing Bank lost its authority to buy SBIC debentures in April and the new arrangement was not in place until September. Thus, the industry lost its access to low-interest leverage for almost six months. During that period, SBIC licensing slowed to only seven new operations, as compared to eighteen during the same period in 1985. In addition, the 1985 total of twenty-six new SBICs was down from forty-five in the previous year.

This funding uncertainty has prompted the industry to promote in Congress the complete privatization of their financing by creating a Corporation for Small Business Investment (COSBI). This bill would create an organization similar to the Federal National Mortgage Association often called "Fannie Mae." COSBI would operate in a similar fashion, raising capital by selling in the private capital market securities that have limited government guarantees against default.

This legislation will be considered in 1987. However, there is no assurance that other pressing issues such as restructuring the Reform Tax Act or trimming the deficit will not delay actions on COSBI even further. In all likelihood, the industry will continue to experience its annual uncertainty on funding issues.

Most SBICs are relatively small; in fact, over 40 percent have less than $1 million in private capital under control. Only 12.4 percent have more than $5 million in private capital. For MESBICs, the size comparison is even more dramatic. Almost 65 percent have less than $1 million in private capital and only 1.4 percent have over $5 million. There are two major implications that emerge from this size constraint. In the first place, staff sizes are usually small. With a growing number of business plans to be reviewed, individual plans can only be given a brief review. A plan that may have taken an entrepreneur three to six months to complete may get only a ten to fifteen minute first reading. As a result, good first impressions are important.

Since the typical SBIC is small, the typical project that a single SBIC will undertake alone is also small, usually in the range of $100,000–$250,000. In fact, a single SBIC can invest no more than 20 percent of its total capital in a particular venture. Larger projects are handled through a syndicate of SBICs working together with a lead SBIC. Under such an arrangement, projects in the range of $2–3 million are quite common.

Venture Capital Subsidiary of an Operating Corporation

The number of major corporations undertaking formal venture capital investment divisions has doubled since 1980. In 1983, there were seventy-eight corporate venture capital funds in operation in the United States, constituting over 20 percent of the total venture capital pool (*Venture Capital Journal* July 1983). The primary purpose of these funds is to invest in technology or products in the market of the parent company. Although no specific capital commitments are published, they are limited to 5 percent of the parent company's capital. Many of the major industrial corporations, such as IBM, Xerox, AT&T, Monsanto, and the major oil companies are active in this area, so there are millions of dollars potentially available for emerging businesses. In 1984, over $475 million was actually committed by U.S. corporations in venture opportunities.

In addition to the major industrial corporate involvement in this activity, several major financial institutions have formed venture investment subsidiaries in recent years. This action, as opposed to the formation of an affiliate SBIC, has been taken to escape the restrictions of government regulations that limit the investment decisions of a firm. It is too soon to determine whether this close connection between the bank venture investment activity and the parent organization will prove successful. However, if the venture group is able to employ the investment discipline of the venture capital industry, including the longer-term investment horizon, there is good reason to believe that the two industries will be able to complement one another in the twin goals of business formation and business expansion.

Major corporate involvement in venture funding is increasing because it is seen as a way around their traditionally slow-moving development programs. It is becoming a proven alternative means of fostering new technologies and entering new markets. It is a way for the emerging business to get more money. Attracted by the right technology and the right market, large corporations can potentially invest much more than private venture capitalists. In addition, corporate venture capitalists can provide technical assistance and quick access to lucrative markets.

The Nature of the Venture Capital Industry

It is difficult and sometimes tenuous to identify the underlying characteristics of the industry. However, with the experience of the past twenty-five years, we can set down several prevailing attributes of the venture capital industry.

1. The investment horizon is usually long term in nature. In order to develop a significant business enterprise, which is absolutely necessary given the reward structure of the industry, the venture investor is usually locked into an investment for a five to seven year time frame. Because of the dynamic process of risk capital, an investor seldom remains involved with a company for over ten years. The opportunities for high returns on investment have usually dissipated by that time and the venture capitalist is ready to recycle funds into other opportunities. There is a recent tendency, however, to see shorter investment periods—along the lines of one to three years.

2. The typical venture investment is made in firms with compound annual growth rate potential of at least 30 percent. The venture investor is interested in opportunities that will provide between 30 and 50 percent return on equity. A firm earning a return on equity of 10 percent can grow no faster than that without distorting its debt-to-equity ratio substantially. Thus, high growth potential is absolutely necessary to generate the required return on equity.

3. The venture capitalist usually represents the firm's first equity financing from an outside source other than friends or relatives.

4. Venture capital investors tend to have divergent interests. Some specialize in specific industries, while others invest in any venture that meets their risk/return criteria. Recently, however, there has been a significant move toward high technology investments.

5. Equity capital is available for a full range of investment situations from development-stage financings such as startups and first-stage financing to later-stage expansions, acquisitions, and leveraged buyouts. This move to later-stage investments has become more popular because it tends to

be a much safer investment than development-stage financings. In addition, the growth of the industry has increased competition and forced individual venture capitalists to broaden the scope of their investments to include later-stage financings simply because of the lack of good development-stage opportunities.

6. The two most important considerations for the equity investor are the management team and market potential.

7. Venture capitalists are usually active investors. They are capable of providing management and technical assistance in the areas of planning, personnel, marketing, and financing.

8. There are certain geographic limitations that should be considered before contacting a venture capitalist. Most are interested in ventures with companies located within a few hundred miles of their own office. This is true especially of the lead investor in any situation. However, many will participate in an investment outside this geographic limit along with several other venture capitalists. The primary centers of venture capital activity have been New England, Chicago, and San Francisco, with secondary centers in Dallas, Minneapolis/St. Paul, and the Washington, D.C. area. Recently, the Pacific Northwest, Southern California, and Atlanta have emerged as areas of increased interest.

Approaching the Venture Capitalist

There are several things to remember when approaching the equity investor. The venture capital industry provides funding for fewer than 2,000 new ventures per year. Thus, even the most active venture capitalists get involved in only five to ten new ventures per year. These investments are made after considering hundreds of proposals. The Center for Entrepreneurial Studies surveyed venture capitalists to determine the most important criteria in judging entrepreneurs and their business plans. The results of the survey are given in Table 10–5. Of the six most frequent responses, three deal with particular aspects of the management team and one deals with the product market.

Thus, as the entrepreneur prepares the business plan to attract venture capital, the most important considerations are in the areas of management and marketing. While this holds true, the plan presented to the venture capitalist is significantly different from the one presented to the local banker. This difference lies not in content, but in emphasis.

The Management Team. Although the venture capitalist is ultimately interested in the return that can be expected from his investment, the financial

Table 10–5
Venture Capitalists' Criteria for Judging
Entrepreneurs and Business Plans
(percentage frequencies)

Capable of sustained intense effort	64%
Thoroughly familiar with market	62
At least 10 times return in 5–10 years	50
Demonstrated leadership in the past	50
Evaluates and reacts well to risk	48
Investment can be made liquid	44

Source: *Wall Street Journal,* May 15, 1985.

section of the business plan will not be given the closest consideration, at least initially. If the venture concept has any appeal to the investor whatsoever, the first thing that will be researched is the management team. The venture investor will be primarily concerned with the business experience, educational background, character, and integrity of the managers and owners of the business enterprise.

Before any final financing arrangements are agreed upon, an extensive background search will be conducted on each owner, manager, and key employee. It is often said that a venture capitalist will invest in a top-notch management team with a second-rate product much more readily than in a second-rate management team with a top-notch product.

Market Analysis. The purpose of this section of the plan is to build credibility for the entrepreneur's marketing concept and approach. In order to accomplish this, the venture capitalist must be convinced that there is a market for the product/service; the entrepreneur understands what motivates customers to buy it; and there is a strategy in place that will result in successful penetration of the market and capture of the projected market share.

The issues to be addressed in this section will differ only slightly from those presented in Chapter 2, "The Business Plan." There are three specific areas in which the venture capitalist will require more detailed information: market size, market plan, and market strategy. The size of the current total market is the first step in calculating expected market share. While this should be included in any plan regardless of funding source, the venture capitalist will prefer that assumptions about market share be based on primary research rather than published data. The venture capitalist places much more emphasis on the results of surveys and discussions with potential customers, distributors, and suppliers than on conclusions drawn from secondary source information. In this case, published data are used to verify the accuracy of direct survey results.

The market plan describes how the sales projections will be accomplished. This section includes a detailed explanation of the marketing approach, answering the questions: What, when, where, how, and who? Service policies, pricing strategies, distribution networks, and advertising and promotion requirements should also be discussed in detail. The other critical element in the market analysis is a discussion of market strategy. It is important to display a basic understanding of how the market is stratified.

This section of the business plan is critical in the venture capitalist's evaluation of the proposal. Its major purpose is to enhance the credibility of the overall proposal by lending support to sales and financial projections—the area on which the venture capitalist will ultimately base a final decision on the merits of the project.

The Financial Plan. This section of the proposal is basic to the evaluation process of any investor. Its format and content will vary only slightly when the source of funds is the venture capitalist. As an equity investor, the venture capitalist has only a marginal interest in the collateral available for security in the event of liquidation. Of primary concern is the expected value of the business after a certain period (usually five to seven years after the injection of capital takes place). This calculation will enable the venture capitalist to answer two questions: 1) Is the company large enough to make this investment worthwhile? and 2) What percentage ownership is required to meet the investor's rate of return on investment criterion?

From the perspective of the venture capitalist, the information presented in this section will assist in the "pricing" of the investment opportunity. This decision is based on the risk/return objectives of the investor. In addition, several other factors are of key interest in determining the company's value. First, the goal of the venture capitalist will be to keep the value of the business as low as possible while still providing adequate incentives for the current ownership. Second, any pricing strategy will also take into consideration other future financing requirements of the firm.

The first step in the pricing of an investment will be the determination of the future value of the business at the end of the investment period. The business valuation process is probably the most critical step in the pricing procedure. For a more complete discussion of business valuation see Chapter 13, "Transferring Business Ownership."

Suppose the venture capitalist estimates that the business in question will be valued at $10 million in five years. Given the degree of risk involved, suppose the investors are requiring a 40 percent compounded rate of return on investment. The initial funding request is $500,000.

After determining the value of the business, the next step is to discount this future value back to the present. Using the present value formula:

$$PV = FV/(1 + r)^n$$

where

PV = present value.
FV = future value.
r = required rate of return on investment.
n = number of years in the investment period.

Using this formula, the present value of this company is around $1,850,000, [$10 million/$(1 + .40)^5$]. In order to realize a 40 percent return on his investment, the venture capitalist will require a stock interest in the company of 27 percent ($500,000/$1,850,000).

Individual venture capitalists usually express their return requirements using traditional rule-of-thumb estimates. It is often stated that the venture capital investment must produce a return of five to ten times invested capital in three to five years. This rule of thumb can easily be translated into a compounded rate of return estimate as was done previously. Table 10–6 shows the results of several of these calculations. A return of five times the investment in five years works out to be a 37.97 percent return; ten times the investment in five years is a 58.49 percent return.

Table 10–6
Venture Capital Rules of Thumb on Investment
Translated into Compound Rates of Return

Times Investment	Investment Period	Rate of Return
5 times	10 years	17.46%
10	10	25.89
5	5	37.97
6	5	43.10
7	5	47.58
8	5	51.57
9	5	55.18
10	5	58.49
5	3	71.00
10	3	115.44

As stated earlier, one of the most important elements of the financing plan is its internal consistency. The summary of the assumptions to the prospective financial statements is the critical component in the financing section that ensures this internal consistency.

Evaluating Risk

The venture capitalist's assessment of risk plays a very vital role in the entire evaluation, pricing, and negotiation process. Thus, before seeking funds from a venture investor, it is wise to have a thorough understanding of the process of risk identification and measurement. All prudent equity investors will evaluate the probability of receiving any returns on their capital before any funds are committed. One result of this is an almost certain "risk adjustment" to the earnings projections, which means that the financial projections will be adjusted downward before any analysis is conducted.

All investment opportunities have some degree of risk attached to them. The closest thing to a riskless investment is the purchase of United States Treasury securities. Most venture capital investments have significantly more risk attached to them than Treasury Bills. The higher the risk is, the higher the required return on the investment will be. In fact, unless there is a high probability that the risks can be overcome, the venture capitalist will not make the investment, regardless of the potential return.

The riskiness of a venture can be attributed to the functional categories of the operation:

1. *Technological risk* is evident in the early research and development stages of a venture. This is the risk that either the entrepreneur does not possess the technical skills to successfully complete the development (or startup) phase of the project or the funds requested are insufficient to fully capitalize the development phase.

2. *Management risk* refers to the possibility that the proposed management team will not be able to successfully organize the production and marketing aspects of the operation. The ultimate success of the venture depends on the ability of the team to generate output and sell it. It is for this reason that most venture capitalists are seldom passive investors; they tend to take the lead in supervising the management of the operation.

3. *Financial risk* becomes relevant after the development phase of the venture is completed. With a completely developed concept, the company will undoubtedly require additional financing to successfully bring a finished product to market. A very popular financing strategy used in the

industry is that of "staged financing" to coincide with the completion of specific events. As each phase of the project is completed and the management team displays an ability to achieve certain goals, the probability of success increases.

4. *Manufacturing risk* is the risk attached to actual large-scale production of the technology. This risk examines the likelihood of being able to efficiently turn the prototype into a marketable product.

5. *Marketing risk* refers to the probability that the product can be successfully marketed. In evaluating this risk, the investors will be interested in whether a market exists for the product, the size of that market, and the competitive environment in the market.

6. *Obsolescence risk* is inherent in most high technology ventures where competition is active and a product's life cycle is short; the dynamics of the market lead to rapid product obsolescence.

The venture capitalist will evaluate the overall riskiness of the proposal by examining all the preceding aspects of risk. One would expect that as a business grows and matures, the degree of risk will be reduced. With each successive phase of the life cycle completed, the venture will be viewed as less risky. Thus, the farther along in the development process a venture is, the less a venture capitalist will require in terms of stock interest to attain a given expected rate of return on investment.

R&D Limited Partnerships

The R&D limited partnership is rapidly becoming an accepted method of funding research and development expenses. However, it was not until the landmark Supreme Court case of *Snow v. the Commissioner* in 1974 that this form of investing really came into existence. Section 174 of the Internal Revenue Code, passed by Congress in 1954, allows for the deduction of R&D expenditures. The IRS ruled in the case of Edwin Snow, a limited partner in an R&D arrangement, that the company actually performing the research and development was not actively offering a product for sale or generating revenue, and therefore was not "carrying on" a trade or business. Thus, the R&D had to be capitalized as part of the final cost of the product and could not be deducted as a legitimate business expense.

The Supreme Court reversed the IRS decision, ruling that Snow was entitled to deduct the expenses as long as they were paid or incurred "in connection with" a trade or business. As a result of this ruling, the definition of a partnership was expanded to include a startup organization, increasing the appeal of this organizational form as a vehicle for funding companies that do not yet have a marketable product.

Structure of the R&D Partnership

R&D partnerships are usually limited partnerships. Unlike a corporation, the R&D partnership is not a taxable entity. Thus, the income or loss generated in connection with the business is allocated to the various partners, who in turn report these figures on their individual tax returns. Any losses generated by the operation can be used to offset other income earned by the individuals.

As with any limited partnership, there are two primary functions to be filled in the organization: the general partner and the limited partners. The **general partner** manages the organization and assumes unlimited liability for the obligations of the operation. The general partner is most often the sponsoring company. However, it is becoming increasingly popular for an outside third party, usually a professional consultant who has packaged the deal and located the investors, to serve as the general partner. The **limited partners** are the investors in the project. To ensure their status as limited partners, they only provide capital and do not actively participate in the management of the business enterprise.

The entity possessing the base technology is referred to as the "sponsoring company." The research and development does not have to be high tech-

Tax Reform and Tax Shelters

The Tax Reform Act of 1986 severely limits the ability of individuals to benefit from tax shelters such as R&D limited partnerships. The Act actually defines three categories of trade: passive, active, and portfolio. Income or losses are assigned to one of the three categories on the basis of the nature of the activity used to generate them.

The most significant aspect of the Act concerning tax shelters is that it only allows losses from passive business activities to offset income from other passive activities. Losses can be carried forward (but not back) for five years to offset future passive gains. A **passive activity** is defined as one in which an individual does not materially participate in the conduct of the business or activity. The Act establishes conclusively that an interest in a limited partnership is a passive activity.

There is some flexibility in the passive loss limitation for taxpayers who have adjusted gross incomes of less than $100,000. These individuals can offset up to $25,000 of nonpassive income against losses from real estate activities in which active participation is involved. The $25,000 allowance is phased out at a 50 percent rate for incomes between $100,000 and $150,000.

This legislation will materially alter the way in which tax-sheltered investments are evaluated and chosen. R&D limited partnerships are not destroyed as a funding vehicle, but their use will be limited to those investors who have nonpassive gains to offset. In addition, the before-tax feasibility of venture opportunities will become more important in the decision-making process.

nology, but it should be a patentable idea leading to a marketable product. In return for the investment, the technology is made available to the partnership through a licensing arrangement.

The R&D contract must be carefully designed to ensure favorable tax treatment. The sponsoring company will agree to perform R&D to develop technology for the investors. All work is done on a "best efforts" basis; that is to say, there are no guarantees that the research will be successful in developing a product. Thus, the investors' capital is truly at risk.

Under Section 174, the limited partners are allowed to deduct the full amount of their investment in the year the payments are made under an R&D contract. It is not necessary for the sponsoring company to spend the funds in order for the investors to qualify for the current year deductions as long as there is a legitimate reason for prepaying the costs of the contract.

The R&D Arrangement

The typical R&D partnership arrangement allows the sponsoring company the option of buying back the technology to manufacture and market the resulting product. This is usually accomplished either through a lump sum payment or a percentage of the revenues generated from the sale of the product. The lump sum payment can be made either in cash or company stock. Any royalty arrangement usually calls for payments ranging from 6–10 percent of gross receipts, with either minimum or maximum payments being made during a specified time frame.

The investment of the limited partners is made in several installments. The typical arrangement calls for an initial cash payment and the signing of a recourse note obligating the investor to pay an additional sum at a specified future date. This allows the investor to deduct the full amount of the investment in the current tax year.

Advantages and Disadvantages

Since 1981, the use of R&D partnerships to fund early-stage development has grown significantly. In 1981, the market for R&D partnerships was only $160 million. Conservative estimates project that this figure will increase to over $2.25 billion by the end of the decade. Many analysts believe that this form of financing will surpass the venture capital industry as a source of seed capital and early-stage financing for companies involved in research and development. This, of course, will depend on continued favorable tax treatment of the R&D arrangement by the legislative authorities.

Although its popularity is increasing, the R&D partnership is not the best source of financing for everyone. The following is a list of advantages to the sponsoring company:

1. Less dilution of stock ownership is expected than with any other equity source. The sponsoring company is able to retain greater control of the project.

2. The risk of failure is borne by the partnership because the partnership owns the technology. Thus, the sponsoring company pays only in the event of a successful development.

3. If the contract is properly structured, the investment is "off balance sheet financing." That is to say, the funds do not show up as debt on the sponsoring company's financial statements. As a result, the company is likely to have an improved ability to borrow from conventional sources because of a substantially improved debt-to-equity ratio.

4. The company's ability to generate cash should be improved. Debt service on the typical loan begins immediately after receiving the loan. Royalty payments under an R&D arrangement do not begin until the product is successfully marketed.

There are also disadvantages to this type of financing:

1. The cost of funds to the sponsoring company is high, and is usually much more expensive than debt.

2. The use of invested funds is restricted solely to R&D expenses.

3. R&D partnerships are expensive to establish, both in terms of time and money.

Taking all these facts into consideration, R&D partnerships are still a viable source of funds for a few emerging firms. Most investors, however, are still initially looking for ventures that make good business sense, and then they look into the tax-shelter consequences. A quick examination into whether an opportunity has good R&D potential includes the following questions:

1. Does it fill a recognized need in the market?

2. What is the market potential?

3. Is there a profit potential of at least five times investment?

4. Is there patent protection?

5. Is the technology flexible? Can it be used in more than one application?

6. How much money will be at risk?

Implementing a research program based on R&D partnership funding begins with the preparation of a well-written business plan. The focus of the plan should be on the technology and its applications in the market. After this is adequately explained, the cost of the project and the potential returns to investors should then be analyzed.

Limited Stock Issues

If equity is not available from any of the previously mentioned sources, before deciding upon a public offering of stock, the entrepreneur should be aware of the mechanics of private placement as a means of circumventing the strict registration requirements of the public offering. The registration requirements governing the sale of stock to the public are discussed in detail in Chapter 12, "Public Offerings."

Private Placements

Regulation D of the Securities and Exchange Act of 1933 adopted in March, 1982, governs the offer and sale of stock exempt from full registration with the Securities and Exchange Commission (SEC). It offers the closely held business owner a means of accessing the public equity market without undergoing the expense of a full registration. Based on the results of an SEC study, over $15 billion in securities were issued in 7,222 filings during the first twelve months of operation. The average issue size was $2.5 million, with over 90 percent being less than $5 million (SEC 1984).

The criteria established to qualify for Regulation D exemption are:

1. No general advertising or soliciting is permitted.
2. A legend should be printed on the stock, stating that the securities are "restricted securities" and have not been registered with the SEC. This is done to ensure that initial purchases are being made as an investment and not with the intent to resell the shares to the public.

If these two conditions are met, a firm can sell up to $500,000 of securities in any twelve-month period. There is no limitation placed on the number of persons purchasing the securities.

Under Rule 505, a firm can sell up to $5 million worth of securities in any twelve-month period by limiting the offering to a maximum of thirty-five non-accredited investors. The principal factor in determining the accreditation of an investor is based on the ability of the investor to understand and properly evaluate the investment opportunity without a prospectus. These so-called "sophisticated" investors are those individuals who have the "knowledge and experience in financial and business matters [that show] that they are capable of evaluating the merits and risks of the prospective investment." Although all non-accredited investors must be furnished with a prospectus, the financial reporting requirements are not as strict as those of a full registration. Only financial statements from the most recent fiscal year need to be certified by an independent public accountant.

Rule 501 provides a list of those qualifying as "accredited investors." The categories include institutional investors (such as banks, insurance companies, and registered investment companies), private business development companies, pension plans, certain endowments (those with over $5 million in assets), company insiders (directors, officers, and general partners), and certain wealthy individuals (those who have a personal net worth of more than $1 million or annual income greater than $200,000). If only accredited investors are sold stock, an unlimited amount can be issued without registration.

One additional point should also be noted. Although a private issue is exempt from full registration requirements under federal law, a registration statement must be filed in each state in which stock is to be sold. These so-called "blue sky" laws must be satisfied regardless of the size of the issue. Most states have agreed, however, that if the issue qualifies under Regulation D, it fulfills the provisions of state law.

Intrastate Offerings

A firm offering securities only to investors living within a single state may be exempt from federal registration requirements, and thus may only need to fulfill the registration requirements of that state. Under the exemption offered by Section 3(a)(11) of the 1933 Act, there is no limit to the size of this type of offering. In order to qualify, most companies generally comply with the Commission's Rule 147. This "safe harbor" provision requires that the following guidelines be followed:

1. The offering company must be incorporated within the state in which the stock is offered and sold.
2. The executive offices of the corporation must also be located within that same state.
3. The corporation must generate at least 80 percent of its revenues from operations located within that state.
4. The corporation must have at least 80 percent of its assets located within the state.
5. At least 80 percent of the proceeds of the issue should be targeted for use within the state.

6. The issue should be sold only to state residents and resale to non-residents is restricted for a period of nine months.

The purpose of the intrastate offering is to provide local financing for local companies. The strictness of the requirements should indicate that the SEC is bound to this notion and that a stock offering of this nature should not be attempted without the advice of competent counsel.

Summary and Conclusions

During the developmental stage of the business life cycle, equity investments are the most commonly used method of funding a venture. The equity sources discussed in this chapter included informal investors, venture capitalists, R&D limited partnerships, and limited stock issues.

The one characteristic these equity sources have in common is that they are oriented toward risk capital investments. Their function in the capital market is to provide high risk capital for business development purposes. As a result, their required return is also quite high relative to the more conservative debt capital sources; this return comes in the form of capital gains through stock ownership.

Informal investors function primarily in the seed and startup stages of the life cycle of the business. For most small business owners, this financing source is made up of personal friends and relatives. For the entrepreneurial venture, another segment of the market opens up—the adventure capitalist. This informal network of wealthy individuals has the capacity to fund millions of dollars of venture opportunities. The problem for the entrepreneur searching for funds is locating such an "angel."

The venture capital industry, historically considered an early-stage investor, has expanded its investment strategy to include later-stage ventures. Although the SBIC industry has always been interested in investments at later stages of the business life cycle, the private venture capitalist is moving in that direction because of the growth in the industry and the intense competition for the relatively few good early-stage investment opportunities.

The R&D limited partnership is simply a way of structuring an investment opportunity to take advantage of certain provisions in the income tax code. In order to qualify for special tax treatment, the venture must have a relatively large research and development component. R&D limited partnerships are established to provide seed capital for the purpose of developing new technology. Investors in such an arrangement are able to deduct their investment in the year they join the partnership. If the technology is successful, the partnership owns the rights to the product and can either license it or sell it.

Finally, limited stock offerings were discussed as an alternative to the full registration requirements of the Securities and Exchange Commission. For those firms who wish to go public but do not have either the requirements or the resources for a full registration, private placement and intrastate offerings provide sound alternatives. These exemptions to the full registration requirements have been well accepted and are providing an option for the smaller firm to have access to the public equity market.

References

Directory of Operating Small Business Investment Companies. Washington, D.C.: Small Business Administration, December, 1984.

SBIC Digest. Washington, D.C.: Small Business Administration, Investment Division, October, 1982.

Securities and Exchange Commission, Director of Economic and Policy Analysis. *Analysis of Regulation D.* Washington, D.C.: Government Printing Office, May, 1984.

"Special Report on Venture Capital Industry Resources," *Venture Capital Journal* (July, 1983).

U.S. Federal Reserve System. *Financing Small Business, Parts 1 and 2.* Report to the U.S. Congress, Committees on Currency and Banking and the Select Committees on Small Business, 85th Congress, 2nd Session, April 11, 1958.

"Venture Capitalists Invest $2.8 Billion in 1983," *Venture Capital Journal* (May, 1984), pp. 7–10.

Wetzel, William E. and Seymour, Craig R. *Informal Risk Capital in New England.* Durham: University of New Hampshire Center for Industrial and Institutional Development, 1981.

11
Debt Sources

In many cases, small firms are not small because of the inherent efficiencies of small size, but because they are in the development stage of the business life cycle. Small firms share several common characteristics. They tend to compete in localized markets and thus require a funding source in or near their markets. The technology is often simple and barriers to entry tend to be quite low, resulting in a highly competitive environment.

The financing options have often been limited because of these factors. Large firms have many financing options available to them that are not available to small, emerging firms. These options include the sale of bonds and commercial paper, and the use of the general creditworthiness of the firm to borrow without pledging specific assets for collateral.

This lack of access to general capital markets forces small firms into situations in which they rely more heavily on certain types of financing. As the firm matures, other types of financing become more available because the perceived risks are categorically reduced or eliminated. Development-stage financing comes primarily from personal savings, informal investors, and government agencies. As the firm progresses into the early-growth stage, federally guaranteed bank loans, trade credit, and institutionalized equity funds become more available. During the expansion stage of the business life cycle, bank credit and other debt capital sources become much more viable options for the firm.

In this chapter, we will examine the common debt sources available to the owner of the entrepreneurial venture. There will be separate discussions on commercial banks, government sources, and other programs of special interest.

Commercial Banks

Commercial banks are the most common source of borrowed funds for small and emerging business firms. Approximately three-fourths of local businesses rely in some way on loans from local banks (*The State of Small Business* 1985). Because of the perception of greater risk in dealing with small firms and the extra administrative expense associated with smaller loans, many large financial institutions simply refuse to lend in this market. In fact, large commercial banks (with assets over $1 billion) rarely pursue smaller loans at all.

Short-term commercial lending has always been the primary focus of the industry's activity. Approximately 40 percent of the assets of the commercial banking industry are commercial and industrial loans. Lack of available data makes it difficult to actually measure bank involvement in the small business sector. From the limited information available, it is estimated that, as of December 1986, commercial banks have over $562 billion in commercial and industrial loans outstanding. Of this amount, small banks had approximately $74 billion outstanding, primarily to local small businesses (*Federal Reserve Bulletin*). In addition to the amount of capital devoted to this activity, its importance is reflected in the manpower requirement allocated to the commercial lending function in the typical bank.

Over 90 percent of all commercial loans made by banks go to **small firms,** which are defined, in this case, as businesses with total assets of less than $1 million. However, in terms of dollar volume, small firms receive less than one-half of the total funds made available to businesses. This means that although larger firms receive less than 10 percent of the commercial and industrial loans, they get over one-half of the dollar volume.

Traditionally, community banks (independent institutions with deposits of less than $100 million) have focused on the small business customer. These small banks provide over three-fourths of all loans to small business. There has been a move recently, however, for the large money-center banks such as Chase Manhattan and the Bank of New York to form special small business divisions to service the lower end of the market.

The commercial banking industry does not become a reliable source of financing until the later stages of the business life cycle. In a study by Len Fertuck (1982), a sample of bank loan officers indicated that over 80 percent of their commercial lending was to firms in the expansion stage of the business life cycle. Although a large number of inquiries about the availability of development-stage loans are made, only 12 percent of banks' loans are actually made at this early stage.

Even though cash flow from operations is the primary source of repayment for most commercial loans, banks in general can hardly be classified as "cash flow lenders." Commercial banking is dominated by "asset-based lenders." That is to say that almost all bank loans are secured with some type of tangible collateral. The secondary source of repayment (the collateral) takes on such an important role in the lending decision that many loans are actually described by the type of collateral securing them: inventory loans, accounts receivable loans, automobile loans, equipment loans, and real estate loans, to name a few.

A disproportionate percentage of small firms have to pledge specific assets as security when borrowing from a bank (as opposed to the much larger firms). Although they do not pledge specific assets, larger firms are typically able to show longer operating histories over which management capabilities can be better assessed. Additionally, large firms have larger asset bases, much of which is usually not specifically pledged to secure another loan. Thus, a loan can be effectively secured by the "general credit" of such a firm.

Owners of closely held businesses (regardless of organizational type) should be prepared to personally guarantee all business loans secured through a commercial bank. In many cases, this tertiary source of repayment plays a critical role in determining whether or not a loan is made. This is especially true in the case of development-stage fundings that are made through banks.

Bankers tend to be risk-averse because of the legal restrictions placed on the use of depositor funds. In addition, a lending officer's portfolio of clients tends to be a reflection of his ability and judgment. Pay and promotion are determined to a great extent by one's ability to develop new business for the bank and simultaneously avoid losses. As a result, entrepreneurs find that bank loan officers rarely lend to firms in the early development stages unless there is either significant personal net worth on the part of the borrower or a co-signer on whom to base a personal guarantee. When asked to explain the difference between bankers and venture capitalists, Roger V. Smith, president and CEO of the Silicon Valley Bank in San Jose, California, responded in this manner. "We're [meaning bankers] like Hertz Rent-a-Car. When they rent you a car, they charge you for usage, and they expect to get the car back. When we give you a loan, we charge interest, and expect to get our money back." (*Inc.* 1986)

Since bank financing is so important to the long-term viability of a business firm, an entrepreneur should begin early to develop and nurture sound banking relationships. The entrepreneur should begin by recognizing that banks have a variety of services to offer businesses of different types and sizes. The retail services offered by a bank are an important consideration in choosing an institution; these include hours of business, location, credit facilities, lock box arrangements, credit card services, and lending limits. However, these factors should be weighed against the human factor, and the entrepreneur should make sure that someone at the bank will take the time to become personally acquainted with his or her business operation.

The entrepreneur should begin by finding a bank where his business is appreciated. This requires carefully matching the business with a financial institution that is large enough to handle the service requirements of the firm and yet small enough to be interested in the account. Consideration should also be given that the long-range prospects of the firm and the bank develop at roughly the same rate. There is nothing more frustrating for an entrepreneur than for his firm to outgrow a bank, or worse, for the bank to outgrow the firm.

In order to foster the development of a sound working relationship with a banker, the entrepreneur should make an effort to keep him informed with respect to the financial status and progress of the firm. Usually this means that the business owner will submit periodic financial reports to the bank, including details about future plans and changing conditions that will have an impact on the operations. These reports should be submitted on a regular basis (monthly or quarterly), at least as often as statements are available from the accountant.

The banker should also be given copies of the firm's operations plan, along with income and cash flow projections and periodic updates. It is important that the projections be realistic and that they be attained. This becomes important as the firm begins to require capital from the bank in order to finance growth or expand into new markets. First of all, the banker will be well acquainted with the business and the planning process that has been established. Second, the entrepreneur will be recognized as an individual that can put together sound financial projections and, more importantly, meet those projections.

The results can be rather remarkable when an entrepreneur accepts these principles and puts them into practice. By following these simple steps, bank funding (especially during the early-growth phase of a firm's life cycle) can be relatively simple to secure. Without prior knowledge of a firm, a banker will subject a loan request to a rigorous formal review procedure that will require the submission of a complete business plan.

Government Sources

Federal involvement in business creation dates back at least to the 1800s, when the government helped to create the western railroads through land grants and direct subsidies. Periodic intervention has increased progressively since that time until today, the federal government is responsible for over $1.3 billion in startup financing via direct loans, subsidies, and loan guarantees. This assistance is offered through over 350 different programs (*Handbook for Small Business: A Survey of Small Business Programs of the Federal Government* 1984).

The Importance of Keeping the Banker Informed

The ingredients for a successful startup were all there: the entrepreneur was an MBA graduate of a prestigious northeastern university, he had ten years experience supervising the assembly operation of a Fortune 500 corporation, he was leaving a well-paying job and putting his life savings into the venture, and he had a well-prepared business plan to document its feasibility. With over one-third of the initial capitalization being owner's equity and modest loan request ($65,000) that was likely to be guaranteed by the SBA, this proposal seemed destined for quick approval. Even with all these aspects working in the entrepreneur's favor, it took seven months and five commercial banks before the request was approved.

Discouraging as this was to the entrepreneur, he conscientiously provided the banker with monthly financial statements comparing actual performance with projected performance, along with reasons for any variances. Financial projections were adjusted when new data were available (almost always increasing sales estimates).

Less than one year after the original loan was made, the company was experiencing a rapid increase in sales that was impossible to sustain given the level of operating capital available to the firm. The need for accounts receivable financing was obvious. Less than two weeks after the request for a $100,000 revolving line of credit was made, approval was given.

Sales continued to increase and soon capacity limitations began to restrict growth. If these levels were to be sustained, the firm would have to expand facilities. Less than two years after receiving the original loan, the entrepreneur went back to the bank with a request for a major capital expansion. The $200,000 request was made on the basis of the monthly report (of which the banker now had more than twenty) and was approved that same afternoon.

The review time for the proposals had been cut from seven months to two hours in the period of a few years. Granted, the loan officer had almost two years of experience with a successful entrepreneur; but more importantly, he was familiar with his openness and respected his forecasting ability, as shown by his willingness to share the details regarding the management of his operation.

Although many agencies have programs to help in business formation, most federal assistance is concentrated in the following major programs:

1. Small Business Administration
2. Economic Development Administration
3. Department of Housing and Urban Development
4. Department of Energy
5. National Science Foundation

Small Business Administration

The bulk of federal financial support for small business is concentrated in the Small Business Administration (SBA). In 1983, business loan approval—direct and guaranteed—totalled over $2.74 billion, as compared with $1.78 billion in fiscal 1982. Appropriations are scheduled to increase to $3.13 billion by 1988.

Federal policy toward small business can be summarized as follows:

> The essence of the American system of private enterprise is free competition.... The preservation and expansion of such competition is basic not only to the economic well-being but to the security of this Nation. Such security and well-being cannot be realized unless the actual and potential capacity of small business is encouraged and developed. It is the declared policy of the Congress that the Government should aid, counsel, assist, and protect, insofar as is possible, the interests of small-business concerns in order to preserve free competitive enterprise. [Small Business Act, Section 2(a)].

The Small Business Administration was created by the Small Business Act of 1953 to implement this policy. Located within the Department of Commerce, the agency has three primary lending objectives:

1. To stimulate small business in depressed areas.
2. To promote minority enterprise development.
3. To promote the contribution of small business to economic growth and a competitive environment.

Eligibility for the programs administered by the SBA is determined by a set of size standards established to determine whether or not a firm is "small." The approach taken to determine size standards takes into consideration the following principles:

1. Standard Industrial Classification codes at the four-digit level are used to define industries.
2. Size standards will vary across industries to reflect the unique structure of each industry, but a single standard for each industry will determine eligibility for all SBA programs.
3. The majority of the size standards are expressed in terms of number of employees. The notable exception to this standard is the construction industry, where a gross-receipts measure of size is used.

Transposing these considerations into a set of numerical size standards for individual industries is a complex task. Present eligibility standards vary considerably by industry, but in general are as follows:

1. Retail—Less than twenty-five employees; major exceptions are general

merchandise stores, grocery stores, automobile dealerships, restaurants, and mail-order houses.

2. Wholesale—Less than fifty employees, with numerous exceptions.

3. Services—Less than twenty-five or less than fifty employees, depending on industry; major exceptions are business services, certain recreation services, and health services.

4. Mining and Manufacturing—Less than 500 employees with numerous industries having lower limits.

5. Construction—Average annual receipts of less than $6 million.

For more detailed information see "Small Business Administration: Small Business Size Standards; Size Standards Revisions" (1982).

A variety of business loan programs are administered by the SBA. They include regular business loans, handicapped assistance loans, small business energy loans, disaster loans, and local development company loans. Table 11–1 presents a breakdown of the major aspects of SBA lending activity.

Disaster Business Loans. Although disaster loans make up the largest single aspect of the agency's portfolio, disaster loans to businesses are only of minor importance in the area of business lending. The vast majority of the disaster loans made each year are disaster home loans. These are loans made to individuals for the purpose of repairing damage done to residences that were

Table 11–1
SBA Loan Activity
(in millions of dollars)

Type of Loan	1986 Actual	1987 Estimated	1988 Estimated
Direct Loans			
Handicapped	$ 14.33	$ 15.00	$ —
Economic opportunity	13.60	24.00	—
Development company	207.09	43.00	—
Veterans	19.10	19.00	—
Total direct	$254.12	$101.00	—
Guaranteed Loans			
Handicapped	$ 1.04	$ 5.00	$ —
Economic opportunity	32.04	56.00	—
Development company	146.12	330.00	373.00
Energy	—	14.00	—
Regular business	2,129.50	2,473.00	2,494.00
Total guaranteed	$2,308.70	$2,878.00	$2,867.00

Source: Fiscal 1988 Budget of the United States Government.

located in specially designated "disaster areas." This designation results from natural phenomena such as floods, hurricanes, and tornados.

Local Development Companies—502 Loans. It is widely recognized that locally owned businesses contribute substantially to the economic well-being of a community. A healthy business climate plays an important role in expanding employment opportunities, increasing income, and broadening the local tax base. In order to encourage a grass-roots effort to assist local businesses in modernizing facilities, diversifying product lines, and, in general, expanding operations, legislation was enacted to enable local communities to form Local Development Companies (LDCs). The direct loan activity in this program is scheduled to decline substantially over the next few years from $207 million in 1986 to $43 million in 1987. This scheduled reduction in direct loan activity is not the result of a reduced emphasis in community development on the part of the federal government. It comes about primarily because of the increased emphasis in guaranteed lending and the introduction of the certified development company (Section 503) program, which will be discussed in a later section. Guaranteed development company loans are scheduled to increase from $146 million in 1986 to $373 million in 1988.

The local development company loan program of the Small Business Administration was created under Section 502 of the Small Business Investment Act of 1958; it authorized the SBA to make loans to LDCs for the purpose of assisting specific small businesses. The stated purpose of the program is:

> To encourage economic growth and prosperity in a community by making available low-interest, long term loans to local development companies for the purchase of land, the construction, expansion, or remodeling of buildings and the purchase of operating machinery and equipment for use therein by a small business (see *Loans to Local Development Companies*, 1975).

The requirements for establishing a Local Development Company are:

1. A minimum of twenty-five individuals interested in community development must join together in organizing the LDC.
2. At least 75 percent of the shareholders or members must either live or work in the LDC's defined area of operation (a specific geographic area within the community, city, or county).
3. The LDC must be organized as either a profit or a nonprofit corporation in the state in which it will conduct business.

In many areas of the country, local development companies are organized and operated by local chambers of commerce or boards of trade, the local affiliate of the National Urban League, the state industrial commission, or simply a citizens' group that is interested in furthering the cause of economic development within the local community.

In order to be eligible for loan funds under Section 502, the LDC must demonstrate both that the funds will be used for construction purposes, including renovation and land acquisition, and there are identifiable small business firms (as defined by SBA size standards) that will use the facilities. The beneficiary firms typically contract to use the facilities by lease or lease-purchase agreement, or occasionally by sale with periodic installment payments.

Since the primary motivation of the members of the LDC is an interest in community development and not profit, many of these corporations are nonprofit. The income that is received for the use of facilities must be sufficient only to cover the repayment of all loans with interest; pay taxes, insurance premiums, maintenance charges, and establish reasonable reserves in these areas; cover the general and administrative expenses of the corporation; and recover the company's capital (including a fair rate or return in order to maintain a broad ownership base).

Funds under this program are available through bank loans with SBA participating loans or an SBA-guaranteed bank loan. The LDC typically injects only 10 percent of the total cost of the project, with the remainder coming from the previously mentioned loan sources. The SBA portion of the project is limited to $500,000, with a maximum loan maturity of twenty-five years.

A business owner seeking LDC assistance should realize that a business plan must be reviewed by three lenders: the LDC, the bank, and the SBA. The entire review process may turn into a prolonged ordeal and take several months. Anyone interested in this program should contact the Small Business Administration for the location of LDCs in their geographic area.

Loans to Minorities. The Economic Opportunity Loan (EOL) program was established to assist socially and economically disadvantaged individuals in establishing and expanding their business ventures. In order to qualify for this program, a person must be a member of a qualified minority group. Blacks, Hispanics, Native Americans, Aleuts, Asian-Pacific Americans, Asian Indians, Vietnam era veterans, and women have been defined as eligible minorities for purposes of this program.

The EOL program places a limit on the maximum loan amount available for any single business of $150,000 (under certain circumstances, this can be increased to $300,000). Loan terms can be extended for up to ten years, and interest rates are usually well below market rates.

In order to secure an EOL loan, an entrepreneur must establish eligibility for the program and then show that capital is not available in the private market. SBA funding for this program is established annually by the Congress and is extremely limited. As a result, the SBA carefully screens each loan request, usually funding the smaller "mom-and-pop" operations for amounts substantially less than the maximum allowable. In 1986, minority-owned businesses received $45.5 million from the economic opportunity loan program. The more viable requests are reviewed in the regular business loan program.

Regular Business Loans. There are two basic types of loans in the regular business loan or 7(a) program: direct loans and guaranteed loans. Loans made directly by the SBA come from funds appropriated by the Congress specifically for this purpose. The demand for direct monies always exceeds their availability, so there is invariably a waiting list of loans that have been approved and are waiting to be funded. In fiscal year 1983, less than 10 percent of the loans and 5 percent of the dollar volume were approved as direct loans. By 1986 the direct lending program was phased out almost completely.

The SBA cannot legally lend to a firm if funds are available from private sources. In order to establish that funds are not available, an entrepreneur must present one to two letters of rejection from local commercial banks with the loan application (depending on whether the city size is less than or greater than 200,000). The maximum loan amount is $150,000 and can be extended over a period of ten years. Interest rates are usually well below market rates.

The majority of the SBA involvement, however, is in the area of "bank guaranteed loans." The SBA can guarantee up to 90 percent of the principal balance (up to a maximum of $500,000) for up to ten years (fifteen, if the loan is for construction purposes). Appropriations for this program are determined by the Congress. In 1986 over $2 billion in loans were guaranteed by the SBA in this program. The SBA requires that the financial institution requesting the guarantee accept as much exposure as possible. This enables the limited appropriations to be extended to aid as many businesses as possible.

Small Business Energy Loans. The amended Small Business Act created a lending program to assist small businesses that were developing, manufacturing, selling, installing, or servicing certain types of energy conservation devices. Twenty-five of these loans were approved in fiscal year 1983, totalling approximately $4 million. Congress has appropriated $14 million in the 1987 budget for this program.

Handicapped Assistance Loans. Assistance to handicapped individuals is also provided by the SBA. In fiscal year 1986, over $15 million was approved for handicapped entrepreneurs. This amount is scheduled to increase to $20 million in 1987.

Neighborhood Business Revitalization. The federal government has established a joint SBA–HUD–EDA program to assist distressed cities in encouraging business development. Even though this program has been formally discontinued, similar loans are being made through other agencies.

Certified and Preferred Lenders Programs. In 1979, the SBA began a Certified Lenders Program (CLP), which gives qualifying commercial banks (and a few non-bank financial institutions) increased authority in loan processing. Banks that have an excellent track record in loan losses on SBA-guaranteed loans and a commitment to the local small business community, as shown by their use of the guaranty program, are eligible for the CLP designation.

The benefits to the bank include an increased ability to service the local small business community by streamlining the usual processing procedure. The SBA is pledged to respond to a completed guaranty request within ten working days. However, if the requesting bank is a "certified lender," the response time is only three days. During fiscal 1983, the CLP included 530 commercial lenders. Over 2,800 loans were approved for $360 million.

In fiscal year 1983, the SBA began what is referred to as the preferred lenders program (PLP). In order to be chosen as a "preferred lender," a bank must be a successful participant in the CLP and have a demonstrated ability to handle all aspects of the SBA loan procedure: process, approval, service, and liquidation. A preferred lender has only to complete the required paperwork and the SBA will automatically approve every request for guarantee. An entrepreneur who is interested in a guaranteed loan should try to establish a banking relationship with a bank that has one of these classifications.

The SBA Loan Application. The SBA loan application includes the following information:

1. A brief summary (one to two pages) of the business proposal, including a statement of sources and uses of funds.
2. A summary of the collateral offered as security.
3. Personal financial statements for each major shareholder (with more than 20 percent ownership), partner, officer, or owner.
4. Business financial statements (balance sheet, income statement, and reconciliation of net worth) for the past three years; financial statements and an aging schedule of accounts receivable and payable that are less than ninety days old; and monthly earnings and cash flow projections for at least one year.
5. A schedule of debt, including the date, amount, current principal balance, interest rate, monthly payment, maturity date, and collateral.
6. A brief business history, including expected benefits of the loan.

7. Resumes of owners and key management personnel.
8. Other information may be required, depending on the circumstances associated with the specific request.

Economic Development Administration

The Economic Development Administration (EDA) was established in 1965 under the provisions of the Public Works and Economic Development Act. The primary purpose of EDA is to encourage business development in depressed areas that have high unemployment and low family incomes. The result is that the goal of the program is to assist private enterprise development in the creation of new and permanent jobs.

Financial assistance through the EDA comes in the form of grants, loans, and loan guarantees for commercial and industrial facilities and working capital. The federal government can guarantee up to 90 percent of the principal on loans for the acquisition of fixed assets and working capital. Current budget amounts are less than $150 million, half the fiscal 1980 appropriation. The future of the program seems doubtful as Congress begins to reassess its involvement in private capital markets and consolidate its programs.

Department of Housing and Urban Development

Housing and Urban Development (HUD) programs for business are administered through grants to local municipalities. The Urban Development Action Grant (UDAG) program, created by the Housing and Community Development Act of 1977, grants funds to municipalities who in turn lend or grant the money for building construction or product manufacturing (see "Places that Give Money Away," *Venture* June 1980).

The stated purpose of the UDAG program is "to assist distressed cities and distressed urban counties in revitalizing their economic bases and reclaiming deteriorated neighborhoods." The focus of the assistance is on projects that address the commercial, industrial, or residential needs of the community. The federal appropriation for the program in fiscal year 1984 was $440 million.

Business development funding through this program is available in economically distressed areas. Project eligibility is determined in part by the impact of the proposed project on the special problems facing low- and moderate-income individuals. The extent to which the private sector is participating financially in the proposed project is also a primary concern.

The community development block grant (CDBG) program was created by the Housing and Community Development Act of 1974 and was later revised in 1977 and 1981. Its revised scope of activity is the result of the consolidation of eleven previously existing programs, including the Urban

Renewal and Model Cities programs. The primary purpose of CDBG is to develop "viable urban communities, by providing decent housing and a suitable living environment and expanding economic opportunities." Funds are directed to local communities and spent by the municipalities in accordance with their Community Development Plans for specific community development activities.

The range of eligible activities is quite extensive. Most of the funding is directed toward neighborhood revitalization projects and improvements in community service and facilities. All projects must either directly benefit low- to moderate-income neighborhoods or meet other urgent community needs.

The 1977 revision added a separate category for economic development to the eligibility list. Commercial and industrial facilities that are identified as necessary in the implementation of the community's overall economic development program may be eligible for direct funding. In addition, the program permits the recipient of certain block grants to serve as a conduit for funding local development companies and MESBICs, with the requirement that these funds be used in neighborhood revitalization projects or minority business development.

The combined appropriation for fiscal 1986 was $3.60 billion for commercial development and rehabilitation in targeted cities. Even though UDAG is scheduled for termination in 1988, the appropriation for CDBG will remain over $3 billion. The funds are distributed by local city councils, based on their assessment of local community needs.

Department of Energy

The Department of Energy (DOE) annually budgets approximately $20 million in three separate programs in the area of energy-related technology. The Appropriate Technology Grants program provides small grants for new energy sources or conservation measures. The Office of Transportation of DOE provides grants to demonstration projects for electric vehicles. In conjunction with the National Bureau of Standards, grants are awarded to inventors of energy-saving devices to perfect their products, start a company, or license the technology.

National Science Foundation

For smaller companies engaged in technological innovation, the Small Business Innovation Research (SBIR) program is potentially an excellent source of financing. The program was enacted to encourage small business participation in the research and development activities of the federal government.

The program has been set up in three stages. Companies are first allowed to compete for initial feasibility awards of up to $50,000, the purpose of which is to test their innovations for six months. If the projects are feasible, awards of up to $500,000 are possible. The purpose of the second phase is to provide operating capital to cover developmental expenses for a two-year period. Full commercialization, the third phase of the program, is to be supported through private sector financing.

The SBIR program is specifically targeted at identifying private-sector firms that have the best capability of taking scientific advances to the marketplace. The program was begun on an experimental basis in 1979 by the National Science Foundation and was expanded by the Small Business Innovation Development Act in July 1982. Up until October 1982, when the program was opened to all federal agencies with R&D budgets over $100 million, 3,028 grant proposals from approximately 1,000 companies were reviewed. Of that number, only 475 proposals were accepted (15.7 percent).

In 1983, 8,814 proposals were submitted and there were 727 approvals. Total dollar awards amounted to $44.4 million. Funding is expected to rise through 1986 and will total over $1 billion. Announcements of agency solicitations can be secured by getting on a mailing list at any SBA office.

Programs of Special Interest

Two additional programs that are of special interest have been singled out because of their potential impact on the private sector. Certified development companies and industrial development bonds will be discussed separately.

Certified Development Companies

The certified development company (CDC) program is a recent addition to the list of federal funding options for the small business. An amendment to the Small Business Investment Act of 1958 was enacted on July 2, 1980, expanding the provisions of Section 503 and creating the certified development company program.

The philosophy of the program is substantially different from that of the other lending programs supervised by the Small Business Administration. Rather than serving as a "lender of last resort," the SBA-certified development company provides long-term, fixed asset financing to qualified small businesses. In order to qualify for the program, a business must be organized as a for-profit concern (proprietorship, partnership, or corporation) and meet certain size standards. The business must have a net worth of less than $6 million and an average after-tax profit over the past two years of less than $2 million. A manufacturing firm must have no more than the prescribed number of employees based on SBA size standards.

Certified development companies are organized either as private, nonprofit corporations or for-profit stock corporations. The CDC must have a minimum of twenty-five members or stockholders from a defined area of operation (usually a county or smaller area). The CDC will also have a professional staff qualified to package, process, close, and service loans. Accounting and legal services are also provided, usually under a contractual arrangement with an independent firm.

The unique feature of the CDC program is the method of funding that the Act has made available to the SBA. When a project is approved for funding, the CDC is authorized to sell 100 percent SBA-guaranteed debentures for up to one-half of the total capitalization of the project. These debentures are sold to the Federal Financing Bank (operating through the Chemical Bank of New York), and the SBA acts as agent for the CDC.

The remaining portion of the capitalization must come from non-federal sources such as personal and stockholder equity or commercial loan sources. The private funding source receives a first mortgage on all assets and the SBA debentures hold a subordinated, second-mortgage position.

Proceeds from the sale of the guaranteed debentures can be used for the acquisition of land and buildings, construction, renovation, and the purchase of machinery and equipment. In addition, funds can be used to pay interest expenses on interim financing and professional fees for services such as appraisals, accounting, and architectural and engineering consultations.

The typical CDC project is structured as follows:

Bank loan	50 percent
SBA guaranteed debentures	40 percent
CDC funds	10 percent

The required CDC participation is a minimum of 10 percent of the total cost of the project. The source of the CDC financing can be loans, stockholders' equity, or, more frequently, funds from the small business concern receiving the assistance.

The CDC provides assistance primarily through two basic plans: the re-lend plan and the lease plan. Under the re-lend plan, the small business buys the assets and holds the title, subject to the provisions of the bank and SBA liens. In this case, the CDC serves solely as an agent through which the SBA-guaranteed debentures are passed on to the small business. Under the lease plan, the CDC retains the title to the assets and leases them to the small business. Whether the arrangement is a lease-purchase or lease with an option to purchase, the CDC manages the entire project and makes the completed facility available to the small business.

Entrepreneurs interested in pursuing this financing alternative should contact the financial assistance division of their local SBA office for a listing of certified development companies.

Industrial Development Bonds

The concept of Industrial Development (IDB) financing involves the issuance of tax-exempt bonds by a local municipality or nonprofit corporation. The proceeds of the bond issue can be used to purchase plant, machinery, or equipment that in turn is leased or sold to a private corporation. Thus, the local municipality or nonprofit corporation serves as an intermediary through which funds are made available to local businesses at below-market interest rates.

Since it was enacted in 1913, the Federal income tax code has allowed an exemption for interest earned on bond obligations issued for the benefits of state or local governments. The use of tax-exempt bonds to provide financing for private business purposes originated in the South in the 1930s. Federal regulations allowed this use to continue in order to assist agriculturally dependent communities in competing with the major urban centers to attract industry and expand employment opportunities.

In response to an increased volume of IDB issues, the Congress passed the Revenue Adjustment Act of 1968 (P.L. 90-364), limiting the circumstances under which IDB interest would be tax-exempt. Tax-exempt status is provided for financing numerous business projects, such as manufacturing and other commercial facilities, industrial parks, hotels, sports facilities, airports, docks, sewage treatment, and pollution control facilities.

Most states have enacted enabling legislation to examine and determine the eligibility of each proposed project. For example, the state of Texas recently enacted legislation to allow the use of IDBs to finance business activity within the state. Nearly $1 billion in bonds had been issued within two years of the passage of the Development Corporation Act of 1979.

For an entrepreneur interested in financing a business through an IDB issue, the first step is to carefully research the project to determine eligibility for funding under state and federal statutes. The second step is to contact the local industrial development corporation (the municipality or other nonprofit corporation specifically established to administer the program) and request that the project be reviewed. Before a local industrial development corporation can formally act on a project, an application must be filed with the state authorities. This application is in effect an extensive business plan with the following specific contents:

1. A brief project description including location, intended use, number and type of jobs created, estimated annual payroll, estimated cost of the proj-

ect, and approximate dates of commencement and completion of construction.

2. A description of the corporate entity requesting the financing. This includes general identifying information such as a certified copy of the corporate resolution to undertake the project.

3. A detailed description of the business that will use the facilities. This includes a history of the business, an analysis of the business and industry, a description of the management team, and detailed financial information, along with three years of financial statements.

4. A description of the proposed bond issue, including amount, debt service schedule, rating, and security. A letter from the underwriter stating that the bonds are marketable is also required.

5. A copy of all agreements, leases, contracts, and other instruments.

6. A statement examining the economic impact of the project on the local community, specifically addressing its influence on employment, the tax base, and other related business activity.

7. A statement establishing that the project will be located in an area that qualifies under federal statutes for IDB financing.

After all parties agree at the local level, the industrial development corporation authorizes the bond issue and requests approval from the local city council. If approved by the local city council, the request is forwarded to the state level, where final authorizing for the bond issue is in the hands of the State Development Commission.

Tax-exempt IDB financing provides significant advantages to the business seeking such funds:

1. Up to 100 percent of the cost of land, building, and equipment, as well as development and financing costs may be covered by the issue.

2. Repayment schedules are tailored to meet the needs of the corporation.

3. IDB issues are exempt from Securities and Exchange Commission registration requirements.

4. Bonds can be issued prior to construction. The IDB financing is thus used as both interim and long-term financing.

5. Since the bonds are tax-exempt, the corporation is able to take advantage of lower financing costs.

In addition, the municipality is able to take advantage of an increased tax base, increased employment opportunities, and expanding commercial activity in the community.

Limiting the State's Use of IDBs:
Killing the Goose that Laid the Golden Egg

Over $19 billion in industrial development bonds were issued nationwide in 1981. By 1983, this total increased to $22.8 billion. The use of IDBs, however, results in reduced federal income tax payments to the U.S. Treasury. A study by the Congressional Budget Office estimates that federal revenue loss associated with the cumulative sale of state and local IDB issues in 1983 was approximately $4 billion. This of course does not take into consideration the impact of the increased local tax base or personal incomes as a result of the development activities.

National estimates of the net tax effect of IDB issues, which consider not only reduced income tax revenues caused by the tax-exempt nature of the interest earnings, but also the increased tax revenues in the form of sales taxes, property taxes, and income taxes as a result of new job formation, are not available because few states have the appropriate methodology required for these purposes. The state of Texas, however, does have an econometric model that has been developed by the Comptroller's Office for revenue projection purposes. Using this model, it has been estimated that the state's 1,191 IDB issues between 1980 and April, 1984, which total $4.3 billion, have had a positive net tax effect of $973 million for the State Treasury. In addition, permanent employment in those projects has increased by over 64,000 jobs and employment in supporting industries has increased by over 100,000.

Texas represents only 10 percent of the IDB activity in the country. If the net effect of IDBs in Texas is representative of that in the country as a whole, the positive tax effects at the state level more than offset the negative effects at the federal level. It should also be noted that the net tax effects in Texas do not take into consideration the increased income tax base resulting from the 170,000 permanent jobs created (Texas does not have a state income tax).

The Reform Tax Act of 1986 had a significant negative impact on the IDB market. Activity in the market fell to just under half of the 1985 level of $17.5 billion. Under the new law, commercial banks are no longer allowed to deduct the interest they pay to borrow funds to buy private-use, tax-exempt bonds. In addition to the tax change, the legislation limits the amount of tax-exempt bonds each state can issue on behalf of private concerns. This forces the state development authorities responsible for promoting the IDB issues to come up with new ways to increase their attractiveness. This will undoubtedly mean higher yields on IDBs and fewer projects financed.

Other Funding Sources

Other institutionalized lenders are also active in varying degrees in the private debt capital market. We will discuss the savings and loan industry, business finance companies, business factors, insurance companies, and community development corporations as sources of debt capital to the closely held firm.

Savings and Loan Associations

Since the early 1970s, research results regarding the policies and practices of the savings and loan industry have argued persuasively for broadening the lending authority of the industry. Deregulation and diversification of the loan portfolio were seen as the keys to the long-term viability of the industry.

Despite the advance warning, federal policymakers did not act quickly enough to enable the industry to avert a major loss in capital during the 1980–1982 recession. Savings and loan associations have only recently been granted the opportunity to significantly diversify their asset holdings. This change was accomplished through the enactment of the Depository Institutions Deregulation and Monetary Control Act of 1980, which permitted savings and loans to expand the services offered to commercial customers. This legislation, along with the Garn-St. Germain Depository Institutions Act of 1982, made over 100 changes in the banking laws that directly affected the savings and loan industry. The recognized problem was the mismatch in the maturity structure of the industry's assets and liabilities. Assets were long-term in nature (fixed-rate mortgages), while liabilities were short-term. The principal changes in the legislation granted commercial and consumer lending powers to savings and loans that were previously reserved for commercial banks. Prior to this legislation, federally-chartered savings and loans were limited in their abilities to provide financial services, principally short-term commercial and industrial loans, to commercial customers.

Overall, the nation's thrift institutions have been very cautious in using these expanded powers. As of March 1984, federally insured savings and loan associations nationwide still had less than $4.5 billion (less than 1 percent of their total assets) in non-mortgage commercial and industrial loans. At the same time, gross loans for the industry amounted to over $710 billion. This conservatism is primarily caused by the lack of expertise in the commercial lending area and the high overhead cost of acquiring and developing that expertise. Thus, it does not appear that the industry as a whole can be considered serious competition in the commercial loan market at this time. However, a significant number of individual institutions scattered throughout the country are competing vigorously with commercial banks in the consumer and commercial loan market.

To the individual entrepreneur this means that, while the industry will remain a specialized mortgage lender for some time, many individual savings and loan associations will be diversifying slowly into the commercial and industrial loan market. Thus, this industry should not be ignored as a potential source of funding. In fact, the savings and loan association should be considered as an alternative to the more traditional sources provided by the commercial banking industry.

Business Finance Companies

Finance companies are often referred to as "asset-based lenders." They provide assistance to closely held businesses in the form of secured loans to finance inventory, accounts receivable, machinery, equipment, and real estate. In many ways, the industry is in direct competition with the commercial banking industry in the area of loans to businesses. There are three different types of finance companies operating in the market: sales finance companies, consumer finance companies, and commercial finance companies. All three are active in lending to business in varying degrees, with commercial and sales finance companies being the most active.

All finance companies, regardless of type, are interested in the borrower's ability to repay the loan. However, they tend to extend credit primarily on the basis of the strength of the collateral offered, rather than the ability to repay as projected by the prospective cash flow statements. As a result, firms that have been denied credit from other institutions (primarily banks and credit units) because of a poor track record or highly leveraged financial position may find a finance company eager to extend credit.

Sales finance companies allocate more than one-half of their funds in the area of sales credit financing, with automobile wholesale and retail sales credit representing the majority. About one-fourth of their funds are used for lending to businesses. The 1,200 sales finance companies account for approximately 60 percent of the total funds available in the finance company industry. Most of the larger finance companies are of this type. (The General Motors Acceptance Corporation is a well-known sales finance company.)

Although consumer finance companies number over 2,500, they account for only one-fourth of the funds available in the industry. Most of their funds are used in making relatively small cash loans that are secured by the borrower's personal property. In some cases, loans in excess of $10,000 are secured by second mortgages on the borrower's homestead. Loans of this type can be used to finance a business only in certain regions of the country. In many states, a homestead exemption limits the use of second mortgages on residences to improvements on the property itself.

The approximately 600 commercial finance companies are more specialized in their lending activities. Almost 90 percent of their lending is in the form of business credit, with accounts receivable financing being the most common form of credit used. The use of accounts receivable financing is very popular because of its high degree of liquidity.

In addition, commercial finance companies offer intermediate term loans for the purchase of commercial, industrial, and farm equipment. In most cases, the loan terms rarely extend beyond three years and the purchased equipment serves as collateral for the loan. Other areas in which commercial finance companies become involved include equipment leasing, factoring, and automobile dealer floor planning.

In most cases, it is not necessary to provide an extensive business plan when approaching a finance company for a loan. A firm's ability to borrow funds is determined on the basis of the appraised value of the collateral offered, historical financial statements, credit references, and resumes of the owners and key managers. The major exception to this rule occurs when the firm is borrowing from a commercial finance company that has the intention of seeking a guarantee from the Small Business Administration. As an example, the Commercial Credit Corporation has a signed guaranty agreement with the SBA and actively seeks guarantees. In such cases, a complete SBA loan proposal is required.

As financial markets become more competitive as a result of deregulation, many sales and consumer finance companies are expanding more rapidly into the field of commercial lending. Once almost solely concentrated in the field of consumer installment credit, these two types of finance companies will be a competitive force to be reckoned with in the future. The industry currently has over $100 billion in total loans outstanding.

Business Factors

Business factors are among the oldest types of financial institutions in the United States. Although business factoring has been in existence for many years, it is largely misunderstood and unappreciated outside of the domestic apparel industry. In fact, this form of underwriting is largely responsible for the growth of that industry.

A commonly held belief is that the one hundred or so firms comprising the industry are lenders of last resort. A 1985 survey by Dun and Bradstreet Credit Services revealed that only 7 percent of the 1,060 responding firms admitted to dealing with factors. A factor performs three primary functions:

1. Purchasing accounts receivable.
2. Selecting credit risks and collecting receivables.
3. Providing advisory services.

A business that uses a factoring company actually sells its accounts receivable for cash that is immediately available. The factor is not extending a loan; it purchases the receivable "without recourse." This arrangement implies that the factor will purchase only the receivables of a firm whose customers are determined to be creditworthy. Since the factor absorbs all bad debt losses, it takes responsibility for all the associated credit and collection functions and expenses.

Factoring improves the current financial position of the firm by reducing the cash required to support a given volume of sales. A typical factor allows sales volumes of ten to fourteen times net worth, while a commercial bank may want to see no more than six to eight times net worth. A firm that factors its receivables can support a faster rate of growth than one relying strictly on bank financing. In addition, by only committing receivables, the other assets of the firm are left unattached and available to secure additional borrowing.

Since the factor assumes the risk of customer default, the cost of such an arrangement is greater than that of simple receivables financing at a commercial bank (with which it is often confused). A fee or commission is charged for performing the credit and collection function. This is generally expressed as a percentage of the full face value of the invoice sold (1–2 percent). In addition, interest is charged on all funds advanced to the firm.

The factor is primarily interested in the credibility of the business owner and the nature of the client's customer base, including the diversity of the invoices submitted for factoring. The capitalization of the business is not the critical factor in the factoring decision; the strength of the receivables themselves is the main issue.

The mechanics of selling an invoice to a factor are:

1. After an order is received, it is submitted to the factor for credit approval (assuming that this is a customer that has not been previously approved).
2. After the customer has been judged creditworthy, shipment is made and the invoice is sent to the factor.
3. The amount of the invoice is credited to the firm's account and can be immediately withdrawn, minus a reasonable reserve, which is usually defined as 20–40 percent. The reserve is held as insurance against returned merchandise and other claims. Once payment is made on the invoice, the firm can withdraw the remainder of the invoice, minus fees and interest charges.

The decision of whether or not to use a factor should be made by comparing the cost of the factor assuming the credit and collection function of the firm with the cost of operating it as part of the firm's internal operations.

Life Insurance Companies

Life insurance companies are potentially an extremely good source of business financing. With over 1,600 companies operating in the United States today, the industry accounts for over 12 percent of all funds made available by financial institutions. Virtually all of the funds available through the industry are long-term in nature, and thus they account for a considerable share of all external long-term capital.

Around 25 percent of the funds of the industry are used to finance mortgages on commercial property. When considering a mortgage loan, the insurance company's primary concern is focused on the property being financed. All properties are carefully examined by an independent appraiser, with special emphasis on the type of building construction (facilities with multiple uses are highly preferred).

Life insurance companies are usually not interested in properties that have appraised values of less than $150,000. Loans are typically made for 70–80 percent of the property's collateral value, with terms extending from twenty to thirty years. Regulations limit the amount of risk on investments, so loans are made only to corporate entities that have been in existence for a minimum number of years (usually five). In addition, a demonstrated historical and present earnings record is required of the borrower.

For holders of certain types of life insurance policies, another possible source of capital is the policy loan. As a policy accumulates cash value, the holder can borrow up to 95 percent of its cash value. The funds can be used in any manner the holder finds appropriate—either for business or personal reasons. Interest rates are usually quite low and loan terms are indefinite. Policy loans are either paid back according to a schedule determined by the borrower or, if they are not paid back, the value of the life insurance coverage is reduced by the amount of the loan. Policy loans make up only about 6 percent of the investments of the industry as a whole.

Community Development Corporations

Even though the United States is the wealthiest nation on earth, there are many areas in the country, both urban and rural, that can be accurately described as "pockets of poverty." These areas have, for the most part, remained untouched by the advancing industrialization that is responsible for the increasing living standards we enjoy.

In an effort to reduce the number and size of these less developed areas of the economy, the Congress enacted into law the Economic Opportunity Act of 1964, creating the Office of Economic Opportunity (OEO) to administer development programs in these areas. Economic development was not specifically designated as a major responsibility of the OEO until the Act was amended in 1972 under Title VII, changing the agency's name to Community Services Administration.

It was also at this time that the community development corporation (CDC) became the agency's major vehicle for community development. A community development corporation is an organization created to address the economic development needs of a particular community. A CDC can be organized as a profit or nonprofit corporation or as a cooperative. Regardless of organizational structure, the CDC is privately owned by a group of individuals living or operating businesses in the target area for the purpose of planning, promoting, and stimulating economic activity.

In fulfilling this stated purpose, the CDC's main function is to expedite the transfer of capital from both local sources and sources outside the community into projects that will improve the quality of life and increase the social and economic participation of the residents of a geographically defined area. By improving the economic, social, and other resources of the local community, it is hoped that the poverty cycle fostered by the social welfare system can be broken. The CDC accomplishes this by operating solely under the guidance of a community-based board of directors.

Many urban CDCs become involved in housing development and rehabilitation projects that are relying on funds from federal government sources such as Community Development Block Grants, Urban Development Action Grants, and Housing and Urban Development funds. By planning business development to coincide with infrastructure improvements, the CDC is able to attract capital from private sources and foster a more balanced growth in the community.

A CDC located in a rural area faces a set of problems that is quite different in nature. The characteristics of a low-income rural population usually include low educational attainment, few job skills, and low density. As a result, such a community will have a difficult time identifying community needs and attracting outside firms into the area. Thus, rural CDCs have tended to concentrate on developing the infrastructure of the community in ways that will increase the area's attractiveness to outside concerns such as shopping malls, industrial parks, and utility hook-ups.

There are several advantages to dealing with a community development corporation. Regardless of the state of the economy, the CDC is looking for good investment opportunities. In fact, during downturns in economic activity when other lenders are becoming more conservative, often the CDC is actively seeking ways to improve the economic conditions of its target area. Since most CDCs are located in areas with high unemployment rates and low income levels, the creation of jobs and managerial and entrepreneurial opportunities takes on a high priority. In addition, community support plays a significant role in determining whether or not a CDC will become interested in a particular project. As a result, it is possible to fund startup ventures through a CDC as long as the potential benefits to the community are substantial. Finally, CDCs have a significant amount of flexibility in structuring the financing package. Loans are typically provided at attractive terms and, in many cases, the CDC will take an equity position in a company to ensure the success of the venture.

By their very nature, CDCs are located in less developed areas of the economy. Regardless of the type of CDC (rural or urban) the area will have many of the characteristics of a depressed area, including limited access to many big-city conveniences, and a generally unskilled local labor force. These characteristics limit the range of business opportunities that can be successfully undertaken.

Although the CDC may respond more slowly than the venture capitalist, it should be approached in much the same manner. In addition to the traditional business plan, the business owner should carefully address the development needs of the local community. However, for the entrepreneur who is willing to locate a venture in the target area and address the concerns of the local community, funding through a CDC can be extremely advantageous.

Summary and Conclusions

In this chapter we have explored the many possibilities in financing through debt capital that are available to the owner of the entrepreneurial venture: commercial banks, government agencies, savings and loan associations, business finance companies, factoring companies, life insurance companies, and community development companies. Because of the nature of the reward available to the funding source, the risk that is willingly absorbed is small. Thus, firms seeking debt capital are likely to be more successful in the later stages of the business life cycle. Only in those circumstances in which the entrepreneur can tap into a federal government program is it feasible to seek debt capital at an earlier stage.

References

Board of Governors of the Federal Reserve System. *Federal Reserve Bulletin,* various issues.

Certified Development Company Program: Program Guide. Washington, D.C.: Small Business Administration, Financial Assistance Division, January, 1984.

Eisenbeis, Robert A. "New Investment Powers for S&Ls: Diversification or Specialization?" *Economic Review* (Federal Reserve Bank of Atlanta), vol. 68 (July, 1983), pp. 53–62.

Fertuck, Len. "Survey of Small Business Lending Practices," *Journal of Small Business Management* (October, 1982), pp. 32–41.

Gladstone, David J. "SBA Programs for Financing a Small Business." In *Guide to Venture Capital Sources,* Fifth edition, edited by Stanley E. Pratt. Wellesley, MA: Capital Publishing, 1981.

Handbook for Small Business: A Survey of Small Business Programs of the Federal

Government, Fifth edition, Washington, D.C.: Government Printing Office, 1984.

"Hands On: A Manager's Notebook," *Inc.* (September, 1986), pp. 99.

Industrial Development Bond Financing in Texas. Austin, TX: Texas Industrial Commission, November, 1981.

Joint Committee on Taxation. *Trends in the Use of Tax-Exempt Bonds to Finance Private Activities, Including a Description of H.R. 1176 and H.R. 1635.* Washington, D.C.: Government Printing Office, June 13, 1983.

Loans to Local Development Companies, Washington, D.C.: Small Business Administration, February, 1975.

"Places that Give Money Away," *Venture,* June, 1980.

"Small Business Administration: Small Business Size Standards; Size Standard Revisions," *Federal Register,* May 3, 1982.

The State of Small Business: A Report of the President. Washington, D.C.: Government Printing Office, March 1985.

U.S. Congress, Congressional Budget Office. *Federal Role in State Industrial Development Programs.* Washington, D.C.: Government Printing Office, July 1984.

12
Public Offerings

The term **going public** is commonly used to describe the act of offering the stock of a privately held business to the public for the first time. It specifically refers to those instances in which a firm is required to file a formal registration statement with the Securities and Exchange Commission (SEC) under the terms of the Securities Act of 1933.

A public stock offering is an alternative financing strategy for a closely held business at any stage in the life cycle. This is particularly true during the expansion phase of the development process. Although a number of businesses in the early stages have the earnings potential necessary to go public, most companies will be well into the growth stages before they reach the required size for a successful public offering. Public sale of stock is also a very popular way to secure the necessary capital to complete a merger or acquisition.

According to the Securities and Exchange Commission's *Monthly Review*, there were 169 small firm issues, amounting to $1.9 billion in 1979 (**small firms** are defined as companies with less than $5 million net worth). By 1986, because of both the continuing efforts by the SEC to encourage more small firm participation and an increased public acceptance of small firm issues, 689 offerings were made, amounting to over $22.2 billion. Of the IPOs made in 1986, small issues (less than $50 million) were responsible for over 85 percent of the activity. The heaviest concentration in activity was in the financial services industry, with 172 issues for over $5.76 billion.

The key reason for going public must be an evident justification for funds combined with a shortage of other appropriate sources of capital. A public offering can also result from a desire to diversify into other markets or expand existing product lines. An entrepreneur could also desire a market for private stock to create liquidity for estate planning purposes.

In this chapter, we will discuss the prerequisites for taking a company public. The forms of federal registration will be examined in detail, followed by an analysis of the advantages and disadvantages of a public offering. Finally, we will look at the functions of the investment banker and examine the underwriting process.

Prerequisites for Going Public

Although a company of any size or stage of development can attempt a public offering, in most cases it is not feasible to do so unless certain prerequisites have been satisfied. Most investment bankers have a predetermined standard for minimum size of the stock offering they will undertake because of the cost of a public issue and the risk involved. In order to satisfy this criterion, the company offering the stock should be in the size range of $15–20 million in annual sales volume, with near term potential of $50–100 million. To satisfy this characteristic, the company must have a growth potential of 30–50 percent for several years.

When evaluating the potential for an initial stock issue, the key criterion is the perceived amount of risk. It is important that as much risk as possible be eliminated. Technological and manufacturing risks should be minimized before attempting a public issue. By narrowing the area of concern, the entrepreneur is able to focus on marketability of the product and capability of the firm's management.

Potential investors will be interested in liquidity, which is determined in large part by the depth and breadth of the market for the stock. Marketability of an issue is enhanced by an extremely marketable product that can support the kind of growth rates necessary to attract attention to both the company and the issue.

The critical factor in any successful issue is the quality and philosophy of the entire management team, especially the top managers. Their experience, integrity, and depth of leadership is critical; especially important is their ability to deal with the anticipated rates of growth that are necessary to make the issue attractive to potential investors.

Historical earnings are also extremely important in the evaluation process. Not only is the size of the earnings important, but also the stability, source, and trend of those earnings are critical. A history of stable earnings growth, with a 10 percent after-tax profit (of at least $1–2 million) is essential in most cases.

The single factor that can override the preceding prerequisites is the nature of the product itself. The development of a new product in a growth industry or the enhancement of an existing product will enable a firm to successfully issue stock without fulfilling all the other criteria.

Forms of Federal Registration

Under the Securities Act of 1933, all public offerings must be registered with the Securities and Exchange Commission (SEC) unless specifically exempted. In addition to complying with federal law, the issue is subject to the regulations of the states in which the stock will be sold. These "blue sky" laws, which vary significantly from state to state, are usually administered by the securities commissions of the various states, and typically operate under the office of the Secretary of State. Certain aspects of the process are also subject to the rules and regulations of self-regulating professional organizations such as the National Association of Securities Dealers and the various exchanges.

The registration process begins with the filing of a registration statement with the SEC. The content of this statement varies depending on the type of business, the amount of information on the company currently available to the public, the type of stock issue, and the class of investor. Stock registrations will generally be either Form S-1 or Form S-18.

S-1 Registration

Form S-1 registration is currently the most comprehensive type of registration. There is no limit to the amount of capital that can be raised through an S-1 offering. Securities can be sold by either the issuing company or the current shareholders. Form S-1 must be filed in Washington, D.C.

There are two principal parts to the registration statement: 1) the prospectus and 2) the supplemental information. The prospectus is the formal business plan that is prepared to serve as the primary selling document for the stock issue. The purpose of the prospectus is to present the company in the best image possible. However, in doing this care must be taken to guarantee full disclosure of all pertinent information. The primary obligation for ensuring complete and accurate disclosure lies with the company, its management, and the principal shareholders, regardless of who prepared the application.

The prospectus is not to be used as a marketing tool in the same sense that a company brochure or marketing circular is used. The prospectus is to be written in such a way that all the negative aspects of the issue are presented along with the positive aspects. Investment bankers and securities analysts who read such documents regularly are used to this style and will not be alarmed by the presentation.

Perhaps the most demanding requirement of the S-1 registration is the content of the financial statement section of the prospectus. The following financial information must accompany this form of registration:

1. Audited balance sheets for the past two fiscal years.
2. Audited income statements, statements of financial position, and statements of shareholders' equity for the past three fiscal years.
3. Unaudited financials dated within 135 days of the effective registration date, including statements from the corresponding period of the preceding fiscal year.

The SEC does not require that the prospectus information be presented in any particular order. However, the following outline has been suggested by the accounting firm of Deloitte, Haskins and Sells (see Wat 1983):

1. *Cover page.* The key facts about the company and the issue should be included on the outside front cover. This includes the company name, the type and number of shares to be sold, a distribution table (the selling price, underwriters' discount, and net proceeds to the company and the selling shareholders), and date of the prospectus. The inside front cover should include a detailed table of contents.

2. *Prospectus summary.* The summary should provide a brief description of the business and industry, pertinent data concerning the offering, details concerning the use of the proceeds, and selected financial information about the company.

3. *The company.* This section should provide an extensive discussion of the business, its product line, lines of distribution, and historical development.

4. *Risk factors.* Any negative aspects of the offering should be described. These can include lack of operating history, reliance on key personnel or customers, or market uncertainty.

5. *Use of proceeds.* This section explains what will actually be done with the proceeds of the issue.

6. *Dividend policy.* The company's past and projected dividend policy (or lack of one) should be explained.

7. *Capitalization.* The capital structure of the company before and after the offering is summarized in this section.

8. *Dilution.* The reduction in the value of the new purchasers' shares must be clearly presented. Dilution results from the difference between what new shareholders will pay for the stock and the original price that existing shareholders paid.

9. *Selected financial data with management's discussion and analysis.* The purpose of this section is to give management the opportunity to disclose all pertinent data regarding the financial history of the firm. This includes financial information on the company's past five years of operation.

10. *The business.* Information on the company, its product line, and the industry environment is provided in this section. Much of the same information that is included in the business section of the typical business plan is required here.

11. *Management.* All relevant information concerning the management team and the firm's major shareholders is provided in this section.

12. *Description of capital stock.* All relevant information on the value of the stock and the rights and transferability of the issue is presented.
13. *Underwriter information.* This section explains the distribution plan of the offering, discloses information on the underwriting syndicate, and explains the underwriters' obligations.

All supplemental information is included in Part II of the registration statement. This includes the disclosure of all additional information on the expenses of the issue, indemnification by the directors and officers, and un-registered security sales within the past three years. Also included are additional exhibits such as the underwriting agreement, the articles of incorporation and bylaws of the issuing company, and all other documents specifically referred to in the prospectus.

S-18 Registration

The S-18 registration option was adopted in 1979 with the idea of relaxing the filing requirements on certain smaller stock issues. Form S-18 can be used on offerings up to $7.5 million as long as no more than $1.5 million of the proceeds is scheduled to go to existing shareholders. Since its inception, this form of registration has increased in popularity, increasing from $50 million in 1979 to $1.35 billion in 1983.

There are certain restrictions on the type of business that can file under this form. The regulations require that the corporation must be doing business principally in the United States or Canada and it cannot be an investment company or a limited partnership. This form of registration can be filed at any SEC regional office.

The financial statement requirement is less demanding under this form of registration. Form S-18 requires an audited balance sheet for only the past fiscal year and other audited statements for the past two years. The selected financial data with managements' discussion and analysis is not required. In addition, the business section requires significantly fewer details.

Regulation A Offerings

Entrepreneurs desiring to sell stock under Regulation A are not going public in the technical sense of the term because there is no requirement to file a registration statement. However, the securities that are issued are tradeable and the company does become publicly held.

All offering materials must be filed at a regional office of the SEC. The disclosure requirements and processing procedures are less complex than those of full registration. The major advantages of this form of registration include the fact that the required financial information need not be audited and decreased expenses are involved in filing. As a result, this form of registration is often referred to as "short-form registration" or "mini-registration."

Regulation A can be used on stock offerings as long as no more than $1.5 million is raised within any twelve-month period. In addition, each shareholder can sell only $100,000 of personally held stock. Although the full registration statement is not required, each purchaser is supplied with an "offering circular" that must be approved by the SEC before distribution.

Registration with the appropriate authorities is required in states where the issue will be offered. The use of an underwriter who is a member of NASD will require NASD review.

Advantages and Disadvantages of Going Public

Under most circumstances, almost any other source of equity funds is preferable to the public sale of stock. Financing through retained earnings or the private placement of stock should be considered before turning to the public for additional equity capital. However, sometimes even the owners of successful businesses find themselves in the position of having to resort to a public offering in order to finance growth.

The decision on whether or not to go public is possibly one of the most important decisions that an entrepreneur will make. When considering a public offering, the advantages and disadvantages should be evaluated carefully.

Advantages

In addition to raising equity funds, the major advantage of going public is that it establishes a market for future financing. There are several implications to this benefit:

1. The firm's access to the market for borrowed capital is improved substantially. Increasing the stockholders' equity in the business improves the firm's liquidity position and, as a result, lenders tend to view the company as more creditworthy.

2. As long as the stock performs well in the market, subsequent issues are more easily placed.

3. Because the market establishes a value for the stock, it can be used more readily in negotiating mergers and acquisitions. This enhanced liquidity also means that stock option plans can be used much more effectively as part of an employee compensation package, making it much easier to recruit and retain qualified personnel.

The company's prestige is enhanced significantly by going public. The main result will be an improved public relations image with customers, suppliers, and creditors. A public offering tends to result in higher stock prices and maximum capital raised with a minimum of dilution. This means that the current owners will have to give up less of the company to get the same amount of capital than they would with any other type of equity funding.

Disadvantages

The disadvantages of taking a company public are not insignificant. The major drawback in going public is that the process itself is costly in terms of both time and money. The total cost of the issue can run as high as 20–25 percent. In addition to the underwriters' commission of 7–10 percent, a number of out-of-pocket expenses will be incurred. The following figures are based on the research of Deloitte, Haskins and Sells, assuming an issue of $5–10 million:

1. *Legal fees.* The attorney's responsibilities include the preparation of the registration statement and negotiations with the underwriters, in addition to all the administrative details that accompany the issue. Cost of the attorney's services will be between $75,000 and $100,000.
2. *Accounting fees.* The accountants will participate in the preparation of the registration statement and, of course, all financial statements. Accounting costs will vary from $25,000–50,000. If audited financials are to be prepared, the cost will increase substantially.
3. *Printing costs.* Printing of the prospectus, registration statement, underwriting documents, blue sky survey, and stock certificates will cost up to $100,000.
4. *Miscellaneous expenses.* Other expenses, including SEC and NASD filing fees, state filing fees, issue and transfer taxes, and indemnity insurance will run as high as $30,000.

Thus, total cost of an issue of $10 million could run as high as $1.3 million.

In addition to the time and money costs, the entrepreneur must be willing to substantially increase the level of information being provided to the public. This includes details concerning company operations that were previously thought to be confidential for competitive reasons. As a result, suppliers, customers, employees, and even competitors will have ready access to information on revenues, expenses, profitability, market potential, production decisions, channels of distribution, and much more. This is not only a result of the initial offering prospectus, but is also caused by the SEC requirement of regular and frequent reporting to shareholders.

This increased reporting requirement will necessitate certain changes in the way in which business is conducted. In order to comply with the quarterly reporting requirement established by the SEC, the company will have to establish formal lines of communication with all the relevant parties who play an integral role in this process to ensure that reports are timely and complete. This will also require that a portion of certain key managers' time be taken up in the reporting process.

To some extent, the increased frequency of reporting will result in a loss of control over the daily operations of the company. Short-term decision making will be undertaken to some extent with the impact on shareholder expectations in mind. Reasons for major shifts in marketing strategy or changes in operations are difficult to communicate to a larger number of shareholders. As a result, management will make operating decisions with a close watch on share prices.

Public sale of stock is an unreliable source of capital for most emerging companies. The number of companies that successfully sell an initial public issue can be counted in the hundreds annually. Public offerings are extremely sensitive to general market conditions, which include the state of the economy, inflationary expectations, and the level of interest rates. These are factors over which the offering company has no control; however, they must be seriously considered before a public offering is made.

Functions of the Investment Banker

There are occasions when an entrepreneur will take a stock issue directly to the public without the assistance of a financial intermediary. This is frequently done with a Regulation A stock offering to save the cost of an underwriter. However, it is generally more efficient to use the services of a qualified investment banker to perform the duty of middleman in the process of selling an initial stock issue.

Investment bankers are often divisions of larger, full-service financial corporations such as Merrill Lynch, Rotan Mosle, and E. F. Hutton. The major function of the investment banker is to underwrite the stock issue. The underwriting process involves the investment banker purchasing the stock from the offering company and reselling it to the public. There are three types of underwritings:

1. A "firm commitment" underwriting is one in which the sale of the entire offering is guaranteed by the investment banker to bring a fixed amount of money to the company. Under this arrangement, the investment banker absorbs all the risk in placing the issue.

2. Stock can be sold on a "best efforts" basis, in which the investment banker is responsible only for the shares sold at the offering price.

3. An "all or nothing" underwriting is one in which the company is not required to sell any of the issue unless the investment banker can sell all of the issue.

The method of underwriting chosen depends largely on the nature of the stock issue, the general conditions prevailing in the market, and the reputations of the company and the investment banker.

It is thus the responsibility of the investment banker to oversee the marketing of the issue through its pre-established channels of distribution. The investment banker must make sure that the initial issue is placed at a fair price to the offering company and that the placement leads to a stable or rising price for the stock. This factor is crucial in establishing a sound after-issue market and maintaining access to the market for future financing.

Selection Characteristics

Most stock issues are sold through a syndicate of investment bankers working through a managing underwriter. It is important that a firm choose an investment banker well in advance of the time it wishes to go public. By developing a relationship with an investment banker, the entrepreneur is in a position to take advantage of the general advice and counsel that is available. The major advantage of such a relationship is that the investment banker is able to assist in a smooth transition from a closely held business to a publicly held corporation.

There are many considerations that are essential in choosing an investment banker. The following are several characteristics of a good investment banker:

1. *Reputation.* The reputation of the managing underwriter is of critical importance to the firm attempting to sell an initial issue. Investors rely heavily on the reputation and ability of the investment banker in choosing an untested stock. Because most issues are sold through a syndicate, the ability of the investment banker to put together an effective group of sellers is critical in ensuring the success of an initial issue.

2. *Experience.* The success of an issue is determined by the ability of the investment banker to accurately price the stock. This critical aspect of the underwriting process is largely a function of the experience the investment banker has in working with companies in the same or closely related industries.

3. *Research capability.* The investment community will expect the managing underwriter to be the primary source of information about the offering company and the industry in which it operates. It is extremely important that the investment banker have a well-trained research staff that has both experience in the industry in question and a good reputation in the financial community.

4. *Distribution capability.* Even though the investor profiles of investment bankers are quite different, all will distribute the issue through their own particular client base. This client base will be composed of institutional investors and/or individual investors. Care should be taken in evaluating the quality and depth of this client base because the performance of the stock on the after-issue market is critical.

5. *Market-making capability.* In order to make a market in the over-the-counter market, an investment banker must be willing to invest a sufficient quantity of its own capital in the stock so that meaningful long or short positions can be taken to ensure liquidity and price stability.

6. *Advice capability.* It is important to develop a strong working relationship with an investment banker. The ability to consult with your investment banker before, during, and after the issue goes a long way in determining whether or not the transition to a publicly held company will be a successful one. There will always be a need for advice regarding certain aspects of the company's operations and their impact on investors' attitudes toward the stock.

As can be seen from the preceding discussion, there are many considerations that must be taken into account in choosing an investment banker. The process should be started early and carried out diligently. The rewards of a strong, long-term relationship with an investment banker are immense.

The Underwriting Process

If an investment banker has not been chosen, the first step in the process will be to discuss the possibilities of the firm going public with several potential underwriters. This step should be taken well in advance of the actual decision to go public. After an investment banker has been chosen, the first planning meeting should be held. The purpose of this meeting is to get together all the parties who have roles in the process. This includes company representatives who will be responsible for preparing the registration statement, the company's legal counsel, the underwriters and their legal counsel, and the independent accounting firm responsible for preparing the historical financial statements and financial forecasts that will be used in the offering prospectus. Appendix 12A presents a schedule of events and responsibilities for a typical initial public offering.

The process for the entire public offering can be summarized as follows:

1. After an initial organizational meeting to take care of many of the administrative details concerning the issue, the process of preparing the prospectus begins. It can take up to sixty days to complete this step of the process.

2. When the prospectus is completed, the registration statement should then be filed with the SEC, the state commissions, and the NASD.

3. As the underwriter finalizes the distribution syndicate, the prospectus is distributed and presentations are made in key cities.

4. After SEC review, the prospectus is revised and pricing decisions are incorporated into the final version.

5. Securities are distributed to be sold to the public.

Summary and Conclusions

The public sale of stock is an alternative means of securing necessary capital for closely held businesses in any stage of development. Although there are many advantages that go along with a public issue, it is not without its disadvantages. Before deciding on this means of capital procurement, the entrepreneur should carefully weigh the pros and cons of a public offering. Once the decision is made to go public, the first step is the choice of a reputable investment banker to serve as managing underwriter of the issue. This selection is critical in determining the success of the initial issue and, more importantly, the performance of the stock in the after-issue market.

References

Wallace, Peter W. "Public Financing for Smaller Companies." In *Guide to Venture Capital Sources*, Fifth edition, edited by Stanley E. Pratt. Wellesley, MA: Capital Publishing, 1981.

Wat, Leslie. *Strategies for Going Public: An Entrepreneur's Guidebook.* Deloitte Haskins & Sells, 1983.

Appendix 12A
Sample Schedule of Events and Responsibilities for the Initial Public Offering

The following is a typical schedule of activities for an initial public offering. It is assumed that audited financial statements are available for the prior historical years and that current operating results will be available before the initial registration statement is filed.

Abbreviations Used:

OC	Offering Company
SS	Selling Shareholders
CC	Company's Counsel
A	Accountants
U	Underwriters
UC	Underwriters' Counsel

Date	Activity	Responsibility
1	Organizational meeting to discuss schedule of events and responsibilities;	All
	Begin steps to accomplish the following: review corporate records to correct any deficiencies and revise inappropriate provisions;	CC
	appoint transfer agent and registrar;	OC
	arrange with banknote company for preparation of stock certificates;	OC
	select a financial printer;	OC
	Begin preparation of: cover page, back cover, and underwriting section of the prospectus;	UC
	capitalization table, audited financial statements, and schedules;	A

	description of business and remainder of prospectus and exhibits;	OC, CC
	directors' and officers' questionnaires;	CC
	powers of attorney for registration statement and amendments; selling shareholders' power of attorney and custody agreements;	CC
	resolutions for Board of Directors' meeting;	CC
	purchase agreement and agreement among underwriters;	UC
	syndicate list;	U
	underwriters' questionnaire;	UC
	comfort letter;	UC
	blue sky survey;	UC
10	Distribute directors' and officers' questionnaires;	OC
	Mail letter to shareholders relating to participation in secondary offering;	OC, CC
17	Distribute typed draft of registration statement, including year-end financial statements, to all parties;	OC, CC
	Determine representative to act for selling shareholders at time of offering;	OC, SS
22	Meeting to review draft of registration statement;	All
	Due diligence session with key company personnel;	All
	Due diligence meeting with accountants and discussion of comfort letter;	A, U, UC
24	Receive officers' and directors' questionnaires and furnish copy to underwriters' counsel;	CC
	Shareholders' meeting;	OC
	Meeting of Board of Directors to adopt resolutions authorizing appointment of transfer agent and registrar, execution and filing of registration statement and related amendments, execution of purchase agreement (subject to final approval of price and discount), power of attorney to sign amendments, and other matters;	OC
25	Complete and distribute draft purchase agreement and other underwriting papers;	OC
	Distribute revised draft of registration statement to all parties;	OC, CC

	Send custody agreements and powers of attorney (including questionnaires) to selling shareholders;	OC, CC
28	Meeting to review revised draft of registration statement;	All
35	Distribute revised draft of registration statement to all parties;	OC, CC
56	Send revised registration statement, with interim financial statements, to printer;	CC
	Send draft of underwriting documents to printer;	UC
57	Deliver first proof of registration statement and underwriting documents to all parties;	Printer
58	Obtain signature pages and power of attorney for registration statement and amendments from directors and officers;	OC, CC
	Receive selling shareholders' custody agreements, questionnaires, and powers of attorney; furnish copies to company counsel and underwriters' counsel;	OC
	Prepare transmittal letters to underwriters and dealers to accompany preliminary material; give mailing instructions and labels to printer;	U
59	Meeting at printer to review proof of registration statement, with final revisions to printer;	All
60	Furnish all corrections and changes to printer, ship certified check for filing fee, letter of transmittal, registration statement, and exhibits to SEC;	CC, UC
63	Registration statement filed with SEC;	U
	Issue press release;	U
70	Proceed with blue sky registration and NASD filing;	UC
	Contact SEC to determine review period;	CC
	Begin two-week road show;	OC, U
78–81	Underwriters' questionnaires returned;	U
	Prepare request to SEC for acceleration of effective date;	CC, UC
	Prepare supplemental information for filing with SEC, if requested;	CC, UC

	Meeting of Board of Directors (Pricing Committee) to approve final prospectus; approve purchase agreement and authorize execution; and ratify acts of officers in connection with offering;	OC
90	Receive letter of comments from SEC and prepare Amendment No. 1 to registration statement;	All
91	Meeting at printer to review draft of Amendment No. 1;	All
	Determine public offering price of common stock and discount;	OC, SS, U
	Accountants deliver final form of comfort letter to underwriters' counsel;	A
	Complete blue sky registration;	UC
92	Agreement among underwriters signed;	U
	Purchase agreement executed;	OC, SS, U
	Amendment No. 1 filed with SEC and registration statement declared effective;	CC, UC
	Send telegrams to underwriters and dealers;	U
	Issue press release and tombstone ad;	U
	Public offering commences;	U
	Give printer labels and printing information for final prospectus;	U
94	Supply transfer agent with legal opinions and other required documents;	CC
	Mail to SEC ten copies of final prospectus;	CC
	Mail final prospectus to NASD and blue sky authorities;	UC
	Furnish company with names and denominations for stock certificates;	U
	Distribute closing memorandum;	UC
	Begin preparation of legal opinions, certificates, and other closing papers;	CC, UC
100	Closing	All

Source: Leslie Wat, *Strategies for Going Public: An Entrepreneur's Guidebook*, Deloitte, Haskins, and Sells, 1983, 47–53. Reprinted with permission.

Part IV
Special Topics

13
Transferring Business Ownership

A transfer of business ownership can take place at any stage in the business life cycle. The placement of this discussion is in no way meant to imply that all or even the majority of ownership transfers take place at the end of the business life cycle. The motivations of buyers and sellers differ according to their personal circumstances and general business conditions. Buyers are always faced with the option of starting a business instead of buying one. Sellers, likewise, can simply choose to close the doors instead of going through the process of finding a buyer and negotiating a sale.

As a general rule, the longer a business is in existence, the more valuable it is on the market. This of course assumes that there has not been a dramatic change in either the market or operating environment that would adversely affect the firm's growth potential. This chapter examines some of the issues related to transferring business ownership, including the reasons for buying and selling a business, essential factors to be considered by both buyer and seller, the process of valuation, and problems in ownership transfer.

Reasons for Buying an Existing Business

Why would someone choose to purchase an existing business rather than start one from scratch? Although purchasing a business may run counter to "true" entrepreneurial instincts, it has certain advantages that should be taken into consideration:

1. The ongoing concern has a track record, so many of the uncertainties that go along with carving out a market niche and building an image are reduced or even eliminated completely. New businesses are usually started in untested locations. No amount of planning and research completely eliminates the risk of a new, untested location and market.

2. Financial data are verifiable according to past performance. With historical data as a basis, financial projections are easier to generate and more believable when used to attract capital.

3. An existing firm has proven channels of distribution, a productive labor force, a working relationship with suppliers, and more importantly, an existing cash flow.

The acquisition of an existing business is not a guaranteed formula for success. The primary risk that occurs in an acquisition takes place during the investigation phase. The danger in purchasing an existing business is that the decision to buy will be made hastily. The result will be an inadequate investigation: failure to gather the right kinds of information, failure to verify the information gathered, and failure to properly analyze the data available. An inadequate search can lead to the purchase of a business for which the buyer is ill-suited or worse, paying too much.

Reasons for Selling a Business

There are numerous reasons why an owner of an established business might be interested in selling. From the buyer's perspective, understanding what might motivate someone to sell a business will provide a head start in the search process. There is often a stigma against publicizing the availability of a business because of possible business disruption: customer relations, supplier expectations, personnel problems, and competitor response. As a result, most profitable businesses are seldom advertised for sale. Their availability is made known only to a select group of individuals working closely with the operation.

Selling a business may be the most important financial decision ever made by an entrepreneur. The reasons for selling can be categorized according to the life-cycle stage of the business. Businesses that are sold in the development stage are usually experiencing problems. Most have never gained sufficient market acceptance to become viable. An extended period of negative cash flow exhausts the equity capital available. With no other sources of capital, the entrepreneur either liquidates the business or, if lucky, sells for little more than asset value.

Businesses that successfully move beyond the development stage are ready to enter the period of accelerating growth, assuming sufficient expansion capital is available. Entrepreneurs who lack the capital to take advantage of this opportunity will either maintain their business as a marginally profitable operation or sell it to someone who has the capital for expansion.

Entrepreneurs who have successfully taken a firm into the expansion stage are not always equipped managerially or financially for the challenges of a mature operation. It is at this stage, where sales growth is greater than the industry average, that the individual can "cash in" on the achievements of the past and move on to other challenges. The alternative, of course, is for the company to retrench and continue as a successful operation at a lower level of activity.

In the later stages of resource maturity, the advantages of selling can be quite compelling. In many cases, owners who are advancing in years will sell their businesses in order to reduce their personal financial risk. To prepare for a more leisurely lifestyle in their later years, these owners will sell to diversify their personal assets. The increased liquidity afforded by selling a privately held company and acquiring stock in a publicly owned firm eliminates the prospect of a forced sale of the business to pay estate taxes.

An equally important consideration is when the business should be sold. At any given time, the business is worth what the market will bear. In other words, the real value of a business is what the maximum bidder is willing to pay at the time the business is being sold. Thus, timing is important. The best time to borrow money is when it is not needed. Likewise, to ensure the maximum price for a business, the best time to sell is when there is no urgency to sell.

The Decision to Buy or Sell

The most critical mistake made in buying or selling a business is rushing into the decision without knowing all the facts. It is important not to become impatient. The process of buying or selling a business is time-consuming, and any decision in this area should not be made hastily. It is also important to avoid becoming emotionally involved with a particular venture. One of the worst things that can happen is to become infatuated with a particular opportunity and ignore other, more relevant information. Special care should be taken to ensure that the evaluation of the transaction is based primarily on objective factors.

Factors for the Buyer to Consider

Much of the work that is done in conducting a thorough search for an acquisition is actually carried out prior to identifying a specific firm to consider. The prospective buyer's first task is to identify an industry or type of business to look for and then to develop formal screening criteria for use in the evaluation process.

Identify an Industry. The business search should focus primarily on those opportunities in which the individual can take advantage of his or her personal business experience. In other words, the search should be concentrated in an industry in which the operating requirements are compatible with the purchaser's expertise. A college graduate who has a degree in marketing and an extensive employment background in retail sales and distribution should investigate opportunities in which this expertise is important. An industrial engineer who has experience in assembly-line manufacturing should choose an industry where production knowledge is critical.

Some may argue that this match is not important because specific expertise can often be secured in the acquisition. Key management personnel who will stay after the acquisition are an important consideration and one of the most important assets that can be bought. However, competence is not the only thing that is being purchased; compatibility is an equally important aspect and much more difficult to predict. Thus, it is probably a good idea not to count too heavily on the current ownership to provide management expertise for any extended period of time. If the current management team is a key factor in the success of the venture, the buyer must take precautions to ensure that they will be able to survive the ownership transition.

Develop a Screening Criteria. Before beginning a search, the buyer should develop a set of guidelines to be used in analyzing and comparing the various opportunities that are identified. These guidelines include: 1) a financial analysis, 2) a marketing analysis, 3) a production assessment, and 4) a management-administration evaluation. The buyer should develop a set of criteria to systematically examine each of these areas. This discipline will help to ensure that each opportunity is evaluated objectively and thoroughly.

A business acquisition should be analyzed in the same manner that any other investment would be evaluated. Although the factor of primary interest is the future earnings potential of the venture, other areas play a critical role in determining whether financial projections can be realized. Customer profiles, channels of distribution, production capacity, and labor supply are examples of key areas to investigate. Using the business plan format as a guide, the buyer should establish a checklist of desirable characteristics and factors for examination.

Factors for the Seller to Consider

The entrepreneur who is serious about selling a business has a great deal to do before placing it on the market. This includes the preparation of a detailed selling prospectus, which is essentially a business plan that emphasizes the strengths of the operation and places the weaknesses in perspective. Like the regular business plan or offering prospectus discussed earlier, the selling prospectus includes detailed information on finances, marketing, production, and management.

Financial Information. The determination of profit potential requires complete and accurate financial information. If audited financial statements are not available, certified copies of federal income tax returns (Schedule C for a sole proprietor, Form 1065 for a partnership, or Form 1120 for a corporation) should be provided.

Information should be included to allow the prospective buyer to conduct a complete financial analysis. An owner who is either unable or unwilling to provide the required financial data is either hiding something or is not serious about selling the business. Without this data, it is virtually impossible to accurately assess the profitability and value of a business.

Marketing Information. In the area of marketing, the selling prospectus includes information on product lines and product mix, customer concentration and customer mix, principal competitors, franchises, patents, trademarks, copyrights, marketing strategies, and channels of distribution.

Production Information. Operational details such as information on technology, production capacity, physical facilities, supplier relationships, subcontractor relationships, work-in-process, and production back-logs are important in determining production capability.

Management/Personnel Information. A vitally important area of evaluation is the management/personnel area. Key personnel should be available for interviews so the prospective buyer can have the opportunity to determine their expertise, management style, and most importantly, their personal objectives. Details on all labor agreements, especially employment contracts with officers and managers, should be provided. Data on employee benefits such as vacation and holiday policies, employee stock option plans, insurance and retirement benefits, overtime pay, and sick leave should also be included. A complete labor force history should be available, including past grievances, contract negotiations, and current policies and practices.

The Role of Business Advisors

Finding a potential business opportunity or buyer is not an easy task. Since general advertising is not often used, the information must be made available in other ways. A careful study of a firm's existing management can tell a lot about the possibility of a sale. An owner nearing retirement age who has no heirs active in the business; a recent illness, disability, or death; absentee ownership; or conflicting management objectives among partners may be indicative of a purchase opportunity.

Information of this sort is not readily available on the open market. In most cases, only certain company insiders have access to these details. While the specific details of a company's operations are strictly confidential, often commercial bankers, certified public accountants, and attorneys have advance indications that a business is for sale. Most of the larger commercial banks have trust departments whose officers serve as managers for individual estates. In many cases, this also includes operating and managing an ongoing business until a successful acquisition can be arranged. CPAs and attorneys, as financial and legal advisers, are both in a unique position to know of pending situations that will lead a business owner to seek a buyer.

Many of the details that must be taken care of are beyond the expertise of the typical entrepreneur—whether buyer or seller. In order to reduce the probability of problems during or after the ownership transfer, it is wise to solicit some expert professional help in areas in which it is needed.

An accountant can provide assistance in conducting a financial statement analysis and, if needed, in preparing earnings projections. In addition, he or she can provide invaluable insights about the potential tax benefits and problems of the specific acquisition plan that is being negotiated.

An attorney is equally important in the process of transferring business ownership. The attorney will examine all existing leases, titles, and other important documents, including contracts with suppliers, customers, marketing representatives, and employees. Another important task is to determine the existence of any pending lawsuits or other legal liabilities, such as liens against assets and unpaid income or property taxes.

The Role of Advertising

More general advertising is also an option for certain types of businesses. Many local, regional, and national publications run frequent advertisements identifying businesses that are for sale. Most local newspapers have a "Business Opportunity" section in the daily classified advertisements. Smaller newspapers may carry only a few actual opportunities; the bulk of the listings will be advertisements for brokers, consultants, and real estate agents who represent individuals interested in selling their businesses. Larger metropolitan newspapers will have much more extensive listings, which are usually separated into industry categories. National publications such as the *Wall Street Journal, Inc., Venture,* and *Money* will also have information on businesses that are for sale. These listings are often regional in nature, depending on the edition that you receive.

Other advertising opportunities are available that can minimize the potential adverse market reaction to an ownership change. Trade sources should be considered as a means of providing information on business availability. This includes sales and manufacturers' representatives and company suppliers. It is also appropriate for some businesses to advertise in certain trade publications and journals, many of which are available only to members of the industry associations.

Using Business Brokers

Business brokers are often used by sellers of businesses to act as their agents in the entire process. In many ways, a business broker serves the same purpose as a real estate agent in the sale of a commercial or residential property. In fact, many business brokers are also licensed real estate agents. A good broker can provide valuable services such as 1) providing a listing of businesses that are for sale, 2) assisting the seller in establishing an asking price for the business, 3) finding and screening buyers, 4) assembling the basic information needed to evaluate the businesses, and 5) ensuring that the proper legal steps are taken in the ownership transfer. In return for these services, the seller agrees to pay the broker a percentage of the purchase price (10 percent is the standard amount).

A listing with a reputable broker is no guarantee that the opportunity is either a sound business venture or that it will be priced correctly. There are several things to remember about the brokerage relationship, the most important being that the broker is the agent of the seller. As such, he is representing the best interests of the seller, and not necessarily the buyer. In addition, the broker is presenting only the facts that have been provided by the business owner and there is no guarantee that the information is accurate. Working through a broker does not release either the buyer or seller from any of the responsibilities of conducting a thorough investigation. In fact, brokers do very little financial analysis. Their responsibility is to present the information as it is given, and not to express an opinion on the soundness of a particular venture.

Valuing the Privately Held Business

Business valuation is a difficult task because there is no generally accepted formula for valuing the stock in a privately held business. The Internal Revenue Service has taken a keen interest in the general approach to business valuation because most valuations are performed for tax purposes. The IRS recognizes certain methods and critical factors that assist in making a reasonable valuation. Legally speaking, the true test of valuation is not precision, but reasonableness. The following critical factors to consider in valuing a closely held business have been established by the IRS:

1. The nature of the business and the history of the enterprise from its inception should be carefully examined. This includes consideration of the stability, growth, and diversity of the operation. Key aspects of this investigation are the type of business, the product/service being offered, a valuation of assets, an analysis of the capital structure, the condition of plant facilities, sales history and trends, and management capabilities.

2. The general economic outlook and the condition and outlook for the specific industry is an important consideration. A critical part of this step is to evaluate the company's standing relative to its major competitors.

3. The book value of the stock and the financial condition of the business should be calculated. This aspect of the analysis requires comparative balance sheets for the past three to five years and a current balance sheet (prepared within the past thirty days).

4. The earnings capacity of the company should also be evaluated. This will require income statements for the past three to five years and a current income statement (prepared within the past thirty days). If the financial statements are unaudited, copies of the firm's income tax returns are required.

5. The dividend-paying capacity of the firm should be evaluated (as opposed to the dividends actually paid).

6. It should be determined whether or not the business has goodwill or other intangible value. This calculation is based on excess earnings, prestige in the marketplace, brand or trade name image, and a record of operations (number of years of successful operation).

7. Stock value depends critically on the proportion of the ownership to be sold. Minority interests are typically less valuable on a per-share basis than majority interests.

8. The price of stock in a similar, publicly held corporation can be used to estimate appropriate multiples of earnings for valuing a business by the formula method. First, several companies with similar business operations, financial results, capitalization, and economic outlook should be identified. Then, their price/earnings ratios should be averaged. Finally, this average should be multiplied by the valued company's earnings, to arrive at an estimate of stock value.

The Valuation Process

Determining the value of any ongoing business is somewhat subjective—an art, rather than a science—and is dependent on the circumstances of each individual case. In order to ensure that important considerations are not overlooked, the valuation process should be conducted in a thorough, systematic manner. The following steps should be carefully followed:

1. Establish the date of the valuation. This date depends on the purpose of the valuation; it may be retroactive because of the death of an owner or it may be the current date.

2. Determine what is to be included in the valuation: assets or stock, all or part. It is also a good idea to make a list of the items being included in the valuation such as assets, liabilities, and goodwill.

3. Obtain and analyze financial statements for the past three to five years.

4. Interview owners, managers, and other key individuals, including the company's banker, creditors, suppliers, and accountant. These are the only people who can produce administrative records and contracts and explain company history, policy, and performance.

5. Adjust financial statements to reflect current economic values. This will entail valuing assets at market rather than book value, eliminating liabilities due to owners, and adding unstated liabilities, such as financial leases, that do not show up on the balance sheets. All unusual items, such as personal expenses of the owner and excess salaries, should also be removed from the income statement.

6. Present adjusted financial statements in comparative and common-size format. Industry comparisons should also be included if they are available.

7. Obtain professional appraisals. It is not uncommon for book values of tangible assets to differ significantly from market values.

8. Prepare prospective financial statements, taking into consideration any changes in operations or capital structure that will affect the firm's financial conditions.

9. Assign a value to goodwill and other intangible assets such as patents, trademarks, and brand names.

10. Evaluate the data, apply one or more of the established valuation techniques (discussed in the next section), and establish an opinion on the value of the business.

Techniques of Valuation

Certain techniques are commonly used to establish the value of closely held businesses. No single technique can be used to establish the "true" value of a business in every situation. A good method of determining the value of a business is to use several different valuation techniques, compare the results of the individual calculations, and establish a reasonable value for the business. The following is a sample of the most commonly used methods in business valuation. Each valuation method will be illustrated using the financial data from a small sheet metal stamping operation given in Exhibit 13–1. The Heart O' Texas (HOT) Manufacturing Corporation has been in existence for seven years under the management of Spencer Jones, its sole owner. After retiring from the military, Mr. Jones moved to central Texas and started the operation. Sales have grown steadily, but the company is performing well below its potential, given the size of the local market.

Marketplace Formulas

The use of established rules of thumb to approximate the value of a business is a common practice in many industries. This technique involves multiplying sales, gross profit, operating profit, or net profit by the appropriate multiple to arrive at a value for the business. Industry practices determine both the multiple and the appropriate sales or profit figure to use.

There are several factors that enter into the process of determining the proper multiple: 1) the nature of the business, 2) the amount of risk involved, and 3) the stability of earnings. There is no table of absolute multiples that can be applied in every situation. The best policy is to check with professional sources who are familiar with the type of business to be valued in order to establish the proper multiple. These sources include business brokers, trade association publications, IRS rulings, and P/E ratios of the stock of similar publicly traded companies.

In most cases, these multiples will range up to five times before-tax earnings or ten times after-tax earnings. Certain high growth, high technology companies will have multiples ranging up to fifteen or even twenty times after-tax earnings. Use of these higher multiples is not a common practice for most closely held businesses. In fact, in *Buying and Selling a Small Business,* the Small Business Administration recommends that no small business be valued at more than five times before-tax annual earnings. There is no need to place such a dogmatic restriction on earnings multiples because there are other valuation techniques that can be used to check the reasonableness of any given valuation.

The Internal Revenue Service recognizes the use of corporate comparisons as a valid method of valuing a business in situations in which it is deemed reasonable and appropriate. This technique involves identifying a publicly traded corporation in the same or similar line of business and applying the price/earnings ratio of the comparison corporation to the earnings of the company to be valued. In order to ensure a valid comparison, the services of an independent accountant are required to review the accounting practices of the comparison corporation and determine whether they are similar to those of the company to valued.

Assuming that these issues have been satisfactorily addressed, the marketplace formula technique can be applied to the problem of valuing the Heart O' Texas Manufacturing Corporation. Using the SBA formula of five times before-tax profit, HOT Manufacturing Corporation has a value of $371,400 ($74,280 · 5). Ten times after-tax earnings establishes a value of $587,800, ($58,780 · 10).

Book Value

The book value approach, which is often referred to as the *net worth approach,* establishes the value of a business using only the information available from the firm's current balance sheet. This simple technique involves subtracting total liabilities from the book value of total tangible assets in order to establish a value for owners' equity, which represents the value of the business.

This approach works well in situations in which the business being valued has no established value for goodwill (a new business or a distressed business). There are several serious drawbacks to this approach: 1) by using the book value of tangible assets, no allowance is made to reflect their fair market value; 2) certain accounting practices such as LIFO accounting can undervalue inventory and accelerated depreciation can undervalue fixed assets and, as a result, significantly impact on book value; 3) the firm may be carrying uncollectible accounts receivable on the books (those over ninety days old); and 4) liabilities may be understated as a result of the use of certain types of off-balance sheet financing and leasing arrangements.

The book value of the HOT Manufacturing Corp. can be calculated as follows:

Total Assets	$770,100
Less: Intangibles	114,000
Total Tangible Assets	$656,100
Less: Total Liabilities	327,400
Book Value	$328,700

EXHIBIT 13–1

Heart O' Texas Manufacturing Corporation
Income Statement for the Period Ending 12-31-86

Net sales		$750,000
Cost of sales:		
Inventory (1-1-86)	$ 97,400	
Purchases	165,000	
Direct wages	180,000	
Other direct costs	70,000	
	$512,400	
Less inventory (12-31-86)	116,000	
Total cost of sales		396,400
Gross profit		$353,600
Operating expenses		202,850
Depreciation		56,720
Operating profit		$ 94,030
Interest expense		19,750
Before-tax profit		$ 74,280
Income taxes		15,500
After-tax profit		$ 58,780

Summary of Operations for Last Two Years:

	1984	1985
Net sales	$620,000	$660,000
Operating profit	63,240	71,280
After-tax profit	32,250	42,900

Prospective Earnings for the Next Five Years:

	1987	1988	1989	1990	1991
Before-tax profit	$89,000	$105,000	$120,000	$140,000	$155,000
After-tax profit	$70,000	$ 81,000	$ 90,000	$102,000	$111,000

EXHIBIT 13–1 continued

Balance Sheet 12-31-86

Assets
Current assets:

Cash on hand and in banks		$ 37,000
Accounts receivable	$150,000	
Less allowance for doubtful accounts	1,500	148,500
Inventory (FIFO)		116,000
Refundable deposits		10,000
Total current assets		$311,500

Fixed assets:

	Cost	Depreciation	Book Value
Land and building	$ 91,800	$ 17,500	$ 74,300
Machinery and equipment	490,000	245,000	245,000
Automotive equipment	31,400	10,400	21,000
Office equipment	15,000	10,700	4,300
	$618,200	$283,600	$344,600
Other assets (goodwill)			114,000
Total assets			$770,100

Liabilities
Current liabilities:

Accounts payable	$ 17,000	
Current portion of LTD	22,400	
Taxes payable—FICA	4,400	
Total current liabilities		$118,800

Long-term liabilities:

Notes payable to banks	$156,000	
Less current portion	22,400	133,600
Note payable to owner		75,000
Total liabilities		$327,400

Shareholder's Equity

Common stock	$150,000	
Retained earnings	292,700	
Total Shareholder's Equity		442,700
Total Liabilities and Shareholder's Equity		$770,100

Adjusted Book Value

This method is an attempt to adjust the value of a firm's tangible assets and liabilities to their economic worth or market value. This involves making the proper adjustments and subtracting liabilities from assets to establish an adjusted book value. The adjusted book value method is more accurate in reflecting a company's economic worth than the straight book value approach.

Neither of the book value approaches reflects the value of the firm's intangible assets such as goodwill, patents, copyrights, and new product development. Despite this limitation, this method is an excellent way to value businesses that are fixed-asset related. This includes certain holding companies and other firms that are related to real estate such as hotels, motels, office buildings, and apartment complexes.

The adjusted book value calculation for the Heart O' Texas Manufacturing Corporation is:

Book Value	$328,700
Less:	
Increased Allowance for Doubtful Accounts	18,000
Reduction in Inventory Value	23,200
Subtotal	$287,500
Plus:	
Increase in Fixed Assets to Market Value	52,000
Note Payable to Owner	75,000
Adjusted Book Value	$414,500

After examining an aging of the accounts receivable and an inventory schedule, two downward adjustments in asset values were made. It was discovered that 12 percent of the receivables were over ninety days old; thus, $18,000 was subtracted from accounts receivable as doubtful accounts. Inventory valuation was adjusted downward by 20 percent to reflect obsolescence. Fixed asset values were increased to reflect an increase in their market value and the note payable to the owner was added back, reclassifying it as shareholder's equity. With these adjustments, the value of the firm is estimated at $414,500.

Capitalized Earnings

The capitalized earnings approach is the first of three earnings and cash flow methods that will be discussed. These three methods share a common underlying assumption: the value of an operating enterprise is determined by the present value of the earnings or cash flows that it will generate. In other words, an individual who is interested in buying (investing in) a business is not concerned with the value of the assets per se, but with the income that those assets are capable of generating once they are arranged together in a productive manner.

The capitalized earnings approach is the simplest of the three to calculate. This method utilizes the formula:

$$CV = R/i$$

where CV is the capitalized value of the earnings stream that is being evaluated, R is the annual earnings stream, and i is the capitalization rate.

The major difficulty in using this method of valuation is in defining the appropriate capitalization rate that accurately reflects the alternative risk-adjusted rate of return for the buyer. Other problems include the assumption that the earnings stream will be constant and last indefinitely.

Using before-tax profit as the earnings stream to be capitalized and 20 percent as the risk-adjusted opportunity cost of funds for the buyer, the value of HOT Manufacturing is calculated as:

$$CV = \frac{\$74,280}{.20} = \$371,400$$

Discounted Earnings Stream

This method of calculation addresses the problems inherent in the capitalized earnings approach, namely that the earnings stream is constant and assumed to last indefinitely. The first step in this approach is to estimate the future earnings stream and the buyer's required rate of return on investment. The length of the projection period is based on how long the buyer is willing to have his capital investment at risk before achieving full recovery (usually three to seven years).

After estimating prospective earnings for the desired period, the following formula is applied to calculate the discounted present value of the earnings stream:

$$PV = \sum_{i=1}^{n} R_i/(1 + r)^i + S/(1 + r)^n$$

where PV is the present value of the future earnings stream calculated for n periods, R_i is the estimated earnings for the ith period, r is the required rate of return on the investment, and S is the value of the business at the end of the nth period.

The accuracy of this approach depends heavily on the accuracy with which future earnings are estimated. In order to reduce the impact of this weakness, the evaluator might generate optimistic, pessimistic, and most-likely sales estimates and then use them separately to determine a range of values for the business.

Based on a five-year investment period, a 20 percent required rate of return on the investment, and a value for the business at the end of the investment period, the estimated value of HOT Manufacturing is shown in the following calculation. The earnings stream used in the calculation is the estimated after-tax profit given in Exhibit 13–1.

Future Value	$\$ \cdot discount\ factor = PV$		
1987 earnings	$ 70,000 · .833 =	$ 58,310
1988 earnings	81,000 · .694 =	56,214
1989 earnings	90,000 · .579 =	52,110
1990 earnings	102,000 · .482 =	49,164
1991 earnings	111,000 · .402 =	44,622
1992 business value	775,000 · .402 =	311,550
Discounted Earnings Stream		$571,970

Assuming the business will be valued in 1991 at five times after-tax earnings, the current estimated value of HOT Manufacturing is $571,970. If a higher discount rate were used (for example, 25 percent), the valuation would be lower. Increasing the earnings stream from five to seven years, with an appropriate adjustment in the business value at the end of the investment period, will result in a higher business value.

Discounted Cash Flow

Earnings generating capacity is not the same as the ability to generate cash. The discounted cash flow method uses the same technique as the discounted earnings stream except that cash flow is used instead of earnings. Ideally, the cash flow estimate that should be used in the calculation is operating cash flow, and not after-tax profit plus depreciation. Based on earlier discussions, it should be evident that operating cash flow is the superior estimate for the firm's ability to generate cash. The mechanics of this calculation are identical to those of the discounted earnings approach. The only difference is that operating cash flow is used instead of after-tax earning.

Valuing Goodwill

Often the biggest discrepancy between the value established by the seller and that of the buyer is in the amount of goodwill or intangible value attributable to the business. The seller sees the established, successful business as worth more than the asset value and the buyer sees only "blue sky." The only objective way to place a value on goodwill is to estimate the value of the excess earning power of the business—the ability of the operation to generate earnings in excess of the average for this type of business.

The original formula for valuing goodwill, referred to as the *residual method,* has recently been challenged in the Tax Court by the Internal Revenue Service. Thus, at this time, there is no proven and acceptable way of determining a goodwill value. Although all current suggested methods are somewhat arbitrary and open to discussion, one has found a significant degree of support in the business literature. A simplified discussion of this approach is found in Howard (1982) and is summarized here.

1. Adjust operating profit to reflect a more realistic estimate of operating expenses. Adjustments include overstated costs because of inventory valuation methods, accelerated depreciation, excessive owners' salaries, and lucrative benefits. Planned price increases can be factored into the sales estimates. A stepped-up maintenance schedule adds to operating costs.

2. Obtain an estimate of the market value of fixed assets from a professional appraiser.

3. Obtain an estimate of the prevailing bank loan rate that applies to commercial and industrial loans of comparable size and risk.

4. Estimate the cost of owning the fixed assets by multiplying the market value of the fixed assets by the prevailing commercial loan rate.

5. Calculate the excess earning power of the business by subtracting the cost of owning the fixed assets from the adjusted operating profit.

6. Determine the appropriate multiple to estimate the value of the excess earnings. Howard presents a table of risk-adjusted multiples ranging from zero to six (from an extremely risky venture to one with relatively low risk). The final multiple is based on an average of six categories: the estimated risk of continuous earnings into the future, the growth potential of earnings, general conditions in the industry, the competitive conditions in the market, the company's track record, and the desirability of the business. A uniform rating of three in each of these categories would reflect a high likelihood of steady income into the future, steady growth in inflation-adjusted earnings, steady industry growth in excess of inflation, normal competition in the target market, an established track record, and a respectable operation in a good environment.

The value of the excess earnings for HOT Manufacturing using this approach is:

1.	Operating profit for 1986	$ 94,030
	Plus: Excess salary to owner	25,000
	Life-insurance premiums	2,400
	Subtotal	$121,430
	Less: Required repairs and maintenance	10,000
	Adjusted Operating Profit	$111,430
2.	Market value of fixed assets	$396,600
3.	Prevailing bank loan rate	12%
4.	Cost of owning fixed assets	
	$396,600 \cdot .12 =	$ 47,592
5.	Excess earning power	
	$111,430 - $47,592 =	$ 63,838
6.	Determine the appropriate multiple	3
7.	Value of the excess earnings	$191,514

Developing a Composite Approach

A major reason for an objective method of valuing a business is to reduce the conflict between buyer and seller during the different stages of negotiations. One strategy might be to estimate the value of a business by adding adjusted book value to the value of goodwill. If the purchase is strictly an asset purchase, the appraised value of tangible assets should be used instead of adjusted book value.

The composite approach to valuing HOT Manufacturing will result in an estimated value of $588,114, if the appraised value of assets is added to value of goodwill, and $606,014, using adjusted book value.

Final Comments on Valuation

The preceding discussion on business valuation should have made it clear that there is no single "best" approach that can be used to determine the value of a business. The best that can be expected is a range of values that establishes a basis for discussion and negotiation.

Note from the summary presented in Exhibit 13–2 that in the case of HOT Manufacturing, the balance sheet approaches gave consistently lower

EXHIBIT 13–2

Summary of Valuations for HOT Manufacturing Corporation		
Technique		**Value**
Marketplace formulas		
Five times before-tax profit		$371,400
Ten times after-tax profit		587,800
Book value		328,700
Adjusted book value		414,500
Capitalized value		371,400
Discounted earnings		571,470
Composite approach:		
Goodwill value	$191,514	
Adjusted book value	414,500	
		606,014

estimates of value than the income statement approaches and that the composite method produced an even higher valuation. Book and adjusted book values were $328,700 and $414,500, respectively. Earnings approach values ranged from $371,400 to $571,470. The composite approach value was $606,014.

This pattern should not be taken literally and expected in every situation. However, patterns usually emerge and values typically cluster within a given range. The goal of the valuation process is to narrow the range of estimated values to reduce the friction between buyer and seller in the negotiation process.

A reasonable price for a business is defined by the prospective payback period. Based on projected after-tax profits, the purchase price should be recoverable in three to seven years. Anything over seven years is overpriced; anything under three years is a bargain.

Other Considerations in Valuation

In addition to the pricing of a business, there are other considerations that play key roles in determining if a transfer of business ownership will take place. These factors include such intangibles as the prestige of the type of business and the reputation of the individual operation. An exceptionally large market share or an extensive or loyal customer base will also be highly valued. A proprietary product, or one with a strong growth potential is also very attractive.

One final factor that should not be ignored is the terms and conditions of the sale. These include the size of the down payment required, whether the owner will finance the acquisition through an installment purchase, the interest rate, and the length of the payout period.

Purchasers with little equity may find it difficult to secure funds through conventional sources. In these cases, finding a seller willing to accept a small down payment and carry an installment note may be equally or even more important than the actual purchase price. Most sellers will not be willing to accept the higher risk of such an arrangement without compensation. Thus, such a buyer must be willing to pay for this privilege by agreeing to a higher acquisition price.

The length of the payout period and the number and timing of installments are essential elements in funding a business purchase. Since cash flow is likely to be a problem in the early stages of an acquisition, delaying the installments or graduating their size can be considered as a means of allowing the new owner to keep as much operating capital as possible for business purposes. The length of the payout can have a dramatic effect on the size of the installment note. For example, to amortize a $1 million note carried at 10 percent in five years will require a $21,250 monthly payment. The same note amortized over a ten year period requires only a $13,215 monthly note. This translates into almost $100,000 in cash flow annually that can be used for the operation instead of amortizing debt.

Terms and conditions of sale are often as important as purchase price and should not be taken lightly. It is for their expertise in this area that accountants and legal representatives earn their pay.

Structuring the Transaction

There are four generally accepted ways to structure an ownership transfer: cash sale, partially leveraged buyout, earnout, or stock exchange. In a recent survey of twenty-four closings, the Capital Alliance Corporation of Dallas, Texas cites that cash payments were a part of twenty-three transactions, notes were included in fourteen, earnouts in four, and stock exchanges occurred in only one.

As a general rule, the greater the percentage of cash involved in the final payment is, the lower the purchase price will be. Increasing liquidity, and thus, reducing risk is usually high on the priority list for sellers.

Although complete cash transactions often take place, it is more common for cash to be used as a down payment. In this case, the seller will take an installment note secured by company stock for the balance of the purchase price. Under these circumstances, the purchase price will be higher, because the seller will have funds at risk over the installment period.

The earnout is discussed quite frequently (over three-fourths of the time in the Capital Alliance study), but makes it into only a small percentage of the actual closings. Under an **earnout,** the seller takes a cash down payment and notes, but also agrees to run the company for a specified time period. During that period, if the return on investment for the new owner exceeds an agreed-upon value, the seller will participate in the profits. This type of transaction takes place when the seller thinks more of the profit potential than the buyer. The extra income allows the seller to profit from the future earnings of the company should they actually materialize and keeps the base purchase price low to the buyer.

If the buyer is a corporation whose stock is traded publicly, the transaction can be closed using stock instead of cash and notes. The buyer gets the business and the seller gets the liquidity afforded by the stock and a tax-free swap. These transactions usually take place when the buyer's stock is perceived to be less risky than that of the seller.

Tax-free exchanges can take one of several forms. One of the most common forms is the **merger.** This is a situation in which one corporation actually becomes a part of the other corporation in exchange for stock in the acquiring (surviving) corporation. An alternative method is referred to as a **consolidation;** in this form, the two corporations form a completely new entity. A **stock-for-stock** acquisition is used when the shareholders of the acquiring corporation simply want to obtain control of the other corporation and thus exchange stock in one company for controlling interest in the other. In this case, both corporations maintain their separate and individual identities.

The actual form of reorganization and the amount of stock exchanges determine the final tax treatment. This entire subject is extremely complex and subject to change at almost any time. Thus, an entrepreneur considering one of these forms of reorganization should both be familiar with the tax code and also obtain the services of a competent tax adviser.

Leveraged Buyouts

Considerable attention has been given lately to the technique of the **leveraged buyout.** This method of buying an entire company or an operating division of a company has been used successfully by outside investors and professional managers to gain control of an ongoing concern.

The idea behind a leveraged buyout is to acquire a business with relatively little cash equity. Borrowed capital, secured by the assets of the company, usually accounts for most of the purchase price of the acquisition. The leveraged buyout, when successfully used, takes a firm with a solid asset base

1986 Tax Reform and Business Liquidation

The 1986 Tax Reform Act included three major changes that will significantly impact entrepreneurs who buy and sell businesses. First, top individual tax rates are now lower than top corporate rates, which will mean more proprietorships, partnerships (especially limited partnerships), and Subchapter S corporations in situations where those forms are possible. Second, there is no differential between the capital gains tax rate and the ordinary income tax rate. While the two types of income are treated the same, losses are still treated differently. Capital losses can only be used to offset capital gains. Finally, the so-called General Utilities doctrine has been repealed. This principle previously allowed corporations to avoid paying tax on the capital gains from the sale or liquidation of a company. Only the shareholders were liable for the tax on the capital gain.

These changes will affect business mergers and acquisitions in several ways. Under the old tax law, there was a conflict between buyer and seller over how to allocate the purchase price among the assets. The buyer wanted as much as possible reflected in tax-deductible items: fixed assets, employment contracts, and non-competitive agreements. The seller wanted as much of the payment in the purchase price as possible to take advantage of the lower capital gains tax treatment. Now that capital gains do not receive preferential tax rates, the conflict over the allocation of purchase price will be minimal.

The repeal of the General Utilities doctrine will probably have an escalating effect on the price of most privately held businesses. Under the reformed tax law, corporations must now claim the capital gains they receive from a sale or liquidation and pay 34 percent on the realized gain (the difference between the purchase price and the tax basis of the assets). The shareholders will still be taxed on the gains from the sale of their stock. The difference is that now they will be taxed at their individual rate of 28 percent, rather than the previous 20 percent capital gains rate. Company liquidations are now taxed at two levels instead of one. The effective rate under the new law is about 52 percent, compared to 20 percent under the old law.

The impact of the new tax law can be illustrated by an example. Suppose a corporation is sold for a $20 million capital gain. Under the old tax law, the owners would be liable for a capital gains tax of 20 percent of the gain, or $4 million. Under the new law, the corporation would first be liable for a 34 percent tax on the gain, or $6.8 million. The shareholders would then be liable for ordinary income tax of $3.7 million on their net gain (a $13.2 million gain taxed at 28 percent). The total tax on the gain is now $10.5 million, over two and one-half times the previous tax.

The only way to avoid the double-tax is for the buyer to agree not to step up the value of the assets to current values. Buyers will be reluctant to agree to give up this advantage; this will leave stock swaps as the preferred way to structure the ownership transfer. For some small companies that have values less than $10 million, the new provisions do not take effect until 1989.

that is used for collateral and allows the new owners an opportunity to build earnings and cash flow to service the debt and provide a substantial return on the investment.

This method of acquisition has been a very popular way for the operating managers of a corporate division to acquire the operation from the parent company. These corporate spinoffs make a great deal of sense when viewed from the perspective of the tax advantages available to the new owners. The tax advantages stem from the ability to generate significant depreciation write-offs for income tax purposes. When a company changes hands, the depreciation value of the capital assets is usually stepped up to reflect their current market values. This increase in basis increases the depreciation expense allowable for income tax purposes and is often a major factor in the feasibility of many leveraged buyouts.

Take the example of a manufacturing facility built fifteen years ago for a cost of $3 million. Under the old tax code, the facility had a useful life for tax purposes of thirty years and thus an annual depreciation rate of $100,000. Under these circumstances, the facility would have a book value of $1.5 million. Assume that now the owner sells the facility in a leveraged buyout for $9 million. The new owners can depreciate the facility at cost in only fifteen years according to the accelerated cost recovery system introduced in 1981. The annual depreciation is now $600,000, or six times the original amount.

Cautions to the Buyer and Seller

The tax and legal consequences of buying an existing business are too complicated and important to deal with adequately in this brief note. A competent attorney and accountant who have experience in business acquisitions can prove invaluable in providing assistance and counsel. It is important, however, that the entrepreneur have a basic understanding of the areas of concern in order to be able to communicate effectively with these professionals.

Tax Consequences

For all the attention paid to tax considerations, they are still not the fundamental concern of the individual who is buying or selling a business. For the buyer, the real payoff comes as a result of the time put into analyzing the feasibility of the acquisition and negotiating a favorable price and terms. For the seller, the payoff comes from the way in which the business is packaged and presented to ensure a fair exposure to the workings of the market.

In most cases, however, tax considerations play a significant role in determining the structure of the acquisition and may be a bargaining issue in the final negotiations. Both parties are obviously interested in reducing their respective income tax liabilities. Prior to the 1986 Tax Reform Act, it was to the seller's advantage to have the bulk of the purchase price considered a capital gain in order to take advantage of the more favorable tax rates. The buyer was interested in stepping up the basis of all capital assets in order to take advantage of more favorable depreciation write-offs. Any payment for goodwill, which is not a tax-deductible expense, can now take the form of an employment contract, to the benefit of both buyer and seller. Previously, a lower capital gains tax rate placed a wedge between the interests of buyer and seller in this regard. Buyers wanted employment contracts with their tax deductions and sellers wanted goodwill with its capital gains treatment. Since there is no longer a differential between rates paid on capital gains and ordinary income, *salaries* is no longer a dirty word for sellers. Under the new tax code, attention has shifted to other issues, namely, how to avoid double taxation in a business liquidation.

Conflicts are inevitable as negotiations come to a close. For this reason, competent, experienced counsel is vitally important to both parties.

Rules for Successful Mergers and Acquisitions

Any move to acquire a company must make good business sense. The following guidelines for successful acquisitions are suggested by Peter Drucker (1981):

1. A merger makes sense only if the acquiring company has something significant to contribute, other than capital. This contribution can be in the form of management, technology, or marketing. Mergers should never be made on the strength of what the acquired company will contribute to the acquiring company.

2. All successful mergers are based on what the two companies have in common. This commonality can be in the area of production, but more often it will be either markets or technology.

3. To ensure success, the decision makers in the acquiring company must respect the product, markets, and customers of the acquired company. There must be a "temperamental fit."

4. The acquiring company must be prepared to provide skilled managers to the acquired company. One should not expect that the top managers of the acquired firm will be content to stay on as division managers. The capable managers will either be the previous owners who are now wealthy as a result of the merger or professional managers who are able to find other meaningful work. Both are likely to move on to other endeavors within a very short period of time.

5. If top managers are to stay with the new firm, they must be convinced from the start that opportunities for personal advancement are available. This will require that a substantial number of promotions be given soon after the merger. These promotions should be given across company lines to show the younger professionals that their avenues for advancement have not been blocked by the merger, only enhanced.

These simple business principles have far-reaching implications. Their validity has been historically tested and their applicability is true under varying economic conditions.

Legal Issues

It is important not to overlook certain legal issues when a business is changing ownership. The following is a list of important areas of concern:

1. *Bulk Sales Act.* Most states require the seller to furnish the buyer with a notarized list of creditors and to notify the creditors of the pending sale. The purpose is to ensure that the business owner does not sell the business and disappear with the proceeds, leaving creditors unpaid.

2. *Stock purchase.* The major concern in buying the stock of an existing corporation is the problem of buying unknown liabilities such as product claims, patent infringement, labor law violations, and tax deficiencies. In addition, the buyer may find that the market value of the capital assets is much greater than their depreciable value.

   A stock purchase carries with it the opportunity to take advantage of any tax losses that may have accumulated from previous years for use in reducing current and future tax liabilities. The benefits of nonassignable contracts, leases, franchises, and licenses are also carried over to the new owners.

   Although there are problems with the purchase of stock, precautions can be taken. For example, the seller can reduce the buyer's anxiety by establishing an escrow arrangement to indemnify against certain liabilities. An **escrow** is a device in which part of the purchase price is held by a third party, usually a bank, as a means of satisfying any future claims.

3. *Asset purchase.* Many of the problems of hidden liabilities can be avoided by simply buying the assets of a company rather than the stock. In such a purchase, the legal continuity of the business is broken. The implication of this is that the seller's liabilities are not carried over to the new operation unless they are specifically agreed upon in the closing documents. The buyer is able to revalue assets and increase the basis for depreciation and can also specifically assume such liabilities as leases, mortgages, and installment notes.

The Buy-Sell Agreement

The important aspects of the business transfer can be clarified in the buy-sell agreement. The agreement should include the following:

1. *Introduction.* Identify the buyer and the seller, the nature of the agreement, and the type of transaction.

2. *Sale of the business.* Identify the assets being purchased and the basis for recourse against shortages or title defects (attach detailed schedules).

3. *Purchase price.* Provide a breakdown of the purchase price, with values placed on each asset item (assuming an asset purchase).

4. *Method of payment.* Specify the method of payment and the financing contingencies (provide a security agreement if owner-financed).

5. *Adjustments.* Since there is usually a time gap between the closing of the agreement and the actual transfer of ownership, there will inevitably be a need to adjust such items as inventory, rent, insurance premiums, and utility deposits.

6. *Assumption of liabilities.* Define which outstanding liabilities are being assumed.

7. *Seller warranties.* Specify that the seller will indemnify against such things as title defects, undisclosed liens or litigation, fraudulent information, and other undisclosed liabilities. (This section should be extensive in a stock purchase.)

8. *Seller's obligation pending transfer.* State that the seller is to conduct the business as normal, maintain accurate records, and give the buyer access to the premises during this interim period. In addition, specify that the seller will comply with the bulk sales laws.

9. *Risk of loss.* Protect against such items as inventory depletion, injury to goodwill, disasters and other casualty losses, and creditors' actions during the period between closing and transfer.

10. *Covenant not to compete.* Specify that the seller will not establish a competing business in the same market for a specified period of time.

11. *Closing.* Set a date of final possession.

12. *Indemnification by seller.* Establish that the seller will reimburse fully any cost or damage sustained by the buyer that is a direct result of any breach of warranty or contract by the seller.

13. *Escrow.* Require the seller to place part of the purchase price in escrow as a security for performance for an established period of time.

14. *Settlement of disputes.* Decide the means by which all disputes that arise will be settled (via arbitration or some other means).

Summary and Conclusions

The subject of buyouts and acquisitions is both an interesting and complex area of study. The purpose of this chapter was to introduce the reader to this subject matter and provide some general guidelines for analyzing and valuing acquisition candidates. Because of the overriding tax and legal implications and the various issues concerning reorganization and merger, the entrepreneur is well advised to secure the services of a trained professional who has experience in buyouts and acquisitions before proceeding too far into the process.

References

Drucker, Peter F. "The Five Rules of Successful Acquisition," *Wall Street Journal,* October 15, 1981.

Howard, James. "Defuse the Hostility Factor in Acquisition Talks," *Harvard Business Review* (July/August, 1982), pp. 54–57.

Liles, Patrick R. *New Business Ventures and the Entrepreneur.* Homewood, IL: Richard D. Irwin, Inc., 1974, pp. 186–201 and 374–384.

Moore, Thomas J. "Pricing a Privately-Held Corporation." Seminar on "Corporate Mergers: Insights from Experienced Participants." Dallas, TX: Capital Alliance Corporation, June 19, 1986.

Olson, Irving J. "Valuation of a Closely Held Corporation," *Journal of Accountancy* (August, 1969), pp. 35–47.

Rockwell, Willard F. Jr. "How to Acquire a Company," *Harvard Business Review* (September-October, 1968), pp. 121–132.

Scott, Richard. "Pricing the Going Concern," *Journal of Small Business Management* (June, 1977), pp. 37–40.

Small Business Administration. *Buying and Selling a Small Business.* Washington, D.C.: Government Printing Office, 1984.

14
The Changing
Financial Environment

F ederal policy makers are slowly realizing that much of the innovation in the product market and growth in the labor market can be traced back to the small business sector. Federal involvement has traditionally been focused in direct aid such as financing and procurement assistance. Because of growing federal deficits and increased awareness of inefficiencies and improprieties that have surfaced in some of these programs, there has been a movement toward reducing direct federal involvement and allowing increased state and local initiatives and private sector solutions to take over. The results have been mixed, but the future of federal programs seems to be clear—they will be phased out. As they are eliminated and consolidated, the challenge is to maintain a stable environment that will encourage and promote enterprise development.

The purpose of this chapter is to examine the financial environment in which entrepreneurs must compete, including local initiatives to encourage enterprise development, changes in the commercial banking industry brought on by deregulation, new concepts in venture capital, and income taxes and securities regulation.

Trends in Enterprise Development

The following discussion looks briefly at three of the state and local government and private sector initiatives that may serve to replace and even improve upon direct federal involvement in private sector activity.

Enterprise Zones

The movement toward enterprise zones has been gaining momentum since the early 1980s, when Ronald Reagan made them a part of his plan to revive business in designated depressed areas. The concept of the **enterprise zone** is simple: set up specially designated areas within communities across the country as targets for economic development. The enterprise zone concept goes far beyond the industrial development approach already in use by the states. The major difference is that it stresses the use of federal tax and regulatory incentives to encourage business development.

Even with presidential support, enterprise zone legislation has failed to advance past the congressional committee level. While Congress has debated the pros and cons of the concept, twenty states have passed legislation creating over 1,300 enterprise zones in over 600 communities. The states themselves have little to offer relative to the federal government in the way of tax incentives for businesses locating in enterprise zones. Federal proposals recommend an exemption from all capital gains tax and 75 percent of all income tax, plus tax credits of up to $450 per employee. State and local tax breaks are significantly less than those proposed in the Congress.

However, state governments are offering exemptions from sales and use taxes, exemptions from utility taxes, increased availability of industrial development bonds, and reduced regulatory red-tape. Estimates by the Department of Housing and Urban Development in 1984 showed that the sixteen states with zones in existence for more than a year attracted over $3 billion in investment and retained or created over 80,000 jobs. Although data on enterprise zone activity are difficult to find, even the casual observer cannot help but notice the improved prospects for inner-city investment that have resulted from the state enterprise zones.

Six zones in Connecticut have created and retained 8,500 jobs and attracted $135 million. Enterprise zones in Arkansas are responsible for fifty-two business startups, over 3,000 new jobs, and $100 million in investment in barely one year of operation. The other states with enterprise zones are experiencing varying degrees of success. In states without enterprise zones, six have passed legislation to enable their creation and nine are considering such legislation.

It may very well be that federal tax incentives are not necessary in the successful establishment of enterprise zones. A study by the National Federation of Independent Business (NFIB) found that business location decisions are largely made on the basis of availability of capital and a qualified labor force, immediate marketability, adequate police protection, and affordable insurance. Because of opposition in the Congress and from certain business groups, such as the NFIB, the best way to proceed at this time may be to allow the states to establish enterprise zones at their own pace. Whether enterprise zones will ultimately play a significant role in the redevelopment of the decaying inner cities of the country remains to be seen.

The White House Conference:
The Second Time Around

In January 1980, President Jimmy Carter called for representatives of the small business community to convene in Washington, D.C. for the first White House Conference on Small Business. The purpose of this historic meeting was to open up the lines of communication between small business owners and the federal establishment. That conference resulted in a list of sixty recommendations, of which two-thirds have been incorporated into government policy over the intervening years.

Delegates chosen from the small business community met for the second time in August 1986 to discuss federal policy as it affects small business. Areas of recommendation included:

1. *Liability insurance*—there should be uniform product liability standards nationwide, limits on awards in personal injury cases, and caps on attorneys' fees.

2. *Future of the SBA*—the Small Business Administration should maintain its status as an independent agency.

3. *Innovation*—the Small Business Innovation Research program should be reorganized and its scope expanded.

4. *Finance*—restrictions on small business access to capital should be eased. This includes uniform securities laws and a simplified registration for public equity offerings and the creation of a Small Business Participating Debenture.

5. *Economic policy*—a constitutional amendment to balance the budget should be passed. Reductions in the federal budget deficit should be accomplished through spending cuts, not tax increases.

Whether this conference has as much impact as the first is yet to be seen. However, one thing is certain. Observers of this conference witnessed an historic change in the perspective of the small business community. The discussions were no longer focused on special tax incentives and set-asides. Instead, the critical issues centered on small business' role in determining the federal government's overall economic policy. Issues such as the balanced budget, interest rates, and the money supply dominated discussions in the domestic policy area. Trade policy and the value of the dollar on the foreign exchange market dominated the international agenda. If the tone of the conference is any indicator, it may be true that the small business community finally understands the difference between being small and thinking small.

Business Incubators

An increasingly popular way of encouraging enterprise development in economically depressed areas is the formation of business and technology incubators. The concept of a business incubator was developed to promote and encourage new business startups and reduce the rate of failure during the early stages of the business life cycle. A **business incubator** provides controlled environments with adequate support systems and low overhead costs for new and emerging firms.

The typical incubator facility is an existing and often previously vacant office or warehouse space. They are often located in economically depressed areas of the city and, more often than not, in or near enterprise zones. The motivation behind the formation of an incubator is to reduce the costs of operation during the initial stages of a firm's life cycle. This is often accomplished by providing flexible lease space for startup businesses at below-market rates. Support services such as office and bookkeeping assistance are almost always available on an as-needed basis. Professional services such as loan packaging, financial planning, and legal assistance may also be offered.

Access to capital sources is often cited as the most important aspect of the business location decision. Most incubator facilities provide some form of financial assistance to their tenant firms. This assistance usually takes the form of technical help and referrals. While fewer than one-third of the incubators maintain an investment fund, almost all assist in filling out paperwork for federal loans and guarantees, preparing business plans, and networking with commercial lenders and venture capital investors. In addition to this direct financial assistance, many firms will have better access to industrial development bonds and other forms of state and federal assistance because of their association with the incubator.

The first business incubators were formed in 1978; by the end of 1985, there were over seventy-five in operation across the country. Studies indicate that the number is expected to increase ten times over the next few years. The increased popularity of the business incubator is caused primarily by the significant benefits accruing to the local community as a result of their formation. The most commonly cited benefits are:

1. The reclamation of underutilized or vacant facilities into more productive uses.
2. The diversification of the local economic base.
3. The revitalization of economically depressed neighborhoods.
4. Increased employment opportunities.

The establishment of an incubator is no guarantee of immediate success for either the new and emerging businesses or the incubator management. While the purpose of the incubator is to create an atmosphere conducive to business success, that success is ultimately determined by the marketplace. There is no question that business creation and expansion within an incubator will have economic consequences far beyond the walls of the facility itself—an expanded tax base and more job opportunities. Even though incubators are not the cure-all for depressed business activity, they can play a significant part in an overall business development plan within the local community if properly managed and supervised.

Intrapreneurship in Corporate America

Intrapreneuring is an attempt to integrate the entrepreneur into the traditional corporate structure to form a unit that takes maximum advantage of the strengths of both parties while minimizing the inevitable friction that will develop between them. There has always been an uneasy relationship between the entrepreneur and the large corporation. It is widely accepted that the entrepreneur is the idea person—a visionary who has the initiative to take a calculated risk on a venture. As a result, the entrepreneur does not fit well into the traditional corporate structure.

The entrepreneur is an innovator, but the goals of the typical corporation tend to inhibit innovation. The corporate structure is divided into distinct, manageable entities with specific duties and responsibility. The result is a structure that sacrifices flexibility for uniformity and stability.

The emphasis on uniformity and stability slows down the innovation process. The structure does not break down at the idea generation stage. The traditional corporation does create an environment in which ideas are generated. But these ideas are focused primarily on modifying current products and technology and not on developing completely new ideas or applications.

The breakdown is accentuated at the implementation stage—the crucial stage where the product idea is marketed to benefit the consumer, the corporation, and the economy. Corporate managers always keep one eye on share prices and are thus concerned about issues that affect current profitability. The initial negative cash flow that accompanies most innovations during the early stages of the life cycle does not lend itself well to traditional corporate objectives.

In addition, personality differences between corporate manager types and entrepreneurial types lead to considerable friction within the structure. The successful manager has worked up through the corporate hierarchy to a position of authority and prestige. By impressing the right people with his administrative ability and personal expertise, he attained promotions; with each promotion came an increased zeal for the structure and stability of the corporate hierarchy. Contrast this with the typical entrepreneur, who is highly competitive and inwardly motivated to achieve at any price. This is the type of person who will challenge the hierarchy or simply try to circumvent authority if it stands in the way of success.

The corporate hierarchy and the entrepreneur are destined for conflict. The predictable result of the conflict is a series of rejected innovations, which are closely followed by a disgruntled entrepreneur leaving in frustration and starting a small business. How long can the corporation afford to ignore its entrepreneurial talent and lose these innovations to the small business community? The challenge is how to harness the entrepreneurial spirit and make it effective within the corporate environment.

Many large corporations that are trying to orchestrate the successful marriage between the traditional hierarchy and the entrepreneur are finding that it requires substantial compromise on the part of both parties. Corporate management must learn to tolerate higher levels of risk and provide an environment conducive to innovation, giving individuals freedom to pursue ideas and applications. The entrepreneur must be committed to the corporation and show a willingness to work in a structured environment by abiding by corporate policy. This includes giving up the dream of becoming an instant millionaire and baron over a personal empire. In other words, the corporation must provide a flexible environment in which the entrepreneur is able to pursue ideas with little outside interference. The entrepreneur must keep in mind the goals and objectives of the parent organization and focus on projects that will add value to the company as a whole.

This partnership is working in many areas of the country. The corporation is able to supply technological and capital resources. In return, the entrepreneur provides the energy and initiative to develop new products and applications. Using this innovative talent, the corporation is able to assemble a diverse, high level research and development group with the finance and marketing support needed to proceed from the idea stage to the market. Success breeds success and the corporations that are able to harness their own entrepreneurial talent in an effective manner will be the ones that will serve as "'agents of change' and our hope for the future" (Pinchot 1985).

The Changing Commercial Banking Environment

In recent decades, banking activities were largely a local phenomenon. Banks were able to establish offices across state borders, but offered only very limited services, such as consumer lending, leasing, and mortgage banking. Full retail banking was completely out of the question because it would require deposit-taking, which was interpreted as interstate banking, and was clearly prohibited by law.

Since the enactment of the Depository Institutions Deregulation and Monetary Control Act of 1980 (Monetary Control Act) and the Depository Institutions Act of 1982 (Garn-St Germain Act), the financial services industry has seen revolutionary changes in the nature and substance of its business operations. Although interstate branch banking is still limited, banks have managed to get around the restrictions in several ways. One approach that has been used by the large money-center banks is to set up loan production offices (LPOs) around the country. Banks such as Citicorp, Manufacturers

Hanover, Chase Manhattan, and Bank of America are establishing LPOs to handle commercial and industrial lending outside their home states.

Other banks are using the strategy of acquiring savings and loan associations and commercial finance companies. Citicorp has a consumer finance subsidiary that has over 100 offices scattered around the country and has acquired a savings and loan association in California that has over 90 branches. Manufacturers Hanover recently acquired the C.I.T. Financial Corporation, which has over 300 offices nationwide. The main advantage of this strategy is simple. When the ban on interstate banking is finally lifted, these financial institutions will be immediately competitive, with retail offices, a computer network, and a customer base.

Recent advancements in technology such as the automatic teller machine allow customers to deposit, transfer, and withdraw cash at remote locations miles from the main banking facility. This capability has fostered the establishment of electronic networks whereby funds can be transferred among banks located in different states.

State laws are being revised in many parts of the country to permit regional banking across state lines. The typical arrangement allows an out-of-state bank to acquire a local bank as long as the acquiring bank's home state has a reciprocal law. Banks in New England have enjoyed this flexibility since the early 1980s. Other areas of the country, specifically the Southeast and the Midwest, are at various stages in setting up their own regional banking networks.

Bank deregulation has permitted the industry to offer financial services previously limited to "non-banks," including the sale of securities, insurance, and real estate. Deregulation has also sparked a merger movement for small banks in order to compete more effectively in the new environment and for larger banks in order to prepare for interstate banking.

The bank holding company has become the primary organizational form within the industry, accounting for over 73 percent of the offices and 86 percent of the assets in 1983. Even though the merger and acquisition movement has led to an increased centralization of authority within the industry, there is still a significant amount of activity in new bank creation. There were 1,680 new banks established between 1978 and 1983, with 405 formed in 1983 alone.

The newly established banks are competing successfully with the larger financial corporations by filling niches in the market. Although the larger banks are able to offer a wider variety of services, the smaller banks can concentrate on the segment of the market virtually ignored by the giants— the small business community. Thus, there is no reason to believe that deregulation will be the downfall of the small community bank. Efficiency in operations and product innovation does not belong exclusively to the large, diversified financial corporation.

For the typical entrepreneur, these changes tend to blur the distinctions among the various bank and non-bank financial institutions. It is becoming more difficult over time to distinguish between a bank and a savings and loan association or a bank and a credit union. More importantly, how will these recent developments affect the owner of a closely held business? Will the new environment lead to better or poorer access to the capital markets? How will interest rate deregulation affect loan pricing for the smaller firm?

One of the major results of deregulation is that the financial markets have become much more integrated nationwide. Smaller markets can no longer isolate themselves from outside competitive forces. To the benefit of local depositors, this increased competition will drive up the average cost of funds for many community banks. Whether or not this increased average cost of funds will increase borrowing costs for local businesses is open to debate. It is doubtful that the marginal cost of funds—the cost of obtaining additional funds for lending—will rise as a result of deregulation. If this observation is correct and loan pricing is subject to market constraints, interest rates paid by borrowers are not likely to change substantially. All things considered, the typical small business will in all likelihood benefit from the increased competition resulting from the deregulated environment.

New Concepts in Venture Capital

As the competition for investment opportunities increases within the venture capital industry, firms are responding by turning their focus away from the traditional developmental stage investment to growth and acquisition financing. Also, venture capitalists are collectively using new techniques to help identify viable investment opportunities.

Commercial Banking and Venture Capital

The increased competition brought on by deregulation in the financial services industry has raised the average cost of funds for the commercial banker. At the same time, expanding markets and sluggish loan demands have exerted downward pressure on loan rates. The result is a margin squeeze that is working to significantly reduce the profitability of the bank's commercial loan portfolio.

With these forces at work, an increasing number of banks are shifting a portion of their investment portfolio from the low risk/low reward commercial loan market to the high risk/high reward venture capital market. This is not an easy transition for most commercial bankers, who have traditionally focused on a firm's past performance when making credit decisions. In contrast, venture investing is by its very nature future oriented. Investment decisions are based on expectations of future profitability rather than results of past profitability.

By 1985, approximately seventy commercial banks had established venture capital funds. In doing so, these banks took advantage of federal regulations that allow a corporation to place up to 5 percent of its capital into a venture capital subsidiary.

The issues a commercial bank must consider before establishing a venture capital subsidiary are far too complex for a complete discussion in this chapter. However, there are several that are worth mentioning. Although the return on a successful investment is high (often more than the return on billions of dollars in commercial loans), the typical investment period is usually considerably longer than the banker is used to—five to seven years as opposed to the one to three years usually considered by the bank. In addition, the trained lender is not prepared, professionally or psychologically, for the problems he or she will face when dealing with firms in the early developmental stages of the business life cycle.

Payoffs in this segment of the financial market can be extremely high and volatile, which is something that bank shareholders may not readily understand. However, despite these risks, the larger money-center banks and even many regional banks are moving to establish these subsidiary operations. It is doubtful that this trend (if it can be called that yet) will change the way the majority of the commercial lenders conduct their business. However, this aspect of a deregulated environment adds one more item to the menu of financial services offered by the industry.

Venture Capital Fairs

The venture capital fair is becoming an increasingly used tool within the industry. The fair concept is similar to an industry conference. Members of the venture capital community gather at a conference site to listen to entrepreneurs explain the merits of investing in their new and emerging companies.

The first venture capital conference was organized by the American Electronics Association in Monterey, California in 1976; it is typical of the many fairs that are springing up all over the country today. Larger than most conferences, the Monterey conference is divided into two three-day sessions, each of which is attended by sixty new businesses and hundreds of venture capitalists.

Each conference has a formal application procedure established to screen prospective companies to ensure that only the highest quality investment opportunities are chosen for presentation. The screening committee reviews numerous business plans and/or formal presentations and chooses a select few participants for the program.

The formal presentations are the focal point of the conference. The venture capitalists attend group sessions in which each entrepreneur has an opportunity to present his story in a few minutes. These presentations almost always include a multi-media slide or video show, complete with four-color graphs and charts showing sales and profit potential.

After these mass presentations, the venture capitalists can sign up for longer, more detailed presentations by the companies they have a particular interest in. Venture capitalists attend these conferences to make deals. The competition for good investments is so great that negotiations can move along fairly rapidly.

Most venture money is still invested in the traditional manner through the established syndicates of investors. However, in geographic regions where venture capital activity has been slow to emerge, venture capital fairs are being used as a means of speeding up and simplifying the process. Fairs are becoming especially popular in the South and Southwest, where the Big Eight accounting firms are taking a leadership role in their sponsorship and organization.

Venture Capital Clubs

Another increasingly important area of activity is the venture capital club, an organization specifically designed to encourage interaction between venture capitalists and entrepreneurs in a community. Venture capital clubs are being formed all around the country, especially in areas where the venture network is inactive or inefficient. Dues-paying members include both entrepreneurs and investors who attend monthly luncheon or breakfast meetings to interact and make venture deals.

The Association of Venture Capital Clubs, based in Stamford, Connecticut, has members in all fifty states. Although they share a common goal of promoting activity in the venture capital community, each club has its own unique style and activities that reflect local resources. Most clubs do not advertise and are often difficult to locate to ensure that only the most interested individuals join. It is not likely that the club concept will replace the traditional venture capital network. However, in those areas of the country where the industry is in its infancy, this concept is destined to play a significant role in speeding up the development of the industry.

Federal Policy toward Business

Federal policy plays a key role in promoting a strong, dynamic private sector in the economy by relying on policies that encourage the efficient working of the free enterprise system. All too often, federal policymakers have erred on the side of increased intervention in the private sector, resulting in high inflation, high interest rates, and low rates of economic growth. These policy errors include the growing federal budget, with the related problem of the complexities of the federal tax code and expanding budget deficits and the erratic way in which monetary policy has been conducted.

Volumes of data have been compiled and much has already been written on this topic (see in particular, *The State of Small Business: A Report of the President*, various issues). However, for purposes of this discussion, we will focus on the impact of federal policy on the availability of capital and the changes that are probably on the economic horizon.

Federal policy has a significant effect on the environment in which entrepreneurs make their financing decisions. As we have already seen, banking regulations play a key role in establishing the guidelines within which the industry operates. In addition, federal tax policy and securities regulations play significant roles in determining the availability of credit and equity funds to the business community.

Federal Tax Policy

The federal government has possibly the single most powerful tool for determining the flow of capital into various sectors of the economy—the federal income tax code. It has been an accepted fact down through history that the power to tax is the power to destroy. In this case, it is more precise to hypothesize that taxation has an important bearing on certain business decisions such as the form of business organization, the source of capital for business formation and expansion, and the form and essence of employee compensation. Tax considerations are clearly important in many business decisions. What is not so clear is the measurement and ultimate impact of the various aspects of the income tax code.

Recent tax legislation has focused on what is popularly called "the supply side." **Supply-side** changes are policy prescriptions that focus on increasing the long-run productive capacity of the economic system by providing increased incentives to work, save, and invest. On the tax side, these changes were implemented in the Economic Recovery and Tax Act (ERTA) of 1981. With over 85 percent of all businesses in the United States filing as sole proprietorships, partnerships, and Subchapter S corporations, the individual income tax rate reductions for which ERTA was responsible represented over $600 billion in business tax relief over the 1981–1986 period.

In addition to the marginal tax rate reductions, ERTA included provisions to lower corporate income tax rates, reduce the capital gains tax rate, liberalize the investment tax credit, and allow firms to accelerate the rate at which they depreciate certain types of capital equipment. These incentives were all targeted at the business sector to encourage increased investment in productive capacity. More capacity should result in increased productivity

Income Tax Reform: The Revolution Begins

October 1986 represents a significant time in the annals of income tax policy in the United States. It was at that time that the Congress passed and President Reagan signed into law the most sweeping tax reform bill in the post–war era: the Tax Reform Act of 1986 (the Reform Act). The most significant aspect of the Reform Act is the dramatic cut in income-tax rates, both individual and corporate.

For taxpayers filing individual returns, the change represents a continuation of the reforms initiated by the Economic Recovery and Tax Act of 1981 (ERTA). ERTA lowered top marginal tax rates from 70 to 50 percent. The Reform Act lowers the top bracket further to an effective marginal rate of 33 percent. Instead of having fourteen brackets ranging from 11 to 50 percent, the new structure has two brackets of 15 and 28 percent. In addition, certain high-income families that have incomes over $71,900 ($43,150 for individuals) will be subject to a 5 percent surcharge.

Capital gains will be taxed at the same rate as ordinary income. This represents a reversal of the recent trend of falling rates on this source of income. Capital gains realized in 1986 were taxed at a maximum rate of 20 percent. In 1987, they will be taxed at the individual rate, or a maximum rate of 38 percent. The maximum rate will be dropped after 1987. In addition, passive losses on real estate and other tax shelters can be written off only against income from other similar investments. These two changes represent major setbacks in the venture capital community. Both will work to discourage rather than encourage investment in entrepreneurial ventures.

The top corporate rate has been lowered from 46 to 34 percent. There is still a graduated rate structure for small corporations. Incomes less than $50,000 will be taxed at a 15 percent rate and incomes between $50,000 and $75,000 will be taxed at a marginal rate of 25 percent. At this point, the rate structure becomes a bit more complicated. On income between $75,000 and $100,000, the marginal rate is 34 percent. For income up to $335,000, the graduated rate structure is phased out by initiating a 5 percent surcharge for an effective marginal rate over this range of 39 percent. Incomes over $335,000 are taxed at a flat rate of 34 percent.

The Reform Act repeals the investment tax credit and significantly modifies the accelerated cost recovery system (ACRS) from the 1981 Act. Eight classes of property are defined, with the typical recovery method being double declining balance with a change to the straight-line method for most machinery and equipment.

The administration promoted early versions of the bill as "tax simplification." As passed, the Reform Act is anything but simple. In fact, most entrepreneurs will find tax planning and preparation more complex than under the previous Act.

and profitability, more employment, and higher rates of real growth for the economy in general.

The tax provisions have such a significant impact on business and individual decision making that they must be constantly monitored. The biases introduced into the economic system by the tax code have the capability of distorting resource allocation decisions and channeling activity into ineffective and inefficient areas. The challenge for policy makers is to be able to recognize the undesirable consequences of the tax code and have the courage to make adjustments, regardless of the political overtones.

Securities Regulations

The federal government occupies the most strategic position in determining the economic environment in which business operates. One of the chronic problem areas of small business financing has been the poor availability of reliable equity funding sources. The Securities Act of 1933 provides three major exemptions that provide relief to small issuers from the standardized disclosure requirements of full registration. However, the SEC has been more concerned with monitoring the size of the issue and the number of investors involved than with the size of the issuer. The smaller the firm is, the greater the relative burden of the disclosure provisions of the Act will be.

The SEC has recently proposed a change in the classification procedure for reporting. Instead of structuring the disclosure rules by asset size, revenues, and number of shareholders, it has recommended that firm size also be defined by number of employees. The establishment of a graduated reporting and disclosure procedure is consistent with the goals of protecting investors and assisting smaller issuers.

The passage of the Employee Retirement Income Security Act (ERISA) of 1974 significantly reduced the flow of venture capital funds into developmental stage financings by prohibiting pension funds from investing in venture capital firms or any other speculative venture. The total venture capital pool remained relatively constant at $2.5 to $3.0 billion over the period from 1969 to 1978.

Capital gains tax reductions in 1978, coupled with regulatory changes in ERISA that allows venture capital investing, resulted in a dramatic increase in the availability of funds to the industry. Between 1978 and 1980, the venture capital pool expanded by approximately $1.6 billion. Favorable tax treatment should enable the venture capital industry to continue to attract a sizeable share of the capital market funds available for equity investing.

Summary and Conclusions

Environmental factors play a key role in determining the extent of enterprise development in the economic system. Governing bodies at federal, state, and local levels influence the environment through economic policy in general and the enactment of programs that target specific groups of areas.

The challenge for policy makers is to achieve a stable overall environment in which private sector initiatives can grow and prosper and, at the same time, implement specific programs that do not distort economic incentives and resource allocation. The general problems that must be dealt with include inflation, interest rates, unemployment, and productivity. Specific issues include access to capital, research and development, and equal business opportunities. The challenges are great, but the rewards can be measured in terms of economic growth and prosperity.

References

Allen, David N. and Rahman, Syedur. "Small Business Incubators: A Positive Environment for Entrepreneurship," *Journal of Small Business Management* (July, 1985), pp. 12–22.

"Enterprise Zones for All," *Wall Street Journal*, November 7, 1985.

Pinchot, Gifford III. *Intrapreneuring*. New York: Harper and Row, 1985.

The State of Small Business: A Report of the President, Washington, D.C.: Government Printing Office, various years.

Index

About the Author

James W. Henderson is the Ben E. Williams Professor of Economics at the Hankamer School of Business at Baylor University. He has worked as an economic consultant, business analyst, and market research specialist. Prior to joining the Baylor faculty in 1981, he was vice president of finance and development at the Dallas Minority Business Center, a Department of Commerce-funded business development organization. Dr. Henderson completed his undergraduate work at the University of Houston, where he majored in finance. He then received both M.A. and Ph.D. degrees in economics from Southern Methodist University. His publications include articles in the *Journal of Development Economics, Economics of Education Review, Journal of Financial Education, Journal of the Southwestern Society of Economists, Baylor Business Review,* and *Cashflow.*